G. J. Stodart

James

Bp. S. E, Africa

JAMES HANNINGTON

D.D., F.L.S., F.R.G.S.

FIRST BISHOP OF EASTERN EQUATORIAL AFRICA

A HISTORY
OF HIS LIFE AND WORK
1847—1885

BY

E. C. DAWSON, M.A., Oxon.

INCUMBENT OF ST. THOMAS'S CHURCH, EDINBURGH

*"Show me some one person formed according to the principles he professes. Show me
one who is sick and happy; in danger and happy; dying and happy; exiled and happy."*

EPICTETUS

ELEVENTH THOUSAND

NEGRO UNIVERSITIES PRESS
NEW YORK

Originally published in 1887
by Seeley & Co., London

Reprinted 1969 by
Negro Universities Press
A DIVISION OF GREENWOOD PUBLISHING CORP.
NEW YORK

Library of Congress Catalogue Card Number 69-19355

TO HIS CHILDREN

THIS RECORD

OF

THEIR FATHER'S LIFE AND WORK

IS

AFFECTIONATELY DEDICATED.

PREFACE.

No apology is surely needed for writing the life of James Hannington. If it be true that every life which has been lived conveys to the world some message which should not be lost, much less can we afford to lose the record of a life like his—a devoted life crowned by a heroic death. With regard, however, to my own part in connection with this work, a word or two of explanation may be necessary.

It seemed to his relatives and friends to be especially desirable that his Memoir should be entrusted to one who had known him personally and intimately. Without this knowledge, his biographer must have failed in presenting him in any recognizable form before the public eye. A mere enumeration of his acts, such as might be easily culled from his diaries, letters and published articles, or from printed notices regarding him, would convey scarcely any idea at all of the man himself. A verbatim record of his sayings would probably produce an impression utterly false, except to those who knew the speaker and understood the moods in which he uttered them. The materials of which Bishop Hannington was formed were not run into the mould in which ordinary men are shaped. In few things was he just

like the majority. Almost everything he said or did was
stamped with the impress of his own distinct individuality.
That individuality his friends now treasure among their
most precious memories. They can never dissociate his
words from the tone of the voice which accompanied them,
or from the sly twinkle, or it might be, the impatient flash
of the grey eyes which introduced them. They can never
think of his acts without recalling the active, energetic
figure, so full of life and movement, which carried through
with an inimitable enthusiasm of forceful purpose whatever
was uppermost in his mind. They would not have had one
thing about him different; but his ways were his own, and
his words were his own, and nothing would be easier than
that a stranger, by separating his words and his ways from
himself, should be perfectly accurate in every statement,
and yet represent him to the world in a manner which
would not only be unsatisfactory, but even misleading and
unfair to his memory.

When, therefore, his widow requested me to undertake
the editorship of his Life and Work, I accepted the responsibility, trusting that my own intimate knowledge of the
man might more than compensate for any want of skill
which I might display in the treatment of my subject.
Perhaps, also, hoping that my own love for him might
enable me to make an appreciative study of his remarkable
character.

It only remains for me to say that, in the compilation of
this Memoir, the Bishop's diary has been quoted whenever
it has been possible to give the narrative in his own words.
I have also to offer my warmest thanks to the Hon. Secretary of the Church Missionary Society, who has placed the

whole of the Bishop's official correspondence with the Society at my disposal; and especially to Mr. Eugene Stock, who has most kindly revised such statements as refer to the history of the Society. Other friends have also contributed letters and personal reminiscences, for which I am grateful.

With regard to the illustrations which are scattered throughout the volume, they are all, with one or two exceptions, reduced from the Bishop's own sketches. Some of the pen-and-ink drawings are exact facsimiles; and even the full page engravings follow his pencil very closely.

The details of the Bishop's death are collated from the different accounts given by those who were either eye-witnesses, or who repeated what had been told to them by those who were present. These accounts slightly vary, but they do not contradict each other in any material point. At the very last moment, when this book had already gone to press, the precious little diary, to the pages of which the Bishop committed his last writings during his imprisonment in Busoga, was most unexpectedly recovered and sent home. The printing of the book was at once stopped, and the last sixty pages have been rewritten so as to incorporate into them the valuable knowledge thus acquired. Space has not permitted me to enter the whole journal unabridged, but very full extracts have been made from it. I may say, indeed, that nothing which could throw any light, either upon the Bishop's state of mind, or upon the circumstances of his case, has been omitted.

I now commit this book to the prayers of God's people. It has been my endeavour, in the pages which follow, to let James Hannington reveal himself as he was, in order that those who did not know him in the flesh may learn the secret of that nature which laid so firm a hold upon the hearts of a large circle of devoted friends, and which seldom failed to leave its deep impression upon all those with whom he was associated.

My own earnest desire is that the example of his noble self-denial may stir up others to emulation, and brace those who read to follow in his footsteps and to " lay aside every weight, and run with patience the race that is set before them."

E. C. D.

Edinburgh, Nov., 1886.

CONTENTS.

—◆—

PART I.

LIST OF ILLUSTRATIONS.

PART I.

JAMES HANNINGTON

CHAPTER I.

PARENTAGE AND CHILDHOOD.

(1847—60.)

" I judge him of a rectified spirit."

BEN JONSON.

" Ring in the valiant man and free,
The larger heart, the kindlier hand ;
Ring out the darkness of the land,
Ring in the Christ that is to be."

In Memoriam.

THERE were Hanningtons in England in very early times.
Domesday Book records their existence. Whether my dear
old friend, whose too brief life I am now trying to set forth,
was directly connected with any of these is likely to remain
for ever uncertain. Nor does it greatly signify to know.
The chief interest of pedigrees to the wise is, surely, to
trace by their help the transmission of certain individual
characteristics and the development of them. If, therefore.
we do not possess a careful record of the lives and characters of a man's ancestors, we can easily dispense with their
mere names. Those only are of any real value to us whose
persons and deeds, manners and words, throw some light
upon the life of the man in whom we are interested, and
offer some clue to its unravelment.

The first among the ancestors of James Hannington

who steps with any definable form out of the shadows is his great-grandfather. We find the following reference to him in his Journal :—" About the middle of the eighteenth century my great-grandfather and two brothers sailed in a boat from Dover and came into Shoreham River to seek their fortunes ; in those days, doubtless, a very great undertaking. Here my great-grandfather married a lady of high family. She was the last of the ancient stock of the De Meophams, Saxon nobles in the year 970 A.D., the best known to posterity of whom was Simon De Meopham, sometime Archbishop of Canterbury, whose tomb may be seen in Canterbury Cathedral."

Of this great-grandfather we wish that more had been recorded, since he seems to have possessed at least one marked characteristic in common with his great-grandson. The diary continues :—"Almost all that I have heard of him is that he was a man of superhuman strength. On one occasion, passing by where a cart was stuck fast in the mud, and six men unable to move it, he bade them stand clear, and lifted it out by himself." Like his descendant James, who was always eagerly to the fore in any accident, or upon any occasion when active assistance was required, he evidently could not resist the impulse to step in and bear a hand.

After his death, which took place early, the great-grandmother was left with two sons, Charles and Smith Hannington. The elder of these is described as " a man of brilliant talents and inventive genius, but who constantly failed in all his undertakings." In fact, his careless extravagance drained his mother's resources, and made it necessary that his younger brother should be apprenticed to a trade in Brighton.

This younger brother, the grandfather of James, was of different metal : steady, keen and industrious to a wonderful degree. His grandson writes of him: "He toiled in a most

marvellous manner." In after days the impression left by
the old man upon the younger generation, who were often
urged to take example by him and to walk in his steps, was
that of " a shrewd man of business, who never wanted a
holiday, and never thought that other people wanted one.
Thoroughly liberal, upright and religious ; no man more so ;
a firm and strict master, greatly loved, but also greatly
feared." In which description, in spite of the unlikeness, we
cannot but recognize the texture of the stock from which
the subject of this biography was hewn. One trait very
remarkably characterized both grandfather and grandson,—a
devoted attachment to the mother. This mother-love was a
controlling influence of great power in the life of James. He
can never write of his mother but his pen frames some new
term of endearment. She is to him " the gentlest mother,
the sweetest, dearest mother that ever lived." If he is in
any trouble, " her darling hand " has always power to soothe
him.

And it is told of the grandfather that, when quite a young
man, he had a highly advantageous offer of partnership from
the owner of a large business in the North of England, but
he refused it, tempting as it was, because his mother could
not accompany him, and he would not leave her alone.

Mr. Smith Hannington married a lady of renowned
beauty, of which traces remained even in James's time, and
by her had five children, the eldest of whom, the father of
James, settled in Brighton and carried on the business which
had been there commenced. For some time he continued
to reside in Brighton, in accordance with the wise old adage
too often neglected in these days, " Prepare thy work without, and *afterwards* build thine house." * There seven
children were born, but in the year 1847, just before the

---

* Prov. xxiv. 27.

birth of James, ability and attention to business having produced their usual result, Mr. Charles Smith Hannington purchased the property of St. George's, Hurstpierpoint, which henceforth became the home of the family.

James Hannington writes: " I was born on the third of September, 1847. The only peculiar circumstance connected with my birth was the fact that my father was in Paris at the time. Can this have anything to do with my passionate love of travelling ? Because none of my brothers seem thus affected."

Hurst, as the inhabitants call it for brevity's sake, is a pretty little village in the south of Sussex. On the side next to Brighton, from which it is distant some eight miles, the horizon is bounded by the wavy line of the high downs. Beyond these, hidden behind their windmill-crowned ramparts, is the sea. On the other side lies a wide stretch of fair view—such a view as is peculiar to the south of England. Pretty undulating country, well wooded, here and there the warm red of old brick farm-steadings catching the level rays of the setting sun, and glowing into crimson on tall chimney-stalk and tiled roof ridge ; everywhere free flowing curves topped with foliage, melting, in the far distance, into the dim uncertainty of broken tree-line.

The mansion of St. George's is pleasantly situated near the entrance to the village. It stands within its own large garden and grounds. At the back a glass door opens upon a flight of wide steps descending to the lawn. All around are shrubberies full of deep nooks, wherein children may hide and play. Not far off are two lakelets, among the spreading weeds of which, and between the broad lily leaves, myriads of mysterious creatures skim and dart, and send up bubbles to the surface from strange and unknown depths. Then, outside the iron railings which bound the lawn, are the fields spangled with golden buttercups, and beyond all stretches the illimitable country that opens out upon the world. A very child's paradise !

Here, there, and everywhere, through this pleasance, went little baby James, with the keenest of inquiring eyes : of that we may be sure. There was no nook in the grounds, from the holly bush where the blackbird had swung that cunning nest of hers with the four mottled eggs in it, to the bank where the humble bee burrled out from some hole behind the broad dock leaves, into which his paddling, sturdy little feet had not taken him. Before long there was no secret of moss or flower or hidden chrysalis, in garden or shrubbery, that had not been probed by his busy, eager fingers. He was a born naturalist. One of the earliest sayings of his, treasured up and recorded by his father, is, " I have just seen a big bird, which could only be a thrush or an eagle ! "

To the end of his life he could not resist turning aside to see some strange insect, or to note some new plant, or examine some interesting geological specimen. Of this faculty for observation and interest in that book of Nature, the pages of which are opened wide-spread before him who has eyes to see, we shall find many traces in his letters and journals. " Beetles " and " mosses " always bulked largely in his estimate of the desirability of any spot in which to spend a holiday.

His very youthful peccadilloes took their form from this early developed love of "specimens." Other boys might steal sugar or jam when the cupboard was by chance left unlocked ; his baby hands itched for the wondrous things behind the glass doors of the library museum. He says, " No portfolio or cabinet was safe from my nasty little fingers." Once it was a rare Babylonian seal, at another time a trayful of selected minerals, which were abstracted, and with much glee hidden away among the miscellaneous articles which formed his peculiar treasure.

This tendency to observe and "collect" was both inherited from and encouraged by that "sweetest, dearest mother," who made a companion of her wayward, erratic little son, and both fostered and directed his natural love of science in many branches. As he grew older, the delight of James was to pore over the treasures of his ever-increasing cabinets with his mother, and to arrange and classify the specimens and relics which they had collected, during their travels, from land and sea.

Taking his education, however, as a whole, we cannot feel satisfied that the best plan was adopted in the upbringing of the child. There seems to have been much liberty, checked by an occasional vigorous application of the birch rod, but little systematic teaching or sustained and orderly training. Now, liberty tempered by the birch rod can never be a very safe system under which to bring up any lad, especially a headstrong and passionate boy with a marked individuality like that of our little James. We are inclined to think that a little less of both in the days of his childhood would have saved him the necessity for more than one lesson hard to be learnt in the days of his manhood.

He himself blames the old-fashioned severity with which any fault, when brought home to him, was punished. "I am not quite certain," he says, "that it did not destroy my moral courage. I have none, and I think that it was from fear that I lost it. To this very day I am afraid out of my wits to ask my father for the simplest thing; and yet I know that there is no likelihood of his refusing me." He also attributes a certain reserve of character and unwillingness to unfold himself to the inspection of others, to the same cause. With regard to this self-criticism we may say that he perhaps may have been reserved to this extent, that he never found it easy, either by letter or in conversation, to convey to another what he felt most deeply. He

was not given to unburdening himself, except to his most
chosen intimates, who were the privileged recipients of his
confidences. This may have been natural, or it may have
been the result of his peculiar training. We are inclined to
think that both may be held, in a measure, responsible for
it. Lacking in moral courage I do not think he was—
certainly not to any conspicuous extent : rather the reverse.
It may have been that moral courage was not natural to
him. In that case there belongs to him the greater honour
of acquiring it.

The man who is naturally gifted with *physical* courage
has no fear of exposing his *body* to rude assaults. And
perhaps we may define *moral* courage as a certain fearlessness in exposing the *inner* self to possible laceration or
rebuff. Insensibility to fear is popularly accounted bravery ;
but he, surely, is no less brave, rather more so, who, though
he vibrates through all his nervous system, and shrinks from
exposure to pain or violence, yet schools himself to encounter them without flinching. And as the courage of that
general, who, preparing to lead his men into the hottest fore-
front of the battle, thus addressed his trembling knees: "Ah!
you would quake worse if you only knew where I am going
just now to take you,"—is justly considered to have been of
a higher order than the stolid insensibility which carried
others calmly enough into the jaws of death—so, he who
resolutely masters his *moral* cowardice, and faces his duty
manfully, must be considered the most truly morally brave.
If it be true, then, that James Hannington, who possessed
the attribute of physical courage in so marked a degree, was
naturally deficient in that moral courage which is the more
important of the two, we can only say that to him belongs
the credit of overcoming his natural weakness in a very marvellous manner. To those who observed him closely, there
were not wanting signs that it was an effort to him to expose

himself—that is, his sensitive, inner self— speaking from the heart to the heart, as must be done when a man wishes to influence another soul. But with whatever severity he may have judged himself, to his friends he always appeared as a man who might be relied upon to do his duty unflinchingly; to speak out what was in his mind, and to abide by the issue. He would sometimes class himself with such characters as Mr. Feeble-Mind, or Mr. Ready-to-Halt; but to us he appeared rather Mr. Valiant-for-Truth, with his sword ever ready to his hand.

The mixed and broken nature of his early education had, at least, this advantage. It set him free to think for himself, and possessing as he did unusual powers of observation, and naturally disposed to make use of them, he gained, while still a lad, a sturdy independence of character, and a knowledge of men and things, quite beyond those of his own age.

The first thirteen years of his life, then, were spent at home, and in travelling and yachting with his parents.

Many stories are told of his fearless and excitable nature. He was always, with the best intentions, in some mischief. Always on the verge of a serious accident; almost always escaping without much harm done, since the perfectly fearless rarely suffer by their own rashness. It is recorded how, at the age of seven, he clambered unnoticed up the mast of his father's yacht, and was at last discovered high aloft, suspended on some projection by the seat of his trousers. And many other such adventures. He must have kept his mother constantly upon the tiptoe of nervous expectation as to what would happen next.

He was eleven years of age when he was permitted to make his first yachting trip alone with his elder brother, Samuel. He says: " My father hired for us a small cutter, of about thirty-two tons. A very slow old tub she was, and, therefore, named the 'Antelope.' Sam was at this time between sixteen and seventeen years old, but very manly for his age. Everything on board was of the roughest description. We used to wait upon ourselves, make our own beds, and do all that sort of thing. Sea pies and plum duff were our standing dishes. All this mattered little to us ; we were as happy and contented as the days were long. The first day, being slightly qualmish, I lay on the deck in the sun, and the next morning was in the most miserable plight, my whole face one mass of blisters, piteous to behold." So, starting from Brighton, they went round the Isle of Wight, past Portland, and as far as the Land's End ; visiting Torquay, Dartmouth, Penzance, St. Michael's Mount, and almost every place of interest accessible to them. The brothers also made an excursion to the famous Loggan Rock, hard by the Land's End ; and James tells the story of that unfortunate practical joker who paid so dearly for his folly—that Lieutenant of a Revenue Cutter, who landed a party to throw the great rocking-stone over the cliff, " to make a grand splash." He only succeeded in moving the mass a few inches, but it rocked no more. The owner of an inn, to which the balanced stone attracted visitors, sued the luckless lieutenant for damages, and he was condemned to replace the stone in its original position. This he did with partial success, but only by special machinery, and at such cost that " he was reduced to beggary." James draws a suitable moral from this, and concludes : " Alas ! I am scarcely in a position to preach ; I have been so fond of playing practical jokes myself." He continues : " We returned in our own time to the Isle of Wight. My father came down to Portsmouth and settled with Redman (the captain and owner). That very night I was awaked by a great disturbance on deck, a crash of bottles, and a sound as of fumbling in our wine locker.

Ah! I always told Sam, thought I, that our wine went too fast; there they are in the act. Urchin as I was, I don't think that, in those days, I knew fear. I struck a light, never went to see whether Sam was awake, but marched into the forecastle and looked at the men. They were both sound asleep, and a stranger lying on the floor asleep too. I then slipped up the forecastle ladder, and should have sallied right up to the offending parties, had not Sam waked and seen me, and called me back, fearing I might get hurt. I had, however, time to see old Redman fearfully tipsy; a woman with him on deck, and a man in a boat holding on by the side. As I did not dare disobey Sam, I crept back into bed, and we heard the woman say, 'I *will* have the silver spoon, uncle Joe; give us the silver spoon.' Here the boatman interposed, saying it was past three o'clock, and he would wait no longer; so the female had to go without the spoon, and Redman stumbled down to his bin, amid straw and broken bottles. Next morning, daring young imp, I called him out of his berth before I was dressed. However, he did not appear until about one o'clock, and tried to look as if nothing had happened. Sam did not quite know how to introduce the subject; we were both very young, and did not like to rebuke such an elderly sinner. At last I went up to him with all the assurance of eleven years, and asked him before everybody why his niece wanted our silver spoon. He tried to look surprised, and said, 'I don't understand you, sir!' But Sam now found his opportunity, and opened up the subject till Redman was, I remember, ready to drop on his knees that nothing more might be said. We forgave him. We had enjoyed the cruise beyond measure, and the little adventure of ' Uncle Joe' only added spice to it."

The result of this trip was that young James quite made up his mind to " go to sea." This might, perhaps, have been his lot, but the death at sea of an elder brother had determined his parents not to allow another son to enter the navy. So the country lost a daring seaman, but she has gained thereby the priceless legacy of the memory of a Christian martyr.

Another adventure we must chronicle, not merely as illustrating the courage of the boy, but as explaining a conspicuous physical defect—the absence of the thumb upon his left hand.

He was bent upon taking a wasp's nest, and had just been initiated into the mystery of making damp gunpowder squibs, or " blue devils." Full of his new acquirement, he sought out Joe, the keeper's son, and together they got possession of a broken powder-flask. "In a few minutes," he says, " blue devils were in a state of readiness, but we must needs, before starting, try one with touch-paper. The result was not so satisfactory as we had expected, and Joe Simmons says I tried to pour a little powder on the top of it. The spring of the flask was broken, and in an instant a terrific explosion took place. The flask was blown to atoms, and I was to be seen skipping about, shaking my hand as if twenty wasps were settling on it. Simmons senior rushed up at the report, and binding up my hand in his handkerchief, led me off to the house, about a quarter of a mile distant, my hand all the while streaming with blood, so as to leave a long red streak in the road. When I reached the garden I was so faint that Miles, the gardener, took me up and carried me. The first person I met was my mother. She at once saw that something was wrong, and, in spite of my saying that I had only cut my finger a little, she sent off for the doctor. I was soon under chloroform, and my thumb was amputated. It was quite shattered, and only hanging by the skin. I was very prostrate from the great loss of blood, but, through the mercy of God, I soon got well again. I never suffered with the lost thumb, I may say, at all. I used to feel the cold in it; but that also has passed away, although even now I cannot bear a blow upon it without considerable pain. It is a great wonder that I was not taken off by tetanus!"

About a year after this, in the summer of 1860, James went with one of his brothers and their tutor for a tour through Wales. One or two extracts from his diary are worth quoting, as instancing that keen sense of humour which was one of his striking characteristics. Upon the top of a coach, near Aberystwith, they encountered a certain Unitarian. At him the tutor, a young man reading for orders, straightway launched himself. The conflict was an unequal one. The stranger turned out to be the "father of two senior wranglers, whom he had educated himself." The fiery orthodoxy of the tutor, in spite of his newly-acquired theological battery, was no match for the dogmatism of the father of the wranglers. James writes, evidently with gleeful remembrance of the scene : " Mr. —— rushed at him single-handed; words waxed very warm; the Unitarian's arms flew about like the sweeps of a windmill. We were ordered not to listen to the profane babbler, but we could not help hearing our tutor scream in a very loud voice, ' But you won't let me get a word in edgeways.' '*And I don't mean to,*' replied his adversary, in still louder tones. I fear he had the fight pretty much his own way, for our tutor said that he was a nasty, rude man, and forbade us to speak to him again." Do we not *see* them? That raw young man, with his thin veneering of theological lore, and that hot-blooded Welsh mathematician, butting against each other in direst conflict?

Again, how graphically he tells the story of that abominable old Welshwoman, "an ancient dame, rheumatic and lame," who "was got on top of the coach by means of a ladder and ropes, two or three men pushing and pulling

with all their might"! The driver, an ex-colonel in the
army, rated at the old dame, and "vowed he would not
stop the coach for such a time. However, they at last
got her up, and she sat coughing and groaning. We soon
began to speculate about her descent, and it became a matter
of conjecture as to how she was to be got down. Two or
three hours afterwards we arrived at Harlech, and the horses
were changed. While this was being done the colonel and
other passengers darted in to get some refreshment. Old
mother was cruelly left on the box to take care of herself.
Thinking, of course, that she was safely housed, the money
for her fare had not been taken. Not two minutes elapsed—
in fact, the colonel only gave himself time to swallow a hasty
glass of beer, when he returned to look at his new team.
Lo! that ancient dame had jumped down, baskets, bundles,
and all, and had given him the slip. If he cursed her in his
heart because she took such a long time to get up, he cursed
her ten times more because she took such a short time to
get down! It was the joke of the day—even the colonel
could not help laughing, although he had lost his money."

Poor little James had now reached the age when
children begin to be uncomfortably conscious of their
own personal appearance and deficiencies. Though he
was in later life singularly free from susceptibility of this
kind, and never seemed to wince beneath any most pointed
personalities that might be thrust at him by maliciously-
minded friends, there is a touch of boyish pain in the following record. An overflow of third-class passengers had
filled their compartment with a number of roysterers, who
cursed and swore forth profane vulgarities all the way home.
"I perfectly well recollect," he writes, "that one of these
cursers, much to my annoyance, noticed that I had lost my
thumb, and I was very impressed, as he was the first
stranger" (brutal fellow!) "that had remarked it to me."

CHAPTER II.

SCHOOLDAYS.

(1860—62.)

"My bonnie laddie's young, but he's growin' yet."
Old Scotch Ballad.

VERY shortly after the Welsh tour referred to in the last chapter, the tutor left to take a curacy. What was to be done with the boys? James was now thirteen, and not very easy for a tutor to manage. Good-natured and warm-hearted, but withal quick tempered, and an inveterate tease : capable of great industry when the subject—as that of natural history—interested him ; but otherwise seemingly incorrigibly idle, and utterly averse to apply himself to the dull routine of the classical mill : it was evident to his parents that he and his brother Joseph ought to go to school. It was only, however, after long thought and some demur that it was finally decided that they should enter the Temple School at Brighton.

"Alas !" he writes, "it was only a private school, and we were allowed to go home every Saturday to stop till Monday morning."

The home-bred boy was at first, naturally enough, very unhappy. The memory of the day when he was left, pale, nervous, and shivering, in the schoolroom, among his new companions, always clung to him. Do not most of us recal such a moment? The kindly manner of the head-master, however, made things easier for both the brothers, and they soon fell into their places.

Hannington criticizes with some severity the private tutor and private school system, with frequent visits home, under which, by a mistaken kindness, he had been brought up. He writes in his journal, " I knew absolutely nothing, the result of private tutorage, and I was put into the fourth class, which was bottom but one." Again, speaking of the time when he left school, he adds : " I only remained at school until I was fifteen and a half, and then left for business, with as bad an education as possible ; I may say as bad as my father's was good. I was no more fit to leave school than to fly, and yet I was then in the first class. So much for private tutors and private schools. I believe that both systems are equally pernicious." All of which I transcribe without either endorsing the opinion or otherwise, except so far as to remind the reader that what is one boy's poison may be another boy's food. As regards a boy of Hannington's type, it can scarcely be doubted that the system he condemns was open to serious objections. As he says of himself : " I was naturally idle, and would not learn of myself, and I was unfortunate enough always to be sent to places where I was not driven to learn. Would that I had been driven ! " In the later years of his short life, his industry and application were unwearied and immense. No one could accuse him of trifling with his time, or of the smallest degree of self-indulgence. He was scrupulously painstaking in the execution of any work which he undertook, and his undertakings he meted out to himself with no scant hand. But no one can doubt that his university course, upon which so much of a man's future depends, would have been quite other than it was, perhaps even a brilliant one, had he possessed the advantage of a more thorough and systematic early training.

Hannington had plenty of intelligence ; was as sharp as a needle ; quick to learn what he chose to learn ; and what

he once learned he always retained. Volatile and excitable
as he was, he could be serious enough when the occasion
seemed to demand it, and in the midst of all his extrava-
gances a certain solid good sense generally kept him within
bounds, so that he never committed any act which could
cause himself or others serious regret. He soon became a
prime favourite at school, both with the masters and boys.
That the former should have been the case is more strange
than the latter. He soon proved himself to be a confirmed
" pickle." He thus reports himself : "I was always very
excitable and noisy, and was called ' Mad Jim.' In fact,
I was one day reported to the Head-Master as ' verging on
insanity,' and was severely punished." He cnce lit a
bonfire in the middle of his dormitory ; at another time
pelted the German Master with his rejected papers ; and
we are not much surprised to learn that, on one particularly
unlucky day, he was " caned more than a dozen times,"
till, smarting in every inch of his body, he had serious
thoughts of running away.

The Head-Master, however, was most judicious and
kind. Whatever was lacking in his pupil's education, the
fault could not be laid upon the threshold of the pedagogue.
He liked the giddy boy, into whose truly lovable nature he
saw, and easily secured his affection in return. Hannington
was sensitively conscientious and trustworthy. Hatred of a
lie was inborn and inbred in him. He might always be
entirely relied upon to carry out anything that he had once
undertaken, and that not only in the letter, but in the spirit.
His word was, in the most rigid sense, his bond. This
fidelity of mind was developed in him very early.

The following instance seems quite a remarkable one of
a schoolboy's endurance for conscience sake.

Every school has its bully. A certain R. R. filled this
rôle during the time Hannington was at the Temple School.

Being rash enough to attack this boy, Hannington got, what perhaps upon that occasion he richly deserved, a tremendous thrashing. Both of his eyes were closed up, and sundry egg-like bumps upon his head bore witness to the hardness of his adversary's fists. That same afternoon he, unluckily, had to go home to pay his weekly visit. Horrified at the dreadful appearance of her son, his mother made him promise that he would never fight again.

Now, there never was one more absolutely devoid of physical fear than James Hannington. Yet, holding himself bound by that promise of his, he returned to school defenceless. Everyone knows what must be the fate of a schoolboy when once the young imps about him have clearly ascertained that he will not fight. He was soon made thoroughly wretched. His pusillanimity, for such it seemed, was taken advantage of in every way. He went about like a muzzled mastiff, submitting to be treated by his tormentors like a coward and a cur.

At last he could stand it no longer. " One day," he says, " I had allowed myself to be bullied nearly to death by B. P., a boy about my own size, when all of a sudden I turned round and said, to the astonishment of the whole school, that I would fight him. He was backed by his cousin, only son of Baron P.; I don't think I had anybody to back me, but I very soon gave him a thrashing, and I never recollect being bullied afterwards." He always remembered that act as a " broken promise," but who can doubt that such a promise was a greater burden laid upon a schoolboy's shoulders than he could be reasonably expected to bear !

CHAPTER III.

BUSINESS AND PLEASURE.

(1862—67.)

"Always roaming with a hungry heart,
Much have I seen and known."
Ulysses.

"One has to spend so many years in learning how to be happy."
GEORGE ELIOT.

IT too often happens in life that the square man is put into
the round hole ; and not only put there, but rammed down
into the hole, and worked back and forth in it, until his
angles have somewhat accommodated themselves to the
misfit. So the wheels of life go round, somehow, not
without a good deal of friction, and some expostulatory
creaking. Happily the subject of this memoir proved altogether too polygonal to be fitted, by any most careful easing
whatever, into the hole which circumstances seemed to have
prepared for him. He already possessed a moderate com-
petence. The portion of goods that belonged, or would
belong to him was likely to be sufficient for his wants.
But the road to fortune lay plainly through the counting-
house, and his father's established and high-class place of
business.

To the counting-house at Brighton, then, he was sent
at the age of fifteen, and there he remained more or less
during six years. He was wholly unsuited, by almost every
characteristic he possessed, for the monotonous routine of a
commercial life. Generous, impulsive, erratic, the careful
men who managed that great business house, had they

taken him into partnership, would have discovered before
long that they had bound a very zebra to their cart yoke.
" Canst thou bind the unicorn with his band in the furrow ?
or will he harrow the valleys after thee ? " The experiment has often been tried.   The result has, we venture to
say, seldom been satisfactory.   Happily, in Hannington's
case, the " fork " was not too persistently applied to that
ever-recurring nature of his.   After six years he was allowed
to choose that path for which the Divine Hand had
fashioned him.

   On looking through the record of these six years they
seem to have been filled up with almost more pleasuring
than " business."   Hannington writes : " As soon as I left
school I was allowed to go with my late master, W. H.
Gutteridge, on a trip to Paris.   I was intensely delighted ;
so much so that at first I could scarcely realize it.   Once,
when a little boy, having caught an unusually fine fish,
thinking that I must be asleep and dreaming, I pinched myself as hard as I could, and repeated the pinch two or three
times, to make quite certain that I was awake.   And now,
as I stepped on board the steamer at Newhaven, I felt
much the same inclination to pinch myself, it seemed so
impossible that I was really on my way to spend six or
eight weeks abroad.   Visions of cardinals shut up in cages,
of the horrors of revolutions, the Hunchback of Notre
Dame, the Morgue, magnificent chocolate shops, all these
and more confusedly floated through my brain."   A
marginal note to the diary, evidently written much later,
adds what was always a dominant thought with him, " My
dearest of mothers was pleased too, and I think that knowing this gave me such great joy."

   This trip is described in his notes at great length.   No
doubt all the information those notes contain can be
gathered from a guide book, but it is not too much to say

that few guide books, drawn up by experienced and profes-
sional travellers, could give much more information, or pay
minuter attention to details than does the diary of this boy
of fifteen. There was almost nothing in the towns he
visited which he did not see, and, what is more, which he
did not think worth the seeing. He was at this time very
far from being a mere gaping schoolboy. If he did not yet
see much beneath the shell of things, he at least took an
intelligent interest in everything. He congratulates himself
upon having had such an excellent travelling companion
as Mr. Gutteridge; but we might also congratulate Mr.
Gutteridge himself upon the companionship of that uncon-
ventionally fresh young mind.

They went to a boarding-house kept by a certain
Madame Boys, from whence he writes to his mother :—

"DEAREST MAMMA,—You will be very glad to hear
that we had a capital passage. We played chess on board
the steamer all the time : neither of us sick. We went to
church Christmas morning at the Ambassador's Chapel,
and to the Madeleine in the afternoon. We had a very
grand dinner party in the evening. Madame Boys is a kind,
good-natured, vulgar, blowing-up-servants little woman—
all very desirable points to make me happy. I mean to
bring you home six snails with rich plum pudding stuffing
in them. With my very best love to all, especially papa,
Your affectionate son,   JAMES HANNINGTON."

The Archbishop of Paris was just at this time at the
point of death. The following thoroughly boyish remark
occurs in one of James's letters home : "I am rather glad
that the Archbishop is dead ; we are going to see him lying
in state." Which they accordingly did, and his funeral
afterwards. They missed nothing, these two.

A short six months were now spent in the house of

business, and then another trip abroad with Mr. Gutteridge
was planned and carried out.

This time they went to Brussels, Antwerp, Luxem-
bourg, Trèves, and many other places, about all of which
Hannington has much to say.   Nothing escaped his obser-
vant eyes, and everything was carefully noted in his pocket-
book.   At Wiesbaden he notes (the gaming tables were
then in full swing) : " Those who seemed to be regular pro-
fessional gamblers were the ugliest set of people that I ever
saw in my life.   A gambling table is a curious sight.   I
recollected those awfully eager and ugly faces for many a
long day."

From Wiesbaden and Frankfort the travellers made their
way to Baden Baden, " nestling in the heart of the Black
Forest like a beautiful but deadly snake on a bank of purple
violets."

Then on to Lucerne, whose fairy-like charms seem to
have inspired the following not unmusical verse :

> " Oh ! for a painter's brush, or poet's pen,
>   That I might now pourtray
>   The glories I saw then.
>   The silver moon, the cloudless starlit sky,
>   The deep, the rippling lake ;
>   Grim Pilate standing by,
>   Hoar-white his rugged peak with glistening snow,
>   Like some fierce lion's fang,
>   Unbared to meet the foe."

From the Wengern Alp James saw his first avalanche,
with which, having, like most travellers, formed marvellous
conceptions of falling mountains, he was at first rather disappointed.   He saw the great Rhone Glacier, not then
shrunk to its present lesser proportions.   From thence the
two crossed over the St. Gothard Pass into Italy, saw the
Lakes and Milan, and penetrated as far as Venice.   Returning across the Simplon, they visited Chamounix, and

made a glacier excursion as far as the " Jardin," an excursion no less fascinating because so often " done." Thence home by Geneva and Paris. The whole trip of two months (June and July of 1863) was evidently not wasted upon the boy, but was a real factor in his education.

The First of September that followed was a notable day in the lad's diary. He was allowed to take out a game-license for the first time, and shot his first bird. The occurrence was, moreover, impressed upon his memory by the explosion of a cartridge in the opened breech of his gun, whereby his face was severely cut and burnt, and for some little time he was quite blinded.

Mr. and Mrs. Hannington had now taken to a yachting life, and spent much of their time on board. James, who was devoted to the sea and its adventures, was frequently passing backwards and forwards between Portsmouth, where the yacht often lay, and Brighton.

" *Sunday, Nov. 1st*, 1863.—Caught in a tremendous squall returning from church at Portsmouth. Never was there such a churchgoer as my mother. She simply would go if it was possible. I wonder that we never capsized during those rough-weather journeys."

The next entry in his diary records his commission as second lieutenant in the 1st Sussex Artillery Volunteers.

" *March 28th*, 1864.—My first day in uniform."

" *June 11th*.—Rapid progress in soldiering. Battalion inspected, and I had command of my company."

Hannington made an excellent artillery officer. He was a great favourite with the men, from whom, however, he exacted implicit obedience. He early displayed considerable organizing power ; and always gave that attention to seemingly trifling details which goes so far to ensure the success of any undertaking.

July and the first week of August of this year were
spent on board the yacht *Zelia*, and in a continental tour
with his parents through part of France, Germany, and
Switzerland. His taste for travel was as keen as ever ; and
everything was noted in the never-absent pocket-book for
future reference.

"*Aug.* 11*th.* — My father gave me a single-barrel
breech-loader gun ; 17 guineas. My delight is great."

"*Sept.* 3*rd.*—My seventeenth birthday. Shot eighteen
brace of birds, four hares, one landrail. 5 feet 10 inches high,
weight 11 stone 6 lb. Sam gave me a garnet ring ; Phil a
gold locket."

In October of the same year he was with his parents in
another yachting excursion. They visited the island of
Alderney, and, in spite of very rough weather, managed to
enjoy themselves. James writes while they were still off
Portsmouth :

" *Saturday*, *the* 22*nd.*—Weather looks worse, though sea
rather smoother. Landed in boat, and, returning, got caught
in a terrific squall, and had great difficulty in reaching the
yacht. Found mother and the crew greatly frightened for
us ; the former in tears. We were an hour behind our
time."

" *Sunday*, *the* 23*rd.*—It blew furiously. No landing for
church. Which means that it *did* blow."

Coming home across the choppy waters of the Channel
they were nearly cut down by the West Indian Packet just
as they entered the Needles. "We had watched her approaching for more than an hour, and as we were beating
up on the right tack, and every foot was of importance to
us, the captain trusted to her giving way, but she evidently
expected us to do the same, and kept on. The huge

monster dashed by within a few feet of us. The men shouted, and my father as coolly as possible fired a blue light, and we were saved."

The following entry appears in the diary for December 30th :—" Father went on deck with five sovereigns in one hand and the paper in which they had been wrapped in the other. He threw the sovereigns overboard and kept the paper. He was much vexed."

The verses which conclude his diary for 1864 show that, though he might not at that time have had any real and vital religion, yet that he was religiously minded, and not disinclined to think seriously. They are worth quoting.

> " My heart, Lord, may I ever raise
> To Thee in humble thanks and praise
> For keeping me throughout this year.
> Lord, guard and guide me while I'm here,
> And when to die my time is come,
> Oh! take me to Thy heavenly home."

A further proof that his mind was beginning to bestir itself, and his spirit to grope after something reliable upon which it might lay hold, is to be found in the remarkable entry made against March 6th, 1865. "Left off mourning for Cardinal Wiseman." He adds a little later : "The fact is that about this time I nearly turned Roman Catholic ; but my faith was much shaken by reading Cardinal Manning's funeral sermon for the above. Also by his own last words, ' Let me have all the Church can do for me.' I seemed to see at once that if the highest ecclesiastic stood thus in need of external rites on his death-bed, the system must be rotten, and I shortly after gave up all idea of departing from our Protestant faith."

Only once again did he ever experience any leaning toward the Roman Church, when for a single moment he thought that he recognized in the quiet seclusion of a

certain cloister the soil suitable for the growth of the
spiritual life, then working still more restlessly within him.
But, in sooth, James Hannington would never have made a
" good " Catholic of the Roman type, much less a monk
who would have been tolerated for a single day by any
" Superior." He was never wont to " think by the
bonnet," * and his sturdy independence of reasoning, and
sound, masculine common sense, would have soon burst
through the cramping enswathements of the Roman system,
or procured him a speedy and emphatic eviction out of that
fold. All this time scarcely a single entry in the diary refers
to the " business." Almost all his time seems to have been
spent on board the yacht. Evidently James was far more
keen to cultivate " horny hands and weather - beaten
haffets " † in many a conflict with the salt-laden winds and
blue racing waves of the open Channel, than a bold commercial style of penmanship, and an automatic accuracy in
totting up figures. He says with some pride : " I can now
sail a boat uncommonly well. To-day I proposed going
across to France in the wherry, and got well scolded for the
suggestion."

In April of this year (1865) he paid a fortnight's visit to
a friend at Virginia Water, Capt. Welsh, " Admiral of the
Queen's Rowing-boats."

" *April 8th.*—After dinner a croquet party. Prince
Alfred came in in the middle of it. Saw the Queen.

" *April* 10*th.*—Another croquet party, which was suddenly interrupted by the arrival of the Queen. We had to
scamper off indoors ; but from my bed-room window I
could hear the Queen laughing and chatting in a most merry
way to Capt. Welsh."

---

* " He thinks by the bonnet, like a monk in Sorbonne."
† Cheeks.   PASCAL (*Old French Proverb*).

"*April* 17*th.*—Rode with Vernon. Called on the Mills. Coming back, was playing the penny whistle, when suddenly met the Queen. I wonder what she thought of my performance ! "

The month of June was spent on board the *Zelia.* A family party was made up for a trip by sea to the west coast of Scotland ; and then once more the serious business of life began, and James turned his unwilling feet to the unwelcome warehouse. He says : " I left the dear yacht and returned to Brighton. I hoped to do well ; but, alas ! it was not from the bottom of my heart. I never could like the business." His head was full of the sunny western sea ; and great green Atlantic rollers breaking over the half-hidden fangs of treacherous reefs ; and the sloping deck of the yacht under pressure of sail, cutting her way through the seething water ; and rocky islands, purple against flaming skies ; and everything but the adding up of those never-ending columns of figures, and the acquirement of knowledge of the texture of merchantable fabrics in that terrible warehouse. Had a business career been seriously planned for him, he would, perhaps, have been kept more rigorously to the grindstone ; but no doubt his parents were at this time willing to allow him to discover for himself, by actual experience of life, in what direction his natural bent tended. He had, accordingly, far more liberty than is granted to most boys at the age of eighteen, who are not intended for a life of idleness.

It is very noticeable that, under this treatment, Hannington never displayed the least tendency to pass his time in lounging about, frequenting the clubs, or in any way leading a fast life. His time was never unoccupied—never hung heavy on his hands. He was never one of those who affect to be superior to the occupations and amusements of every-day life—who yawn, and find nothing to interest them in the world. He always had something to do—always something in hand ; and what he did undertake he carried through with a heartiness and delighted enthusiasm which never failed to infect others and stir them up to co-operate. It was this faculty which made him the very life and centre of any circle of society into which he was introduced. His friends often found themselves, under his influence, working might and main for the achievement of some object in which none of them had taken the slightest previous interest, but which Hannington had made the all-important object of the hour.

About this time he threw himself heart and soul into the work of his battery. He passed his examination for promotion, and about the end of the year received his commission as captain. His delight was boundless when, at the Artillery Volunteer Camp at Shoeburyness, the Brighton men won both the Palmerston Prize of 40 guineas and the Queen's Prize of 100 guineas. His own detachment behaved itself very creditably, and showed signs of careful drilling. I find this entry after the return from the camp : "I presented a gold pin to Bomb. C. for good shooting." At this time, also, he began to show signs of that interest in the welfare of young men which in after years was so marked a feature of his ministry. He took a great deal of trouble in procuring for them suitable recreation rooms, and personally inspected, tested, and bought the various articles necessary for their equipment. He organized concerts, readings, and games, and made himself a prime favourite with the men under his charge.

Hannington was always fond of telling a good story against himself. Here is one : On Easter Monday, 1866, at the Grand Review, the Prince and Princess of Wales being present, he was appointed major to the battalion. Right proudly he jingled along upon his gaily-caparisoned charger. Scarcely, however, had they started, when that horse, unmindful of his own dignity or that of his master, took the bit between his teeth and bolted. Away flew James in full view of the admiring Prince and Royal party. First his horse made for a gap which led over the cliff; from thence, being hardly turned by the waving arms of some fisherfolk, he dashed down the pavement and ran full tilt into a cart; grazing this, he was nearly knocked from the saddle by violent contact with a cab horse; and next, still sticking bravely on, he charged home into a mounted officer. At last, not without effort, this mad career was checked, and the major rode back to his post, girth broken and accoutrements all awry, amid the ironical cheering of the delighted crowd. So he tells us. But if he appeared, through his charger's misdemeanour, in a ridiculous light that day, he at all events seems to have enjoyed the occurrence as much as any of the onlookers.

The same spring, the Hanningtons made up a family party for a long yachting trip to the Mediterranean. James's diary has the following :—

" *May 9th.*—Left Brighton with Sam and Jos, and found father and mother at Lymington, busy putting a few finishing touches. Among other things that they have added to one of the best fitted and most comfortable yachts afloat, is a steam launch. Scarcely another yacht has one."

This, of course, was in 1866. They landed first at Belem, on the Tagus, and saw all that was to be seen. " Got permission and went over the Castle, which is exceedingly picturesque, and built of marble. They are much behindhand in gunnery—only some old 12-pounders on wooden carriages, painted red. The sentry sits about and smokes in the most casual manner. I got into conversation with the guard, and showed them the manual and platoon. One spied my thumb, and at once affirmed for me that I had lost it in war."

Gibraltar, Algiers, and many places are described with much patient minuteness. At the latter place he bought a young jackal, which was brought home with him as a pet. On this cruise his botanical notes begin to multiply ; and he evidently used the microscope systematically, and to good purpose. From Naples, James and his brothers ascended Vesuvius, and disported themselves in the crater, which was then in a slight state of eruption. At Civita Vecchia they went on board the Pope's yacht, *The Immaculate Conception*, " handsome outside, but very dirty in." The officer in command paid a return visit to the *Zelia*, and was much astonished at the completeness and sumptuous arrangements of the English vessel.

After some days spent in Rome, they directed their course to Genoa. James writes : " The war has broken out, and the town is in great excitement. The citizens are garrisoning the place, but present anything but a military appearance. The Garibaldians seem, to the visual eye, an awful crew."

But we need not enter into the details of this trip. The boy of nineteen chronicles all he saw, as though it had never been seen before, and never might be again by eye of mortal. He is still very boyish, pleased to be courted and admired by foreigners as " one of the lords from the English yacht." He still has a great deal to learn, but he is evidently teachable, and by the grace of God he will learn his lesson.

On the last day of August, Hannington was again in Brighton ; and the next day, being the first of September, we find him, indefatigable and keen, carrying his single-barrel breech-loader over the turnips and stubbles. He writes : " Sam and I killed between us 25½ brace of birds."

"*Nov. 3rd.*—Riding over from Brighton to shoot, my

horse fell, and rolled over with me on my leg. I never said anything about it, lest I should be forbidden to strain the leg by going out shooting. Killed eighteen brace of pheasants."

" *Nov.* 9*th.*—Went to Mayor's banquet, and delivered my maiden public speech, by returning thanks for the ladies ; received great eclat."

" 1867, *Jan.* 8*th.* — Breakfast and meet at Sir J. Simeon's. In at death."

" 9*th.* — Went across in Royal yacht *Alberta* to Southampton, and returned with Sir Stafford Northcote."

" 11*th.*—Crossed again with Sir Stafford ; inspected the docks. Treated with fearful civility, the effect of travelling in the Queen's yacht. Returned in the evening with General Gray."

" 14*th.*—Left Cowes in the *Alberta* with Lady Caroline Barrington, and returned to Hurstpierpoint."

And now follows a very singular entry. I quote it with some hesitation, as liable by the unthinking to be misunderstood. Those, however, who have had some experience in tracing the strange and complex movements of the human soul, and who have noted how, side by side, are to be found there the workings of the trivial and the tremendous, will know how to read this passage. It runs thus :

" *Feb.* 9*th.*—I lost my ring out shooting, with scarcely a hope of ever seeing it again. I offered to give the keeper 10s. if he found it, and was led to ask God that the ring might be found, and be to me a sure sign of salvation. From that moment the ring seemed on my finger ; I was not surprised to receive it from Sayers on Monday evening. He had picked it up in the long grass in cover, a most unlikely place ever to find it. A miracle ! Jesus, by Thee alone can we obtain remission of our sins." He adds, in a note written several years afterwards : " This is a quotation from my diary, written at the most worldly period of my existence." It was written, remember, for the inspection of no eye but his own, and, therefore, expressed, without doubt, the unfeigned conviction of the moment. As we have seen before, he was, in spite of his volatile exterior, by no means devoid of religious thoughtfulness. If he had not, as yet, any intelligent apprehension of his true relationship to God, he never wholly neglected the externals of religion. He had always " a secret apprehension " that there was a better way. Keenly as he enjoyed his surroundings—and no man ever entered with more zest into the pursuit of the moment—he was never wholly satisfied with a life apart from God. It is deeply interesting to notice in this strange, unreasoning appeal to the Unseen by the careless younker in his momentary vexation over the loss of a trinket, the early traces of that assured and reasonable, though childlike, trust in God which so distinguished him in later life, and marked him pre-eminently above his fellows as *a man of faith.*

He next mentions that he was " carrying on an interesting correspondence with Frank Buckland about a surface net when yachting." I believe that he never became personally acquainted with the eminent practical naturalist. Had they met, they would have found in each other congenial spirits.

After a short trip to Paris in the spring, James Hannington and his brothers started for a cruise in the Baltic, and a visit to some of the cities of Russia. The following entry in his diary marks the event:—

" *June 4th,* 1867.—Yacht *Zelia,* 195 tons. Under way 9 a.m. Abreast Brighton, 3.40. Off Beachy Head, 5.15."

Christiania, Copenhagen, Stockholm, etc., were all inspected with intelligent eyes. While at the latter place, he wrote : " The King, when we went over the palace, had

just left a cabinet council, and during the discussion had
sketched a tree and a face on a sheet of paper. The
guide's contempt when I asked for this was supreme. If
he was a fair example, Stockholmers are not overweeningly
proud of their monarch."

They then spent a week in St. Petersburg and Moscow,
keenly entering into the delights of everything that was
going in the way of entertainment, and toward the end of
July set their faces again homeward. An incident which
throws light upon Hannington's character occurred on the
return voyage. The elder brother, who was in command of
the expedition, having been recalled home by domestic affairs
which required his presence, the leadership fell to James. He
at once took the reins, and held them with no uncertain hand.
He writes: "The men have of late been very disorderly,
and getting worse, so, on my assuming command, I instantly
gave them my mind on the subject, and told them that in
future any man breaking leave would be discharged. The
first to do so, as it happened, was the captain, who remained
ashore, and, by his own confession, helplessly drunk." The
captain had no doubt that he would be able to make it
all right with the young commander. But he reckoned
without his host. Discipline was at stake. Hannington
felt that now or never was the time to assert his authority,
and in such circumstances he was not accustomed to hesitate for a moment. To the astonishment of the whole
crew, and not less so of the culprit himself, the captain was
there and then sent ashore with all his belongings. After
this dreadful example the crew gave no more trouble. They
recognized the fact that they had one at the head of affairs
who might be expected to execute what he threatened, and,
after the manner of sailors, they liked him none the worse
for it. He was fortunate enough not to suffer himself on
account of this prompt act of justice. He writes: " I met

Captain Van Deurs, a very gentlemanly man, and well recommended, whom I engaged, and an immense success he turned out." The next day they stopped a fishing smack off the coast of Denmark to buy some cod. The fisherman asked whether the yacht belonged to the King of England. "' No, there is no King ; England is ruled by a Queen.' 'Then it must belong to the Prince of Wales. *That*,' pointing to me, 'is the Prince of Wales.' No answer on Van Deurs' part confirmed them in their idea, and left them full of joy to return to their native village and pass the rest of their lives as the men who had seen and talked with the Prince who had married their own popular Princess! "

"*July 26th.*—Fell in with a tremendous gale, which came suddenly upon us with a rising glass. All sails were set at the time, and I was alone on deck, the men being at tea. I rushed forward and shouted, ' All hands shorten sail! ' and in half an hour's time we were laid to with the water washing over us most uncomfortably. Carried away our jibboom while pitching into a sea ; it was a splendid stick too. Three men were washed overboard by a huge wave while clearing the wreckage ; but the next wave flung them back on to the deck. After laying to for sixteen hours, and drifting about helplessly, scarce knowing how matters would end, there was a slight lull. I ordered the jib to be set, but it was blown to ribbons ; so we waited a little longer, and then set the storm jib and were able to continue. For two days we were without the sun, but the captain made the land by our soundings. The soundings were very interesting. The lard at the bottom of the lead brought up light silver-like sand off the Danish coast, which gradually grew darker, until almost black off the coast of England."

With this trip we may bring Chapter III. to an end. It marks the conclusion of a period in his life. As his character was formed and his disposition became more marked, his nature asserted itself more and more definitely against a " business " career. Of whatever else in life's arena he might be capable, in that at least he felt that he could never excel. His heart was not in it. Surely something else might be found for him—some other vocation— a real *vocation* to which his heart might respond, as to that for which he was created and brought into this world ; not a mere *line*, grooved out for him by the industry of his forefathers.

But how the emancipation took place must be reserved for another chapter.

CHAPTER IV.

EMANCIPATION.

(1867—68.)

" He was never a Sceptick in his Principles, but still retained a
secret Apprehension that Religion · . . was founded in Truth,
and this Conviction . . . could not but occasion some secret
Misgivings of Heart."

DODDRIDGE (*Life of Colonel Gardiner*).

ONE thing, and one thing only, had, for some time past,
prevented Hannington from shaking himself free from the
harness which galled him, and in which he felt that he could
not hope to run life's course with any prospect of credit or
success. Both his training and temperament made him unwilling to run counter to the wishes of his father, and he
could not bear the thought of inflicting the slightest pain,
or even of causing the shadow of disappointment to fall
upon the mother whom he adored. About this time, however, he made a tentative effort at freedom. He wrote to
his father with regard to the general impression of his
friends as to his unfitness for a commercial life, saying, " I
know that I am laughed at, and looked upon as fit for
nothing but collecting curiosities." In fine, he desired that
something else more congenial to him might be found, upon
which he might exercise his superabundant energies. He
says in his diary : " Sam proposed that I should take to
farming ; and there was nothing I thought I should like
better. But my father, who had had a taste of farming
himself when young, would not hear of it. My mother

wrote, saying : ' Your letter was kindly and sensibly expressed, but it brought floods of tears to my eyes. The bare
thought of my sweet boy going where his father and mother
could not see him from time to time distracts me; father,
too, said he could not bear it.' Seeing that my mother took
it so tremendously to heart, I was ashamed that I ever suggested giving up my work ; and so for the time I gave up
all thought of leaving home, and endeavoured to settle down
once more quietly and contentedly. My mother's and father's
love devoted my heart to them. I felt that I had sinned
grievously in even suggesting what might give them pain."

The matter, however, was not to rest here. "There
is a Divinity that shapes our ends," and Hannington was
not to be shaped by any parental wishes—dutiful resolutions on his own part notwithstanding—into the ordinary
type of a British merchant citizen.

The first blow struck upon his shackles was, after all,
dealt by the hand of his father. It happened in this wise.
The family had been hitherto, at least nominally, Indepen-
dents. Mr. Hannington had built a chapel in the grounds
of St. George's, in which Nonconformist services were
held. Finding, however, after a wide experience of men
and things, that they had no serious quarrel with the Church
of England, he and his family decided that they would
seek admittance into her communion. At the end, therefore, of 1867, St. George's Chapel was licensed for public
worship by the Bishop of Chichester, and the charge of it
became a curacy—virtually a sole charge—under the Rector
of Hurstpierpoint. James writes :

" *Sunday, Oct. 26th.*—The last Sunday of the dissent-
ing ministers in St. George's Chapel. Mr. Hart preached
the farewell sermon with a good deal of true emotion.
He and his wife were pensioned by my father, the pension

to continue for the last survivor's life. Little did I think
that I was ever to occupy that pulpit. Perhaps the old
man prayed for me."
  " *Dec. 14th.*—Opening service at St. George's. Mr.
Methuen, the rector, preached a splendid and most suitable
sermon ; spoke very kindly of my father. Preached also in
the afternoon to a crowded congregation."

  The consequence of this important step on the part of
his father was that Hannington was brought much into
contact with Churchmen of whom he had known little
previously. He says: "This year (1868) was most eventful to me. Through the change from dissent to the Church
I got to know the clergy of the parish church and college.
I yearned for ordination. My mother had once or twice
spoken about it, and felt my mind on the subject,
so I knew that she would offer no objections." After
some self-examination, however, he was led to conclude
that his increasing dissatisfaction with, and loathing for, the
business at Brighton had more to do with his desire for
Orders than any other motive. "I had it fixed upon my
mind that I was to be ordained," he says, " but as for real
motives I had none, or next to none. I was, I fear, a mere
formalist, and nothing more."
  However that may have been, there are not wanting in
dications in his diary that he was thinking seriously at times.
His was far too honest a nature to permit him to take any
step which did not secure the hearty concurrence of his
will and intellect. He could never have become a " mere
formalist." He had too much humanity about him, and too
much enthusiasm within him to have permitted that. A
mere secular organizer he might have perhaps become ;
enforcing zealously, and by the power of his own personality,
dogmas which lacked the power of the Spirit of God to

commend them. But from this, too, he was saved, as will appear in the course of our narrative.

To outward appearance he was still as gay, thoughtless, and reckless as ever. Delighting to startle his friends by some extraordinary feat of personal courage or endurance, by eccentric acts which could only emanate from " Jim," it was not easy to associate with this madcap the serious business of life. But the following entry will show that in his heart he was neither a careless nor indifferent spectator of the mystery of life, or of the set of the world-tide toward Eternity.

" About this time," he writes many years later, " John Thurston * came to stay with us ; very ill ; he lingered a long time ; when he was told that his case was hopeless, he not only seemed resigned, but, as far as one could tell, just touching the hem of the Saviour's garment. He died on June 6th, 1868, and was buried in Hurst churchyard, in our family vault. I was in Brighton the night he died, and at the exact time of his death I had one of those peculiar warnings—an internal thrill—which told me certainly that he was gone. My diary reads thus :

" *June 6th.*—John worse ; about one p.m. he took his leave of me. About four, at his own express desire, he received the Sacrament from Mr. Methuen, surrounded by us all. I was obliged to go to Brighton at five. As I was sitting at supper I had a heavy palpitation of the heart. Something said to me, ' John is dead ! ' I took out my watch frightened. The hour was ten p.m.

" *7th, Sunday.*—Got up at 4.30 a.m. ; walked down to see John, if not gone, though I was sure he was dead. Went straight to the doctor's room. Heard that he died at *two minutes past ten o'clock !* "

---

* A cousin.

The Lenten season of this year Hannington kept with much severity, fasting rigorously in private every Wednesday and Friday.

On April 23rd he wrote to his mother, saying: "I have decided in favour of the Church. I believe that God is with me in this matter."

On July 5th he received the Holy Communion for the first time. He wrote in his diary: "I am afraid whether I am fit. I was not so fixed in thought as I wished." Shortly after, something that he read in a " fairy tale," or some train of thought started by some expression in the book he held in his hand, led him to self-examination. He came to the conclusion that his frame of mind was not what it should be, and that he needed bracing up to his duties, both religious and secular. He writes, " Prayer refreshed me." It was not yet very intelligent prayer ; but it was the petition of a soul seeking, though with much blind groping, after a higher life, and, as such, was doubtless heard and answered by the Eternal Father.

The next day's entry runs thus : " I have to-day been much better in work. It comes easier to me when I watch and pray."

At this period of his spiritual development the functions of the Church evidently exercised a strong fascination over him. He made a point of being present when anything was being done by the clergy in the neighbourhood. Within a fortnight we find him at the laying of two foundation stones of ecclesiastical buildings, and listening with admiration to speeches made by the Bishops of Chichester and Oxford. He threw himself with his accustomed energy into this newly-found channel for his activity. He inaugurated, in connection with the Church Harvest-Home Festival, the first sports that had been known in Hurstpierpoint. He was to be seen frequently at Services in the parish church, or at choral and other festivals. He waited diligently upon the lips of such distinguished preachers as might come within possible distance of his home. His mind was apparently just in that condition in which a permanent bias, one way or the other, might have been imparted to it had he been brought into contact with one strong enough to exercise a controlling influence over him, and willing to use it.

But his time had not yet come. If the town of Mansoul was beginning to feel the stress of the siege, it was by no means yet taken, or even ready to be taken by assault. The volatile and fun-loving nature of the young man soon resumed its sway over him, the newly-fanned flame of ecclesiastical ardour soon paled and died down, and though he certainly never repudiated religion, it is equally certain that, for some years to come, he laid no claim to be esteemed " religious."

One important acquaintanceship, formed shortly after he came of age, was destined to exercise a very happy and altogether beneficial influence upon his character. He was introduced to Dean Burgon, then Fellow of Oriel, at the house of his brother-in-law, Archdeacon Rose. Hannington writes concerning him : " He is so kind, and seems to take a great interest in me, and gives me kind advice, which I hope that I shall follow. He soon perceives a fault. He stops to play with all the small children he sees. Mrs. Rose frequently says to him, ' Dear John, I wish they would make you a canon ;' and he seems to regard himself as not at all worthy of such promotion. Sunday was spent by us all, Burgon and myself included, in taking classes in the Sunday-school. He preached in the afternoon, and then took me with him for a walk."

Kind attention bestowed upon a young man is seldom wasted. In Hannington's case his esteem for Dean Burgon helped to ballast him, and was no insignificant quantity in his University life.

His college friends used to watch him, with an amused surprise, wending his way every Sunday evening to the Greek Testament class which Dean Burgon held in his rooms in Oriel. But he was not to be dissuaded. I do not recollect that he ever missed that class when he could by any possibility attend it. How can it be doubted that, though his spiritual nature was not as yet sufficiently awakened to enable him to enjoy Bible study for its own sake, those Bible classes did him good? They and the society of the good and sincere man who conducted them, and whose original personality commended him in an especial manner to the heart of Hannington, were safe-guards and a sort of sheet-anchors, which helped to keep him from drifting whither so many have suffered shipwreck.

So, then, with the full consent of his parents, the first step was taken which severed him from a commercial life, and it was decided that James Hannington should, in due time, seek for ordination as a clergyman of the Church of England.

CHAPTER V.

LIFE AT OXFORD.

(1868—69.)

" Not in the sunshine, not in the rain,
   Not in the night of the stars untold,
Shall we ever all meet again,
   Or be as we were in the days of old.

" But as ships cross, and more cheerily go,
   Having changed tidings upon the sea,
So I am richer by them, I know,
   And they are not poorer, I trust, by me."

WALTER SMITH.

ON the 22nd of October, 1868, James Hannington's name
was entered as a Commoner in the books of St. Mary
Hall, Oxford. My own personal recollections of him date
from this time. Eighteen years have passed since then.
Later events have crowded out from my mind many of the
earlier memories of my life, and the lichen growth of time
is slowly but surely effacing some of the most deeply-grooved
impressions. Nevertheless I can still without difficulty
recall the moment when I first heard the sound of his
voice. Why the impression of that moment should have
lingered with me I cannot tell, except that his voice was a
singular one—in *timbre* quite unlike any other voice which
I have ever heard.

I was seated, a solitary freshman, in a dark little room
which was usually allotted to the last comer. The single
lance-window looked out upon the " Quad," with its paved
walks, square patch of grass, and central clump of dwarf

shrubs. A little disconsolate and lonely was I at that moment, wondering what sort of companions those might prove among whom my lot was to be cast during the next three years or so. As I sat in somewhat melancholy mood amongst the cups and saucers, decanters, and tumblers, brand new kettle and teapot, and other paraphernalia of a student's housekeeping, which had been sent in that afternoon by various tradesmen, my attention was arrested by a passing group of men who cast a heavy shadow through the narrow window. They were talking loudly, but one voice separated itself distinctly from the others. I was keenly alive to every new impression, and the tone of that voice remained with me.

It was half plaintive, half petulant, but, withal, wholly attractive. I fell to picturing to myself what kind of man the owner of that voice might be. The following day I was introduced to him, and for the first time set my eyes on James Hannington.

Let me try and describe him as he was when he made his first appearance in St. Mary Hall, as a freshman, in the autumn of 1868. A tall, well-proportioned young fellow, with somewhat loosely and pliably set figure, that gave promise of both activity and power. Careless in his dress—rather affecting a soft white hat, broad-soled boots, and a general *abandon* of costume. His face was the very index to his character. I have before me, as I write, some dozen photographs which were taken between the years '68 and '85. During that time the face has filled out and matured, but it is substantially the same. He was then in his twenty-first year, of pale, rather sallow, complexion. A mouth, the pouting lips of which seemed half-humorously to protest against life in general. A pair of clear grey eyes, which twinkled with latent fun, though deep set beneath projecting brows which suggested unusual powers of observation and penetration. A nose not too prominent, but sharp and inquiring, the nostrils of it readily expanding when moved by indignation. (He used, after his first African journey, to delight in telling how the natives would compare it to a spear!) The chin firm set, and jaws square, without any too-marked massiveness. The ears, not lying close to the head, but set at rather an angle. A face combative, yet attractive. Volatile, yet full of latent strength. Assertive, yet retiring. Altogether, quite a noticeable face and figure : not by any means to be ignored. The outer clothing of a nature capable of great things, if seized and moulded by the Divine Spirit. What otherwise—who might venture to prophesy?

Carlyle professes to attach much significance to a man's laughter. He says, "How much lies in laughter; the cipher key wherewith we decipher the whole man! . . . . The fewest are able to laugh what we call laughing."* Hannington would so far have satisfied his requirements. None who have heard his laugh can surely ever forget it. When he laughed the spirit of laughter took full possession of him, and shook him sorely before it would let him go. His laughter was contagious, he so evidently enjoyed it ; it came welling up with such wild, uncontrollable waves, that one found himself irresistibly compelled to give way and join in too, aye, till the tears ran down his cheeks, out of pure sympathy.

His voice was, as I have said before, unlike any other ; at least, any other that I have ever heard. It was not unmusical; of considerable power too ; but with a certain plaintive quaver in it,—a certain staccato thrusting forth of single words and short sentences that was strangely characteristic of its owner. A sort of intermittent fountain, it corresponded with his movements.

---

* *Sartor Resartus.*

These, like his voice, were not smooth or even. He was far from being awkward ; there was even a certain easy power in all that he did which was not far removed from graceful bearing, yet it was as though he studiously avoided conventional attitudes. When he walked, he walked with his whole body and shoulders, but whether he walked, stood, or sat, he was distinctly himself—never quite like anybody else. When I first saw him, he was leaning against the lintel of the door which opened from his own staircase upon the Quadrangle. He was surrounded by a group of men, all seniors, with whom he was chatting, and evidently on the best of terms. To my freshman's eyes, beholding with awestruck reverence those second and third year men, Hannington's audacity in thus taking the college by storm seemed boundless. It was evident that, though a freshman, he had already been received into their circle, and that the seniors regarded him as an acquisition to their society.

Perhaps this was partly owing to the fact that he came up to Oxford with more experience of the world than many others ; it was more probably owing to the irresistible magnetism of his genial good fellowship, coupled with his decided individuality and force of charcter ; but, from whatever cause, there can be no doubt that he almost immediately began to excrcise an influence over his fellow-students, and that he shortly established for himself an ascendancy over them which he maintained without a rival until the end of his University course.

It cannot be said that Hannington was an industrious student. On the contrary, the golden opportunity of those undergraduate years was missed by him, as by so many others who vainly regret, but cannot recal, what they then despised. Not that he was ever a dunce. What he chose to learn—and he learned everything that interested him—he knew accurately and thoroughly. In chemistry, botany, natural history and general science he was singularly well grounded, and, as a student of medicine, he would probably have taken a high degree. But for classics he had very little taste. He had never gone through that course of patient gerund-grinding and grammar-grating by which public schoolboys are broken in, and he was by nature very impatient of any yoke which compelled him to plod continuously along the line of a given furrow. Some seven years, moreover, had elapsed since he left school, and what slight smattering of classic lore he had there acquired must have, by this time, almost passed from him. Add to which fact the consideration that the whole previous training of his life had not been such as to fit him for close study, or to accustom him to endure the strain of continual intellectual effort.

We have it on no less an authority than that of Pliny, that " the mind is aroused to action by the active exercise of the body." This may be accepted if we understand by "active exercise" sufficient exercise to counteract the evils of a sedentary life. But we are inclined to think that more than this is apt to have a contrary effect upon the mind, and by over-development of the bodily faculties, check the development of the mental. There is no time when we are less disposed to think continuously or deeply than when we are making some great physical effort, or enjoying the excitement of a life of constant movement. Hannington had hitherto given himself little time to think, while at the same time he had never been idle. That he was slow in developing those mental powers which, if earlier matured, might have secured for him the honours of the " schools," may be attributed largely to those constant excursions and voyages by which his love of adventure had been indulged. It must also be borne in mind that he had

had, until now, no direct incentive, or even encouragement, to study. On the contrary, he had been taught that he might dispense with learning, the absence of which had proved no bar to the success of either his father or grandfather. It is not surprising, then, that it took some time for him to shake himself down into the course of the University curriculum, and that his degree was somewhat delayed in consequence.

Hannington's rooms in St. Mary Hall bore witness to his wanderings. They were large and airy ; oak panelled from floor to ceiling. In one corner, over a drawer cabinet full of curiosities and specimens, hung two gilt and painted Icons from Moscow. Opposite was a curious drawing of a terrier's head, burnt with a branding iron upon a panel of some hard wood, and picked up I know not where. Conspicuous was a portrait of his mother, a dignified and handsome lady, with much facial likeness to her son. Elsewhere, a rack full of whips and sticks of every size and shape. A miscellaneous heap of narwhal's and swordfish's horns, old weapons and what not, filled up a corner. A shady place was found for a considerable glass tank, wherein various fish, including a young jack, disported themselves. Add to all this pictures, china, bric-a-brac, and ornaments of the usual type, a plentiful stock of lounging chairs, with a good, capacious sofa of the old-fashioned square kind ; bookcases fairly well filled, especially with works on natural history ; portfolios full of scraps, and deep, red-cushioned window embrasures in which to double up the limbs and cozily con the same, and you will have a fair idea of what those rooms were like.

Here Hannington kept open house. Here his friends were wont to assemble, and here a frank and kindly welcome always awaited all who were congenial.

While Hannington had in him all the elements of popularity, and never failed to make himself liked, he did not

go out of his way to make friends. He was not much inclined
at this time to " suffer fools gladly." He would form strong
and apparently instinctive antipathies against certain persons,
antipathies for which he could offer no more valid reason
than that given in Martial's celebrated epigram :

> " Non amo te, Sabidi, nec possum dicere quare ;
> Hoc tantum possum dicere, Non amo te." *

Well, he may have been sometimes unjust, but, on the
whole, I am inclined to think that he was not often at fault
in his estimate of a man's character.

Nor was he a man to be trifled with. He possessed a
quick, passionate temper of his own, which it was never
difficult to rouse, and those who thought to take advantage
of his free and open manner, or of any eccentricity of his,
were soon disabused ; they were rarely rash enough to
tempt him a second time. When seriously angry, he was
capable de tout, and was quite formidable. All his friends
thoroughly understood this, and regulated their conduct
accordingly.

But through all his actions there ran a strong under-
current of genuine kindliness, unaffected simplicity, and
genial love of his kind which at once attracted others to
him. He was one of the few men who, while a leader in
an exclusive and hoi-polloi-despising college set, was
acquainted with and popular with all down to the last-
arrived freshman. He could be keenly jealous, too, for the
prerogatives of his party, and his friends will recall some
sufficiently stormy scenes when the authority of the " Red
Club " was invaded by some daring revolutionary spirits,
who objected to privileged oligarchies. Notwithstanding

---

* Which may be freely translated by the well-known couplet :

> " I do not like you, Dr. Fell,
> But why I don't I cannot tell."

this, there was no man who succeeded better in effacing differences, and in creating among the community a healthy *esprit de corps.* Wherein his "great strength" lay did not appear at first, or upon a brief acquaintanceship. He seemed to be wholly given over to the spirit of fun—to deliberately yield himself to the perpetration of nonsense. He loved to startle and shock the sensibilities of the staid followers of established precedent. When the mood was upon him, he could be as troublesome as a schoolboy, and his spirits were quite as untameable.

He must surely have tried to the utmost the patience of the much-enduring and long-suffering Principal, whose tact in dealing with him cannot be too highly admired, and who won for himself Hannington's warm esteem and regard. He was accustomed, good-naturedly, to chaff everybody, and loved to play queer practical jokes upon his friends. But with all this there was an underlying earnestness of purpose which, coupled with an iron inflexibility of will, soon made itself felt. It was generally recognized, before he had been long in residence, that he had something in him, that he knew what he wanted, and that, when once he had made up his mind that a thing ought to be done, he was not to be denied.

He might, with boyish glee, bring a whole armful of fireworks into college on the 5th of November, and let them off in defiance of all rules and regulations; he might complete a festivity by galloping round the Quad upon a chair at the head of his companions in riot; he might be known chiefly to the unthinking as the organizer of wild pranks, the getter-up of burlesque theatricals, the hospitable entertainer at noisy feasts; but, beneath all this, were sterling qualities which soon left their impress upon the little world in which he moved, and caused his influence to be more deeply and widely felt than that of many older and more talented men.

He was, moreover, unselfish, open-handed, and generous to lavishness. He was always ready to be paymaster whenever his companions would consent to lay that burden upon him. Those who needed his assistance and made claim upon his purse seldom or never met with a refusal. This readiness to impart of course laid him open to the attacks of one or two " notorious sponges." But only at first. He was, as we have said, a pretty keen judge of character. If once his suspicions were aroused they were hard to allay, and then his contempt would be bluntly outspoken. His caustic wit was not to be easily endured by those whose designs upon himself or others he thought that he had fathomed.

Even his " scout," and the funny old Mother-Bunch of a bed-maker, while they found him the most considerate and liberal of masters, for his manner with servants was always courteous and winning, soon discovered that he was no fool, and not to be squeezed at their pleasure. Ah, me! that bed-maker! With her heavy wheezing voice in which she would perpetually " beg parding," and the slowly creaking shoes upon which she and her pails would ascend the groaning stairs! Like all the other servants, she " did like Mr. Hannington, but he were a curious young gentleman—yes, that he were."

In his younger days Hannington was a most inveterate tease. He would sometimes irritate his victim to the utmost verge of all possible endurance ; but then he thoroughly understood the principle of give and take, and never objected to be teased in return. I cannot recollect him to have lost his temper, or even to have shown signs of annoyance in this game of thrust and parry. If some friend's own galled withers were wrung oftener than he liked, he had at least the satisfaction of knowing that he might try his hardest to find some sensitive spot in the skin

of his tormentor.   At this time he was very quick to resent
and avenge an insult, but he seemed even to thoroughly
enjoy to be made the target for whole sheaves of arrows of
legitimate " chaff."

Some men are privileged.   By general consent they are
allowed to say and do with impunity things which would
not be tolerated from others.   Hannington was one of these.

It was impossible to be cross with him.   Even the
Dons extended to him an unwritten licence.   Upon one
occasion, I recollect, the Principal remonstrated with him
by letter upon want of attention to study, and inquired
how long he intended to continue "a gentleman at large."
To this the irrepressible *alumnus* at once replied, " I hope
that you will in future regard me no longer as a gentleman
at large, but a gentleman at ' smalls ' ! "   Who else would
have dared such a rejoinder ?

His wit was quite unsparing.   As I had at that time
some small aptitude for catching likenesses, while he was an
adept at rapid rhyming, he persuaded me to join with him
in framing a book to be entitled the " Skimmery Album."
In this most of the men were to be found humorously
depicted and described.   Few escaped the pillory, from the
Principal downward.   In looking back upon that work of
art, I am not quite sure that either the rhymes or the
drawings were always polite, or even in the best of taste,
but of this I am quite sure, that no one took the jest amiss.
It was " only Jim."   None of his darts were poisoned.   If,
perchance, they caused a moment's irritation, they left
behind them no envenomed sting, or anything that could
rankle or cause permanent pain.   The man who essayed to
leave his room, and found that his " oak " had been firmly
screwed to the doorpost by some stealthy practitioner from
without, and himself a helpless prisoner, after vowing vengeance upon the unknown impertinent, would relent when

he discovered that he had been victimized by the incorrigible Jim.

The luckless one who returned from an evening party to find that some mischievous sprite had transformed his trim chambers into a very miscellany, and " made hay " of his goods and chattels, would smile resignedly when he traced the hand of the irrepressible joker.

The very boatmen at Salter's would grin when he came down to the river, and make ready to smile at the pleasantries of the St. Mary Hall captain. He was well known everywhere, and I make bold to say, wherever he was known he was well liked.

Hannington's thoroughness in carrying out whatever he undertook has already been alluded to. Under his captaincy the boat club throve and prospered. When the post of captain fell vacant and was offered to him as the result of a unanimous vote, he made a little speech to the effect that he would accept the position, and endeavour to do his duty in it ; but on one condition only. If he were to be captain, he should expect to be implicitly obeyed. He would resign the moment he failed to inspire confidence in the club, but he would never consent to be captain in name only. The boat needed a strict captain, and, if they elected him, he did not mean to give them cause to find fault with him in that respect. His speech was hailed with acclamations ; and he proved himself as good as his word. He not only sought out the best men and coached them assiduously, but he kept them close to their work. Absentees were hunted up, warned, and duly exhorted to mend their ways. Punctuality was insisted upon. Training was rigidly exacted, and rules made, which, like those of the Medes and Persians, might not be altered. However, if the captain made great demands upon others, it was certain that he never spared himself, and so gave no occasion for grumbling.

And how he would row !   Like everything else that he
did, he did it with all his might.   As he was wont to say:
" I would row my heart out sooner than that we should be
bumped."   I find in his diary mention of one ludicrous
scene over which we often laughed.   The long line of
" eights " that May morning lay like huge water-spiders,
one behind the other, upon the surface of the still river.
Each was held in its place by boathooks from the bank, and
waited for the signal gun to dart forward in pursuit of the
boat ahead.   We were all rather nervous.   We knew that
we were a better crew than the one above us, but strongly
suspected that we might fall a victim to the still better boat
below.   We sucked our slice of lemon, stripped to the thin-
nest of jerseys and flannels, and grimly determined to bump,
if possible, before we were bumped.   After the momentary
confusion which followed the roar of the gun, and when
we had settled down into our stroke, we soon found that
we had our work cut out for us.   The crew behind was
working grandly; the eight backs swung to and fro like a
well-balanced machine; at each stroke their boat leaped
from the water; it was quite evident that they were overhauling us hand over hand.   Hannington was rowing just
behind me at No. 7, and I knew that he was tearing at his
oar like one demented, but felt too, without being able to
see, that all was not right with him ; what it was I could
not tell.   As we entered " the gut," where the river makes
a sharp turn, the " stroke " of the boat below called upon
his crew for a spurt, that they might catch us while we
were held back by the drag of our rudder.   The chace
became exciting, the two boats almost overlapped, and the
shouts from the crowd on the towing path, as the friends of
the two crews mingled into one, swelled into a prolonged
roar.   As we, hardly escaping from our pursuer, emerged
from " the gut " into the straight reach, I could not help

noticing that the shouts of encouragement from the shore were intermixed with laughter, till by and by the laughter predominated, and, to my no small disgust, the grinning faces of the crowd, as we now hugged the Berkshire shore, were evidently directed upon *our* boat. What had we done? Who was doing what? This was quite too dreadful! I was not long, however, left in doubt. As we passed the post, and I turned to congratulate Jim upon our escape, I beheld him overwhelmed with confusion and shame. In his immense energy he had worked his nether garments almost wholly off, and the latter half of that hard-fought race had been rowed by him, not without frantic snatches at his disappearing raiment, garbed almost as slightly as Ulysses and·his crew, as depicted upon some ancient vase!

He was also a great canoe man. When the floods were out, and all the low country was one vast lake, from which protruded the tops of the highest hedges and the long lines of pollard willows which marked the course of streams, we would betake ourselves to light canoes and seek adventures, shooting the boiling rush of the foaming "lashers," and letting ourselves be whirled down by the mad waves of the swollen and straining river. Here, as everywhere else, Jim was always to be found at the post of danger. The ugly eddy which swirled with sullen roar beneath the arch of some sunken bridge, or the sweep of the deep and treacherous Cherwell, tearing madly through the branches of some submerged tree, which spread themselves like a net to catch and entangle the unwary canoeist as he rounded a difficult corner—these were his delight. He became a perfect master of his tiny craft, and was soon able to paddle while standing upright almost as easily as when seated. How keenly he would enjoy the fun of a canoe race! In this everyone is allowed to do his best to hinder or overturn his competitors ; and here Hannington's mingled boldness and dexterity gave him a great advantage.

He had, too, the young Englishman's love for a stand-up fight. The 5th of November, 1868, saw the last of those " town-and-gown rows " which had been so long a disgrace to the University. The authorities had determined to put an end to the unseemly spectacle, and a strong force of proctors and their myrmidons patrolled the streets. There was, notwithstanding, a good deal of fighting. One undergraduate was killed, and others were more or less injured. Those few gownsmen who escaped the proctors and their " bulldogs " linked arms, and tried to drive the mob up the High Street before them. Hannington was, of course, in the thick of the mêlée. He had witnessed the fatal blow by which the student mentioned above had been struck down, and was filled with a Berserk rage and thirst for retribution. His friend, having just been himself " run in " by a proctor, and secured within the Hall gates, has a vivid remembrance of that indignant figure, with the light of battle in his eye, and his avenging fist stained with the gore of his adversaries, struggling in the hands of those who conducted him back to his college, and compelled him to desist from the conflict.

There was an undefinable charm about this bright, queer, passionate, fun-loving, unconquerable undergraduate. A mutual friend writes of him, " He was in some subtle way the life and soul of our set." With all his seeming volatility, he possessed that indescribable something which Chalmers used to call " wecht," and to which he justly attributed so great importance. That *weight*, without which no man can achieve greatness, but the possession of which makes its owner a force in the world.

And the influence which he exercised was always, even in his most careless days, in the main for good. We have

seen, by the extracts quoted from his diary, that he was
already accustomed to think at times deeply and seriously.
It is true, if I may repeat what I have elsewhere written of
him, " he was not, in his undergraduate days, a man with a
definite purpose. He had not, apparently, any settled object
in the regeneration of the society in which he moved ; his
religion, as Doddridge says of Colonel Gardiner, ' still
hung loose to him.' All the stops of his nature had not
yet been pulled out by the consecration of his life to Christ ;
the tunes played upon that life were still, perhaps, purpose-
less, yet they were, withal, harmless enough. I never
knew him to fall into any of those vices common to young
men. While he was eminently social, he never indulged
himself to excess. During his residence at Oxford he exercised a real and entirely salubrious influence over his fellows.
At the club ' wines,' under his presidency, sobriety became
the order of the day, and to exceed became discreditable.
He was, in his wildest moments, sound at the core, and
there are not a few who will have felt the better for his
companionship." *

We have already had occasion to remark that the boy
James, however addicted to pleasure, was never given to
" loafing." His very idleness was busy. We notice the
same characteristic in the young man. He equally eschewed
the society of the fashionable lounger, who voted energy to
be " bad form," who frequented the High Street, and there
exhibited, with languid grace, the faultless cut of irre-
proachable tailoring ; and that of the self-indulgent and
beslippered novel-reader, as loth to seek his couch at night
as to rise betimes from his bed in the morning.

The following extract from his diary gives the details of
a single Sunday which may be taken as a not unfair example

---

* *C. M. Intelligencer*, April, 1886.

of many others :—" 7 a.m., Holy Communion. 9 a.m., Chapel. 10.30, 'Varsity Sermon by Dr. Gouldburn ; twenty-mile walk with E. Ashmead-Bartlett. 5.15, Chapel. 7.30, Service in St. Mary's. 9 p.m., Greek Testament Lecture under Burgon." Which all must, surely, confess was a fairly well-filled day !

Hannington spent the Christmas vacation of 1868—69 in his usual energetic manner, by rushing over to Germany, and visiting Berlin, Dresden, and other continental cities in midwinter.

He was still, as the Principal put it, more disposed to play the part of the " gentleman at large " than that of the student. During the ensuing term we find notes of two visits to Cambridge, which he, of course, compares unfavourably with his own dear Alma Mater. The rest of the term is occupied with sports of various kind. E. Ashmead-Bartlett and he had struck up a great friendship ; and Hannington threw himself heart and soul into his friend's early successes in athletics, in which he then had an ambition to excel. He records his pleasure when Ashmead-Bartlett ran third in the 'Varsity three-mile race, which secured to him the right to take part in the next Inter-University sports. He tried his hand at the " new French two-wheeled velocipedes," then first introduced into Oxford, and which resembled the perfect bicycle of to-day not much more closely than " Puffing Billy " resembles the express locomotive of the " Flying Scotsman." He gave large wines, and got up and acted in the great hall doggrel English versions of Greek plays. In fact, like other young men of high spirits and social gifts, he entered thoroughly into the enjoyments of this new life. He appreciated its freedom, made all the more piquant by the appearance of restraint imposed by college rules, and was disposed to make the utmost of its possibilities.

Though he afterwards became an efficient speaker, and could even now, upon such occasions as that narrated above at his Boat Club election, speak pithily and to the purpose, he was not fond of speechifying. Like some of his contemporaries, who have since found their tongues, he did not much affect the excellent college debating society, much less the debates at the Union. Action was more in his line than speech. Had he lived in the days of the Scotists and Smiglesians, he would have, doubtless, borne a good club in Logic Lane.* He had the young Briton's thorough contempt for a " mug."

To row in his college boat, and be captain of it, to be the most popular man in residence, and perhaps some day to be elected president of the then flourishing Red Club, these were things compared with which a good degree seemed but as the dust in the balance. Some little time afterwards, when these ambitions were gratified, he writes : "I am now captain of the boats and president of the club. So I am at the head of everything." Ah, well! most healthy young minds pass through this phase of experience. The time was coming when those things which now seemed of least account would bulk most largely in his eyes—when he too would " put away childish things."

In the meanwhile his life went on as before, little changed by his adoption of those outward and visible signs of learning, the cap and gown. The Long Vacation of '69 —as though his whole life hitherto had not been been one long vacation—was spent in a yachting tour, during which

---

* " The followers of Duns Scotus and Martin Smiglesius, who lived respectively in the fourteenth and sixteenth centuries. The students used to adopt their tenets, and when argument failed, would try to cudgell each other into acquiescence. Logic Lane is ' a narrow defile where the partisans used to encounter,' hence its name."—ADDISON (*Essay XCI.*, " *On Managing a Debate* ").

he visited the coast and ports of Holland. Of this trip a
few notes from his diary may be sufficient. While at Antwerp, he writes: " I am rather astonished at myself, on
viewing for the third time Rubens' ' Descent from the
Cross.' I have lately been studying continental pictures
very keenly, and have, I think, a better eye for merit than
formerly. The first time I beheld it with disappointment,
the second time with indifference, the third time with
rapture. The figures I cannot help thinking too muscular,
and the features coarse to vulgarity, but the lifelessness of
the body and the colouring seem to me perfection. I could
not take my eyes off the picture, until the man, thinking I
had had enough for my money, covered it up."

Hannington next took his steam yacht up the Rhine,
and had some exciting adventures on the rapid waters of
that treacherous river. Once the ship caught fire. " We
had proceeded about two miles past Bommel, when the
steward came to me and called me aside most mysteriously.
He thought he had better inform me quite privately that
smoke was pouring up through the ship's floor. I darted
down below and found, as he said, the cabin full of smoke.
There was no doubt that the ship was on fire. ' Send
quickly for the carpenter, and don't tell the others for a few
minutes. Now, carpenter, keep your head cool : the vessel
is on fire ! tear up this floor at once ! ' Then, running on
deck to the pilot : ' Bring up as quickly as possible. En-
gineer, draw fires, and be ready if I want you for a stiffish
piece of work.' We could find no fire under the cabin,
but everywhere smoke. Then we went to the coal bunk,
and directly it was opened the smoke rolled out in volumes.
My heart sank. The coals on fire ! Nothing could save
her from utter destruction ! We turned the coals over,
but found no fire, although the smoke kept rolling out.
Next it began to burst out behind the donkey engine.

Dreadful suspense ! Be calm ! With much difficulty we
tore up the engine-room floor, and then saw the keel in a
blaze ! Bad as this was, it was a relief to have found the
enemy. I shouted to the men, who had gathered anxiously
round, to stand to the buckets, and, stripping off coat and
waistcoat, I took one myself; and then, turning on all the
taps, we speedily filled her with water to the floor, and thus
extinguished the flame. It was an anxious time, however.
The fire appeared to be in close proximity to the coals, of
which we had a large supply. Had they been ignited our
chance of escape would have been small. It resulted from
the ash-pan almost, if not quite, resting upon the wooden
keel. The iron had become red hot, and kindled the
wood. Why, indeed, this had not happened before I cannot tell."

Next comes the following entry :—"Brought up at
Nimegen ; created a most profound sensation. It appears
that the Queen's yacht, the *Fairy*, is the only one that
has yet ascended the Rhine, so the people think that I
must be of the blood royal. On landing everybody was so
obsequiously polite that I had almost too much of a good
thing. However, without assuming to myself any dignity
beyond that of an ordinary English gentleman of great
affability, I inspected with great interest all that is to be
seen in this out-of-the-way little place, unnoticed by Murray
or Bradshaw."

Any generation of over-weening pride was, however,
properly checked by the next adventure. " We steamed
on to the Prussian frontier. Here I had to land, and, in
spite of explanations that the yacht was not either a merchant or passenger vessel, I had to make a manifest of
everything on board—rice, salt, tobacco, wine, etc. Of
course, I did not know in the least what we actually had.
I, therefore, told the man whatever came into my head,

as a pound or two of tea, two loaves of bread, fifty bottles
of wine, etc. I then had to sign my name to four different papers to vouch for the accuracy of my statement.
Anybody can imagine my delight when, having solemnly
made my declaration, I was informed that the custom-house
officers would come on board directly to see if my statement
were true ! It was an insult hard to brook without flying
in a passion. In a few minutes ten officers arrived. I received them as if they were of the utmost importance, but
at the same time as if I was more so. I then told the
steward to take them round, but to show them nothing else
but the joint of meat. I, in the meantime, got hold of one
who seeemed the most officious, and although he declared
in a loud voice that he would not touch a thing, I managed
to pour a glass of my very best down his throat, while his
subordinates were below. We shook hands repeatedly, and
became sworn friends. They finally declared that they
must have a bottle of wine to test its strength, which they
did, and sent it back in half an hour with a charge of about
£1 on my declaration, which I thought moderate."

To his great satisfaction, Hannington was able to bring
the yacht to Cologne at the time appointed to meet his
father. He had had many difficulties to contend with.
The navigation of the river proved both tedious and
dangerous for a vessel of the *Iole's* draught. Many
times they stuck upon sandbanks, or were stranded upon
hidden reefs. The pilot again and again urged him to telegraph to his father to announce the impossibility of reaching
Cologne by the day mentioned. To this he had but one
reply: "*I have undertaken to be there.*" And there, on
the 7th of August, to the surprise of all, he was.

All this was, no doubt, conducive to the formation of
character. It helped to produce in him that self-reliance
and readiness of resource which afterwards so remarkably

distinguished him as a missionary pioneer. But it did not help him much to make up leeway in his classical education.

It is not surprising, therefore, to learn that, when he returned to Oxford in the autumn of '69, and at once took up his old *rôle* as Master of the Revels, the Principal strongly recommended him to seek out a competent tutor in some quiet and retired part of the country, where there would be few distractions, and where he would have no temptation to seek other friends than his books.

For this purpose he suggested the Rev. C. Scriven, Rector of Martinhoe. He could not have selected a better man. But the place! Alas! how could the Principal, with all his kindly forethought, know that this perplexing undergraduate would find in Devonshire peasant folk, and still more in Devonshire cliffs and seas, distractions even greater than college life could offer him?

CHAPTER VI.

MARTINHOE.

(1870—73.)

"A great, broad-shouldered, genial Englishman."

Princess.

MARTINHOE and Trentishoe are two small sister parishes on the wild north coast of Devonshire, about half-way between Ilfracombe and The Foreland. Far from any railway station, they are shut off from the rest of the world by their inaccessibility. The population of the two parishes, at that time held by Mr. Scriven, does not much exceed three hundred souls. These are, however, scattered over a wide extent of country. A lonely place is this corner of North Devon, and out of the way. A place of wide-stretching moorland; dark, weather-scarped cliffs, and rocks worn and torn by the ceaseless sweep of Atlantic billows. Hannington writes of his first impression of the district: "The country round is magnificent, and I soon fell in love with both place and people."

The impression which he himself made upon the party at the Rectory is recorded in another note: "I found out that their opinion of me is that I am very eccentric." However, in a very short time, not only they, but the simple country folk around, learned to love him, and to regard him as, in a peculiar sense, their own. He entered thoroughly into the pursuits of the people, and was soon widely known among them. Before he had been long at

Martinhoe he was welcomed everywhere, in farmhouse and cottage, as a personal friend.

The strange habits and customs of the Devonians, almost unaltered through centuries, interested him greatly ; he studied them sympathetically, while he keenly enjoyed the humour of them. The following is an extract from his diary :—

"*Feb.* 20*th.*—We had a funeral this week. The bereaved gave a tremendous feast on the occasion to those who were invited ; and any others who chose to attend went to the house for tea and coffee. On Sunday they all came to church in a body. They came in very late, and sat together in a conspicuous place, remaining the whole time of the service with their faces buried in their pocket-handker-chiefs ; nor did one once look up. A short time since, the clerk at Trentishoe lost his wife. A few days after the funeral he asked for a holiday, borrowed a horse, and rode round the parish to sound all the young women on the question of matrimony. He arrived at the Parsonage and proposed to both the servants, but was refused. At last he found a lady bold enough and willing to take the step, and she bids fair to make him a good wife.

" There is an immense deal of superstition about here. Neither man, woman, nor child will enter a churchyard after dark, and on Midsummer night they say that the spirits of the departed move about the graves, and are to be seen. Many of the people know charms for different diseases, and are in great repute. Old John Jones can bless for the eyes: and afterwards offered to reveal the secret to me, in which case he would be able to 'bless' no more, the gift becoming mine.

" Mrs. Jones 'to the parsonage ' has a seventh son, who has power to bless for the King's evil. Numbers resorted to him, but finding that he did not get sufficient from them, and that every time he ' blessed ' virtue went from him, and left him weak, he has discontinued the practice."

The belief in witches still holds sway over the minds of the people. They have unbounded faith in charms and spells. I remember once to have had a conversation with Hannington on the subject of the supposed miracles at Knock, Lourdes, and other places. Whatever might be the source of the alleged healings, he warned me against summarily concluding that no cures had taken place.

He said that he had himself seen the strangest cures effected in Africa by medicine men with their fetish ; cures of which, to an impartial beholder, there could be little doubt. He then narrated some remarkable cases of persons who had, under his own observation, been healed by recourse to men or women who were supposed to be endowed with the power to " bless." He was of opinion that certain diseases—in fact, all those diseases which were directly or indirectly nervous—might, in certain cases, be healed by a strong faith in—anything.

The reader will, no doubt, recal the case mentioned both by Pascal, and also by Racine in his history of Port Royal, in which a daughter of Madame Perier was cured of a lacrymal fistula of a very bad kind, which had disfigured her face for more than three years, by a touch from a supposed Thorn from the Crown.

Supposing this cure to have been really effected—and it is testified to by no less authorities than Pascal, Arnauld, and Le Maitre—there is no need to believe that any special virtue resided in the " Holy Thorn." Rather that the extent to which it is possible for the mind to sway the body has not yet been accurately ascertained.

Upon one occasion, and I believe one only, Hannington

was induced to experiment upon the credulity of the people. The result was notable. He had a decided taste for the study of medicine, and had picked up at different times no small practical knowledge of it. The country doctor, indeed, trusted him so far as to seek his assistance in reporting upon and caring for many of the simpler cases of sickness. His repute as a " medicine man " among the country folk themselves was great. They placed unlimited confidence in him. Upon the occasion to which allusion has been made, he was asked to prescribe for a certain woman who *appeared* to be in the last stage of consumption. She had been under medical treatment for years, but had obtained no relief. Hannington filled a phial with water slightly flavoured and coloured, and attached to the cork a small leaden medal, such as is found on some bottles of eau-de-Cologne. This he gravely presented to the woman, merely saying to her, " When you take a dose, first turn the bottle round three times three ; and, whatever you do, *take care that you do not lose that leaden medal, but return it to me when you are well.*" From that hour the woman began to amend ; in a very brief time the medal was returned—an apparently complete cure had been effected. I make no comment upon this, but give the story as nearly as possible in the same words in which he narrated it to me.

After some more or less spasmodic reading, Hannington returned to Oxford on March 19th, and went into the schools to pass his "smalls." During the first day of the examination he had good hopes of success; but on the second day an ill-conditioned organ-grinder took up his station outside the " theatre," and with the horrible iteration of his popular airs drove all thoughts out of the distracted head of the unhappy student. In a fit of irritable despair he rushed out and withdrew his name.

The next term Hannington spent in residence. He was at this time elected President of the " Red Club," which, with the captaincy of the Boat Club, was the highest social honour that we were able to confer upon him.

On the 10th of June he again tried to pass his Responsions, and this time successfully.

The next entry in the diary is again from Martinhoe. Hannington had discovered a new source of delight. The cliffs descended to the sea in sheer, precipitous walls of three or four hundred feet. In few places was access to their base possible, except to bold and experienced climbers. A perilous scramble from ledge to ledge in search for chough's eggs revealed the existence of some remarkable caves, the largest of which was then and there dubbed Cave Scriven. These caves, carved out by the foam-fingers of the tireless sea, fringed with immense fronds of fern, pillared with stalactite, and floored with firm white sand, the safe and undisturbed citadel of birds, were quite inaccessible to any but a cragsman. Hannington at once resolved that they should be seen and explored by the party at the Rectory, and for that purpose set to work to make a practicable path down to the shore. Into this business he threw himself with characteristic energy. The engineering difficulties to be overcome were not small. The cliff was in many places a sheer precipice—nowhere could foothold be obtained except upon treacherous projections or crumbling ledges. However, he writes : " On Sept. 1st we commenced, and secured two able-bodied men and old Richard Jones to help. When Richard was a boy he had been the best hand in the parish at climbing the ' cleve' (cliff), but now he was old and crippled. We thought, however, he might be useful to do odd jobs, so at 7 a.m. we all turned out with ' pick-isses,' ' two-bills,' crowbars, and spades, and made our way to the scene of action."

It will be observed that Hannington had, as usual, succeeded in carrying along with him all his friends, the other
pupils at the Rectory, and even the servants.   His enthusiasm was the most infectious thing in the world.   The
most ridiculous project became, when he threw himself into
its execution, the all-absorbing business of the hour.   Thus,
for the time being, the interest of the parish was concentrated upon this wonderful " path," which was to lead down
the face of a dangerous cliff, from nowhere in particular to
nobody knew where.

Though the leader of this pioneer corps of sappers and
miners was almost incapacitated by a severe attack of shingles,
he refused to succumb, and himself marked out the first section of the path.   The party, amateurs and hired labourers,
then set to work in good earnest, and soon made the first
part of a practicable zigzag.   When they got well down
over the edge, however, the rocks proved very rotten, and
after several narrow escapes, the enthusiasm of some was
damped, and the two able-bodied workmen refused to risk
their lives further.   Old Richard alone remained undaunted ;
and, with his help, and that of George Scriven, the path
was at last completed.   Some graphic extracts from the
diary explain how it was done.   Old Richard was clinging
on to a landslip, and plying his pick as best he could, when
Hannington cried to him, " ' Hold on, Richard, till I come
back to you ; I am going to climb down a bit further, and
see where we can next take the path to.'   Old Richard,
however, was a man who could not stand idle, as I found
to my cost ; for when I had crept down some distance I
heard the rush of a stone, and a considerable boulder shot
past my head, within a foot of me.   I had barely time to
dodge as it whizzed by like a cannon-ball, accompanied by
a volley of small stones, and I could feel the draught of air
it made.   With a shout I apprized Richard that I was

below, and climbed up like a lamplighter, and stood by his side pale and breathless. He was quite cool. 'I don't like the look of that old rougey place where you have been climbing,' said he. Nor do I, thought I to myself, when you are working up above. If you are not the coolest old hand I ever met——! However, I said nothing; but after dinner George and I climbed across this 'rougey place,' with the assistance of a rope, and determined that we would not return until we had cut our own path back. Old Richard now gave in. He took back to the village the news that he was beaten now. So George and I did it by ourselves. Capital fellow is George, and just as determined as myself that we should succeed, even if the whole cliff came down about our ears."

There was much triumph when the work was completed. An opening day was arranged, and a party of twenty visitors descended the dizzy path down to

"The murmuring surge
That on the unnumbered idle pebbles chafes,"

and were introduced to the wonders of the new-found caves.

The following entry appears opposite January 1st, 1871:

"Received the Holy Communion with great misgivings. Reflected upon the manner in which I had spent the past year, and made resolutions, which, alas! soon failed."

A day or two later he was almost drowned while skating. The same evening, however, he went to a Devonshire farmer's party, which he thus describes : " I am going to ' see Christmas,' which is Devonian for ' I am going to a party.' We arrived at 6 p.m., when a hot supper was ready—three hot roast joints, etc. ; after which, games, dancing, and the like went on till midnight, when there was another hot supper as substantially provided as the first.

Then cards commenced till 8 a.m., when there was a hot breakfast." Hannington does not say whether he saw this party out, but apparently it is not uncommon on such occasions for guests to remain even until noon, when they wind up the festivities with a final dinner. The habits of our beef-and-ale-consuming forefathers still linger in hospitable Devonshire.

A week later Hannington found himself in nearly as awkward a position as that of the elderly gentleman who, while probing the clefts of the rocks for anemones at low tide, was seized by the finger and held fast in the tenacious grip of a huge crustacean. Tradition says that he was drowned. The same fate might easily have befallen our adventurous explorer of caves. He says: " On the twelfth of January I asked Morrell and George Scriven to join in an excursion to a cave we called ' The Eyes,' two small holes just large enough to creep through, which penetrated a headland. While there, we discovered below water mark a hole which seemed to penetrate some distance ; so, with no little squeezing and pushing, I wound my way in, and found myself in a large hollow chamber with no other outlet than the one I had entered by. It would have been a dreadful place in which to be caught by the tide. The water gradually rising in the utter darkness would drown one like a rat in a trap. I explained all this melodramatically to my companions outside till they grew quite impatient. ' Well, come out then,' said Morrell, ' for the tide is fast coming up, and we shall have a job to return.' So I crawled down to the entrance and essayed to come out head first. I soon stuck fast, and after great squeezing and squirming, barely managed to get back again inside. Next I tried to get out as I came in, and so worked my way down feet first. It was no go, I was again jammed tight. My two friends then got hold of my legs, and pulled and pulled till I thought my

legs and body would part company. Matters really began
to look serious. I was bruised and strained a good deal, and
escape seemed impossible. And now the full horror of the
situation flashed across us all. My mocking words were
actually to be realized! I said in the best voice I could
that I must say good-bye; but if ever I passed a dreadful
moment it was that one. The tide was creeping up slowly
but surely. Applying all their strength they pushed me
back into the entrance that I might make one more effort
head first. Then it suddenly occurred to us all that I might
try without my clothes. No sooner said than done; and
after a good scraping I soon stood once more by their side.
But it was a narrow escape!"

Nothing daunted by this adventure, Morrell and he set
themselves to conquer "the champion climb amongst the
natives." Twice they were defeated. It seemed to them
that "no mortal man could go up." The third time they
were successful, scaled the dizzy height, and "were made
free of the cliffs."

Hannington kept the next two terms at St. Mary Hall.
He was now twenty-three, but the boyish spirit was not in
the least abated. *Vide* the following:

"*April 25th.*—For a bet I wheeled Captain Way up the
High Street in a wheelbarrow, and turned him out opposite
the Angel Hotel."

The Easter Vacation was spent in a yachting trip with
his own people. They all had a pleasant time on the
bright waters of the south coast. Whenever there was a bit
of rough work to be done, James always undertook it.
"Now, men," he was wont to say, "you remember me up
the Rhine. No putting back to-day, mind!" On several
occasions, while the rest of the party went by rail to avoid
some stormy foreland, he took charge of the yacht; never

better pleased than when a real stiff sea had to be encountered, or a difficulty overcome. As he was not in good health, he next took advantage of doctor's advice to make a yachting voyage to Norway. There he made the most of his time, appreciatively seizing upon all strange ways, quaint sayings, and queer surroundings, and making himself very popular with the Norwegians, whether *pigge*, postboy, or boatman.

One story we may quote from his diary : "The landlord at Gudvangen, Herr S., is quite a character. He dances round one, and his long hair flies about in a most ludicrous way. 'He shall sit up all night if he shall make you comfortable ; ' and to commence adding to your comfort he pats you on the back. Then he is full of bitter remorse because you tell him that the maid (pigge) *will* grease your boot-laces. 'He shall send her away ; he shall do it himself ; it shall break his heart if you are not comfortable.' Herr S. speaks good English, but he likes to add to his vocabulary. Some one said that the Germans were fond of guzzling beer. The conversation dropped, but not the word. It dwelt in Herr S.'s mind. The next morning we were at the river. Herr S. expressed a thousand regrets that it was so clear. Said he : 'If only you could get a little *guzzling* water you shall catch fish.' We found that he thought that ' guzzling ' meant *thick !* "

On July 18th he was back once more at Martinhoe ; reading, cliff-climbing, and botanizing—chiefly, I imagine, the two latter. His zeal for exploring the wave-worn nooks of the perilous coast had infected the others. Parties were constantly made up to reach some new cave, or test the practicability of some hitherto impossible track. Hannington never tired of describing these adventures. On one occasion they were creeping along a narrow ledge of rock overhanging a "vasty deep," when they came to a place where the ledge turned at right angles, and was, moreover, blocked by a mass of jutting rock. A long stride over the obstacle is required. He writes: "As I knew the place best, I stepped on first, and then began to help the others across. All got over safely till it came to R——'s turn. I was sitting on the ledge, and held out my hand to him. He somehow missed the hand, slipped, and lost his balance. The fearful look of terror that flashed over his face, accompanied by a low moan and gasp of despair, I shall not easily forget. I dashed at him, caught him by the arm, and, gripping the rock with one hand, held him for a moment dangling in the air. Fortunately, George was at hand, and seized my wrist, otherwise we must, both of us, have gone over and been lost. Together we hauled him up, and I soon had the satisfaction of hearing him say, as he shook me by the hand: 'Thank you for my life!' I, however, was myself quite as much indebted to George." Good Mr. Scriven did not half like these perilous freaks. But, while the mania lasted, there was no keeping his " pups " off the cliffs. To use his favourite expression, they were " like moths buzzing round a candle."

"*Aug. 5th.*—Helped to put new east window in the church. I had recommended Baillie, and had obtained the design.

"*Aug. 26th.* — Took Lord Tenterden, Mr. Justice Pollock, and some others to see the caves. They expressed the greatest astonishment at the engineering of the path, and the magnificence of the caves."

Next occurs the following :—

" I suggested to Mr. Scriven that I should come to him at once as his curate, and read for my Degree afterwards."

To this he adds in a note written long after: " Very

fortunately the Bishop would not consent to ordain me until I had taken my Degree."

Fortunately, indeed! In this, as in other things, we can trace the good Hand of his God upon him.

And now an event took place which moved him to the centre of his being. The controlling love of his life had been that of his mother. The boyish tenderness for his " dearest, sweetest mother," had not been impaired by time. No other affection had ever usurped his heart. He was the least susceptible of men to the charms of women. No Adonis could have seemed more wholly unassailable by what is called love. His friends and companions were mainly, and, indeed, almost exclusively, of his own sex. Not that he was unpopular with women : far from it. But in whatever light they may have regarded him, in his eyes they were but weaker men, to be treated with chivalrous consideration, but otherwise as companions—nothing more. His whole love was given to his mother. She, on her part, fully reciprocated his affection, and found an ever fresh delight in the devotion of her favourite son. Mrs. Hannington had, for some time, been seriously ill. On the 30th of September of this year, 1871, her doctor pronounced that there was little or no hope of her recovery. James was in an agony of mind ; he could not believe that such grief was in store for him. In a few days the crisis seemed to pass, and his mother, to his intense relief, rallied. He determined, notwithstanding this, to remain by her side instead of returning to Oxford to keep Term. As the days dragged wearily by matters did not improve. It was evident that his mother was sinking. She was very happy and peaceful. As for James, he wrote: "We had but a melancholy Christmas Day, and mournfully closed the year. The doctor gives my mother no hope, and yet there seems to be hope. I cannot but hope—I *must* hope."

He found time, in the midst of this racking anxiety, to run up to Oxford, at the urgent request of his friends there, to settle a quarrel which had occurred in the St. Mary Hall Boat Club. But, having set matters straight, and prevailed upon the then Captain to resign, he at once returned to Hurst. On February 14th his mother submitted to the operation of tapping. She bore it with a patient resignation which was deeply touching to her husband and children. She got, however, very little relief. On the 24th, James writes: "Very, very ill." On the 26th: "I went in to her at eight a.m., and at once saw that the end could not be far off. She was almost unconscious. She kept dozing and rousing, and commencing sentences. Especially she would repeat again and again: ' I will take the stony heart out of their flesh, and will give them an heart of flesh. I will take—I will take the stony heart away—away.' "

So the bright, active, brave spirit, which in so many points resembled that of her favourite son, went down, step by step, to the brink of the still river; and her son would hardly let her go—would have held her, but could not. About three o'clock in the afternoon she ceased her broken utterances ; at about five o'clock her arms, which had gently swayed to and fro, moved no longer, and at seven she died in the presence of all her children. After the last reverent look, the others moved sadly away. As for James, he fell on her face, and kissed her, and cried to her, as though she could still hear him. Scarce knowing what he said, he besought her again and again to come back to him—not to leave him when he most wanted her. By and by came the faithful old nurse, and, with gentle compulsion, led him away.

Mrs. Hannington had always felt an almost morbid dread lest she should be buried before life was actually extinct. She had mentioned this to her son, and he had promised that he would assure himself that death had taken place before the interment. This explains the following note : " I promised my mother to see her six times after she was dead. I saw her seven, and there could not be the slightest doubt that she was gone."

Indeed, it was almost impossible to tear him away from her bedside. He would sit there in the silent gloom, hour after hour, plunged in grief that refused to be comforted. Or he would be found kneeling by that figure so mysterious and still beneath its enveloping sheet. They had to coax and almost to compel him from the presence of the dead in order that he might take rest or meals. On Saturday, March 20th, the funeral took place in the Parish Church of Hurstpierpoint. " Hundreds attended, coming from miles round."

So the desire of his eyes was taken away at a stroke.

It is clear to us now why this should have been. His heart was to be emptied that it might be filled with that only love which does not fade, and which cannot be taken away. Had James Hannington written an epitaph upon his mother's tomb, it would have been couched in some such terms as that most touching inscription in a Paris cemetery—"*Dors en paix, O ma mère; ton fils t'obéira toujours.*" Her memory always exercised over him a hallowing influence. Nevertheless, it was, perhaps, needful for him that the human voice should speak no more words of advice and sympathy, that he might be taught to listen for the sound of that " still, small voice " which whispers to those who have ears to hear: " This is the way, walk thou in it."

In May, 1872, Hannington successfully passed his " Moderations," and resided for some time in the house of Mr. Morfill, of Oriel, with whom he decided to read for his next Examination. After a short vacation he continued his studies with Mr. Rumsey, and determined that he would put an end to trifling, and pass the final examination for his Degree as soon as possible.

The following entry occurs for October 18th :—" Father, Bessie, and Blanche Gould came to stop at Oxford a few days. Took them to hear Canon Liddon, who preached a magnificent sermon." A few days later a letter appeared on his breakfast table, in which his father announced his intention of marrying again, and that the latter lady had consented to become his wife. This second marriage turned out very happily, and by and by Hannington, no doubt, understood that it was better thus than that his father should be left to brood over his grief in a house from which his children had flown to make homes for themselves. But coming so soon after the death of his mother, to whom he knew that his father had been tenderly attached, it is not to be wondered at if, at first, the new alliance troubled him, or that his diary should record his feelings in the words, " I am terribly cut up and cast down."

He set to work, however, in good earnest to bring to a close his already too prolonged University course, and, early in December, passed with credit the first part of " Greats."

On May 15th, 1873, he rowed for the last time in the " eight." " Bumped Keble." " Should have caught Exeter, but No. 3 caught a crab instead." Apparently the crew rather fell to pieces towards the end of the week, for the next entry runs : " Of all atrocious horrors, this is the most disgusting. We have been re-bumped by Keble ! "

" *May* 28*th.*—Lunched at Morfill's. 3 p.m., garden party at Morrell's. 9 p.m., ball at Masonic Hall, given by Ashmead-Bartlett." And so on through a list of " Commemoration " festivities.

On June 12th Hannington took his B.A. Degree.

CHAPTER VII.

THE TURNING POINT.—ORDINATION.—THE GREAT CHANGE.

(1873—74.)

"I have been from my childhood alway of a rumorous and stormy nature."   LUTHER.

"We took sweet counsel together, and walked in the house of God as friends."   *Ps.* lv. 14.

"O most sweet Lord Jesus, by Thy holy Infancy, Youth, Baptism, Fasting, scourges, buffets, thorny crown,—Deliver us."
ST. ANSELM.

"ABOUT this time," Hannington writes, "a different tone began to steal over me insensibly. I prayed more."

About this time also a certain friend of his who had recently received Holy Orders, and who was serving as Curate in a country parish in Surrey, began to think of him. In the solitude of his lodgings, when the day's work was done, and he was alone with his own thoughts, his mind would rest lovingly upon old college friendships. He thought of James Hannington—gay, impetuous, friendly, fun-loving Jim—and gradually it was laid upon his heart to pray for him. Why, he could not tell; but the burden of that other soul seemed to press upon him more heavily day by day. He had not had much experience in dealing with souls; he had but a short time before learned the meaning of "effectual, fervent prayer;" he would have been called "a babe" by St. Paul; not yet even a "young man," much less "a father." But his life had been transformed within him, and filled with a new and most radiant joy. He knew himself redeemed, and in union with the Father of Spirits with whom is no changeableness, neither shadow of turning. He could not now have lived over again that old college life of his as once he had been content to live it. He thought of many friends. To some he spoke, and tried to make them partakers with him of his new-found benefit. For some he sought to pray, but for none can he ever remember to have prayed with such a distinct sense that he *must* pray as for James Hannington. I find the following entry in Hannington's diary:

"*July* 15*th.*———— opened a correspondence with me to-day, which I speak of as delightful; it led to my conversion."

Young men are not, as a rule, good correspondents, and between these twain no letter had passed for nearly two years. Communication was re opened in the following manner. A pair of skates was the ostensible cause. The Curate found them, with other rubbish, in a box full of odds and ends, and, holding them in his hand, remembered that they had belonged to Hannington, with whom, after the manner of chums, he had held many things in common. Then and there he sat down and wrote to Hurstpierpoint, asking his friend in what quarter of the world he might be found, and whither he would wish those same skates to be sent. The letter was forwarded to Martinhoe. In due time came a kindly response. "Glad to hear from you again. Never mind the skates; keep them, or throw them away—anything you like; but tell me about yourself," and so on. Then followed the news that he was meditating ordination; was not sure that he was as fit as he ought to be, with more to the same effect, all written lightly enough, but with a certain something of seriousness which induced the Curate to think that the opportunity he had been seeking might have, perchance, arrived.

He resolved to avail himself of the opening thus given, though not without a certain dread. He was naturally loth to lose the friendship of one for whom he entertained a warm affection. He remembered Hannington's openly expressed dislike of religious enthusiasm, and his contempt for all canting protestations of superior piety. It was not without a mental struggle that he determined to lay bare his own heart to an eye only too probably unsympathetic. It seemed likely that this letter of his might open a wide gulf between them. Still, if friendship was to be lost, it should be at least well lost. So he reasoned, and, with prayer for guidance, just wrote a simple, unvarnished account of his own spiritual experience; tried to explain how it had come to pass that he was not as formerly; spoke of the power of the love of Christ to transform the life of a man, and draw out all its latent possibilities; and finally urged him, as he loved his own soul, to make a definite surrender of himself to the Saviour of the world, and join the society of His disciples. This done, the Curate walked, not without misgivings as to the wisdom of the course he had adopted, to the miscellaneous little shop which did duty in the village as drapery and grocery store, post-office, and what not, and dropped his letter into the box.

For thirteen months no answer was returned. Prayer was made without ceasing, and still under the sense of a burden imposed, but there was no response. The Curate concluded that his letter had been consigned to the oblivion of the waste-paper basket.

He was, however, wrong. During those months events

were happening at Martinhoe. The Hand of God was not idle, and the seed was germinating.

> " Thou visitest the earth, and waterest it :
> Thou greatly enrichest it ;
> The river of God is full of water ;
> Thou providest corn, when Thou hast so prepared the earth ;
> Thou waterest her furrows abundantly ;
> Thou settlest the ridges thereof :
> Thou makest it soft with showers ;
> Thou blessest the springing thereof :
> Thou crownest the year with Thy gladness."—*Ps.* lxv.

But seed, whether sown in the heart of a man or in the furrows of the field, must be allowed time to develop and strike root. The husbandman must not be impatient, but wait for the " crown of the year."

Seed had been sown in Hannington's heart which was not destined to perish ; but that heart still needed further preparation for its upspringing. We may compare the events that followed, with their wholesome laceration of his pride, to the harrow in the Hand of his God.

On September 8th he writes : " The Bishop has put the exam. a week earlier, which will, I doubt, entirely undo me, as I have left my Prayer Book for the last fortnight's reading." He had yet, then, to learn that " cramming," however permissible in other cases, should have no place in an examination for such a charge as that. He goes on to record :—

" *Sept.* 17*th.*—Exeter ; in uncomfortable lodgings. Did a paper at 9.30 ; fairly well. 11.30, another paper ; did well. 1.30, dined with the Bishop. 5.30, another paper. 8 p.m., chapel, with a sermon from the Bishop.

" 18*th.*—Over-read last night. Passed a sleepless night ; woke exceedingly unwell. Three more papers, one of which was the Prayer Book. Unable to do anything ; had been disappointed of a week's reading, and was also very ill.

" 19*th.*—Another bad night. Three more papers ; and on
the 20th was, as I thought, unkindly dismissed by the Bishop
—' I am sorry to say that your paper on the Prayer Book is
insufficient. If you go down to Mr. Percival, he will tell
you all about it. Good morning.' I was so confounded
that I was nearly overwhelmed with despair. Mrs. Dovell
told me afterwards that she thought I should have died or
gone off my head."

Hannington told me, some time after, that the shame
and confusion of his failure came upon him at first as a
sickening blow. He thought that he should never raise his
head again. Then, as he thought of his own unwisdom
and of the Bishop's hard manner towards him, he gave way
to an ungovernable burst of passion. He was filled with
furious madness, partly against himself, and partly at the
recollection of what seemed like an insult inflicted on him.
He was suffering himself to be swept along upon the full
tide of this stormy mood, when suddenly the thought struck
him, as though he heard spoken words of warning, " *If
you can give way like this, are you fit to offer yourself as a
minister of Christ ?*"

He was sobered in an instant. It seemed to him that
his defeat had been ordered in the providence of God. He
resolved to accept it humbly, and to strive to approve himself a more worthy candidate upon another occasion.

Hannington now went back to Oxford, in order that he
might read with Mr. Morfill. The following sad occurrence impressed him : " Loyd, one of our men, nephew to
Lord Dufferin, cut his throat last night. This has thrown
a gloom over the place. He is just alive. He did it from
despair about the schools ; but his mind was evidently
affected."

He wrote, about this time : " How I dread ordination !

I would willingly draw back; but when I am tempted to do so I hear ringing in my ears, 'Whoso putteth his hand to the plough, and looketh back, is not fit for the kingdom of God.' What am I to do? What?"

When it is remembered that Hannington was possessed of a sufficient competency, and that at this time he had as large an income as ever in his life, it will be plain that he was not influenced in his decision to persevere by any monetary considerations.

The temptation to lead the independent life of a private gentleman, and to occupy himself with his favourite scientific pursuits, must have been very strong. Many young men in his position would have easily succumbed to it. As an explorer, or in independent research into the vast realm of natural history, he might easily have distinguished himself, and satisfied any thirst of ambition which might possess him. He was his own master. The whole world was open before him; and he was one who would never have let time drag heavily, or have been at a loss for employment and interest.

It is characteristic of the man that he should have shaken this temptation from him, and, with steady determination, faced what he now dreaded with an almost morbid fear. His conscience would not have absolved him else. "Whoso putteth his hand to the plough, and looketh back, is not fit for the kingdom of God." Those words held him fast to his purpose.

The end of 1873 found Hannington back at Martinhoe, among the Devon farmers. He went to one of those parties described before, and danced the old year out. Having performed this rite, he returned to Oxford, where he took part in a series of gaieties, and then started for Exeter, to face once more the Bishop's Chaplain and his papers.

He was terribly nervous and agitated; could not sleep at all that first night. He faced his papers next morning in such a frame of mind that it was impossible he could do his best. He was one of those men for whom an examination has real terrors. What he knew best and most accurately, on such occasions fled out of his mind, and left him in a state of helpless blankness.

There are some men who never show their powers so well as across a green baize tablecloth, and confronted by two examiners. They pass everything with ease and credit, and afterwards disappoint the expectations of their friends. There are others who, though hopelessly stumbled under such circumstances, and able to bring to the front nothing that they know, yet leave their mark upon the world. Hannington was one of the latter sort.

On the present occasion he was thoroughly well prepared in his various subjects; but by the time the examination drew to a close he had worked himself into such a state of nervous excitement, that it was almost impossible for him to do himself credit.

On the fourth day of the examination he was summoned into the presence of the Bishop. He was told that his paper showed evidence of hard and conscientious reading, but that his matter had been badly handled (how could it be otherwise, poor fellow, when his ideas were utterly muddled and gone astray!) ; and, in fine, that he must remain a deacon for two years, and come up for an intermediary examination. With this information, and—" You've got fine legs, I see : mind that you run about your parish. Good morning "—he was dismissed.

The following day (March 1st) the Ordination took place in the Cathedral.

Through the silent aisles sounds the Archdeacon's voice

"Reverend Father in God, I present unto you these persons present to be admitted Deacons."

Then, after the heart-stirring petitions of the Litany, the Bishop is heard to ask :—

"*Do you trust that you are inwardly moved by the Holy Ghost to take upon you this office and ministration, to serve God for the promoting of His Glory, and the edifying of His people ?* "

A moment's silence, and then from each candidate the answer—

"*I trust so.*"

And there can be little doubt that Hannington made this answer with all sincerity, according to the light he then possessed. That Ordination was to him very awful, and full of solemnity. Behind Bishop and officiating clergy, he saw ONE to whose awful Majesty he had consecrated the service of his life.

" So," said he to himself, as he left the Cathedral, " I am Ordained, and the world has to be crucified in me. O for God's Holy Spirit ! "

The next day he met the Principal in the Quadrangle of St. Mary Hall. " He, having known me in my wildest and noisiest times, said, in his dry way, 'I am not certain whether you are to be congratulated or not.' "

On the Sunday following, Hannington assisted in the Services at Hurst, and preached his first sermon, which he pronounces—probably not without reason—to have been " feeble, in fact, not quite sound." In spite of the congratulations of his friends, he tore it up.

The next Sunday he commenced his duty as Curate of Trentishoe. The people crowded into the little church to see their old friend in his new garb. Alas ! he had not yet much to the purpose to say to them. Services in those parts were conducted in a primitive manner enough. Take the following example :—" I went over to Parracombe.

"Clerk: 'We are going to have service in the school-room this evening, sir.   We like it better.'

"'Oh; well, what does Mr. Leakey do?'

"'Why, sir, he reads, prays extempore, and expounds. He don't preach no sermon, and don't wear no gown.'

"I, dreadfully nervous: 'I think I will read the Evening Service, Jones.   Is there a Bible?'

"'No, sir, there aint; he do bring his own with him.'

CURATE'S ROOMS AT MARTINHOE.

"More nervous than ever, I gave out a hymn.   Then, while they were singing it, in came a surplice, which I put on.   Next a lamp, which was most acceptable.

"I then said I would read the Litany; so I commenced. Then a Bible was found and thrust on to the table, so I was able to read a Lesson.   Then came the most trying ordeal. The table was quite low.   I had not my glasses, and did not like to hold my sermon-case up before me, so I had to lean on my elbows, stick my legs out behind me, and thus read painfully through my paper.   Moral: 'Learn to preach and pray without book.'"

Ah, me!. Was there ever such a Curate before or since! Let us hear him describe himself :—

" Here I am, a lone man, living in a singularly out-of-the-way place, Curate of Martinhoe and Trentishoe; clad in a pair of Bedford-cord knee-breeches of a yellow colour, continued below with yellow Sussex gaiters (' spats ') with brass buttons. Below these a stout pair of nail boots, four inches across the soles, and weighing fully four pounds. My upper garment, an all-round short jerkin of black cloth, underneath which an ecclesiastical waistcoat, buttoning up at the side. N.B.—The two latter articles of clothing I always wear. I am seated in as pleasant a room as you would wish to see. Wilton carpet, old china, piano, arm-chairs, numberless pictures, and large candelabras. Only there is no fire, and it is very cold—but alas! my chimney smokes."

That last item is not to be wondered at, as the cottage in which he took up his abode was close under a steep hill, and a strong down draught was almost inevitable.

Paying a visit to a parish in Essex where he had to respect the conventionalities and don the usual clerical habiliments, he says : " I found it a great burden going about in black clothes and top hat! I never could stop in such a place ! "

I find just here a note of his first missionary meeting, which is interesting in view of his future life :

" *July* 30*th*.—I went to my first missionary meeting at Parracombe. I was made to speak, much against my will, as I know nothing about the subject, and take little interest in it. There was an old Colonel Simpson, who spoke after me, and gave me such an indirect dressing, that I made up my mind never in future to speak on any subject until I knew something about it."

The rough work of a Devonshire parish exactly suited Hannington's temperament. Such adventures as the following were quite to his mind :—

"As I had ridden my pony more than fifty miles last week, and had a hard ride yesterday, I determined, instead of going round by the road, to cross Exmoor, to take duty at Challacombe. When I got on to the moor a dense fog came on, and I soon lost my way. I galloped up hill and down in mist and rain from nine till eleven, which was the hour of Church Service, and then was still as much lost as ever. I determined to give up church, throw the reins on the pony's neck, and let him take me back home. Presently I struck a track which promised at least to lead somewhere, so once more clapping spurs to my pony, I galloped along, and soon came to a gate which led me off the moor. This track brought us to a farmhouse, and there a man volunteered to accompany me, " for," said he, " you will lose yourself again if I don't." I arrived at church, and found the people sitting patiently in the pews, discussing with one another whether I would turn up. They all thought I was lost. I whispered to the clerk how it had happened. ' Iss,' said he in loud tones, ' we reckoned you was lost, but now you are here, go and put on your surples, and be short, for we all want to get back to dinner.' Dripping wet as I was, I put on the surplice over all, and gave them a shortened service. In the afternoon I got back in time for church at Martinhoe."

So he spent his time among those scattered hamlets, doing the best he knew; and doing it with all his heart. Riding on his rough Exmoor pony with his Prayer Book in one pocket of his shooting jacket, and medicines for some sick person in another. Welcomed everywhere. Admired by the young men and beloved by the aged, to whom he was as a son. They forgot that he had come among them as a stranger, and treated him as though he were a born son of the soil.

The life was entirely after his own heart, and yet he was not happy. The people were content with him, but he was not content with his own ministrations to them. He was parson, doctor, family friend, all in one. He felt that he could be of some use to the poor and needy. He sat up long nights with the sick and dying. His purse was always at the command of those in want. He could and did sometimes preach vehement sermons against prevalent vices, such as immorality, and excessive drinking at " wakes " and feasts, but he could not preach the " Word of Life." As he visited the sick and dying, or " read Prayers " in bald-looking, uncared-for country churches, and held up his manuscript sermon to his eyes in presence of sleepy audiences of tired labouring folk, he realized *that* ever more keenly. He was not giving them the Word of Life. How could he, when he did not himself possess the secret of that Life! The burden of his great responsibility weighed upon him more heavily every day. He began to understand, as he had never understood before, that he was not right with God. God's ordained Messenger with no Message to deliver—that was his position. A position, to his transparently-honest soul, altogether insupportable. He began to be in great distress.

Some thirteen months had passed since that letter bearing the post-mark of a Surrey village had reached him. It had not been answered. The friend who wrote that letter had concluded it burnt, perhaps with indignation, or, maybe, with scornful contempt. How could he know that it had been treasured up, read, and re-read, and that it would prove to be the turning-point of a life !

But Hannington's own words will best describe the phase of his mind during this important period of his career :—

· "And now," he says, "comes a tale of surpassing
interest to me. More than a year ago ——— wrote me
a letter. I did not answer it, although the impression it
made never left me. Time passed on, and I knew that I
was not right. I sought and sought most earnestly, at
times being in terrible bondage of spirit, and doubts, and
fears. I began to despair of ever coming to the knowledge
of the Truth. At length I again wrote to ———, and
begged him to come and pay me a visit. Most earnestly
did I pray that he might come and bring me light, as
Ananias did to St. Paul."

This letter ran as follows :

"MY DEAR COLONEL,*—Can you come and see me ?
Even a short visit. I am in much distress of soul and want
your advice. I am so sorry that I did not answer your last
letter. It was not, I assure you, through want of interest
in its contents. It has never been off my table during the
past year, and I have read it again and again. Do come
and see me if you can.—Yours,

"JAMES HANNINGTON."

Alas ! his friend was not master of his own time. He
could not be spared from his work at the busiest time of the
year to make a journey into distant Devonshire. He was
strangely moved by this marvellous response to his prayers.
He now understood how it was that the burden of that
soul had never ceased to press upon him during all that
time. He at once did what he was able. He wrote what
he thought might be helpful to one in spiritual darkness and
distress ; he invited Hannington to come and see him ;
and laying his hand upon the only suitable book which he
then happened to have upon his writing table, sent it with

---

* A nickname by which his friend was known at college.

the letter to Martinhoe. This book was "Grace and Truth," by the late Dr. Mackay, of Hull. A book which, if somewhat crude and dogmatic in its statements, and apt thereby to repel, has at least the merit of stating its facts in a clear and forcible manner. The index finger may be a rude one, but it points plainly and emphatically where lies that narrow path which leads through the Cross of Jesus to eternal life.

Hannington was dreadfully disappointed. He writes :—

"I was in despair. It seemed to sound my death-knell. I thought the Lord would not answer me."

He sent the following to his friend :—

"MY DEAR COLONEL,—Many thanks for thinking of me. I cannot possibly come to you. I wish that I could ; and that for many reasons : one is that darkness, coldness and barrenness have seized hold upon me, and I cannot shake them off. I am, I don't know in what state, unless I am being bound by the devil hand and foot. But I mean to fight him desperately hard, if only I am helped. I cannot do it alone. Oh, for strength to rise and triumph !—Yours very affectionately,

"JAMES HANNINGTON."

Shortly after came the following, in reply to another letter :—

"MY DEAR COLONEL,—I am so much obliged to you for remembering me. I can assure you that I appreciate it deeply. There are few to whom one seems united in a bond closer than that of relationship ; at least, I know very few to whom I can really open my heart as I can to you. . . . . . . I feel depressed at the fact that, when I would do good, evil is present with me. I have no faith, I can lay hold of nothing. I cannot believe that I can ever be saved ; and I feel that I have no right to preach to others.

I try to feel that God willeth not the death of a sinner, but no, I can preach it, and feel it for other persons, not for myself. How few rays of light seem to shine upon me! Will the sun ever break through the clouds so that I shall be able to say, ' Jesus is mine and I am His '? I shall try and visit you if I can. Very many thanks for the book ; I will read it shortly.—Yours very affectionately,

"JAMES HANNINGTON."

As Hannington could not obtain an interview with his friend, he turned to the book which he had sent. In his private diary he writes :—

" I determined to read every word of the book. So I began with the preface. Here I soon perceived that the book was unscholarly, for the argument is built upon Matt. xv. 27, ' Truth, Lord,' which the author treats as ἀληθέια, instead of the exclamation ναὶ. This was enough for me. I therefore threw the book away and refused to read it."

We may observe here that Hannington was wrong. Dr. Mackay does not make the mistake with which he hastily charged him. It might be possible for a reader to suppose that he confuses the two words because he does not take sufficient care to make it clear that the word rendered " *Truth* " in Matt. xv. 27, is not the same word as " *Truth* " in the passage " Grace and Truth." He certainly does not take proper care to guard the reader against the supposition that no play upon the words is intended. But it cannot be fairly urged that he has perpetrated in his preface a piece of palpable and gratuitous ignorance. He apparently intends to deduce from the Syrophenician woman's " Truth, Lord," no more than an unqualified *assent* to the statement of Christ with regard to her.

But Hannington was in no mood to have mercy upon

the book or its author. His heart was sore that he could
not have his friend. The poor book had to stand the kicks.
Moreover the blunt dogmatism of its tone, effective enough
with a certain class of minds, did not fall in with his then
line of thought. He was evidently glad of any excuse
to condemn the book and throw it aside, on the principle
that " any stick is good enough to beat a dog with."

So " Grace and Truth " lay in a corner unread
for some little while. He shall himself narrate what
followed.

"When I left on the 16th of September for Exeter and
St. Petherwyn, I spied that old book and said, '—— is sure
to ask me if I have read it. I suppose I must wade through
it ; ' and so stuffed it into my portmanteau. At Petherwyn
I took the book out and read the first chapter. I disliked
it so much that I determined never to touch it again. I
don't know that I did not fling it across the room. I rather
think I did. So back into my portmanteau it went, and
remained until my visit to Hurst, when I again saw it, and
thought I might as well read it, so as to be able to tell
—— about it. So once more I took the ' old thing,'
and read straight on for three chapters or so, until at last I
came to that called ' Do you feel your sins forgiven ? ' By
means of this my eyes were opened."

His anxiety had been great. His search for the "hidden
treasure" had been long, continuous and painful. His joy
was now correspondingly great. His pent-up feelings
rushed forth in a torrent of thanksgiving. Like a " certain man " of old Jerusalem, who " entered into the temple
walking and leaping and praising God," so he could not
contain his gladness within the bounds of quietness. He
shook off the chains of darkness and bounded into the light.
He says :

" I was in bed at the time reading. I sprang out of bed and leaped about the room rejoicing and praising God that Jesus died for me. From that day to this * I have lived under the shadow of His wings in the assurance of faith that I am His and He is mine."

And truly it was even so. Yet did he not immediately enter into the *full* assurance of faith. For some time after his enlightenment he was, to use his own favourite expression, subject to fits of " bondage." ˙ His old life would assert itself strongly. He could not all at once shake off the habits of thought which had become natural to him. He had his periods of darkness and light, despondency and rejoicing. But he fought a good fight, and little by little he made sure his ground, until finally he emerged from the mists into the full sunlight of the Father's smile. A delightful and altogether helpful little tract entitled " Gripping and Slipping" describes the precarious state of a soul which has not learned the secret of maintaining its grasp upon the Hand of the ever-present Christ. Perhaps only they who have had some humiliating experience of the " slipping" state can fully appreciate the boundless security of him who " grips." To the end of his life Hannington refused to throw in his lot with those who apparently teach the possibility of Peace without Conflict; but when once he had grasped that Hand, he followed the leading of the Spirit with the unfaltering faith of a little child. Thereafter he went straight forward, nothing wavering, to do the duty that lay nearest to him. That he had learned the secret of " the overcoming life" could not but be recognized by those who watched him closely and noticed with wondering thankfulness how the old James Hannington was being,

---

* This note was written just before his second missionary journey to Africa.

day by day, remodelled into a new man ; the same, and yet another.

The following letters will throw some light upon his state of mind at this time :

" MY DEAR COLONEL,— .... The chief object of my letter is to tell you how very useful those two books you have given me have been made to me. I have never seen so much light as I have the last few days. I know now that Jesus Christ died for me, and that He is mine and I am His. And all this you are the human means of teaching me. Perhaps to-morrow I shall be in doubt and despair, but not as I have been before ; for I know that *I believe* and I can tremblingly exclaim, ' Help Thou mine unbelief.' Dear Colonel, what thanks I owe to you, and incomparably little with what I owe to God ! "

" I ought daily to be more thankful to you as the instrument by which I was brought to Christ, and to know that He died for me.   Unspeakable joy ! "

" I have been rejoicing so lately that I fear it may come from Satan puffing me up, for I do so little for Christ.   My prayers and praise are so dead and formal.   I love the things of this world so much, and Jesus so little, that I ought always to be mourning.   ' Sorrowful yet always rejoicing,' I know.   Yet latterly I have been rejoicing, and not sorrowful, although I have so much in me about which I ought to lament.   Do write and tell me am I wrong. Can that peace be false which comes from the knowledge of forgiveness of sins through the belief that Jesus died for me ?   No, never.   I feel that it cannot, it cannot be false (Tit. i. 2)."

" How wonderfully I have been led on from one thing to another, though at the time imperceptibly !   I speak of my choosing the Ministry when I was most unfit for it.

Then again getting sent back from Exeter, when I now see that to have passed the examination then would have been the very worst thing that could have happened to me. Again, our friendship, which for some time had been dormant, renewing itself, and proving so extraordinarily useful to me!   .   .   .   I fear that the tone of this letter is shockingly boastful, and one which I am not worthy to adopt. You will have to set me back into a lower seat! The Lord keep me humble! How much instruction I stand in need of! Cease not to pray for me."

On the nineteenth of October in this year, 1874, Hannington paid a visit to his correspondent in Surrey. The stress of his great anxiety of mind had left its evident traces upon him. He was far from well, and tired too with his journey. He did not, moreover, find it so easy to talk to an old companion and sharer of his jests, as it had been to write to him about the secrets of his soul. This just at first:

"Well, Colonel."

"Well, Jim."

"How are you, old fellow?"

"Glad to see you, dear old man."

Then some conversation upon general subjects, old friends, and old customs.   But, by-and-by, when both had settled into their chairs, and looked each other in the face, the subject uppermost in their hearts could no longer be kept in the background. The barriers of reserve were broken down; and before long they found themselves telling each other without constraint how the Lord had dealt with their souls.

That evening the Curate held a Cottage Lecture in a distant part of the parish. Seeing that Hannington was worn out and haggard-looking, he tried to persuade him to remain at home. He, however, insisted that he should be allowed to go. So arm in arm the two sallied forth. His friend

will not easily forget that walk. As they threaded their way
among the gravel pits, and crossed the mile of rough common and deep and muddy lanes, Hannington's conversation
was always upon the one subject. Having once conquered his
shyness, he laid bare his heart in the confidence of that hour.

When they reached the cottage he would not be persuaded to take any part in the service. He had come, he
said, as a learner ; he would sit among the audience. So he
quietly waited, while his friend went among the adjoining
cottages to gather in some laggards, and then took his place,
somewhere in a corner, among the group of poor folk who
crowded the little room. He was still, in his own estimation, the humblest of disciples.

I find the following note about this in his diary :

" *Evening.*—To my great astonishment ——— took a
Cottage Lecture. I feared that I never could do a thing of
that sort."

His friend now urged him strongly to try, at least when
he was addressing small audiences of country people in
Devonshire, to preach extempore. Hitherto he had been
bound entirely and rigidly to his paper. Even in his private
devotions he seldom ventured beyond his book of prayers.
To his marked energy and decision of character he united
depreciation of himself and distrust of his own motives to a
singular degree. This made the study of his religious life
peculiarly interesting. Every step made toward spiritual
liberty was the result of close and unsparing self-examination. He would remorselessly probe his feelings and every
ramification of them before he would permit himself indul-
gence in any new "liberty." Never did any apply the
scalpel and dissecting knife more ruthlessly to his own " vile
body " than did James Hannington.

It was not long, however, before he saw plainly that it

was his duty to tell people what he knew, as the Lord had told himself—and to tell it as simply as possible ; hence he soon decided to discard the manuscript sermon, and adopt the practice of taking his thoughts only into the pulpit, in the form of notes, leaving the words that were to clothe them to the inspiration of the moment.

That visit was useful to both the friends. The one had realized the meaning of that statement of Carlyle, "It is certain my belief gains quite *infinitely* the moment I can convince another mind thereof." The other left, encouraged to go back to his charge among the Devonshire moors, and tell all men boldly what great things the Lord had done for him.

may, perhaps, be permitted to repeat here some words written by his companion in recollection of this period : —

"Very touching is it now to me to think of those days in the light of his subsequent life. None who saw his strong nature thus receiving the Kingdom of God as a little child can ever doubt that to him it was granted to see that Kingdom indeed. I shall not readily forget the morning on which he departed. Together we got into the little two-wheeled pony cart, and together we drove over the long stretch of breeze-swept common which lie between Hale and the Camp Station, at which he purposed to meet his train. As mental impressions sometimes interweave themselves with scenery, and the memory of the one unconsciously revives the other, so can I never dissociate that drive from the interchange of thoughts for which it afforded the opportunity. The white road, which undulates, now past clumps of fir-trees, now between banks tipped with yellow furze, again over long stretches of common, and the bright freshness of that sunny morning, will be to me ever, as it were, the binding of the volume of the book wherein are written many precious words."

45416

CHAPTER VIII

WORK AT TRENTISHOE AND DARLEY ABBEY.

(1875.)

"There is small chance of truth at the goal when there is not child-like humility at the starting-post." COLERIDGE.

HANNINGTON returned to Trentishoe in a very different frame of mind from that in which he had quitted it. Like that captain of the host of the King of Syria who went back to his master with his flesh "like unto the flesh of a little child," he felt himself to have become a new man. Some little further time, however, was to elapse before he would fully realize all the conditions of his new life, or dare to proclaim the Gospel of the Kingdom as one who had himself been admitted to the fellowship of the Founder.

I do not note that his sermons became all at once markedly evangelistic. It would have been very unlike him if they had. Whatever faults he may have had, preaching beyond his own experience was not one of them. Whether or no he had read old John Byrom's advice to preachers, he so far followed it, that

"he never dealt
In the false commerce of a truth unfelt."

In this lay much of the power of his preaching. He proclaimed what he knew. But this very honesty of his forbids the supposition that his sermons were, at this time, upon a higher level of spiritual life than that to which he himself

had attained. The freedom, the "unction," and the blessing were soon to follow. In the meanwhile he resolved
that he would try what he could do without his hitherto
inseparable pulpit companion, the sermon-case. He says:

"*Sunday Morning.*—I determined, at the eleventh hour,
that, by the help of God the Holy Spirit, I would preach
extempore, in spite of myself and my protestations to the
contrary. I had not, previous to this morning, prayed to
be led to do it, and so I felt it was in answer to ———'s
prayers. I succeeded a great deal better than I expected,
and have only once since, for the last ten years" (this was
written in 1884), " preached a written sermon. My plan has
ever since been to make rather copious notes."

Soon after he commenced extempore preaching he was
warned by the following painful occurrence, that to preach
without a manuscript entails not less preparation but more.
He was paying a visit to his father at Hurst, and was, of
course, asked to occupy the pulpit of St. George's. He
was very nervous, and, moreover, was not well, but, from
one cause or another, that sermon never got beyond the text.
The young preacher—on this occasion a " stickit minister "
indeed—had just sufficient presence of mind to dismiss the
astonished and sympathetic congregation with a hymn.

His friends justly attributed the above incident to the
fact that he was thoroughly run down in health ; and, indeed,
he was, by the doctor's orders, confined to his bed for nearly
a week. He would not, however, let himself off so easily.
He wrote to his friend : " Alas ! my spiritual father, what
a sickly son you have !—a Mr. Idlebones, Ease-in-the-flesh ;
a Mr. Chat-and-do-nothing—a carnal professor."

Similar misadventures have been chronicled of great
men, from Massillon to David Livingstone ; and if this accident were indeed the result of vain confidence and want of

faith, he soon experienced the blessed truth embalmed in the exquisite line of that old Latin hymn—

" Mergere nos patitur, sed non submergere Christus." *

A fortnight later he preached again in St. George's, and this time with considerable power. His father, who now heard him for the first time, was deeply moved ; so he was encouraged to persevere.

In February he was back once more in Devonshire, and had his first experience of a " Parochial Mission." This was conducted at Parracombe by Mr. John Wood and the Vicar, Mr. Leakey, with whom he formed a friendship which lasted until the end of his life. Hannington writes : " I went over there, and was delighted." The next Sunday, in spite of a terrific storm, and heavy snow-drifts which almost beat him back, he made his way again to Parracombe, and preached to the anxious from Rom. v. 1. He was now able to speak as one who had himself found " peace with God through our Lord Jesus Christ." The text was an epitome of his own recent experience. We are not surprised to learn that his sermon was blessed, and made useful to several people.

This Mission gave him considerable impetus. He began to feel that the Great King might have some definite work for him too among His servants. That to him also had been committed a talent.

That wild, harum-scarum Exmoor pony of his, which was always falling, or otherwise putting his life in danger, but which he kept " because it was so game " and " would go down a cliff almost like the side of a house " without flinching, carried him in every direction from cottage to cottage and farm to farm. And he no longer went among the people without a message. The Word of Life was now,

---

* Christ suffers to sink, maybe, but not to drown.

of all subjects, the nearest to his lips. An old man known as "Carpenter Richards" died. There were not many deaths in Martinhoe. Old Richards had been, in his youth, in prison for smuggling. The last words he uttered were, "I love Mr. Hannington." "Oh," writes Hannington in his private diary, "that it had only been, ' I love the Lord Jesus ! ' "

Opposite April 26th I find this entry :

"Sent for, instead of the doctor, to see a man" (here he mentions symptoms), "a hopeless case. I pointed him to the Saviour. My name down here as a medical man is quite established. I am sent for in almost every case ; which gives me the opportunity to speak to them about their souls."

"*May 9th, Sunday.*—Rode about four miles to leave some medicine. Then preached at Parracombe. Rode to Walner. Saw man with inflammation. Found him already dying. He followed me in prayer, and said some nice things. Preached at Trentishoe. Returned to Walner. Found patient unconscious. Evening, preached and held a mission service in my own rooms, during which time, the man, I hear, died." He thus rode some twenty miles that day.

"*May 13th.*—Man came running to me to come at once. A child drowned. I ran straight off at my top speed, and found that the child had fallen into a tank only seventeen inches deep, but life was quite extinct.

"*May 15th.*—Sat on inquest as foreman of the jury, and received a shilling for my pains ! "

"*20th.*—Administered enema to a patient. Preached to the Club at Lynton. Dined with them and returned thanks for Bishop and clergy. Returned home with the doctor and assisted him to make a post-mortem on the

child of the man who cursed me." This latter was
an ill-conditioned coastguard, who had, I imagine, taken
offence at Hannington's new views.

From the above extracts—and they are only samples of
many such—it will be seen that, although the souls over
whom he was placed in charge did not much exceed three
hundred, Hannington was not idle. Though the people were
few, the distances which had to be traversed, and the roughness of the moorland roads and bridle paths, made the work
of such thorough supervision as he gave them far from easy.

There are men who work well under a pressing
sense of obligation to duty ; but it is against the grain. If
their consciences would let them, they would infinitely prefer
to " stand at ease." Such men sink into the easiest available
chairs with a sigh of relief when their annual holiday sets
them free. To them relaxation means cessation from work.

There are others to whom work is a necessity. They
work at their profession with all their might, and they work
at their play with all their might. Hannington was one of
this sort. He was one of those Englishmen whose amusements so sorely puzzle our Continental neighbours.

When June of this year came round, and he thought
himself entitled to a holiday, he cast about for pastures new.
He had often looked wistfully seaward, where the cliffs of
Lundy Island rose in a purple line against the flame of golden
sunsets. Out on the extreme limit of the western horizon,
Lundy seems a foothold from which the happy traveller
might gaze out upon a new and more glorious world, from
which he might take his flight " Far away, on from island
unto island at the gateways of the day." The very " land
of far distances." Such to the poetic mind. To the naturalist it offers a field of great interest. Rare plants await
the botanist. There are " beetles " (under which term

Hannington classed the whole insect family) to reward the entomologist. The sea-shore teems with life, the sea with fish ; the cliffs are the haunts of myriads of sea-birds, which deposit their eggs upon the ledges. There are caves to be explored, bathing and climbing *ad libitum*. What more can a reasonable man desire ?

I took an egg spoon and a bag
In which ... the eggs ...
And in the girl ...
  my trusty friends
Did firmly plant the foot
Then lowered me over
  twelve feet or more
Till dangling in the air
  However would you like the
Just hanging over there

Having persuaded a College friend, T. May, to join him, Hannington sailed from Instow, and received a hearty welcome at the farm on Lundy Island from Mr. and Mrs. Dovell. There they had what the Americans call a "good time." They wore their oldest clothes, fished, egged, botanized and explored to their heart's content. The humorous sketches, which are reproduced in exact fac-simile from a book of rhymes which Hannington wrote for his little nephews and nieces, describe some of the adventures of these two. They had arrived in the height of the egging season. The birds lay their pear-shaped eggs upon the narrow ledges of the most inaccessible cliffs. To reach these the egg hunter arms himself with an instrument called an egg-spoon, like a tiny landing-net, at the end of a long, light rod. He is then lowered over the edge, and fills his wallet with as many eggs as he can reach. Hannington, partly for the sake of the adventure, and partly to add some cormorant's eggs to his collection,

persuaded Mr. Dovell and his friend " Cluppins " to let him down from the edge of a tremendous precipice. They were more nervous than he, and got well laughed at by the enthusiastic eggsman as he scrambled up again with the contents of three nests in his pockets. Whether or not he really played them the trick which he has so spiritedly depicted in the series of sketches, I do not know.

The next day these two big boys determined to explore

the recesses of a dark cave much frequented by seals.
They had to take off their clothes and swim into the
entrance. They found themselves standing at the mouth
of a deep cleft, which wound its way for some distance
into the darkness.   On stooping down to examine the
sand, they saw distinctly
many recent tracks of
seals.   As the passage is
very narrow and of utter
darkness, and the danger
of meeting an alarmed
and frantic seal, in a
place where neither could
pass the other, would
not be small, his friend
very wisely counselled
retreat.   But there was
never any going back
for those who followed
Hannington, unless in-
deed they deserted him
and went back alone.
This, of course, his
friend had no thought
of doing, and so the two
wormed their way in-
ward till they reached a
large chamber called

the Seals' Kitchen. Every moment they expected a charge
of sea-monsters, but when they arrived at the end of their
journey they found that the seals, which had taken refuge
there at high tide, had made their way out again just
before their own intrusion.

As their clothes were off, and there are no summer

visitors to be scandalized on Lundy Island, they next
amused themselves by swimming to various places at the
foot of the sheer cliffs, and climbing up, amid screaming,
circling seagulls, to the ledges where the shags had laid their
odd-shaped eggs.

The next sketch represents a harmless little joke of which
his hostess was the victim. An emu's egg has been given
to Hannington, about which he tells the children :

" While I was busy blowing eggs,
    And this was by my side,
A lady coming at the time
    At once this big egg spied.
' O pray, declare, what have you there ?
    Where *did* you get that egg ?
I *must* get one, let what will come ;
    Please tell me how, I beg.'

' A secret that ; I may not tell,'
    To her I straight replied,
Then having put the egg away
    Soon out again I hied.
My back was turned scarce half an hour :
    She to the cupboard goes,
And to the eggers of this isle
    The emu's egg she shows.
' The strangers took it on the cliffs,
    And, look you, I will pay

A goodly sum to any one
　　Who brings the like to-day.'
The eggers one and all left work;
　　Off with their spoons they run.
The master comes.　Asks in a rage,
　　'What's of those wretches come?
Unwilling strangers should them beat,
　　They hunted high and low
In every single breakneck place
　　Where mortal man could go.

But emus are not wont to lay
　　On fair Britannia's isle;
And least of all on Lundy's cliffs.
　　It really made us smile
To hear next day the fearful tramp
　　Those weary eggers had,
Returning tattered, pale, and thin,
　　And faces very sad."

Another sketch which is full of delicate fun represents himself, "Cluppins," and a boatman, fishing. The conger eel just hauled into the boat is supposed to be asserting his individuality after the manner of congers.

"'Tis my delight on a shiny night
　　For conger eels to fish;
Nor takes it long, if they bite strong,
　　To catch a splendid dish.

But as you haul them in your yawl,
Look out and mind your leg,
They'll bite your calves right clean in halves,
Though you may mercy beg."

Whatever may be thought or the artistic merit of these
drawings of his—and it must be remembered that he never
practised drawing, nor, indeed, handled a pencil to any purpose until he was about twenty-five years of age—it must be
acknowledged that they are full of life and movement.
They tell their own story. What they lack in correctness
they make up in vigour and a certain incisive humour which
gives them a distinct value of their own. This must be my
excuse for publishing them ; as for their author, he intended
these, and innumerable others of the same kind, only for the
eyes of the children at home—his little nephews and nieces
—for whose amusement he wrote his rhymes and illustrated
them. He was in the habit of turning his adventures into
easy-flowing, doggrel verse for the children. His rhymes, if
collected, would form quite a volume. They are prefaced
thus :—

" Nephews and nieces, come this way,
And hear what Uncle has to say.
Oh ! such a funny man is he
As ever you may wish to see.
Johnnie, Katie, Toosie, run
To see your Uncle's book of fun.
And, as it's such a jolly day,
Let's ask for a half-holiday."

At about this time Mr. Hannington definitely proposed to his son that he should return to Hurstpierpoint and take charge of the Chapel of St. George. This did not at the time commend itself to the mind of James. He was now quite happy at Martinhoe. The people loved and trusted him. His work was beginning to tell. The report of his preaching, and the earnestness and power of it, had gone abroad. Crowds would throng the little churches, sometimes overflowing into porch and churchyard, when he was expected. He loved his work too, and the people, and the rough rides over stormy moors, and the wild sea-cliffs and the sounding sea. The unconventionality of that life thoroughly suited his temperament.

He felt, moreover, that, by accepting the charge of St. George's he would be placing himself in a position of peculiar difficulty. The people at Hurst had known him since he was a child; how could he hope to escape the proverbial fate of the unhonoured prophet?

Would he, moreover, prove as acceptable to the more cultured denizens of the neighbourhood of Brighton as he was to the untutored Devonians?

With characteristic thoroughness he examined his own heart on the subject, and strove to weigh the pros and cons with an impartial hand. Perhaps the fact that told most strongly for the acceptance of St. George's was his reluctance to leave Martinhoe. He ever distrusted his own flesh, and thought that, in doubtful cases, it was a good and safe rule to run counter to its special pleading.

He had consulted me in the matter, and even made the proposal that I should myself take St. George's. This I was unable to do. He, therefore, concluded to leave himself entirely in the Hand of God, and to look upon the consent or refusal of the two Bishops of Exeter and Chichester as a sign whether or not he were to take the step. It seemed quite possible that neither of the Bishops would have wished him to undertake a new charge until he had received his Priest's Orders. Thus the matter rested for a while. I find the following prayer upon a loose sheet of paper, upon which are written several arguments on both sides of the question :—

" *Dear Lord, mercifully reveal Thy Will in this matter. Be Thou ever my Guardian and Guide.*"

So childlike was his spirit, and so simple his trust !

As time went by, the answer to his prayer came in the gradual removal, one by one, of all the difficulties in the way of his transfer. When both the Bishops signified their assent, he felt that the matter had been taken out of his own hands. The next thing was to prepare himself for his new sphere of work. St. George's, though a curacy, is virtually a sole charge. He would be thrown entirely upon his own resources. He decided at once to leave Martinhoe, and to spend some time with an experienced clergyman, from whom he could learn something of the varied work and organization of a well-ordered parish.

The Parish of Darley Abbey, a suburb of Derby, seemed to offer precisely what he required. The population consists of about a thousand persons, the families of workers in two factories—a paper and a cotton mill. The parish was a model of perfect organization. The Incumbent at that time was the Rev. J. Dawson, who, by the combination of powerful and attractive preaching with close and frequent house-to-house visitation, had filled, not only the Church, but also his class-rooms, with large and eager audiences. His week-night Bible Classes had enrolled out of that small population the unusual number of a hundred and twenty women and between seventy and eighty men, all regular attendants. His wife also conducted a Sunday afternoon Bible Class for factory girls, at which about sixty were usually present.

The efforts of the Vicar were backed up in the heartiest manner by the Evans family, the proprietors of the mills. By them the social and temporal affairs of the parish were managed with a patriarchal hand. Every house belonged to them, and was held by its tenant upon condition of conformity to certain rules. Among these rules was the singular one that every young man and woman should attend the Sunday School until the age of eighteen. Whatever may be said of such compulsion theoretically, in practice it worked very well. The numbers who voluntarily attended the Bible Classes, Prayer Meetings, and extra Services of the Church conclusively proved that the people were not offended at the rule, and did not resent it. There was no public-house in the village, and all provisions were supplied from one central store, of the best quality, and at "Civil Service" prices.

This parish, then, seemed to offer a good illustration of the manner in which intelligent working-people might be successfully dealt with. Hannington resolved to abide there for a while, and study the system thoroughly.

It was with a heavy heart that he went the round of his old haunts and said good-bye to his friends. The dear old cliffs, upon which he had had many a perilous scramble. The sea-washed caves, down to which wound his famous path. The wide moorland, over which he and his pony had so often galloped. All these seemed doubly dear now, when he was about to leave them, and seek the grimy fields which lie beneath the smoke cloud of ever-vomiting factory chimneys. The people, too, his beloved patients—his warm-hearted Devonshire friends, with their quaint ways—had never seemed so friendly or so desirable as now, when he was to be separated from them. One of his humble

friends, who possessed the power of " blessing," seized the
opportunity while holding his hand at parting, and, before
Hannington knew what she was doing, " said words "
over his finger, which had been dangerously stung by some
poisonous fly.   He was incredulous, but none the less
grateful.

So, on August 17th, 1875, he left North Devon somewhat sadly.   The hearty welcome, however, which greeted
him at the Parsonage of Darley Abbey, where his name was
already well known, did much to cheer him.   He soon took
his place as one of themselves in the family circle, and
became, as usual, a prime favourite.

Dear old Miss Evans was then alive.   Can any one who
ever knew her mention her name without some epithet of
affection ?   That massive red-brick mansion, which stood
within its own park-like grounds somewhat apart from the
village, was, to all intents and purposes, the palace of the
little kingdom of Darley Abbey.   There Miss Evans ruled
supreme.   She was then in her eighty-ninth year ; in full
possession of all her faculties ; the mistress of her household,
—of their hearts and minds, as well as of their bodies.   She
came of a long-lived family.   Her brother, the senior partner
of the firm, had lately died at the age of eighty-seven, and
her sister, with whom she had lived at Darley House since
their babyhood, had, though paralyzed during the greater
part of her life, only recently been removed at the age of
eighty-four.   She herself lived to see her ninety-sixth year.
She seemed to rise superior to the course of Time.   Her
small, erect figure would go hither and thither with the
precision and punctuality of a clock.   Her bright and
sunny face, with its never-failing smile, was to be seen
wherever she was needed.   And where was it that she
was not required ?   She was the very life and centre of
the village and all its work.   In any family difficulty, in any

dispute, in any case in which an arbiter was required, it was to "Miss Ivvins" that the people always went. She had spent her long life among them and for them, and she thoroughly understood both them and their ways. But she must be obeyed. Her large household of devoted domestics —several of whom were almost as old as herself, and had remained with her ever since, three-quarters of a century ago, as an active, bright-eyed girl she had taken up the reins of government—knew this. The villagers all knew this. Sometimes a new-comer, mistaking the gentle demeanour of the little woman, and the kindly look of interest in her eyes, would think to presume. But he seldom transgressed far. He was soon made to feel that those mittened hands, with their tender touch, concealed a grip of steel. In her younger days it may have been that she used her power somewhat unsparingly. It is not always easy for strong common sense and a commanding mind to make allowance for the weakness of others. But now, in her extreme age, softened, chastened, beautiful in her brisk helpfulness, self-respecting and respected, she presented a perfect picture of sweet and honourable womanhood.

The income of her large fortune was spent in doing good. No one will know until the Great Day of the Revelation of all things how many homes were made happy by her, how many were saved from ruin by her prompt interference, how many were assisted to make a start in life. Truly there are not a few who will rise and call her blessed.

Miss Evans was quick to discern the merits of James Hannington. He was always a welcome guest at Darley House. He, on his part, was charmed with Miss Evans, and enjoyed above all things to draw out her rich store of Christian experience.

On one occasion, when we called together, we found several elderly ladies, friends of Miss Evans, gathered round the fire. Their conversation upon some point of spiritual interest quite engrossed us, and we stayed a considerable time. As we at length left the house, Hannington turned to me with a quaint look, and said :

"Do you know, old fellow, I think that I must really be a Christian ? "

"I hope so," I said. "But what makes you think so just now especially ? "

"Well," he replied, with a smile, "what an unutterable bore I should have thought those people and their talk on such a subject a short time ago. But, do you know? I positively enjoyed it."

Hannington had his first experience of a genuine parochial tea-party soon after his arrival. It is the custom at Darley Abbey to issue a general invitation to the people on the day of the Derby races to what is called "the Race Tea." On this occasion over six hundred sat down. After tea addresses were given, among which Hannington noted with interest a description which the Rev. J. E. Linnell, himself once a workman, gave to the working people of his own eventful life.

On the twenty-ninth of September Hannington was instituted as Curate of St. George's, but he resolved to gain more experience of pastoral work before commencing his labours there, so, leaving the chapel in charge of the Rev. F. H. S. Pendleton, he returned to Darley in time to take part in a Mission which was to be conducted by the Rev. C. Melville Pym.

Into the work of this Mission he threw himself heartily. He says : "I gave the opening address. Mr. Bemrose, the publisher, followed. I was thin, but he was splendid." Every day he gave some address—rough and ready, but forcible and to the point,—visited energetically from house to house, and assisted at the after-meetings. On one occasion he seized hold of a notorious drunkard, and would not let him go until he had made a definite promise to come to that evening's Service. That Mission produced a great effect upon the people of Darley, and consolidated the Christians there into a united working body. Hannington was soon himself to conduct many such in other parts of the country.

He also saw and took part in the remarkable work which is carried on by the railway men at the Derby Station. He says: " I went to the Midland Railway breakfast-room, where about a hundred men meet and listen to an address from some specially-invited preacher every morning while they consume their breakfasts. A short time ago the Bishop of London spoke to them. This gathering originated in a half-witted man who used to read his Bible at meal time, and was badly treated, in consequence, by the other men. He went apart into a corner by himself, and was presently joined by another. They both of them got so persecuted that somebody spoke to the officials, and they gave them a small shed. This has now grown into the present meeting of about a hundred strong. I came in and asked if I might be a listener. The foreman said, ' We have been disappointed in our man ; will you speak to us ? ' I had not come prepared, but the Lord helped me ; and they immediately begged me to come again."

During the short time that he spent at Darley, Hannington quite won the hearts of the people. His frank and open manner took them by storm ; his eccentricities only endeared him the more to them. As a mill-worker was heard to say: " We all like Mr. Hannington, and no mistake ; he is so free like ; he just comes into your house, and sticks his hands down into the bottom of his pockets, and talks to you like a man."

He was the life and soul of the family party at the

Vicarage. His queer sayings and his oddities are still remembered by the members of that circle, especially by the Vicar, who thoroughly entered into and enjoyed his humour.

"I know that I am sometimes a little different from other people," Hannington would say, penitently, yet with a sly twinkle in his eye.

" A little different!" the Vicar would reply, shaking with laughter. " Why, I never saw anybody in all my life at all like you."

Or, as putting on a quizzical air, standing astride upon the hearthrug, he brought to light some imaginary discovery which he had made with regard to some member of the family, and then proceeded with infinite glee to work up the most ridiculous superstructure upon this mock foundation, the Vicar, who had been enjoying the whole thing with suppressed delight struggling on every feature, would burst forth from the depths of his arm-chair with a sounding peal, and a " James, you are perfectly incorrigible ; you are not content until you have probed out the tender part of everybody, and then you just go on dig, dig, digging away relentlessly at that spot till you become unbearable. You ought to be ashamed of yourself! " All this with the keenest appreciation of his odd pupil.

Well, has not one of our greatest modern thinkers said : " Eccentricity has always abounded where strength of character has abounded. That so few dare to be eccentric marks the chief danger of the time ! "

And if he did sometimes carry his humour to the verge of irritation, or persist in working out his vein of vexatiousness to the annoyance of the over-sensitive, he was soon forgiven. It was impossible to take offence, for the simple reason that he never meant to offend.

And Hannington could be very gentle and courteous

when he chose to be so. With the aged, or the weak, or
with those in need of comfort, help, or consolation, he was
ever the gentlest, kindest, and most considerate of friends.
In the presence of such he was another man. None who
ever sought his advice in trouble, or by whose bedside he
has sat in their sickness, will readily forget the tender helpfulness of his quiet manner, and the true ring of sympathy
in his voice.

CHAPTER IX.

ST. GEORGE'S, HURSTPIERPOINT.

(1875.)

"Sir, the life of a Parson, of a conscientious clergyman, is not easy. I have always considered a clergyman as the father of a larger family than he is able to maintain."   JOHNSON.

> "And evermore beside him on his way
>   The unseen Christ shall move ;
> That he may lean upon His arm and say,
>   'Dost Thou, dear Lord, approve?'"

                                        LONGFELLOW.

ON the third of November, 1875, Hannington was again in Oxford, to receive his M.A. degree. He found at St. Mary Hall, alone of his former companions, the Rev. David Johnston, Minister of the Church of Scotland in the Orkneys, a Biblical Student, and holder of the Kenicott Hebrew Scholarship, the tenure of which required him to reside in Oxford during the Michaelmas Term of that year. The following entry refers to this meeting:—

"Had a long and profitable converse with David Johnston ; he told me that he never had had any hope of my conversion, I seemed so utterly given over to the world."

Mr. Johnston was not the only one of his former acquaintances who were unaware of the change which had passed over his life, and the tenor of it.

On one occasion, shortly before the correspondence which has been given in Chapter VII., one of Hannington's college friends was spending the month of September

at the country house of an old St. Mary Hall man.
"The great change" had but lately passed over himself. He could not have hidden it if he would. A new
language and words to which his companion was unaccus-
tomed cropped up as the two trod the stubbles, or waded
knee deep through the turnip-fields, carrying destruction
among the partridges. An indefinable aroma of a new life
permeated even their conversation over the pipes at night.
But when, finally, he confessed that he had heard the call of
Christ, and was resolved to follow Him, his companion lost
no time, but wrote off at once to Hannington for advice.
Said he: " I don't know what has come over ———. He
is dreadfully changed in his views. You must come and
spend a few days with us when next he is here, and we will
soon settle him between us." Alas! those three were
never to meet on earth. Had they done so within two
years of that letter, there would, indeed, have been two
against one, but the majority would not have been upon
the side espoused by Hannington's perplexed correspondent!
Over Hannington, too, that Change had passed.

To many of his old friends it seemed like a miracle
when he boldly took his place among the fighting men in
the vanguard of Christ's Great Army.

On the seventh of November, Hannington preached
his introductory sermon in St. George's Chapel. We have
already described the village of Hurstpierpoint. In the
grounds of St. George's House, on the highest part of
them, stands the chapel, a well-shaped building, with high-
pitched roof; simple in construction, but withal appropriate
to its surroundings. Within, a nave seated for some three
hundred persons, comfortable and commodious—benches low
and open. Beyond, a simple chancel, from the arch of which
hangs a light brass chandelier. Throughout the building a
subdued light, falling through the stained glass of single,

ST. GEORGE'S CHAPEL, HURSTIERPOINT.

pointed windows. Chancel door perhaps ajar, letting in a ray of warm sunlight, and revealing glimpses of smooth lawns and flowers, and spaces of sky and far-reaching view.

At the end of every pew hangs a bracket, which can be raised at will to accommodate an additional sitter. And these brackets were seldom out of use during Hannington's incumbency of the chapel !

Here he laboured during the next seven years ; almost unknown to the world, but well known enough in the neighbourhood of Hurst, and winning the affection of his people in a manner in which it is given to few clergymen to do.

One of the most wholly unconventional souls that ever breathed, some of his sayings and doings remind us irresistibly of William Grimshaw, whose eccentricities were known and beloved anywhere within a day's journey of Haworth.

In his old, faded boating coat—his St. Mary Hall "blazer"—he would walk briskly down the village street. All the children knew well enough that the pockets of that coat were filled with goodies. They looked out for him with a shy expectancy. One day, as he walked with a certain dignified ecclesiastic, this time attired in proper clerical uniform, a little girl stole up timidly behind, and pulled his coat tails. "Please, sir," said she, blushing, "haven't you got a bull's-eye for me ? "

He would gather the children about him and give them some brief and fitting instruction with regard to their conduct towards their parents and each other. Thus, they were not to "sneak," not to speak untruths, etc., etc. When he next encountered them they were cross-examined : " Now, then : what were the three things you were not to do ; eh ? " When the answers were correct, the rewarding bull's-eye was never wanting.

There are few men who know how to combine perfect
freedom and familiarity of manner with a self-respect with
which the rudest boor will not venture to take a liberty.
Hannington had learned the secret of this combination in a
very wonderful manner. He could be hail-fellow-well-met
with rough men and lads with enviable impunity. The
workmen of Hurst knew him among themselves by the
pet name of " Jemmy."   He was Hurstpierpoint's Jemmy;
their own Jemmy.   But there was no one in the district to
whom the men raised their caps more willingly, or to whom
the boys looked up with more unquestioning admiration.
Chalmers is reported to have said to one who was maintaining that the clergy should " stand upon their dignity,"
" Sir! if we don't mind, we may die of dignity."
Hannington was quite of that opinion. He sought all
souls, anyhow and anywhere. If he could not win them
in a dignified manner, he had no objection to appear as
undignified as the occasion seemed to demand.

" Oh, the value of one soul! " he somewhere writes;
and his whole life from this time bears witness to the sincerity of his estimate. He would get hold of the boys and
attract them to himself by his kindly interest in their
pursuits—an interest by which they could not but be
flattered; he would gradually wean them from evil companions, by encouraging them to cultivate any taste which
he might detect in them. Boys who showed a liking
for curiosities or natural history were invited to his house,
and allowed to examine his own large and various collections,
and his cabinets of classified specimens. All this with a
good-natured raillery which was very effective in checking
any disposition to conceit on the part of his protégées. His
quizzical smile kept everybody at his own proper level.
No boy with a taste for the concertina, or for scribbling
designs upon his slate, or for rapid summing, was suffered to

delude himself into the idea that he was an embryo Mozart, or Turner, or the future senior wrangler of the village. One of his friends * reports the following characteristic reply to a lad who "fancied himself" as a musician, and to whom he at once consented to allow the use of his own harmonium. "But when shall I begin, sir?" asked the boy. "Oh, well," said Hannington, looking at him with an amused smile, "I shall be *out* on Thursday."

These lads and the young men loved him. He gathered them together into a Bible Class and Temperance Association. They were called "Hannington's Saints," but they were not much afflicted thereby. They were taught to regard the disapproval of the scoffers as the highest compliment that could be conferred upon them. The following extract from his diary will show how closely he was accustomed to watch his lads, and, as he used to term it, to "father" them:

"Went to the Review with several of my Bible Class. I had also with me S. S., whom I am trying to get hold of. We passed on the road a vanful of the wild lads of the parish. It was extraordinary to watch S. S., how wistfully he looked at them, and evidently longed to be with them. He watched them until they disappeared from view. Oh! what a fight the devil is going to make for that young man! Get to Thyself the victory, O Lord! Amen and amen."

There is little room for wonder that Hannington was both respected and beloved when, as we question his people, there come out, one by one, the sacrifices which he made for them and for the Great Cause which he had at heart. Take the following example:

He was very fond of riding. There was no pleasure to

* Mr. W. Boxall.

which he looked forward with more keen delight than to a long gallop over the downs, or a scamper with his sister-in-law through the country lanes. They two would sometimes start from the field beyond the gardens of St. George's, and ride straight across country, clearing everything in their way, in a neck-and-neck race.

But one day Hannington announced that he had sold his horse. He would ride no more. He had need of the money for other things which were not hard to guess. For the future he would go about the parish on foot. As for the stable and coach-house, he meant to knock them into one. They would, if properly fitted up, form an excellent mission room, and just such an one as he had for a long while wanted for his meetings. No sooner said than done. Just behind his house stands the transformed stable to-day. Papered, carpeted, hung with paraffin lamps, provided with forms and harmonium—a model mission hall; and a model also of what may be done by a man whose heart is wholly given to serve the Lord. These and many similar acts were done so quietly and so wholly without ostentation of any kind, that many of his most intimate friends never suspected that he was making any special sacrifices. Of all this from himself they never heard a syllable.

He never posed as a large-hearted man, given to liberality. Indeed, I do not think that he knew that he was liberal. His liberality was not a vestment put on; it was himself; it ran in his blood. To have behaved like a churl would have been to him the most painful thing in the world, if not a sheer impossibility.

I find traces of £50 given to a needy brother "missioner" upon one occasion, and another sum of £40 to a certain ————, " to see him through his trouble."

How many other such sums were expended in a similar manner it is impossible to guess. But, as George Dawson

says with regard to an act of magnanimity on the part of old
Andrew Marvell, " a man cannot do one thing like that
without doing many things like that," and the blessed habit
of giving, like all other habits, grows with the use of it.
He was a preacher, too, who could not fail to secure an attentive audience.   While he was not naturally a ready speaker,
he had, from the commencement of his extempore preaching,
that eloquence which is bred of intense conviction.   His
style might be formed upon no known standard, but it was,
at least, effective.   It was never conventional.   He never
dealt in platitudes.   He spoke as one who had something to
say ; and from the first he caught the ear and held the attention of the most sleepy country congregations.   Of only too
many well-meaning and learned preachers might the rustic
hearer complain with, alas, too much of saddest truth,

" I 'eerd 'um a bummin' awaäy loike a buzzard clock ower my 'eäd,
    An' I niver knaw'd what a meän'd." *

Hannington, at least, took care that the people should know
what he meant.   In these, the early days of his preaching,
he gave no thought to anything but his matter.   He would
let himself be carried impetuously along upon a stormy tide
of speech, the broken waves of which disdained to be confined within the bounds of legitimately constructed sentences ;
and often used he laughingly to take his present biographer
to task for " criticizing his grammar," when such criticism
was very far from his thoughts.

As might have been expected, these things soon righted
themselves.   He rapidly acquired command of language that
expressed his thoughts in concise and pithy sentences; and
many have without reserve endorsed words which I ventured
on a previous occasion to write concerning him : " Latterly his

---

* *The Northern Farmer.*

preaching was not only cultivated and powerful, but, from the originality of his thought, and his close acquaintance with the minutiæ of Scripture, most deeply interesting and instructive."* Whatever faults may have been laid to the charge of his early preaching, neither dulness nor vagueness could be numbered among them.

"Are you going to hear Jemmy preach this evening?" one neighbour would say to another. Or, next day, "He gave it us regular hot last night, didn't he?"

When he preached against any particular vice, no one could entertain the least doubt as to *what* vice he intended to condemn. Unlike the Irish clergy whom Miss Ellice Hopkins so amusingly describes as racking their brains during the potato famine to find some euphonious synonym for the vulgar word "potato," Hannington was never afraid to call anything by its proper name. So far he was a very Latimer. In Devonshire, the "spade" of immorality was called and denounced by the name which belongs to that particular kind of "spade." In Hurstpierpoint, the "spade" of drunkenness was described, not in decent generalities, but in most pungent particularities. "The old fuddlers," as he used to dub the alehouse theologians and pothouse politicians, could not find the least loophole of escape from the understanding of *what it was* which their pastor stood up to condemn.

The following is very characteristic : "One Sunday he gave out the announcement : 'I intend to preach a temperance sermon next Sunday evening ; I am aware that the subject is unpopular, but you know my own views upon it. I shall, no doubt, speak pretty plain, so if any of you do not care to hear me you had better stop away.' Of course, the church was crowded."

---

* *C. M. Intelligencer*, April, 1886.

Here is an instance of his adaptability :—

" I had a curious experience at the workhouse. I gave out a text, and began in rather a sermonizing way. The coughing was so tremendous that I could scarcely hear myself speak. I never heard such a selection of varied coughs in my life. Well, thought I, this will never do, so I altered my tone, and said, ' I will tell you a tale.' The coughs all stopped together—dead silence—and so I went on. As soon as one tale was finished I began another, and so kept their attention to the end without difficulty."

It is told of Sydney Smith, that, when preaching in Edinburgh, in the first quarter of this century, seeing how almost exclusively the congregations were composed of ladies, he gave out as his text, " Oh, that *men* would therefore praise the Lord ! "—laying distinct emphasis on the word " men." That was in questionable taste, but it marked a fact. Bishop Ryle, writing in '53, laments the absence of men from the churches, and there are still parishes in which that complaint might be made. It was not so in the Chapel of St. George's during James Hannington's incumbency.

But to the problem, " Where are the men ? " it may be that an easier solution is at hand than that which presents itself to some perplexed pastors when they painfully discuss the question at their periodic clerical meeting. To the reproaches and exhortations of Pulpit, it may be that Pew has something valid to reply. He might say : If it be true that " a modern sermon is too often a dull, tame, pointless religious essay, full of measured, round sentences, Johnsonian English, bold platitudes, timid statements, and elaborately-concocted milk and water "*—change all that ; preach to us

---

* Bishop Ryle.

something the very opposite of that veracious description, and you will no longer have to ask, " Where are the men ? " Englishmen have not lost their love of a good sermon. They are not harder to please to-day than were the audiences of Latimer, Wesley, Whitefield, or Chalmers. They do not even ask for a fine sermon; only preach to them in earnest, and preach *to the point*, and they will not fail to give you a hearing. In some such terms might Pew lift up his voice in reply to the wailing of deserted Pulpit.

The secret of Hannington's success will probably be found to have been, that what truths were made plain to his own heart, these he sought the power of the Spirit of God to enable him to make plain to the congregation. And he had no lack of hearers. Men and women, young and old, they filled his little chapel to its utmost holding capacity.

The experience, moreover, of his own former life was very useful to him here. He had proved for and in himself that it is possible to believe in God, think seriously, and pray earnestly, without having any definite part or lot in Christ's matter. He, therefore, never fell into the mistake of addressing his hearers as though they were Christians indeed until they had been actually converted to God. He sought for broken hearts, contrite spirits, and souls willing to be saved through faith in the Redeemer ; nor did he seek in vain ; in results such as these his ministry was fruitful from the first.

But, while Hannington was a diligent preacher, ministrant, and visitor, he did not forget that his flock possessed bodies as well as souls. He took an active practical leadership in every local effort to improve the well-being of the people. I find a note about a certain Industrial Exhibition*

* Mr. Mitten writes with regard to this exhibition : " Here at Hurstpierpoint our friend did a good deal, and it is a place where it is very difficult for anybody to do anything without raising obstruction in some quarter or other. He threw himself

which was planned and organized almost wholly by his own
exertions, though, as usual, he succeeded in enlisting the
co-operation of almost everybody, and arousing their enthusiasm in the success of the undertaking.   The idea of this
exhibition was, that everybody in the village should show
their various manufactures, paintings, joiners' work, carving,
and any curious or fancy articles they might possess.   The
people took up the plan warmly, and the exhibition, which
was the first of the kind ever held in the neighbourhood,
proved a great success.   It was repeated in following years,
and no doubt was useful to many as a guide to the discovery
of their own individual talent, and an encouragement to
occupy their hands in some profitable pursuit.

Nor did his interest in medical work slacken.   Here
are some specimen entries from his diary :

" Helped Dr. Smith to cut off a man's finger—gangrene.

" Assisted Drs. S. and H. to cut off Bristowe's arm, as
mortification had gone further.   Afterwards, performed
duties of hospital nurse ; carried off the arm and buried it.

" Dr. Pearce summoned me to come and help at a post-
mortem.   Found two large stones in each kidney.   Very
bad subject.   Dr. P. cut himself, and I had to sew him up
again."

The following is a good example of fearless shepherding :

" A most virulent case of small-pox in an outlying part
of the parish ; a boy taken with it.   I called, and found the
people forsaken by their neighbours.   No milk, and the

---

fully into the idea of the exhibition, and so cautiously approached
the Rector and Resident Curate, that they too entered into the
project heartily, as if it were their own idea ; indeed, his management of this difficult feat filled me with admiration for his skill in
making people do just as he wished, by rendering it impossible
that they could do any other thing to their own satisfaction."

boy's life depending upon it. I fetched some milk, and then, at the request of the mother, saw the boy and prayed with him. The next day it was all over the parish that I had visited the small-pox case. The people were in a dreadful state of mind. The relieving officer called, and in an authoritative way ordered me not to go near the place. I replied that if the law were on the side of the sanitary officials, it was open to them to use it, but where duty called I should go ; and as he went out of one door, I went out at the other, and called at the infected house. The doctor gave no hope. Every preparation had been made to bury the poor lad the same night. The following day the health officer wrote, urging me to take every precaution, but not forbidding me to go, as the law is on my side. Letter from X. Y. Z., asking me not even to speak to her husband in his carriage out of doors for three weeks ————!! After all, the boy recovered."

Whenever the people were in any danger, distress, or difficulty, they knew to whom they might apply for help without fear of refusal. Here is an instance which may give one an idea of the manner in which he would follow up to its conclusion any case which he had undertaken.

In October of 1879 Hannington received a telegram from a certain Mrs. ————, asking him to come at once to her assistance, as her husband had run away with another woman and left her wholly destitute. He lost no time in bestirring himself in the matter, and the man was soon arrested and in custody. Hannington then called upon the prisoner, but found him entirely hardened, and refusing to be reconciled to his wife. He prayed with him, pleaded with him, and spent much time in representing his duty to him from every point of view, but all to no purpose. The next day he was up early, and sought the man's cell before breakfast, in hope that the night's meditation might have resulted in a better frame of mind. The husband was still sullen, and obstinately refused to see him. Nothing daunted, Hannington appeared in the man's behalf in the court, and said all that was possible in his favour with regard to his past history. He was, however, condemned and sentenced to three months' imprisonment with hard labour. Up to this time he had, with strange perversity, persuaded himself that his wife and all the rest of the world were in the wrong, and that he was the persecuted and injured victim of their malice. His sentence, therefore, came upon him as an additional and unwarrantable piece of injustice. He was furious. More impracticable than ever. Hannington lost no time in seeking another interview with him, but met with nothing but reproaches and bitter accusations against all concerned in his incarceration. He was not discouraged, but, as usual, made the man's case the subject of special pleading in his private prayers.

He did not lose sight of him, but kept himself acquainted with the prisoner's movements in the gaol where he was confined, and when the day of release arrived, went up himself to meet him and tender his assistance. After an interview which lasted three hours, he left him deeply penitent. Not long afterwards occurs this entry in the diary :

"Went up to town; took an affectionate leave of ———. He sails for ———, is still very depressed, but I have every hope that real blessing has come out of it."

Nor did he go without substantial help from his friend ; which help he used to good purpose in the land of his regenerated life, and in due time "returned every penny of it."

Disinterested acts of kindness like the above could not fail to win for him something more than the mere liking of the people among whom he laboured. No doubt they were as prone as others to take the attentions of their pastor, and any sacrifice on his part in their behalf, as a matter of course; but they could not help seeing that he was no " hireling shepherd." From his lips the words, " I seek not your's, but you," came as no vain protestation, but as a statement of undeniable fact. Whether they would or no, they could not withhold their hearts from him. If they did not agree with his teaching, or follow his precepts, at least they all loved him.

And he, too, was attached both to the people and to his work among them in no ordinary way. More than once he was offered livings with larger and better known spheres of labour. But though he derived no emolument from St. George's, which had been left to him by his father without a stipend attached to it, and, as time went by, his private income, which had been amply sufficient for a bachelor, proved to be no luxurious provision for a family, he always refused preferment. His constant reply to those who would have him seek promotion was, " I dwell among mine own people."

It may be a fitting conclusion to this chapter to say a few words with regard to Hannington's Church views. Some of the readers of this book will, no doubt, remain unsatisfied until they have been told to what party in the Church he belonged. But if they hope to find in him a partisan of their own special school of thought, I fear that they will lay down these pages with disappointment. Whatever party may lay claim to him, I cannot, after an impartial survey of his whole life, discover that he attached himself *exclusively* to any section of the Church. What I mean by that is that he was not a party man. He never seemed to me to take the slightest interest in Church-party-politics. He undoubtedly found most that was congenial to him in the society of men who are generally supposed to belong to a certain school, but he did not weigh the merits of others in the balances of that school; whenever and wherever he thought that he recognized a spiritually-minded man, he quickly and joyfully accepted him, whether he found him in priest's cloak and biretta, or the broad-cloth of some country local preacher. He was quite willing to occupy the pulpit of any man—whether in the Church of England or out of it—who would allow him to preach a Gospel sermon, even though the views usually advocated from that pulpit differed in many points from his own. He was very impatient of all conventional rules which threatened to hamper his full liberty of Christian action, and was, in the same way, an enemy of any formalism in worship which might tend to cramp his spiritual freedom. Toward the close of his ministry, and especially when he himself had become an administrator in the affairs of the Church, his views underwent some modification, and he learnt to estimate Church order at its full value; but at this time the one thing which he craved above all others was freedom—freedom to serve Christ as the Spirit might direct him. As we have seen, his feelings had undergone a considerable change since the time when he was first brought into contact with the Church. Then he was strongly drawn toward High-Churchism. In his boyhood, he had even once been powerfully attracted by the Roman system. The discipline, apparent union, and the zeal of the English Romanists commended them greatly to him. His mind, however, was too robust and independent to accept Roman dogma; and, still in search of something wherewith to satisfy the desire of his soul, he thought that he had found what he wanted in the " Anglican " Church system. He had not at that time, grasped the truth that the only way to peace with God is through vital and personal union with the Lord Jesus Christ, much less had he found that peace ; but he was thoroughly in earnest, and he required *earnestness* in any religious society of men as an essential condition to joining himself to them.   The self-denial which was entailed upon him in keeping the Fasts and Holy Days of the Church seemed to satisfy for a while his spiritual craving.

This was the attitude of his mind when he went to Oxford, and I am inclined to think that had he been brought under the personal influence of some leading High-Churchman, some man of commanding moral force, who could have at once claimed him by his personality, and fascinated him by the spectacle of a practical, manly life, coupled with such an inner religious life as would have appealed to his imagination—he might have been readily seized, and, at least for a time, held.

This, however, did not happen.   While his mind was still in the balance, and while, moreover, his religious sense was almost drowned in the excitement of his new college life and popularity, so that he was not inclined to think so seriously as before, and was little disposed to delve beneath the surface of things, and patiently dig out truth for himself, he was brought into contact with a set among the under-graduates which professed to be the exponent of the latest and most correct Church ritual.   The young men who composed this set paid great attention to correctness of posture in chapel, and to niceties of observance in public and private worship.   They were fond of dressing them-selves, in the privacy of their own rooms, in abbreviated, lace-trimmed surplices, and getting themselves photographed with crozier and censer.   In the bedroom of one such, we accidentally discovered an altar composed of his trunk, draped with a suitable antimacassar, upon which stood a row of tiny candlesticks and a vase or so of flowers, while above, upon the wall, hung a plaster crucifix!

Those who knew Hannington will understand what must have been the effect produced upon him. His mind, apparently, underwent a swift revulsion. All this jarred upon him and disgusted him. It offered him endless food for railery, and excited his immeasurable contempt. He loved to lampoon the performers and ridicule their "functions." It was not, of course, fair that a system should be judged by the youthful extravagance of its junior disciples, but Hannington was at that time very impressionable, and there can be little doubt that to what he then saw, during his residence at Oxford, may be attributed the origin of that dislike for all unnecessary ritual which he displayed at the commencement of his ministerial life.

Afterwards, his lot fell among Evangelicals. They did not obtain any decided influence over him while at Oxford, but it was among them that he first, after his conversion, felt the power of spiritual life. At this time, if he had been pressed to define himself, he would, no doubt, have termed himself an Evangelical, but while he undoubtedly found himself most in unison with liberal and large-hearted members of that school, he already disliked party names and the spirit of faction, and utterly declined to be bound by the "red tape" of any party whatsoever. He had the widest sympathy with *all* Christians. He loved and respected all those who love the Lord Jesus in sincerity. Toward the close of his ministry especially his feelings toward all Christian workers became enlarged and his antipathies softened. Every *against* seemed to have been swallowed up by one all-comprehensive *for* — for Christ. At the same time this large-hearted charity did not prevent him from being a true son of the Church. His love for his own Church evidently deepened with each year that he served in her ranks; he had no doubt in his own mind as to her superiority, both in order and forms, over those bodies which dissented from her. A Universal Christian first, and a "Churchman" after, he did not for a moment forget that he was the latter.

CHAPTER X.

(1875—79.)

"The Country Parson desires to be All to his Parish."
GEORGE HERBERT.

In the previous chapter I have attempted to describe Hannington as he appeared in his parish, and to ascertain how it was that he came to be loved, and to be a moral force there. We may now, perhaps, with advantage continue to follow the details of his life in their chronological order.

It is deeply interesting to note how entirely his heart was thrown into the business of " fishing for men." His diary at this period is full of jottings which refer to the spiritual awakening of such a one, or his conversations with another concerning the welfare of his soul. The subject is never absent from his thoughts. Such entries as the following stud thickly page after page :

" Spoke to H. H., and was made useful to him. He was certainly converted to God."

" ———— came to see me about her soul. A case needing much patience. Visited ———— in the agonies of death. I have hopes of him."

" My servant, John,* was, I trust, turned to the Lord ; I have prayed for him a long while."

---

* Mr. Mitten writes :—" It was a way also of our friend to take a lad for his servant and transform him, then pass him on to something better. In this way he had a good many, who have, so far as I know, all turned out well. He had a great influence with young men, and collected many to come and read with him."

About this time he was able to be of assistance to his youngest brother, Joseph. Mr. Joseph Hannington writes :

"Some little time before I knew what it was to have full assurance of faith, I came down one Sunday from Brighton to hear my brother James preach. I was in much doubt and distress of mind. One remark in my brother's sermon made a deep impression upon me, and threw light into my soul. It was as follows : ' *The fact of our salvation does not depend upon our own feelings. As for myself, there are times when, if I consulted my feelings, I should say that I am not saved. I should be plunged again into the depths of misery. Feelings are treacherous things, not to be trusted. They are the least reliable of things to rest upon. After some sermon which has met our own case we may have experienced a time of peace ; or our circumstances may have induced a happy frame of mind, we are then quite assured of God's love. Depression of spirits follows, and we quickly lose our hope. But as surely as we rest upon these frauds, our feelings, the Lord will see fit to withdraw them in order that we may learn to rest upon Him. I find that as soon as I go back and take my stand upon His bare Word, I recover my joy and peace. Therefore, let me urge upon you the necessity of staying your faith upon Christ : not upon your most hallowed feelings, but upon Christ Himself and His written promises. Whenever you are in doubt, perplexed, and unhappy, go at once to the Lord ; fix your mind upon some precious passage from his unfailing Word, and God's Truth will disperse any mists of darkness which Satan's lies may have brought upon your soul.'*

"From these words I received much help, as I had for a long time fancied that when I felt happy after prayer, or reading my Bible, or hearing some sermon, I was all right, but in a very little while all these happy feelings fled away and left me more wretched than ever. A short time after this my attention was directed by the Hon. T. Pelham to St. John iii. 36, "He that believeth HATH everlasting life;" and the Holy Ghost opened my eyes in a moment, and I saw the truth of my dear brother's words, and have been enabled to rest from that day to this upon the Word as a rock that cannot be shaken."

Mr. Joseph Hannington goes on to say that, being over-joyed at his discovery, he tried to impart his happiness to all whom he met. He did not receive, however, universal encouragement. One old Christian bid him take heed and not be too joyful, as he would soon probably lose the fervour of these first impressions. Thus he was damped. He says:

"I next wrote to my brother James; and oh, how differently he met my case! A letter soon came expressing his great delight, and telling me that he would not cease to pray for me. He was never at any time very fond of writing letters, but he then wrote quite lengthily for him, and tried to build me up and encourage me to follow the Lord and to learn to know Him better. He used a good deal of persuasion, and took a great deal of trouble to induce me to enter the ministry of the Church of England, but this did not happen, as I could not see my way clearly in that matter. He, however, set me to work at once in connection with his meetings; my part was to waylay souls and catch them by guile in order that they might be induced to remain to be dealt with personally, or to seek an interview with him in his own study. Thus a goodly number were brought to the Lord. He was particularly apt in dealing with souls, and was much used in removing their difficulties and pointing them to a simple acceptance of the Saviour. He would frequently say, ' Now, don't push them forward too quickly, or they won't stand and certify that the work is real.' But, as a rule, the converts stood firmly, and many of them are now experienced Christians and workers in the Lord's vineyard.

" In bygone days our eldest brother, a friend, and myself used to meet nearly every day to dine together at half-past one. We were almost sure to get upon the subject of religion. It was Jim's delight to come round the corner quietly and surprise us all, at the same time remarking, ' Here you are again, upon the same old subject !' And right heartily would he come and join in. He delighted to enter into any conversation that was connected with the salvation of souls and the love of Jesus Christ, his Saviour."

Hannington had a great deal of the boy in him still. He came to Sandgate at the end of 1875 to act as " best man " at my own marriage, and his spirits were exuberantly overflowing. When first he had been informed of my engagement, he had been full of the idea that the safest course for a servant of God was celibacy, and he had written to me, not without austerity, entreating me to beware, lest I should allow an earthly affection to usurp the highest Love. Now, however, he was disposed to regard this my matrimonial alliance with greater leniency—a leniency to which the following entry in his diary, made about a fortnight previously, may afford some clue : " Called for the first time upon Mrs. Hankin-Turvin at Leacrofts ; she and her daughter come to my church, and are earnest Christian people." It is possible, then, that this first interview with Miss Hankin-Turvin had somewhat modified the severity of his views. Or perhaps he had satisfied himself that my intended wife was not—to use his own expression—" a daughter of Belial."

At all events, he threw himself into the preparations for this wedding with an impetuous zeal that was delightful to behold, even if it were at times somewhat embarrassing. He insisted upon helping me to pack my boxes, though— amid laughter, teasing, and constant fresh discoveries of how the various articles might be better arranged, or rammed down so as to occupy less space—the packing made but slow progress. When, at last, my dear wife and I were seated in our reserved carriage, booked for London, and, thinking that we had seen the last of the wedding party, were trying to look as though we were not newly married, a face beaming with excitement suddenly appeared at the window, and our irrepressible " best man " bestowed his parting blessing upon us, covering us with shame and confusion before the grinning porters, with a well-directed handful of rice.

At the end of 1875 Hannington accepted the Secretary-ship of the Hurstpierpoint Temperance Association. Into this new work he threw himself with characteristic energy. He writes : " I am about the only teetotaler in Hurst ; " but, nothing daunted by the fact that total abstinence was evidently very unpopular, he determined that he would wage war to the knife against drink. Mr. Boxall tells how, during the first year, only four pledges were taken, and how, as Hannington persevered, in spite of the most determined opposition, the number of abstainers gradually increased.

He says: "At that time there was a great deal of drunkenness in the village ; no less than seven public-houses were turning out their weekly average of ' finished articles.' One of the first acts of the Bishop we can remember was on one Christmas evening, when, in walking up the street, we saw one of those notorious characters floundering helplessly in the miry road. Together with the Bishop, we were able to drag the poor fellow along to his home, but in a most pitiable condition, being almost encased in mud. Being brought much in contact with drink by visiting among the working classes, his ardent nature was roused into earnestness and zeal, and, in Bible class and pulpit, he vigorously advocated total abstinence. He never went about without a pledge-book. There was no popular sympathy, and those who signed were only met by the derisive cry, ' *He's* joined the saints.' This merely roused him to greater exertion, more meetings were held, teas were given in the mission-room, every inducement was held out. The coldness and indifference of the people on this subject distressed him greatly. He frankly told his congregation that this was the hardest work he had ever taken in hand." *

The publicans could not have adopted a worse course than that of stirring up opposition to his crusade. They did not know their man if they thought that they could either put him down or tire him out. He rose to meet a difficulty with the keen joy of a strong swimmer who delights to bathe in the breakers and shakes aside their force with a rich enjoyment of the contest. He went about everywhere among the mockers, and the more serious opponents of his views alike, with that good-natured persistence of his which so often proved irresistible. " No man could call another a ' fuddler' as he could. With the utmost good-humour he would say, ' Ah ! you're another old fuddler ; won't you come and write in my little book ? ' He had a well-known sign which he used to make ; holding up his left hand he would write with his fingers upon it. Everyone knew that it meant, ' Come and sign the pledge.' "†

---

* Art. in *Church of England Temperance Chronicle*, April 24th, 1886.

† Ditto, ditto.

We may insert here a later entry :

" Preached for the temperance cause in the Church of the Annunciation, a ritualistic church in Brighton. A crucifix hanging over my head. There was an extraordinary gathering. People of all denominations had flocked to see what I should do, and whether I should be true to my colours. Wherever I looked I saw somebody whom I knew. I preached from 1 Tim. v. 23, and as I gave out the text, " Take a little wine," I thought I saw some of them look terrified ; but I went on to show that my brother had a stronger claim upon me than my stomach ! "

At last the time appointed by the Bishop of Exeter drew to a close, and in June, 1876, Hannington went to Chichester to pass his final examination for Priest's Orders. He writes :

" There is a marked difference in tone between the Chichester and Exeter examinations. Here the tone is much more spiritual.

"*June 8th.*—Two of our number disappeared this morning. One, ———, with whom I was at school, and with whom I fought and thrashed !

" *9th.*—Examination finished. I have been highly complimented by all the examiners, five in number, and told that I have come out at the top of the list. Thank God ! It is a lift after my hard experience at Exeter, for which I can never consider that I was to blame.

" 1*0th.*—(Shall I quote it ? Yes ; for that which rendered him so incomprehensible to certain matter-of-fact and unsympathetic minds, who had no understanding of the unconventional, is just that quality which so specially endears his memory to his friends—I mean that lighthearted boyishness which he retained side by side with his

purposeful manhood—and this extract affords a kind of key
to his character. Here it is) : " *Saturday, the* 10*th.*—A day
of rest. I nested in the Bishop's garden, and round the
belfry tower for swift's eggs." I confess that I do not envy
the man who can read this extract with contemptuous
disapproval, or who can suppose that the writer of it
meditated less, or spent a less profitable day after his
Ordination examination, than if he had confined himself
to a respectable promenade within the limits of the gravel
paths.

"*Sunday, the* 11*th.* — Procession from Palace to
Cathedral. Dean preached an excellent sermon, and the
whole service, though exhaustingly long, was impressively
performed. Afternoon, Burgon preached again ; I had tea
and supper at the Deanery, and went for a long walk with
the Dean, who is more eccentric than ever.

"*Sept.* 13*th.*—Opened a meeting in my coachhouse"
(this was the transformed stable and coachhouse, henceforth
to be a mission-room), " and invited the first time only those
to whom I believe the Word has been blessed." (Here
follows a list of names.) " My brother Joseph spoke.

"*Oct.* 4*th.*—Started a Mother's Meeting, the first ever
held in Hurst.

"*6th.*—Commenced a Women's Bible Class. May the
Lord bless these efforts !

"*11th.*—About sixty present at the Men's Bible Class.
I am taking St. John's Gospel regularly through.

"*14th.*—Started a Saturday Night Prayer Meeting for
men, and prayed earnestly that it might continue.

"*Nov.* 16*th.*—Went into Brighton to Bowker's and
Hopkins' meeting. Perhaps I heard selfishly, but I did not
get what I expected."

The following letter may here be quoted with the re-

minder that it was written in a chatty way to his wife, and
that the language used is, as one might suppose, wholly
unguarded.

"I have had a letter from Jos, the result of a conversation
with Beatrice about 'Convention' views.   I am evidently
regarded as very grovelling and in the mire, but I fail to see
that there is any practical difference between us as to the
results of faith.   With regard to the possession of perfect
peace by a believer, we are quite agreed.   So also with
regard to rejoicing always.   But with regard to bonds,* Jos
suffers as much as I do.   I only put the clock in front of
him so that he might not exceed the hour, and it put him in
such fearful bondage that he could scarcely speak.   And if
brother P—— happened to come in during his meeting his
bonds were endless.   The only difference that I can see
between us is that he says : 'Sit still and believe, and it
will come to pass ;' while I say, 'Up and be doing while
you believe.' . . . . .   I must say I enjoy the uphill,
struggling path most of all."

Hannington was present, after this, at more than one
Conference.   He was in perfect sympathy with the aims
of the good and holy men who spoke at the meetings
alluded to above.   Their teaching was the daily practice
of his life.   But he was essentially a man of active, fighting faith, and some of the disciples, in preaching what was
then regarded as a new doctrine, no doubt went beyond
their masters, and exaggerated their gospel of a restful

---

* "Bonds" or "bondage" in Hannington's vocabulary always
meant want of freedom in speaking, praying, or preaching.   He
was "in bondage" when anything weighed upon his spirits or
prevented him from launching himself unrestrainedly into his
subject.

life into a repudiation of that uphill struggle which Hannington knew to be a very practical thing.

"*Jan. 1st*, 1877.—The New Year breaks in upon me. How? How? Under a new epoch I am engaged to be married. I, who have always been supposed, and have supposed myself, to be a confirmed bachelor, cross, crabbed, ill-conditioned! What a change in the appearance of everything does this make! It, however, seems to fill me with the things of this world, and to make me cold and dead. Lord Jesus, grant that we may love Thee each succeeding hour more abundantly. Amen, amen."

So Hannington commences his diary for the year 1877. The allusion to an approaching marriage is explained by another entry which occurs shortly before :

"*Dec.* 26th.—Proposed to Blanche Hankin - Turvin, and was accepted."

Miss Hankin-Turvin was the second daughter of Captain James Michael Hankin-Turvin, formerly of Terlings Park, Gilston, Hertfordshire. She and her mother were at this time residing at Leacrofts, Hurstpierpoint, and were in the habit of attending St. George's Chapel. Hannington had from the first recognized Miss Hankin-Turvin's fitness for the duties of a clergyman's wife, and admired her sterling qualities and earnestness of character. This before he had any intention of giving up his independence as a bachelor. He was not one of those men who are dependent upon the ministrations of women. He was complete in himself, handy and helpful, quite capable of managing his own household. Full of ways and habits of his own, too, which he was aware might not commend themselves to any wife. His heart, moreover, was not disengaged; his work was his wife; in a very real sense he was wedded to

it. He scrutinized jealously any other affection which
threatened to make an exacting demand upon his time and
attention.

He was, however, beginning to discover that a bachelor
clergyman is subject to certain disadvantages from which his
married brother is free. He is liable to annoyances and
hindrances well known to every popular celibate. He may
easily find himself in positions of much awkwardness and
difficulty. He was not able to avail himself of opportunities
of access to certain classes of people to whom he would
have had ready entrance as husband and father. He had
also convinced himself, by observation of other married
couples, that a wife who was like-minded with her husband
might be to him the most effective help in his work that it
was possible for him to obtain.

When these experiences coincided with his own strong
inclination, and added force to the pleadings of his heart,
he delayed no longer, but, as we have seen, proposed to a
lady who he had every reason to believe would satisfy his
most exacting requirements.

In this he was not disappointed. His wife became his
second self. She entered with all her steadfast heart and
soul into his many works. She softened in him what
needed to be softened, strengthened him to persevere when
she saw that he was down-hearted, encouraged him in his
favourite scientific pursuits, bore with a bright and gentle
patience those vagaries of his which might have proved a
severe trial to one less wise than herself, submitted to be
teazed with unvarying good humour, never let him feel
that he was reined in, curbed, or hampered, exacted no
demonstrations of affection from him other than he
freely gave, ever quietly helping, never complaining or
obtruding selfish wants of her own to hinder him from
making any sacrifice, she conferred upon him the greatest

blessing which God has in store for a man in this world—a good wife.

"So these were wed, and merrily rang the bells."

The marriage was celebrated on February the 10th in the parish church. The service was choral. Five clergymen, including the Rector and Mr. Bell Hankin, assisted at the ceremony. The church was crowded from end to end, all Hannington's own flock who were able being present to witness the act. He and his bride made their way through a long lane of warm-hearted and enthusiastic friends to their carriage. With his characteristic love of making himself out to be as odd as possible, he writes : "I walked down to church with my umbrella, and called in as usual at Mr. Mitten's. In the vestry I remarked that if ever I was married again I would have another choral wedding, and finally I jumped first into the carriage, and left the bride to follow ! "

The first letters to his wife were written four or five months later. These letters abound with the peculiar pet names which he was wont to bestow upon all those for whom he cared. Some of these were in sound anything but complimentary, but his wife and his friends knew how to read between the lines. These to his wife commence variously : " My dearest Wifie," or " My very dear Bochim," " My dearest Missus," " My dear Bellinzona," and, now and again, " My dearest Heart's Beloved." They are full of allusions which require almost a glossary to make them comprehensible to a stranger. Hannington had a vocabulary of his own which was expressive enough to those who held the key to it.

He and his friend May spent a few weeks during June in the Scilly Islands. From there he writes :

"MY DEAREST,—It has been a great relief to me to think to-day that you have heard of our whereabouts. I expect day after day Betsy in heat and dust toiled up and got a thump for not bringing back any news. However, now you will be satisfied. I received two letters from you last night, one with the news of poor dear John's death. I was very cut up about it, though I ought not to have been, for it was a wonderful mercy. Trained for a few weeks in the school of affliction, and then taken home to Glory. You may tell Mrs. Parsons, if you will, that I hope to preach a funeral sermon on the Sunday evening after my return, that is July 15th, if nothing prevents.

"Things are going on very smoothly here with us. The weather is excellent. The Botany first-rate, and the Beetles moderately good. There are fewer than anybody might expect, though I have taken several; quite enough to occupy my spare moments. Yesterday Mr. Atkin took us over to the island of St. Agnes. We met there two celebrated old botanists. I addressed them: 'Are you Mr. Ralfs?' 'Yes.' 'Are you Mr. Curnow?' 'Yes. However do you know us?' 'Mitten,' said I. 'Are *you* MITTEN?' 'No,' I replied. 'Oh, dear, what a pity!' said they. I told them that Mitten had asked me to call upon them, and we got on very well together, and they pointed out Arthrolobium Ebrac, Trif., Suffoc., Glom., and a new Lavatera that Ralfs had just found. I cannot be too thankful for this pleasant change, and only wish that you were a more scambleinous Tomboy.*

"And now for one anecdote. A man showed us the way up to our hotel when we arrived—our two selves and

---

* Mrs. Hannington was not then strong enough to accompany her husband.

two medical men.   The landlady, meeting him at the door,
said, 'How many have you brought?' 'Four, Mum.'
'Any ladies?' 'No.' 'Oh, thank goodness!!!'

"After this we dined very comfortably together.

"My kindest love to my dear Ma.   I hope you have
not been frightened.   A thousand kisses from

"Your very affectionate
"HUSBAND.

His diary supplements the above allusion to the two
botanists :

"*July 4th.*—Explored St. Martin's.   Met again the
old gentlemen whom the boatmen contemptuously describe
as old herbalists, and told us that one poisoned himself last
year, and it took all the doctors in Penzance to set him
right!   Found them gathering Ophiog: Lusitan.

"*5th.*—Sailed to Western Islands.   Landed on Gorregan
in search of greater black-back gulls.   The *Schiller* was
wrecked near these rocks; and what a hideous mass of
rocks it is!   On every side you see ugly black heads peeping
up.   They require the pen of Virgil to describe them.

"*11th.*—Left Penzance with F. G. May.   I secured a
carriage by putting an umbrella in the corner.   On my
return, I found that an old lady and gentleman, without
observing my umbrella, had taken my seat.   Presently the
old lady said, 'My dear, that is an umbrella behind you.'
It was produced and carefully examined.   'Most miserable
old thing! give it to the guard.'   'I beg your pardon,' I
intervened; 'that is mine.'"

On Nov. 8th he writes: "Paid a visit to Darley Abbey,
and stayed with Miss Evans, 'the Clerical Hotel of the
Midland Counties.'   The dear old lady seems much the

same. She is now about ninety-one years old. The servants show their age more than their mistress."

The end of November found him in Atwick, where he
and his brother Joseph conducted a short Mission. He
writes :

"My dearest Wifie,—To begin at the beginning, I
had better go back again to Darley. I found things in rather
a sad plight—such a number of backsliders among the young
people—and I could not get to see any of them ; they kept
out of my way. I stopped over Friday, and had a nice
meeting of old friends in the evening, just about forty, but
all believers. Rhoda just been pushed in ; but it won't do,
I expect.

"I met Jos at Hull, and came on to Atwick with him ;
we had a prayer-meeting to begin with. Only two or three
came. I was very tired, and spoke very feebly. Jos had
got on a mackintosh, in which he rustled and fidgeted so
incessantly, the men who prayed shrieked so terrifically,
that I burst out into one hysterical giggling fit—fortunately
not visibly. But what an awful beginning ! I was very
much cast down. Sunday morning, full of doubts and fears,
but was enabled to speak more at liberty than I have ever
been before. . . . Rhoda squeezed in by Jos, but, of
course, I can't receive.* . . . I am in bondage still,
and the more so as Jos keeps me laughing nearly all day
with his wonderful sayings and remarks. . . . We hope

---

* This word "receive" was one of Hannington's own vocabulary. He was always very cautious of accepting or "receiving"
a person as a saved soul upon the bare profession of faith in
Christ. He liked to wait for the proof in the changed life. His
brother Joseph would rush in triumphantly asserting, " Such an one
is saved, or is at liberty." To whom James would reply, " Hush,
Jos, I can't receive in such a hurry." This was especially the case

Rhoda will do. Everybody receives readily but myself, and you know I am always rather unready to receive. . . . I need not tell you both to pray—you are doing that.

"Your very, very, very, very affectionate

"HUSBAND."

In his diary he writes : "A man turned up from another parish, and walked all round the neighbourhood, literally compelling the people to come in. Each service saw more and more, with a small but yet very blessed result. God be praised for even one ! Oh, the value of one soul ! it is priceless."

I find a letter at this time from the Rev. J. Dawson, who had left Darley Abbey, and was then Vicar of St. Peter's, Clifton, inviting Hannington to take part in a Mission to be held in his church in February of the ensuing year. He says :

"We shall want James. We can't do without him. It won't be like a Mission without him, so he must come."

On Sunday, the 2nd of December, his first child was born ; and on the 6th of January, 1878, was baptized by his father under the name of James Edward Meopham. In his diary he writes : "I never seemed to enter into the Service so much as to-day : 'Thine for ever, God of love. Hear us from Thy throne above. Thine for ever may we be, Here and in eternity.' "

"*Jan. 12th.*—Saw Mrs. P. H.'s housekeeper. Dying of

---

when the two brothers were working together, as in this instance. The Rhoda referred to is an old servant who has been nearly thirty years in the service of the family. She had been often prayed for and pleaded with, but remained spiritually dead. During this Mission she was brought to the Saviour. Though Hannington feared to "receive" her precipitately, her case proved to be a real and abiding one—much to the joy of the whole family.

cancer, and now sinking very fast. God, I fully believe, has used me here. She could not speak, but knew me. When I said, 'Eye hath not seen, nor ear heard,' the dying face lighted up with joy. 'We shall meet again,' I added. She pointed upwards with really solemn majesty."

On the 21st of January, 1878, Hannington took part in the Birmingham Mission. The following was his first letter to his wife :

"My dearest Lily,—I hope you arrived safely at your Ma's on Monday afternoon, and that you, old Ma, and Squaliner Grub * are all quite well.

" I am thankful to say that I arrived in Birmingham quite safely. No adventures on the journey of any kind whatever. On my arrival at the Vicarage, I found that I was to stay with a friend ; and so, after some dinner, I was received by an admirable widow lady, and was presently shown into a bedroom as large, I should say, as my father's. Four gas brackets flaring ; a fire large enough to roast an ox ; table, chairs, sofa, etc., etc. ; in fact, everything to make me comfortable. At seven o'clock I was fetched by the Vicar to go to the Mission Hall. Alas ! alas ! my heart rather sunk when we arrived : an empty room, and various signs of a certain dry Churchism. However, after a bit, the room began to fill ; but I could see at once the way had not been prepared. However, I preached with liberty, and had an after-meeting, and tried to get them to stop. The Lord directed me to one soul ; as far as I could see, a genuine case. I think that there might have been more, but the organist got up directly I said that I should now speak to any souls who were anxious, and that the rest might go, and said that there would be a choir practice !

---

* The baby !

"I never heard such a thing in my life. It is uphill work, I foresee. However, we must just go forward, expecting a great blessing, and I really cannot but think that it will be so.

" Kindest love to your Ma, and your dear old self.

" I remain your very affectionate

" HUSBAND.

The diary has some references to the above Mission :—

" Sadly interrupted by a huge, tipsy man wedged into the middle of a crammed meeting. Nevertheless, the Lord gave me immense power, so that I held them together in spite of intense interruption. But the strain was so great that I afterwards burst into tears."

" A man professed to be in difficulty because he had been told that God came from Teman * (Hab. iii. 3)."

" A most interesting case ; a young man named —— kept me up till 11.30 p.m."

Altogether, Hannington's part in the Birmingham

---

* Those who have worked among the illiterate poor will not be surprised at this entry. It is amazing at what strange difficulties they are often stumbled. I have myself met with labouring men who were also unable to surmount this verse about God coming from Teman ! This was in Surrey. There are certain stock difficulties which appear to perplex certain classes of minds. The following is an example of such another : Once, when fishing off Hastings, the boatman put to us this question : " *Whom did Cain marry ?* " Many years afterwards, when visiting the Infirmary of the Farnham Workhouse, I was brought into contact with a tramp who was dying of dropsy. During a somewhat long illness I attended him very closely. He was almost as ignorant as a heathen. The elementary facts of the life of our Lord had to be imparted to him as to an infant. But what he heard he received with the simplicity of a child. He seemed gratefully to accept

Mission of 1878 seems to have been a blessed one, and his name will be remembered by not a few in that town.

"*Feb.* 5*th.*—From a passage I read relating to the experience of Moody, I have been led to cry earnestly to be much more filled with the Holy Ghost. I have long felt that my ministry, my life, my conversation, lacks unction. Thou wilt fill me, O my God!

"*Feb.* 14*th.*—I pray, and keep praying, for the Holy Spirit."

About this time he caught a very severe cold, which developed into an attack of rheumatism, by which he was completely disabled, and confined to house and bed. The doctors, finding that the usual treatment failed, recommended a course of baths at Aix-les-Bains, and a short residence abroad.

With his mother-in-law, to whom he was greatly attached, to take charge of him, he sailed on May 21st, and remained abroad for two months. His unsparing expenditure of himself in his work had thoroughly exhausted his

---

Christ and His Salvation. One morning, when I asked him how he had passed the night, he made this wonderful reply : " I was in awful pain, and sweat all night. I thought the morning would never come. But oh ! I thought to myself *I had never yet sweat blood.*" At last the end drew near. He was lying still and almost without power of speech. His lips seemed to move, and I bent down my head to catch his words. He painfully raised his arm, and drew down my ear close to his mouth. I listened with all my might, and these were the words I heard slowly and with difficulty uttered : "*Can—you—tell—me—who—did — Cain— marry ?*" I was, I confess, startled. But to his simple mind the difficulty was a real one—a last temptation whispered into his soul to make him doubt the great Salvation. So I gently explained as best I could, and, satisfied with the reply, he closed his eyes and died in peace.—ED.

vitality, and it was only by slow degrees that he recovered
his usual elasticity of body and mind. He amused himself,
and kept his mind from altogether stagnating, by compiling a
book of rhymes for the children, in which his own adventures, and those of his poor mother-in-law, were mercilessly
caricatured and described. The latter is always depicted in
a monstrous coal-scuttle bonnet, and portrayed in every
imaginable funniest predicament. Her son-in-law was a
terrible *compagnon de voyage* for a person who was sensitive
about appearing afterwards in pen and ink. About himself
and his baths he writes to his wife :—

"MY DEAREST HEART'S BELOVED,—. . . . .
Ma has told you all about snow mountains and nightingales,
and the old gentleman whom she took for a commercial
traveller, and couldn't bear, and who turned out to be Lord
Charles ———, and then she found out how exceedingly
interesting his anecdotes were ! So I must pass on to give
you a little idea of the baths. As we take them daily, I am
getting quite learned. You get up and dress lightly at a
few minutes before eight. Then, at the establishment, you
are seated on a wooden stool, and two jets of hot water are
let fly at you ; the man asking ' Est-ce bon ? ' meaning, Is
the water too hot or too cold ? And if you object, and say :
' I—i—i—t— s—s—b—*boiling !* ' he says : ' *Non*, c'est bon.'
He then begins to rub and pinch you from head to foot, after
which he lightly rubs you with a towel, and then rings a
bell. At this two men appear with a hooded chair, in which
is laid a blanket. You enter, and are swaddled up tight like
a mummy, so tight that you can't move. You are told to
lean well back, and off you go, full tilt, to your hotel.
Starting from the baths you go down a steep flight of stairs ;
the curtains are drawn in front so that you cannot see, and
you can't move hand or foot, and you feel inclined to scream

to the men to tell them you are going to pitch on your head. One morning, as I arrived near my hotel, a conversation took place between Fanchette, the maid, and my men. 'Who have you got there?' said she. 'Number Fifteen.' 'Fifteen! Why, she ——.' ''Tisn't *she*; it's *he*.' 'He! Then it's *Fourteen*.' I had told them the wrong number, and narrowly escaped being carried into a lady's room! Arriving at the hotel, you have to be got upstairs, which is a somewhat difficult process, and rather trying to the nerves. The curtains are then drawn back, and you are taken up by the shoulders and feet, and lifted like a mummy into bed. There you have to lie for about half an hour, to produce a re-action, when your housemaid, who is a man, comes and unmummies you. I hope that, after a bit, I shall be better, but there are not many signs yet."

Alpine air, however, and rest of body and mind, soon began to tell. On July 21st he accepted a proposal to preach at Pontresina. " I did so to see how I stood it. I preached from Isaiah liii. 6, to a small, but breathlessly attentive congregation." Ten days later he was back once more at Hurst, and ready to renew the fray.

His note is : " Reached England and Home, finding all well, and my precious son much grown."

One of Hannington's favourite fictions with regard to himself was that he had no patience with children, especially babies. " O my, gracious ; there's that baby again," he would say to the indignant mother, when his latest arrived nephew or niece was brought in for his inspection ; or when paying a visit to another sister-in-law, whose husband he was about to join in some distant Mission work, " Well, now, I suppose I must see the *baby*" (with an indescribable intonation on the word baby), " or its father will

be asking me questions about it which I can't answer."
But whatever the mothers may have thought of this profession of indifference to their offspring, the children
themselves were not to be so deceived. They knew better.
No one was more popular in the nursery than Uncle James.
The very children in the village would creep up close to
him and beg for bull's-eyes as he passed. And as for babies,
he loved as much as many another man to feel their soft
little fingers clasp around his own—when no one was
looking. In a letter to his wife, he writes of the baby of
the day : " *You may kiss his little dear face for me.*" A
man who did not love children never wrote such an expression as that. " His little dear face ! " The baby-face must
have been in his mind, all dimpled and soft and fresh for a
kiss, when he wrote the words.*

The following extracts from the diary may be given:

" *Sept.* 12*th.*—Visiting one of my parishioners, I was
asked if God were alive before Jesus Christ, who Paul was,

---

* Several years later, after his consecration to the Bishopric,
while narrating some of his African experiences to a congregation
at Bath, he made the following statement, than which I cannot
recal any more touching in its tender simplicity:—

" When far inland, the mail comes in but once a month. Its
arrival is heralded by two gun-shots, fired in quick succession. No
matter what one may be doing, he leaves his occupation, and
hurries forward to get a sight of his precious letters. There would
be some, perhaps, from my brothers, some from friends, always
one from my wife. But once there was one which, when I saw the
handwriting, I opened first. It was on a bare half-sheet of paper,
the lines running this way and that way ; tumbled and soiled ; but
that one letter I read first, and treasured above all the others. *It
was from my dear little son,* and contained but two lines: ' My
dear Father,—God bless you.' These few words received by me
in the wilds of Africa were more precious than many a longer
letter."

and who the Israelites were!" An ignorance not so unusual as some might suppose. " Visited old Mrs. Sayers,
who lives with two unmarried sons. She is ninety ; they
both over sixty. She said : ' I boxed Joe's ears the other
day, and sent him up to bed, as the boy was troublesome.
There,' she said, ' I forgot they are growing up.' "

"Mr. Dear has left me his Jansenist engravings and
books ; I became intensely interested in them."

The reading of these books seems to have revealed to
Hannington the fact that high-souled purpose and true
spirituality of mind are to be found among men who belong
to widely differing schools of thought. He found much in
the writings of Pascal and the Port-Royalists that delighted
him. He could not but recognize that they too had been
taught of God. He says: " I think that many of my
opinions were slightly modified, and my sympathies were
enlarged."

"Very much exercised about preaching the same truths
Sunday after Sunday. My mind was afterwards directed to
a doctor who uses the same medicines for the same diseases
all the year round ; and, again, to the fact that we eat and
drink the same things day after day and year after year."

On November 23rd he conducted a mission at D——.
"Tremendous cautions about what I was to do, and what
not to do. Above all things not to be excitable. I
was shown the church, and went up into the pulpit. I
took hold of it with a strong hand, to try whether the desk
and sides would stand much knocking about. I perceived,
to my intense amusement, that all this was carefully noted,
and produced a feeling of terror as to what I was going to
do when I preached ; and many further hints were given."

"*Dec.* 26*th.*—Gave a Christmas party to men, to keep

drunkards out of the public-house. About sixty came. After prayer and hymns we spent the evening in looking at books, microscope, and magic lantern."

"*Jan.* 1*st*, 1879.—I make no resolutions for the coming year. I pray for more earnestness, more love, more diligence, greater regularity, and entire consecration to the service of the Lord."

"On Christmas Day old W. D. was converted, to the best of my belief, by the reading of the Collect, Epistle, and Gospel."

"15*th.*—The Rector has decided to have a Mission, and I have written to Ernest Boys."

"23*rd.*—Brighton, to meet the Bishop on the question of the Mission. Praise God, the Bishop has helped us much."

"*Mar.* 1*st.*—Mission commenced. The Bishop administered the Holy Communion to the workers, and in the afternoon gave a splendid address, full of Evangelical truth." "All through the Mission the services were densely crowded. On Sunday evening every corner of the church was packed, and many went away."

"*Mar.* 19*th.*—Called on Arthur Garbett. He told me that the archdeacon was dying, but transcendently peaceful."

"*April* 9*th.*—Introduced to Canon Garbett, who preached at the parish church. A splendid disquisition, but far above the heads of a country congregation."

"*April* 13*th.*—Easter Day. Piercingly cold, and ground covered with snow, which contrasted strangely with the Easter decorations. 58 communicants."

CHAPTER XI.

(1879—82.)

> " But, good my brother,
> Do not, as some ungracious pastors do,
> Show me the steep and thorny way to heaven,
> Whilst, like a puft and careless libertine,
> Himself the primrose path of dalliance treads,
> And recks not his own rede."
>
> SHAKESPEARE.

MR. SCRIVEN came to Hurstpierpoint in May of 1879, and spent some time with Hannington, during which they made together some interesting architectural tours in the neighbourhood. Mr. Scriven is an enthusiastic architect, and he found in his former pupil an untiring and intelligent listener. Everything of this sort interested Hannington. He was full of information obtained by his acquisitive mind, and stored up by a retentive memory in the course of his wanderings. His knowledge of folklore, of the geological peculiarities, of the flora and fauna, and of the local traditions of almost every place through which he had passed, made him the best of companions.

He returned with Mr. Scriven as far as Sherborne, where the two visited the Abbey Church, and, being joined by his old friend and fellow cliff-climber and egg-hunter, Mr. F. May, crossed over to Lundy Island to spend there his summer holiday.

And here again we notice how in the midst of his play Hannington never seems to have forgotten what some would have called his work. The business of seeking to influence souls in behalf of Christ was apparently never alien to any of his moods. His diary makes it abundantly clear that this was not merely the work of his life, but the delight of it. It did not occur to him that to talk on the subject of religion was "talking shop." It was the most natural thing in the world to him to converse about those truths which were to himself as meat and drink. In the midst of jottings of architectural trips and Lundy Island clamberings we find such entries as the following:

" The Lord has led me to speak to Harry G., and has brought him to the knowledge of the truth. Edwin A., too, has been gradually led to believe in Jesus."

There are some excellent persons whose society becomes oppressive, and their conversation a source of nervous apprehension to everybody. They always appear to be lying in wait for an opportunity. Whatever may be the theme of discussion, whether weighty or light, everyone instinctively knows that they will turn it by and by into a " profitable " channel. Their companion for the time being is made to feel that they lie at the catch. Whatever he may say will, he is sure, be used as a handle upon which to fasten some argument which makes for religion. He is put upon the defensive. These good people are, he suspects, only affecting to take an interest in his sports, pursuits, opinions, or general affairs in order that they may bring the conversation round to the " one thing needful," and spring upon him the question whether or not he is saved.

Hannington was not one of this kind. The boys never slipped round the corner when they saw him coming, or trembled when they found that they were committed to a

tête-à-tête with him, lest he should take them at a dis-
advantage and pin them with some question which they
were ill-disposed to contemplate and wholly unprepared to
answer.

At Mission times, when everybody knew what to expect
from him, he would, no doubt, endeavour, both openly and
by strategy, to get to close quarters with the consciences of
young and old, rich and poor. A friend might even find himself unceremoniously pushed into the presence of the Missioner to be " dealt with." But, as a rule, Hannington was
full of real wisdom in his intercourse with the world. His
interest in the sports of the lads and lassies was quite sincere
and unaffected ; he made them feel that he was a big boy
himself, and loved fun for fun's sake. So also with the
elders, he came among them not merely as a prophet, but
as a man to whom nothing that pertained to men was indifferent.

There was no need for him to pull in the subject of
religion, as it were, by the shoulders, and consciously and
painfully lead every subject of conversation up to it. All
his life,—his amusement as well as his labour,—was permeated by his faith in the Unseen.

> " He had perceived the presence and the power
> Of Greatness ; and deep feeling had impressed
> Great objects on his mind, with portraiture
> And colour so distinct, that on his mind
> They lay like substances, and almost seemed
> To haunt the bodily sense." *

Thus it came quite naturally to him, without *preaching*,
to speak to another of the eternal world, and of that City or
which he was himself a citizen. And men, too, in stress
of soul, would come to him, not as to a mentor, but as to a
brother, who having passed through similar times of per-

---

* Wordsworth.

plexity, and being now in possession of the spiritual blessing after which they sought, could help them with his counsel.

On Lundy Island the two friends proceeded to shake off years and respectability, and to behave like untamed schoolboys loosed for a holiday. In one of his letters home he says :

"We are not failing to enjoy ourselves. . . . . . We watch the tremendous seas, and, like young children, venture on to small rocks as the sea is coming up, and laugh at the unlucky wight who remains too long and gets splashed. We bathe too. The other day I was knocked down by a wave and bruised my knee. Beetles are rather out of favour. I hope, my dear, that you are quite well, and have not disappointed your eyes out over the various posts that have brought no letters. . . . . . I often think of sweet Gashum, and I send him and you the most tremendous amount of kisses. . . . . .

"Oh, my dear, the rats have eaten my nailey boots. Who would have thought of it ! But it was a judgment ! Those boots have been nothing but trouble. The fact was that my Pa gave them to me to give away, and I appropriated them to my own use ! They've leaked. They've got wet and refused to get dry. They've been slippery on the shore, slippery on the rocks. I was carrying them through a pool of water; a wave came, and to save my boots I lost my balance, and fell and hurt my knee, and now the rats ! yes, the rats. Never defraud the poor of a pair of boots again ! Perhaps the boots are the Jonahs that keep us bound here.* But I can't give them away now. Whether you shall send the other pair by Mr. Mitten or

---

* They were detained for ten days beyond their time by rough weather, during which no boat could cross from the mainland.

not, I will leave until I land. Alas! that will not be to-day. We can see over to Instow, and nothing is coming.

"An hour or two later. The skiff is reported. We are in the greatest glee. So good-bye. A thousand kisses, and many to dearest little Gashum."

"Gashum," of course, is the baby. Why so called I shall not be rash enough to attempt to guess, but Hannington nicknamed all those whom he loved. It was a special mark of his affection. "Gashum" is mentioned in all the letters of this date in ever varying terms of endearment. In another sentence he says, "I hope dear little baby is quite well. One thing I am quite certain about, and that is that he does not miss his Gogum."

From Ilfracombe these two walked through much of North Devon, seeking out places of architectural interest. When they arrived at Bude, two hot, dusty and travel-stained pedestrians, without a decent show of baggage of any kind, and walked up to the hotel, they were received with scant civility. Hannington looked tramp-like and unpromising. The innkeeper eyed him and was not cordial. He says, "This amused us far more than if we had been received as great men in disguise. I enjoy seeing every side of life."

Hannington and Mark Tapley would have been birds of one feather. But it is certain that that prince of body-servants would not have remained long in his employ. He would have felt that there was no room for the development of his special talent.

The diary continues:—

"*July* 21*st*.—Walked to Shermanbury. The church, I am told, was originally the squire's stable, and I can well believe it. The water was so high on the road that I had to wait until a farmer came along and drove me over, but, coming back, I had to strip. It was four feet deep on the road, an unknown thing in the middle of summer."

One need not pity him. Had he had to swim across with his clothes on his head he would, I have little doubt, have preferred it.

"*28th.*—Found my great-grandfather's tomb in New Shoreham Church."

When Hannington returned home he proceeded to impart to his young men some of the architectural lore which he had acquired. He seldom failed in quickly interesting others in what interested himself. On the Bank Holiday he took a party of them to Three Bridges, and showed them some fine old churches. He says : " My young Christians take a very intelligent interest in architecture, scenery, and botany. I cannot but feel that such things expand their mind."

The following entry occurs for August 8th :

" Went into Brighton to hear Dr. Talmage, many of whose sermons I have read, and some of which I have admired. But why did I go to hear him ! He was about on a par with a third-rate actor. I was woefully disappointed; although, after I got over the roughness of his accent, I liked him better. His power seems to lie in his voice. If, for instance, he says the word *weeping*, he makes the word weep ; but I am sorry that I heard him."

On August 26th a little daughter was born, whom he named Caroline Scriven. " God be praised for all His mercies ! "

" *Oct.* 18*th.*—Last week I gave notice that if anybody liked to bring me half-a-dozen of any sort of vegetable, I would put them in the church for our harvest festival, and on

Monday send them to London to be distributed in poor districts. The response has been far beyond my expectation. Things came in all day, and on Monday, four large hampers were sent to Hambledon of Drury Lane and Fegan of Deptford." *

The manner in which he recognized the direct leading of God is illustrated by the following :

" *Nov. 20th.*—How the Lord directs our paths ! I had said, I will have a rest this afternoon, and then something said to me, ' The Lord has work for you that you do not know of yet.' Dinner was half an hour late, which resulted in my being in the house later than usual, and receiving an immediate summons to a dying woman, whom I pointed to the Saviour."

On April 24th, 1880, Hannington writes : —

" Ernest Boys arrived for a revisiting Mission. The other end of the parish has received him coldly, so we at St. George's opened our doors and received a blessing, although there was nothing of great external interest to record."

" *May 3rd.*—Got hold of J. Q., who boldly rejected the Gospel."

" 13*th*. — Had a tremendous rowing — I can call it nothing else—from a neighbouring clergyman, the root of whose grievance was that one of his parishioners was converted at our Mission."

" 23*rd*. — I could not help noticing the curious

---

* The Parish Magazine of the Drury Lane Mission Church has the following reference to this gift :—" The congregation of St. George's increase their offerings to the poor folk of our Mission every year. All honour to them ! This year they have sent us vegetables, fruit and flowers. We simply danced for joy at the sight of 8 cwt. of choice produce. They must have a glorious minister over them, for ' Like priest, like people.' "

mixture in our congregation to-day. Two Unitarians, two Roman Catholics, Ritualists, Wesleyans, Calvinists, a Quaker, besides Congregationalists and open Plymouth Brethren."

In July, Hannington and Mr. Mitten, the botanist, started together to spend their holidays by the Lakes of Killarney. They spent their time hunting for mosses, much to their mutual satisfaction.

On Sunday, the 18th, Hannington preached at Ballybrach. "It struck me," he says, "that the Saxon was not very acceptable to anybody except the Rev. B. Anderson, who escaped from the sound of his own voice. They appeared to me to be ready to hear of the sins of the Roman Catholics, but never dreamt that Protestants were sinners too, and didn't want to hear it. I may have been mistaken in this supposition, but I think not."

"Visited Muckross Abbey, and found an honest man. His compact, nominal as I thought, was not to take money. He made himself most pleasant, and I offered him something as one does to a railway porter. No! He thanked me affectionately, said that few of the hundreds he showed over the place offered him anything. These he cursed for their meanness from the bottom of his heart, but he would not take a farthing. . . . . . When we left Killarney, I saw at the station a leave-taking. I never did see such a scene of tears, and kisses, and sobs, amounting to howls. Up rushes one and kisses the man who is departing on both cheeks. 'I don't know you personally,' he says, 'but shure, I'm a namesake of your wife's.' I don't know how many miles he had not come just to kiss him. In an open third class carriage they were talking very freely. One man confessed plainly that he thought killing a landlord was no breaking of the 'tin' commandments."

On his return to England, Hannington met Mr. F. May, and spent a short time with him. They started, one day, to walk across Dartmoor, and getting befogged, lost their way. They soon fell into a bog, and were in considerable peril. Hannington was equal to the emergency. He says: "When in the worst place I kept up F.'s drooping spirits by solemnly pulling my tooth-brush out of my pocket and cleaning my teeth. The shout of laughter at my composure, and the breathing time it gave us, pulled us together, and we safely crossed a dreadfully dangerous place. Arrived at Prince Town, and thence to Tavistock, twenty-two miles, where we caught the train and proceeded to South Petherwyn."

The following extract is touching: "How little there seems in my diary about my wife. Her incapacity to walk much, or to travel, causes us to go out together so seldom. It is often a cause of regret to me that it should be so. But while I am at play she is at work, and visits much in the parish among the poor, and almost exclusively among them."

"I have this year preached 158 times, besides Bible Classes. Last year, 136 times."

The next entry in the diary attests in a very remarkable manner the sincerity of this man's life, while it throws a strong light upon his complex character. Amidst all his busy restlessness, there was in him a strong desire after quietude.

Nirvana had no charms for such a nature as his. His idea of the beatific life was not even the enjoyment of green pastures by the side of still waters—if, at least, he had been compelled to sleep there and dream for ever. He displayed much self-knowledge when he wrote, "I enjoy the uphill, struggling path most of all." But, like every true-souled man who has listened to the voice of God, and whose spirit has enjoyed the delight of communion with the Highest, he longed intensely after a life in which all remaining hindrances to intercourse with the Divine Spirit should be removed. There were times when he felt that just to drink in the Love of God, and to receive the communications of His Will, would satisfy all the cravings of his nature, while it exercised to the utmost every faculty within him.   He sometimes was inclined to look upon those very recreations of his which all his friends knew to be so absolutely necessary as safeguards against the over-strain of his excitable nervous system, in the light of hindrances to a perfect walk with God.   Even the active interest which he took in the work of his parish and its manifold details seemed to him sometimes to clash with that pure love of God which should be the motive and mainspring of all endeavour.

O man of true and simple * soul, all who have known what it is to long that they might flee away and be at rest— at rest *from themselves*—will sympathize with what you say :

"1881.   *Jan. 3rd.*—Walked with Cyril Gordon and M. Hankin to Cowfold, and went over the Monastery.   It is a huge place.   It had the most extraordinary effect upon me.   It set me longing for a monastic life.   I think, probably, a reactionary feeling after a long spell of hard work. I exclaimed, ' Lord, let me spend and be spent for Thee.' "

A monk ! A monk of the François Xavier type he might have been.   None other.   And, indeed, of Xavier, allowing for differences of creed and education, he often reminds one. The same simple single-mindedness, the same fiery, impetuous zeal, the same scorn of personal discomforts, the same indifference to luxury and contempt of danger, the same childlike, unreasoning acceptance of the truth as it was

---

* ἐν ᾧ δόλος οὐκ ἔστι—John i. 47.

revealed to their own hearts, and the same magnetic power of communicating their faith to others, characterized both these missionary pioneers.

Had he lived in still earlier times he might have been a Knight Templar, and, with virgin heart and body, have wielded a good lance for the honour of Christ and His Church. But a monk whose life must be spent in fast, vigil, and mechanical prayer, who shuts himself off from the striving of the sin-steeped, perishing world in order that he may the better save his own soul! Never!

He continues: " That night I had forty-two men present at my Bible Class. Shut up in a monastery that could not be. These Franciscans have no contact with the outer world."

In the outer world we next find him—hard at work as ever, and full of it. He had undertaken to conduct the Services in Holy Trinity Church in connection with the Blackheath Mission. His diary reports:

" *Feb.* 18*th*.—Arrived at Holy Trinity Vicarage, Blackheath. I am advertised to take twenty-seven Services in eight or nine days, and they are pleading for more. ' As thy day thy strength will be.' "

" 19*th*.—Holy Communion at St. John's. Met dear Latham, of Matlock, who greatly encouraged me and strengthened my hands. Mr. ——— understands nothing about Missions, and is inclined to be obstructive. Afternoon went to hear Bishop Thorold. He preached a magnificent sermon to Mission workers. Evening, gave an address to workers myself. About sixty present, which encouraged me greatly."

He wrote home, saying:

" I heard an address from the Bishop of Rochester, a most magnificent sermon, touching on all points of the

Mission question. I was afterwards introduced to him, and felt pleased that I had asked for his permission and benediction."

On the 28th he continues:

" For the last eight days I have been incessantly on the move, so much so that I have been unable to keep any record. It was more than hard work, more than uphill, and yet very blessed, I preached four times one day, and three times the next, alternately, making thirty times in all."

The next entry may be quoted as a hint to those who invite clergymen to come amongst them and undertake exhausting labours, with difficulty leaving their own home work, and returning to it spent and nerve-worn, and who forget that there are such things as expenses in connection with travel:

" I was put to £4 expenses, and dear old Mr. ———, just as I was leaving, said : ' You will let me pay your cab fare to the station ? ' This was the first word on the subject, and the evident simplicity and good faith of the dear old man quite took my breath away. ' No,' said I, ' I will pay it.' However, he insisted on my taking eighteenpence."

Most men in such circumstances would have replied : " Pray do not trouble to pay my cab, and I will send you an account of the sum total of my expenses when I reach home." But that was not Hannington's way. Money was not unimportant to him at this time, as his fixed private income did not expand with his family. But he suffered in silence, and the only allusion to this little episode is to be found in his private diary.

" *April 17th, Easter Day.*—Ninety-four communicants. When I came here first I found only twenty-four or thirty."

The next entry affords an instance of the manner in

which his friends were accustomed to lean upon his rugged sincerity when they needed *real* sympathy :

"*April 22nd.*—Telegram from the Rev. ——— to come instantly. When I arrived I heard that his wife had just been found dead. ——— dreadfully cut up ; telegraphed to me for Christian sympathy."

"*24th.*—Preached from Isa. xlix. 15, without especial reference to the sad event. In the midst of the sermon I heard an agonized burst of tears which I thought proceeded from one of the ———s, touched by the reference to a mother's love. Never did I preach in such mental distress, such exquisite agony of mind. I scarce struggled through."

"*May 23rd.*—Visited my father on his yacht at Shoreham. Afterwards found to my great delight Trigonium Stellatum."

On May 25th his third child was born, whom he named Paul Travers.

Dear little Paul ! He is now five years old. In hair, eyes, and contour of face much, if not quite, what his father must have been at his age. When I visited Hurst last spring, and he heard that I was an old friend of his father's, he waited till we chanced to be alone, then crept up and laid his elbows upon my knee. 'Tell me something about father," said he. "Your father," I said, "was a very brave man, and a good man. Will you, too, try to be both brave and good ?" So he listened with large eyes wide-opened and awe-struck, as to the tale of some martyr hero of the holy past. When I had finished, still with his elbows on my knee and his upturned face resting upon his hands, he said, with a plaintive quaver in his baby voice: "Tell me *more* about father." The memory of that father, and the record of the splendid self-sacrifices of his devoted life, will be to his children a priceless legacy, in the possession of which they, though orphaned, are most richly dowered.

On June 4th certain alarming symptoms warned the family that Colonel Hannington * was in a more critical condition than ever in former times of illness. He had been repeatedly operated upon for stone, and his declining years were full of unrest and pain. On Whit Sunday all realized that he was dying, and James administered to him the Holy Communion. He writes :

"*June 6th.*—5.30 a.m. called by doctor. Father worse. Telegraphed to Mary, Sam, etc., who all came. I saw him alone, remaining with him in constant attendance. At 11.30 the doctor insisted upon my going to bed. At 2.30 a.m., June 7th, he ran into my room. 'Come at once.' I leaped from bed, ran to the door, thinking he had left it open, and nearly stunned myself. Recovering, I ran in in time to see the last two minutes of my father's life. As he passed away a heavenly expression spread over his face. Just two minutes before he had said : ' Nurse, I am dying!' When she moved to help him he spoke his last words, ' Let me go.' It was, indeed, we all felt, a happy release from intense suffering."

The funeral took place on June 11th. " About five hundred followed as mourners. After the ceremony at the grave the friends adjourned to St. George's, where Mr. Aldwell, of Southsea, administered the Holy Communion."

By his father's will James Hannington found himself the owner of St. George's Chapel, but also in the awkward position of the possessor of a church without a stipend, or the means of providing one. He was still willing, as hitherto, to give his ministrations without recompense, but

---

* Mr. Hannington was made J.P., and also appointed to the Colonelcy of the 1st Sussex Artillery Volunteers, in 1873.

he felt that, in case he were led to undertake any other work—and it was not to be supposed that he would remain during his life the curate-in-charge of a small country district—it would be extremely difficult for him to provide a proper stipend for a successor out of his own strictly limited private income. He felt that his father had made a mistake, and had, by some unfortunate oversight, omitted to make a suitable provision for the chapel. The discovery of this was, no doubt, a severe blow to him, as St. George's, though a curacy *de jure*, was almost a separate parish *de facto*, and in the continuance of the special organization and work which he himself had initiated he took the most lively interest. However, what had been left undone could not now be done. He simply writes: "The Lord will provide, and I will honour my father to the utmost of my power." With regard to the chapel, it may be sufficient to add that, before his last journey to Africa, Hannington left it by will to his eldest brother, Mr. Samuel Hannington, by whom all the responsibilities connected with it have been heartily undertaken.

When the business connected with the death of his father and the apportioning of his estate was concluded, Hannington accompanied his eldest brother and family in a tour through the Western Highlands of Scotland. He was not in very good spirits, and the change of scene was much needed by him. Here is an extract from his very brief mention of this trip :

" *Sunday*, *July 3rd*.—Having arrived in church, the Free Kirk at Kilchrenan, just after the conclusion of the first hymn, the minister, Mr. Stewart, stopped, leant over the desk and said to me, ' Will you preach ? ' Sam pushed me out into the aisle, and in two minutes I found myself in a Highland pulpit. I preached from Joshua before Ai with great liberty, and the people seemed kindly disposed toward the Saxon. In the evening went to Portsonachan. A young stranger preached a written sermon far over the heads of the people, and a dog" (there were several sheep dogs in the congregation) "worried a rabbit beneath the boarding of the chapel floor !"

"*July* 29*th*.—Baby Paul Travers christened. O Lord, hear our prayer and make all our children Thine, and Thine only."

Two months later we met in Switzerland. Hannington had planned with Mr. Mitten to make a short moss-hunting tour in August, and, when in Edinburgh, had arranged that, if possible, we should spend a while together at Zermatt. The two botanists started on the first of August, and, making their way as speedily as they could to Wasen, "crawled on hands and knees" along the St. Gotthard Pass to Hospenthal. So Hannington describes their progress. Nor without accuracy. When these enthusiasts got into a likely place they would hunt the ground like beagles, lest a single rare or valuable specimen should escape their notice. I find a reference in the diary to an incident about which "Professor" Mitten, as Hannington would call him, used often to be teazed, but which is equally characteristic of both the collectors. While they were exploring the high pastures and snow-flecked rocks of the Riffel, I went up from Zermatt one morning to pay them a visit. When I had almost surmounted the long series of zigzags, and was a few hundred yards distant from the inn, I was made aware of two figures, both busily employed in grubbing around the base of a mossy rock. Their pockets were bulky and distended, and they might have been gold or diamond diggers, if one might judge from the earnestness of their expression, and the energy with which they scraped as if for some buried treasure. I soon recognized the moss hunters. They were on their way to Zermatt. Hannington was habited, as was his wont on such occasions, in a loose brown suit of some rough material, baggy at the knees and elbows, and new some years before. From the soil-stained pockets protruded leaves, stalks, and trailings as of moss. Upon his head was one of those grass hats, like an inverted flower pot, which one may buy at wayside stalls for a franc, and about which he had loosely wound a pocket-handkerchief to shade his sun-scorched face. He welcomed me warmly, and we returned together to the inn to lunch, leaving Mr. Mitten to the society of his cryptogams, and telling him that we would rejoin him at the Hotel "Zermatt" in the evening.

As Hannington had not yet discovered any edelweiss, we strolled after lunch to the one place on the brow of the plateau overlooking the glacier where the flower grows rather abundantly. It was quite late in the afternoon when we returned and commenced the long descent. To our intense amusement we came almost immediately upon "the professor." He was still within a few yards of the rock near which he had been when I first encountered them both! His pockets were more distended than ever, and he had not yet exhausted the treasures of the neighbourhood. The *furor colligendi* at once resumed its sway over Hannington, and when he had finished laughing at his friend, he, too, sunk down upon his knees and recommenced his scraping operations. It was in vain to spur on two such incorrigibles, so I left them to follow when either light or mosses should fail, and pursued my own course downward. Though I had hurt my heel and my feet were encased in no better protection than list slippers, which were continually coming off, I reached the bottom some hours before the botanists, still unsatiated, appeared at the hotel.

Hannington did not remain long enough in Switzerland to become thoroughly bitten with the mania for Alpine climbing, but he could not resist scaling one or two peaks. The perilous always exercised a powerful fascination over him. He often needed to hold himself in strong restraint to keep out of danger when he had no excuse for encountering it, and the mere encountering of which would have been to him a fearful joy. Thus it may be imagined that the precipices which wall in the valley of Zermatt, and which have drawn together so many adventurous spirits, offered a great temptation to him.

While at the Riffel, he sallied out alone one day, and climbed the knife-like edge of the Riffelhorn quite unaided, taking off his boots to enable him to cling to the steep rocks which so sheerly overhang the Görner Glacier. They told him, when he returned, that he had really endangered his life. That a guide, or at least a competent companion, should have been taken with him, and that more than one experienced climber had been killed by a slip of the foot from those treacherous rock slants. But, he writes : " It did not seem dangerous to me." After all—as the Cat says to Rudy, in Hans Andersen's story of the Ice Maiden— " One does not fall down if one is not afraid."

He also ascended the Breithorn and Monte Rosa. While on the latter mountain, he gave proof of that determination and firmness of will which was one of his distinguishing characteristics. As we have already stated, he had commenced a vigorous crusade against intemperance at Hurst, and had himself, for example's sake, become a total abstainer. This pledge he considered binding under all circumstances. He planned the Monte Rosa expedition rather abruptly, and telegraphed from the Riffel to the hotel in which I was staying in Zermatt, asking me to join him. This I was unable to do through having hurt my foot, so he determined to make the ascent alone. The start was effected at an early hour by the light of lanterns, and when the morning was advanced he and his guides found themselves upon the steep snow slopes which lead upward from the Görner Glacier. Hannington was not very well, and suffered considerably from sickness. At one time it seemed as though he would be unable to proceed. " Snow sickness " is not uncommon among beginners, and the usual remedy is a mouthful of brandy. This would undoubtedly have been effectual, and his guides repeatedly urged him to take some. He was, however, resolute, and conquering his weakness by sheer effort. of the will, persevered until he reached the summit. This was soon noised abroad in Zermatt. Indeed, I heard of it the same evening, and rode up to the Riffel early the following morning to inquire for him. I found him busy with his mosses, and none the worse — except indeed in complexion —for his adventure. He got a good scolding for his extreme and Spartan-like application to himself of his own principles, but was, in our secret hearts, admired none the less.

Dr. Francis Hawkins, who was with us at Zermatt, has since told me that, meeting Hannington for the first time, his eye was attracted to a severe swelling upon his hand—the result of a fly-bite—which, from the extent of inflammation, must have caused him no little inconvenience and pain ; Hannington made light of it, but it struck his observer that here was a man of no ordinary endurance and power of self-control. We shall see later on how this same tenacity of will and strength of endurance not only saved his life more than once in Africa, during that terrible time of fever and dysentery, when, left for dead by his bearers, he yet found strength to crawl after them into camp—but how these qualities impressed both his associates and dependents, and constituted him their leader by right divine, as well as by the fiat of the Home Committee.

After his spring holiday, Hannington did not feel himself at liberty to prolong his Swiss tour beyond a fortnight, and so turned his face steadfastly homeward. That same evening, after the slow descent from the Riffel already described, found him and Mr. Mitten at St. Nicolas. The next day they walked to Visp, took train to Susten, and from thence, passing up the smiling valley to Leukerbad, ascended the steep bridle path which scales the stupendous cliffs of the abysmal Gemmi, and spent the night at the little inn which is perched like a raven's nest upon the very summit. All the way the lithe grey lizards glanced like flecks of shadow over the grey stones. Grasshoppers with green and crimson wings flashed in short flight across the path like living emeralds and rubies. Great Apollo butterflies and striped swallow-tails soared and balanced themselves on widespread lazy wings over the deep ravine, or raced up and down the steep hill sides above the nodding grasses. The air was tremulous with the chirping of innumerable hosts of crickets —a tireless invisible choir. Hannington was indifferent to none of these things, but, upon this occasion, botany was the order of the day, and the two " herbalists " concentrated their attention mainly upon the flora of the districts through which they passed. They were so delighted with their " find " on the Gemmi, that they remained there for nearly two days, collecting on the Kandersteg side of the pass. Hannington writes : " Entering some woods the flora was so superb and so different to what we had come across, that the Professor was nearly crazy with delight. . . . . . At Berne, after giving a very little time to the sights, two travellers astonished the natives by visiting all the fountains, and peering down into the water, at times turning up their sleeves and groping in the depths beneath, dragging up tiny fragments of a minute fissidens * which is only known to grow in Berne."

A few days later, Hannington was again in England, and, after a short visit to Martinhoe, where he preached to congregations of his old friends, he settled down once more to work in St. George's.

The two last chapters have been occupied with a somewhat desultory description of various incidents of Hannington's ministerial life. They have been given in the order in which they are referred to in his private journal and letters. Not every event is here recorded, but those have been selected which seem most to display the man, his idiosyncracies, and his method of working. His was a nature for the proper understanding of which it will be necessary to throw all available side lights upon it. Men are, it is commonly said, like the leaves of a forest; among their countless multitudes, no two are precisely alike. Yet some are more widely differentiated from their fellows than others. Among the numerous biographies which have appeared— among the countless memoirs, monographs, and notices of workers in the busy world-hive—we are inclined to think that Hannington's double has not yet been seen. The acts of his life recorded in the foregoing pages may be sufficient to show that his was a distinct personality compounded of many seemingly incongruous materials. Patience and impatience, impetuous haste and dogged tenacity of perseverance, pride and humility, love of applause and disdain of it, vanity and self-depreciation, nervous sensitiveness and moral courage, self-assertive wilfulness and unselfish thoughtfulness for others and forgetfulness of self—all these paradoxical elements went to make up this man who was a continual puzzle to those who knew him only superficially.

---

* *Fissidens Polyphyllus.*

But all these elements were fused together by his deep earnestness of purpose till they formed, as it were, a composite metal, tough, elastic, and enduring, from which, as from a piece of ordnance, the message of his life might be discharged with unerring precision and irresistible force.

The next chapter will be the last which has to do with his home life and work, and in it we will try to make it clear how he was gradually led to the conclusion that he ought to respond in his own proper person to the appeal from the Mission Field for more men.

CHAPTER XII.

THE BECKONING HAND.

(1878—82.)

"I heard the voice of the Lord saying, Whom shall I send, and who will go for us? Then said I, Here am I, send me."—*Is.* vi. 8.

"I am not worthy of the Quest."—*Holy Grail.*

WHEN Hannington heard, early in the year 1878, of the manner in which the heroic labours of Lieutenant Shergold Smith and Mr. O'Neill had been crowned by their violent death on the shore of the Victoria Nyanza, he was deeply moved. He felt within himself the stirrings of a strong desire to offer to fill the gap which their fall had made in the ranks of the little Central-African Mission Army. That desire slowly ripened and developed into a definite purpose.

At the commencement of his ministry he knew very little, almost nothing in fact, about foreign mission work. He bent all his energies upon the duty that lay nearest to him, which seemed to be the shepherding of those few sheep in the wilderness who had been constituted his special charge. To the surprise of some of the friends of his boyhood, he seemed to be content with the uneventful life of a hard-working country parson.* Quite gradually his mind was

---

* As one of them writes : "That the Bishop should ever have settled down to the life of a country parson was a thing that often came up in my mind with unformed doubts and fears, though we never discussed the matter."

enlarged to take in the wants of a wider sphere. He became more and more consciously aware of dark, perishing millions "in the regions beyond," among whom moved heroic men, brethren of a new order of knight errantry, the pioneers of the modern Church.

Now and again he would meet with some friend who would stir up in him an interest in the evangelization of the heathen world, and among the many agencies at work, the great Church Missionary Society began to take in his mind a foremost place. As early as 1875 he had some conversations at Darley House with Miss Evans and Miss Gell— sister of the Bishop of Madras, and now Mrs. Childe— which left their impression upon him, and caused him to resolve that he would make himself better acquainted with what was being done to carry out the last charge of Christ to His disciples.

Such entries as the following occur in his diary from time to time :

" Dunlop Smith orders me to do more for the C. M. S."

" Mrs. Weitbrecht arrived for the Zenana Society. An exceedingly dear old lady. If all missionaries were as she is it would be good for the cause."

" Preached on Day of Intercession my first C. M. S. sermon : 1 Kings xviii. 41."

" Gave —— to the C. M. S., an Easter gift."

Then the following :

" H. G. came to see me, and, to my surprise, told me that he longed to become a Missionary. I told him that I longed to be one too. Smith and O'Neill's death, and some papers I had read, had set me longing."

Then—

" *Nov. 21st*, 1881.—C. M. S. meeting at the Dome,

Brighton; Bruce from Persia. Most interesting. How that man's words went to my heart!"

"*Nov.* 29*th.*—Went to Eastbourne to a meeting of C. M. S. District Secretaries. Holy Communion 10 a.m. At 11 a.m. Mr. Lombe addressed the meeting. He is a grand man ; I only wish we had one like him. After lunch, at which I thought myself happy to be near Mr. Lombe, Mr. Eugene Stock spoke. Clear and incisive. If he had asked me to go out, I should have said, Yes. I longed to offer myself to go."

" 1882. *Feb.* 11*th.*—Cyril Gordon came to me. I opened to him my heart about offering myself as Missionary. It does not seem to me, however, possible that the C. M. S. would accept me. I am not worthy of the honour."

Not worthy of the honour, O holy and humble man of heart! Unworthy of the honour of serving *Christ* thou mightest indeed have deemed thyself; but there has been no society of men who would not have been honoured in possessing such an agent and servant as thou! Had the Church Missionary Society "despised" thee, as thou didst fear, it would have set its sign and seal for ever to its own fatuity. But not least among signs of its vitality will be recorded the fact that it recognized thy power and admitted thee at once into a foremost place amongst the ranks of its fighting men.

Not many days after this interview with Mr. Cyril Gordon, Mr. Wigram, the Hon. Secretary of the Society, wrote to Hannington, saying that it had been reported to him that he was willing to labour in the foreign Mission-field, and offering to afford him the opportunity he desired.

This letter brought his thoughts on the subject to a

head, and he hesitated no longer. During the past four years the conviction had been steadily deepening within him that his constitutional gifts and aptitudes were such as to qualify him in a special manner for work of toil and danger among a savage race. His large and broad knowledge of men, gained during a life of constant movement and varied travel; the habit of command which he had acquired quite early in life; and the influence which he could not help seeing that he readily acquired over rude and untrained natures—all seemed to have been granted to him that he might employ them in some difficult service that would tax his powers to the utmost.

It was true that his presence was apparently needed at home. His work at Hurstpierpoint had been crowned with a large measure of success. His friends did not fail to point out to him that a man may serve God as faithfully and efficiently in an English parish as among heathen tribes in the torrid or arctic zone ; that if every good man went abroad —etc. ! He acknowledged the force of these arguments,*

---

* In a sermon preached at the Church of St. Margaret, Brighton, he used the following words :

"Our little band which is about to set forth needs all your sympathy to encourage them. You may depend upon it that it requires some courage to leave home on an expedition of this sort. I speak from personal experience. When all men are against one, saying that one is making a mistake, that he is utterly wrong, that he is running away from the work which God has given him to do, and is seeking other work for himself, no small courage is needed to go forth. But I should not dare to stand up before you if I believed that I were going out to find work for myself. I firmly believe that I have been sent forth by God. From the beginning I have placed the matter in the hands of God. I dare not weigh my own motives or fathom my own heart, but I ask God to guide me by His Holy Spirit. I pray that if God will not go with me He will not let me go."

and, moreover, had four strong personal arguments of
his own which fought mightily against his project—even
a wife and three little children. He was quite aware, also,
that it was possible that his crowded church, large classes,
and flourishing societies *might* not be equally well cared for
by a successor ; but, on the other hand, he knew that it
would be far easier to obtain the services of an able man
for a home parish than to persuade such an one to respond
to the Society's appeal, and to give up almost all hope of
preferment by burying the best years of his life unknown
among the heathen. As he used to say : " There are plenty
of men who would be glad enough to take my place here,
but there are not many who can make up their minds to
sacrifice home and home prospects, and go into the ' dark
places of the earth.' Missionaries are not, like other travellers, held in high esteem. They are looked upon as a
set of inferior clergy, and generally live unnoticed and die
unrewarded. Few men see much attraction in such a
career. When the C. M. S. appealed for more men, I
seemed to hear the Master asking, ' Who will go ? ' and I
said, ' Lord, send *me*.' "

In reply to Mr. Wigram's letter, Hannington wrote :

"HURSTPIERPOINT, *Feb.* 16*th*, 1882.

" DEAR SIR,—Many thanks for your kind letter. I
shall, if nothing prevent, be passing through London Tuesday next, on my way to hold a Mission. May I call upon
you then ?

" I am, in consequence of this, and also having to prepare for a Mission *here* immediately after, so busy that I
cannot well write at the length such a vastly important
subject demands. I am thirty-four. Offered myself only
pro tem., because married. For Nyanza, because I under-

stand that it must necessarily be *pro tem.*,* and because I believe I have a fair amount of experience and, thus far in life, endurance and nerve likely to be useful for such a field. I append a few names of my more immediate friends for reference." (Then follows a list.) "I can give several more if required. I should, however, greatly prefer that none of these were written to until I have had a personal interview with you. For this reason : I have not announced the matter, because I do not want people's minds unsettled, should it fall through from other causes. God forbid I should boast, but I venture to believe that the Committee will be satisfied with the character my friends will give me. I only wish I were more deserving of their kind esteem,

"I am almost weighed down with the great responsibility of my offering myself; but I pray, 'Lord, send me there, or keep me here; only let me be useful;' and I cannot but believe that we shall be rightly guided.

"I am, dear sir, yours truly,

"JAMES HANNINGTON.

"Will you kindly let me know if Tuesday will suit, and the time? I should prefer morning, as I am going to Nottingham (D.V.)."

Whatever may have been Hannington's faults, he was not one of those who, when they see their duty clearly, still "linger with vacillating obedience."

---

* The following extract from a letter to Mr. Cyril Gordon will explain this :

"I volunteer to help in the expedition for Uganda for the following reasons: It is a place where I believe the general experience I have had would be useful, and where I understand Europeans cannot stop very long ; and I do not see my way clear to offer myself for a long term. Say from three to five years."

On Feb. 21st the diary takes up the thread of the narrative :

"Made my will, and proceeded to Oak Hill House, Hampstead, where Mr. Wigram lives, and, after dinner, had a long discussion about my going out as a Missionary. Wigram gave me a most tremendous sounding on all points of the faith.

"*22nd.*—Went to Salisbury Square, and was interviewed by Lang. Dined at the College. G. Chapman came up. 'Are you offering yourself for Africa?' to which I had to make an evasive answer. Interviewed Mr. F. F. Goe.

"*23rd.*—Interview with Barlow.* I am praying that the Medical Board may be directed rightly concerning me. I went to see them, expecting tremendous criticism, but, rather to my disgust, they only asked one or two questions, and turned round and said, ' You are fit to go anywhere.' "

After these preliminaries, Hannington wrote to the Committee from Southwell, where he had gone to see his friend, the Rev. A. C. Garbett.

"SOUTHWELL, *Feb.* 23*rd*, 1882.

"GENTLEMEN,—In answer to your appeal for men, I place myself at your disposal for the Nyanza work for a period of not more than five years, on the condition that you will undertake to supply my place at St. George's Chapel, Hurstpierpoint.

"Though I offer to serve you on these conditions most freely and to the best of the power given me, yet I would earnestly beg you not to accept my services unless you feel that you have urgent need of them.

"Should you ask me to go out, I shall be able to have

---

* Principal of the C. M. S. College at Islington.

£25 quarterly paid to your Treasurer to help to defray my expenses. I shall also be able to pay £50 towards my outfit.

"With humble prayer that your minds may be rightly guided,

"I remain, your obedient servant,

"JAMES HANNINGTON."

St. George's Chapel was now Hannington's own property, but had been left to him by his father wholly unendowed. His own private income was not large enough to allow him to provide an adequate stipend for a Curate-in-Charge; he, therefore, proposed to the Society that they should supply the duty by means of missionaries who had either retired from the field, or who were at home on prolonged leave, while he served abroad. During the five years which he purposed to spend in Mission work, he offered himself to the Committee without other stipend than the payment of his travelling expenses, towards which he was to contribute a hundred pounds yearly.

Had he not felt bound to consider the needs of those who were dependent upon him, and to whom his means belonged, as well as to himself, he would gladly have poured all he had into the treasury, and have gone forth as a simple evangelist to the nations which "lie in darkness and in the shadow of death." On the 6th of March Hannington again visited the C. M. College. He describes the evening thus :—

"Prayer, 5.45. Tea at 6. Dormitory meeting, 8.30. Prayer, 9.30. Bed, 10. The whole atmosphere of the College strikes me as very holy."

"*Mar.* 7th.—Walked with Barlow to Salisbury Square, 12 o'clock. Went in to see the Committee, who accepted my offer, and said they urgently needed my services, and were otherwise most complimentary. Canon Money offered prayer, and I learnt more news in the prayer than I had any idea of. I gathered that I was to be the leader of the party.

"I returned home, and broke the news to my wife. She was more than brave about it, and gave me to the Lord. I had asked her often before, and she had said she would let me go. I had not mentioned my offer before, because she was all alone, and I thought the suspense would be more than she could bear. I also told the Neves, but nobody else, as we have a Mission coming on."

The Committee of the Church Missionary Society was about to send a fresh party to Central Africa to reinforce the brave two * who held the ground at Rubaga, that latest city of martyrs, by the mystic source of the Nile.

King Mtèsa was then alive; he whose bright, intelligent, though fitful nature, had so attracted Speke when he visited his Court, in 1861, and whose qualities made so deep an impression upon Stanley that he wrote, in 1875, a letter to the *Daily Telegraph*, in which he " challenged Christendom to send Missionaries to U-Ganda."

After the manner of African monarchs, Mtèsa did not make things so easy for the missionary band as his warm invitation had seemed to promise. At first he appeared to lend a ready ear to Christian instruction, but his mind was more occupied with the temporal advantages to be derived from contact with Europeans than with their creed. The Arab traders also at his Court, here as everywhere else, did all in their power to poison his mind against the white men. These Arabs are well aware that their miserable traffic in human flesh cannot long prosper where the influence of Englishmen is allowed to prevail. They, therefore, thwart and hinder the European in every conceivable

---

* Mr. A. M. Mackay, C.E., and the Rev. P. O'Flaherty.

manner, and use all their influence with King and chiefs to make his stay in the country impossible. Every traveller, whether missionary, explorer, or man of science, who has attempted to stop for any length of time with a Central African Prince, has felt the malign power and suffered from the treachery of these slave-trading vampires. Before the coming of the Christians, these Arabs had persuaded Mtèsa to profess himself a Mahommedan. They now intrigued without intermission to turn him aside from his apparent inclination to study and adopt the teaching of Christianity.

To add to the ordinary difficulties of implanting the Christian Faith in the soil of savage hearts, the Roman Catholic Church now thought fit to interfere. We do not wish to speak with bitterness of their conduct; but, with almost the whole of the Dark Continent before them, it was surely a gratuitous piece of vexatious harassment that they should send a band of priests for the express purpose of disputing with the English Churchmen the ground which they had already occupied for two years,* and where they were, at last, after most painful effort, beginning to reap what they had sown and watered with their own blood and tears.

These French priests of the Roman Church, coming by way of Zanzibar, and crossing the Lake from Kagei, arrived at U-Ganda in 1879, and took up their abode at Rubaga. They were not content merely to establish a Mission there, but at once informed Mtesa that he had been deluded and mistaught by the Protestants. The poor King was, as may be supposed, reduced to the extremity of perplexity. He would say : " How can I know whom to believe ? I am first taught by the Arabs that there is One God. The English come to tell me that there are *two*, and now I am to learn that there are three ! " (God, Christ, and the Virgin).

---

* Since 1877.

Messrs. Wilson, Felkin, and Pearson were now in U-Ganda, and they persuaded the King to allow them to return by way of the Soudan, taking with them some chiefs, who might be presented to the " Queeny," Her Majesty Queen Victoria, and bring back to their people tidings of what they saw in Europe. Mr. Pearson was left behind, and, together with Mr. Mackay, set up a small printing press, and taught the people to read. They showed quite an enthusiastic readiness to acquire this new accomplishment, and scholars might soon be seen everywhere poring over tablets with alphabets, sentences, and portions of Scripture. These were not given gratis, but were eagerly bought by the lads and others. So the work went on, with sundry ups and downs—the ups being the result of the general goodwill of the people, the downs that of Arab intrigues and Roman misrepresentations—but, on the whole, progressed. In the spring of 1881 the envoys who had been sent to England returned with Mr. Felkin * and the Rev. P. O'Flaherty.† Leaving Mr. Felkin at Zanzibar, Mr. O'Flaherty proceeded to Rubaga, where he remained with Mr. Mackay, and the work of the Church went forward apace. The two missionaries " described themselves as builders, carpenters, smiths, wheelwrights, sanitary engineers, farmers, gardeners, printers, surgeons, and physicians." They were, in the usefullest sense, " All things to all men." They went on transcribing the Bible, Prayer Book, and Hymns into Lu-Ganda at a great rate, and found that the demand for their printed slips was even greater than they could supply.

On March 18th, at the very time when it had been finally decided by the Home Committee to send out Han-

---

* Now Dr. Felkin of Edinburgh.

† Mr. O'Flaherty died on July 21st, 1886, in the Red Sea, as he was returning home.

nington and his party to their reinforcement, they were reaping the first considerable fruits of their labour. Five converts were admitted into the Church by baptism. The first five of a church which two years later, at the end of 1884, consisted of eighty-eight native members. In few Mission stations of modern times have so many hardships, repulses, and perils, with savage persecution, had to be endured; but in few have the results been more rapid, or the conversions of a more solid and abiding character. The history of the Central African Mission, when it is published, will prove to be (whether a permanent Church be established in U-Ganda or not) the romance of modern missions. This book contains an account of Bishop Hannington and his connection with the Mission rather than of the Mission itself, but we shall, in the course of our narrative, be called upon to show how some of these young native Christians have already stood that most awful and bitter test of sincerity, from the very contemplation of which we shrink with shuddering dread and pity, and have confessed to their trust in Christ even in the flames.

The new party was to consist of six men—the Rev. R. P. Ashe, B.A., St. John's College, Cambridge; three of the Islington College Students (the Revs. J. Blackburn, Cyril Gordon, and W. J. Edmonds); and also Mr. C. Wise, an artisan. Hannington was entrusted with the leadership of the expedition. They were to endeavour to reach U-Ganda from Zanzibar by the old route, viâ Mamboia, Uyui, and Msalala, and from thence by boat across the Victoria Nyanza to Rubaga.

When all had been finally arranged, and the time for his departure settled, Hannington made known his determination to his congregation at Hurst.

On March 26th he announced that he would explain his step, and state the reasons which had led to it, at the

evening service. The chapel was thronged. Many wept
aloud; the people would hardly let him go. Some could
not be made to understand that he ought to go. They had
learnt to look upon him as their own. He seemed to them
to be defrauding them of their right in him in thus taking
himself away.

However, there was no appeal. He could not now be
detained, so they determined that they would do their best
to encourage him, and send him forth in a manner that
befitted their own pastor. They were not rich, but they
did what they could, and, among other suitable gifts, subscribed £85 toward his outfit.

As the public mind was at that time directed toward
U-Ganda by Messrs. Wilson and Felkin's book, which had
been very favourably reviewed in the *Times*, Hannington
took advantage of the fact to appeal in the columns of that
paper for subscriptions to enable him to carry with him a
new boat with which to navigate the Victoria Nyanza in
place of the *Daisy*, which had been wrecked. This appeal
was well responded to, and he was able to take out in
sections a good boat, which has since proved of much
service to the Mission band.*

On May 16th a Valedictory Dismissal was held in St.
James's Hall, Paddington. Eleven Missionaries were committed to the care of the Lord of the whole earth, and sent
forth into the regions beyond. Hannington writes: " I, of
course, had to speak when my turn came, but I scarcely
know what I said." That same evening he returned to
Hurst, and preached in the parish church to a great congregation. All who could cram into the building were
there.

One of his friends writes: " It was with a keen sense

---

* Hannington himself subscribed £25 toward this boat.

of severe personal loss that we heard that he had definitely
made up his mind to go out to Central Africa. I well
remember that part of the day when he preached his final
sermon at Hurst. We travelled down together from town
to Hassock's Gate. He gave me a long letter to read
which had been sent home by one of the missionaries from
Mtèsa's country. All the way down he had been preparing
the farewell sermon which he was to deliver that evening in
the parish church. It was one of the most earnest and
effective addresses to which I have ever listened, and evoked
a thrill of emotion through the whole of the densely-
crowded audience. The text was 1 Sam. xxx. 24, '*As his
share is that goeth down to the battle, so shall his share be
that tarrieth by the stuff; they shall share alike.*' With
characteristic humility he spoke of the time when he first
came among them, hot-headed and inexperienced ; told us
things against himself, which he never laid to the charge of
others, and said how kindly they had all borne with him.
And he added words which must now dwell in many
memories : that if it should be that he lost his life in Africa,
no man was to think that his life had been wasted. As for
the lives which had been already given for this cause, they
were not lost, but were filling up the trench so that others
might the more easily pass over to take the fort in the name
of the Lord."

After the sermon he found a great crowd waiting outside
the church to receive him, and his hand was wrung by
friends and acquaintances who formed one continuous double
line all the way to his own house. He did not get away from
their embraces until past midnight. Early the same morning — for he saw the last of his friends at 12.30 a.m.—
he left for the docks ; but as the diary here becomes more
circumstantial, we may continue the narrative in his own
words.

"*May* 17*th.*—Up at 5 a.m., though I had everything well prepared. Ah, what a heavy heart I had. I longed now to be away, for the worst was yet to come. The pound of flesh, blood and all, must be cut away. First, my dear mother-in-law, not the mother of my youth, but of my manhood, loved with a man's affection. She remained in her own room, and was the first of the home circle to receive the stab. How brave she was; and she, of all, feels that she has least chance of seeing me again. We parted calmly. Next my boy, Tom Lewry, who has served me so lovingly —he wished to say good-bye to me alone ; and then, passionately flinging his arms around my neck, implored me not to leave him. Next was the meeting at family prayers ; how I got through it I do not know. Then dear Mr. Boxall came, so faithful, so silent. Good-bye to him meant all that it could possibly convey. Now came, of all my affectionate friends, H. B. For a month I had seen him nearly every day, and every time, I think, without exception, he has burst into tears about my going, and has offered to work his passage to Zanzibar if I would let him follow me. Now my most bitter trial—an agony that still cleaves to me— saying good-bye to the little ones. Thank God that all the pain was on one side. Over and over again I thank Him for that. ' Come back soon, papa ! ' they cried. Then the servants, all attached to me. My wife, the bravest of all. . . . .

" I was about to jump into my brother's carriage. The publican's son (I was always thought to be the publican's enemy) crept up, and thrust a letter into my hand, a pretty book-marker, and a text, and a letter written by his mother. The thing that broke me down was passing a building. The roughest of the rough men, who I thought would have had a holiday to rejoice at my departure, left work, and crowded round to express their sorrow as best they could ; several were at the train on the platform. Then came two hours quiet, but quiet just then to me was terrible. I rushed to Salisbury Square to see if there were any parting message, and was well rewarded by Wigram saying: ' I felt certain that you would find time to look in once more ; you are ubiquitous.' How the Lord helped me. Surely if I wanted a parting sign to hasten me forward, it was to be found in the great support He gave me. I had thought that preaching in a crowded church, people blocking my way along the road and clinging around me, four hours sleep, and such a leave-taking, would have given me a severe headache and feeling of lassitude. I was, however, entirely free from any bodily pain or weariness, and I had not experienced such freshness for a month. The fountain of my tears seemed held back. I have not said that dearest Sam, the best of brothers, came with me to Salisbury Square. He had been skirmishing about, putting continual extra touches to my already comfortable kit. Now, from Liverpool Street to the docks, he began emptying his pockets of money and forcing little articles of comfort upon me. Then there was the bustle of the ship, and the saying good-bye on the part of others to their relations, for only mine were allowed to go as far as Gravesend. Then came the final farewell to my brother. . . . I watched and watched and watched the retreating tow-boat, until I could see it no longer, and then hurried down below. Indeed, I felt for the moment as one paralyzed. . . . Now was the time for re-action ! No. ' Casting all your care upon Him.' . . . I went below, and set my cabin in order for sea, arranged about prayers, etc., and the rest of the day passed so rapidly that, when night came, I scarcely knew it was gone. ' My God, how tender Thou art ! "

PART II.

CHAPTER XIII.

THE FIRST MISSIONARY JOURNEY. ZANZIBAR TO MPWAFWA.

(1882.)

"So in life ; if some wifeling or childling be granted you, well and good ; but if the Captain call, run to the Ship, and leave such possessions behind you, not looking back."

EPICTETUS.—FARRAR (*Seekers after God*).

As Hannington's journal from this date onward is written much more fully and consecutively, and is, moreover, supplemented by long letters to the Church Missionary Society, we shall be able to continue the narrative to a great extent in his own words. He writes :

"I must leave the farewells. I have not sufficient cold blood in my veins to make red ink enough to write them.

"On May the 17th, 1882, at about noon, I found myself on board the s.s. *Quetta*, a fine Clyde-built ship of 3200 tons, and began to make inquiries about our party. Mr. Ashe was on board, but nobody seemed to know anything about the others. The authorities were in a great state of perturbation, as time and tide wait for no man. I could not help feeling a little nervous when I heard that we were to start for Gravesend without them, and leave a tug in which they might, if possible, overtake us. To my great relief they came steaming up behind us about an hour later." In a letter to the children he adds, " But didn't they catch it from one Captain Brown, who was sent to look after them ! Brown ! They say he was *black*, and his tongue the same colour. And, poor things, it was not their fault at all. There had been an accident on the railway." He continues :

"My companions were the Rev. R. P. Ashe, W. J. Edmonds, J. Blackburn, and E. C. Gordon, with Mr. C. Wise, an artisan. I had also on the ticket the names of Mr. and Mrs. H. W. Lane, who were bound for Mombasa, and Miss ———, a bride who was to meet her bridegroom at Zanzibar. The latter was placed specially under my charge, but I am afraid that the principal way in which I fulfilled my task was by teasing her unmercifully about the bride-cake, which I unfortunately discovered to be on board.

"We had not many fellow passengers on board the *Quetta.* And of these the majority were going to the mission field. Ten L. M. S. men for Lake Tanganyika, all dissenters of different shades of opinion, though chiefly Congregationalists. There was also a Major Smith, Secretary of the Wesleyan M. S., travelling for his health, and, lastly, a Miss Angus, of the Baptist Zenana Society. We thus had many persuasions represented ; and—will you believe it ?—we all dwelt together and parted in peace and friendship.

"On the first night I went to the captain, and made a request for public prayers, which was at once granted.

"Our first morning we held a C. M. S. Council, and have mapped out our day as follows : Private devotions before breakfast. Prayer. Then Wise is to read with Ashe. Edmonds, Gordon, and Blackburn take the boys, and I help Lane. The rest of the morning is spent in studying Swahili.* After lunch we have a meeting for

---

* The language of the coast, and widely known in the interior through intercourse with the traders.

reading and prayer, and the rest of the day is to be improved as we best may be able.

"We have a little pleasant banter with the L. M. S. men. Their expedition is fitted out so much more expensively than ours. They eclipse us in every point. We have to glory in the fact that so much less money has been expended on us, when we would have been permitted to have had more, had we desired it. I feel sure we have enough.* Only may the Spirit of God go with us every step of the way.

"The only cloud that hangs over us at present is the unpleasant suggestion that we may not reach Aden in time to carry on our cargo. The poor bride is in despair, as the bridal outfit is in the hold!"

Hannington wrote his first letter to the Secretary of the C. M. S. from the Mediterranean, and says : "Give me as much advice as possible, and do not ever hesitate to point out my faults and shortcomings ; in so doing, you will be more than ever my friend. Do not expect too much of me. It may be that my share of the work is already done. I think most highly of Ashe ; † should I fail, you will be better represented. God be praised for raising him up to come among us."

Hannington was always ready to express a generous appreciation of the merits of others. In his letter to the Secretary, he has a special word of commendation for each of his companions, and adds with regard to himself, "There

---

* As it turned out, they had not ; and many of their sufferings were due to want of a few extras.

† Mr. Ashe was afterwards stationed in U-Ganda, where he has one through the troublous times which followed the death of Mtèsa.

is only one wretch among the six, and if he is taken away it will be no great loss."

At Aden the whole party for Central Africa were transported into "a dirty old vessel called the *Mecca* ; dirty is not a strong enough word, so I must use *filthy*. She swarmed with cockroaches, black ants and bugs, and was, moreover, dreadfully overcrowded." The vessel was only 1200 tons, or less than half the size of the *Quetta*, and was packed with passengers. The food, accommodation, and management all seem to have rivalled each other in badness. They soon fell in with rough weather and heavy seas, which rendered their position, uncomfortable before, now almost intolerable. Hannington, old sailor as he was, was prostrated with sea-sickness. He says : "I was washed down to leeward twice, and was wet for three days, without any opportunity of changing."

It was in a shattered and dilapidated condition that they made out the Island of Zanzibar, on June 19th, and steamed into the calmer waters of the sheltered roadstead.

Soon, he says, "Mr. Stokes, our travelling companion, came on board, and gave us a hearty welcome. He is to take charge of our caravan. And now about Zanzibar. I had been prepared to find a disgusting place, full of half-starved slaves and beggars, but was never more agreeably surprised in my life. I do not think that I was asked for anything more than once. The streets are narrow, crooked, weird, and some of them dirty, but not half so bad as I had been led to expect. Not worse, I should say, than Genoa, ' the beautiful.' The many quaint sights more than atoned for the few disagreeables. Outside the town, the tropical vegetation, often standing out, on a gentle slope, against the clear, blue sky, or backed by the deeper blue of the sea, presented wonderful pictures of green freshness."

Hannington saw a good deal of the members of the Universities' Mission, by whom he was most kindly received and welcomed. He says : " I preached in the Cathedral on Sunday evening, as a slight return for the many kindnesses which the Universities' Mission have shown us. They had a special Communion for our party in the morning."

The short time spent at Zanzibar was very busily occupied in packing and preparing for the journey. Although Mr. Stokes had relieved Hannington of much of the trouble of collecting porters and goods for the interior, yet the Mission stores which he had brought from England had to be made up into suitable loads of fifty-five or sixty pounds, and all had to be inventoried and weighed to prevent the bearers from stealing the contents of their packs. The African traveller has still to go about, carrying with him a miscellaneous assortment of articles, more or less bulky, with which to purchase food, pay tribute, hire extra assistance, etc., etc. It will be indeed a blessing and an economy of labour when the rupee has found its way into circulation among the tribes of the interior.

The Zanzibari are notorious for their dilatory habits and lethargic indifference to the hurrying of the traveller impatient to be gone. They made no exception to their rule for Hannington's benefit. He writes :

" This is the style of thing. At 6 a.m. you want a package sewn up in canvas. A man promises to send for a Hindu at once. You wait patiently for half an hour, then you think that you had better go and see, and you find that he did not realize that you wanted him so quickly ; however,

he will now send at once. In fact, you see the messenger
start. About an hour later he enters the yard, and you jump
up. He, on the contrary, sits down very complacently, and
wonders why you bounded up so energetically. You
explain what you want. He still sits and looks first at you,
then at your package, and measures both accurately with his
intelligent eye. By-and-by he actually rises and measures
the package, this time with tape. Then he once more
squats and chews betel nut with an activity that you wish
he would apply to your job; and then, in about a quarter of
an hour, he departs to get his needle and thread, promising
to return instantly. It is now about 9.30, and you are
summoned to breakfast, for which you are quite ready. On
your arrival upstairs you find that nobody else has come, so
you drop into the empty arm-chair, and wait with the best
patience you may have. In an hour's time the party has
assembled, expressed its various apologies, and in another
hour has finished its breakfast. On your arrival in the
yard, you find the Hindu has arrived, but has quietly waited
for you to tell him where to begin. So, having stated your
opinion at length with great pains and with many signs, you
are pleased to find that he pooh-poohs your notions, and
prefers his own way; at the same time he reminds you that
it is now noon, the hour that he dines, and that he will
return afterwards. 1 p.m., lunch time. At 2 o'clock you
return, package progressing, but just at that moment a
messenger enters the yard; the Hindu is especially wanted
for a short time. It is quite 3.30 before that package is
finished. Thus, and sometimes worse than thus—did we
have to battle our way, bale by bale, through an immense
amount of packing."

Before he started for the interior, Hannington sought
an interview with the Sultan, Seyyid Barghash. He

had been told that the Sultan was becoming alarmed at the large number of European missionaries who passed through Zanzibar, but however this may have been, he was received very warmly and with distinguished courtesy.

Dressed in full academicals—scarlet hood and Master's gown—and escorted by the pro-Consul, Col. Miles, he made his way to the palace. There a guard of honour was drawn up, and the Sultan came down into the square with much state, and greeted the young English clergyman. He then led the way up those steep stairs, which Mr. Johnston has so graphically described, into his reception room. After all were seated, and glass cups of coffee and sherbet served, the Sultan engaged Hannington in conversation as to his journey and its object. He writes: "After about half an hour the Consul said we must be going, otherwise I think that His Highness would gladly have prolonged the interview. Conversation never flagged for a moment, although, as far as I was concerned, it was carried on through an interpreter. When we left, he rose, led the way into the square, and, shaking hands, wished us good-bye. He was very interested in our expedition. His credulity is surprising. He firmly believes in a gigantic snake in U-Gogo, which is reputed to reach to the sky, and to devour oxen and women and children whole ! "

Hannington made rapid progress with his study of the Swahili language. He says: "I have this morning commenced daily prayers in Swahili. Henry Wright Duta, the baptized Waganda boy attached to me, read them. The study which I gave the language on board has been of immense help to me. Let every missionary be urged to stick close to the language he has to learn on his journey out, in spite of all obstacles."

When all was ready for the start, Mr. Stokes first crossed

to Saadani * with the greater part of the caravan, and on the next day, June 27th, the missionaries followed. Hannington says :

" I went round to Mackenzie's and was greeted with ' You can't go to-day.' ' Why not ? ' ' Fifteen men have run away, and they must be looked after.' However, on looking over Stokes' letter I could not see that he said they were to be hunted up, and so I replied that we should start at once. Then I found where the difficulty arose. Raschid, who had brought the letter, wanted a day on his own account, which I soon informed him he could not have. I ordered a dhow for noon, and by intense energy, actually got everything ready by 1.30.

" I am not going to describe that dhow. It was as bad as most other dhows, and we were packed so closely that if one fell there he had to lie. When we arrived off Saadani we found that the tide was high and that the shore could not be approached nearer than half a mile. The sea was pretty rough, and as we grounded we bumped so furiously that I expected the poor old dhow would have gone to pieces. Stokes plunged through the breakers from the shore and brought out a small dug-out canoe which was, at best, a quarter full of water. I preferred a swimming to a foot-bath, and so, stripping off my clothes, and putting them into a bag, unmindful of sharks, I waded and stumbled over the half mile of sharp coral which lay between our vessel and the beach. In due time, after repeated voyages by the canoe, we all got safely ashore, and found our tents pitched, and a tough goat, that unfailing accompaniment of an African meal, awaiting us."

The next day was spent in getting the men into their

* The channel between Zanzibar and the mainland is about thirty miles.

places and organizing generally. On the following morning
at sunrise the long line of porters wended its way along the
narrow track which led toward the interior. At first their
way lay through country which, but for the tropical nature
of the vegetation, would have reminded the new comers of
a path through an English wood ; then through long grass,
thickly strewn with mimosa trees, till they reached their first
camp at Ndumi. The porters were, as usual, while desertion
to the coast was still easy, very troublesome, and occasioned
the most vexatious delays by their insubordination and slug-
gishness. They made the first night or two hideous with
their cries and songs, and tried to get the rest out of which
they had thus defrauded themselves during the following
working day. Mr. Stokes' long experience in dealing with
the natives here proved invaluable, and matters mended after
a bit.

At Ndumi they had their first experience of the horrors
of an African well. " You might cut the water with a
knife. An English cow or an Irish sow would have turned
from it. However, it boiled well, and added body to our
tea ! " Writing to his children he says : " I had seen ' green
tea,' but never before green coffee. I soon grew tired of
grumbling because the men would bathe in our drinking
water, but I did not like to find there dead toads and other
animal and vegetable putrefaction. Afterwards, when weak
and ill, I used to avoid drinking any liquid. I have been
three and even four days at a stretch without drinking anything at all."

On Sunday the caravan rested at a camp called Mkangi,
" a beautiful spot where we greatly enjoyed our quiet Services. We also had two Kiswahili Services for the boys,
and at the close of the day felt much refreshed, and ready to
proceed with our journey."

On the 8th of July they reached the river Buzini,

" Loud had been the warnings of Stokes that we should not wade through the stream lest we should take fever. One man, at least, had nearly died here from his imprudence in this respect. In consequence of this we were all full of caution. When I arrived I was very hot, and should not, under any circumstances, have thought of entering the water until I was somewhat cooler. The headmen had not yet come up, and I was waiting for them, when my boys volunteered to carry me across. This was a task clearly beyond their powers; but the ambitious Johar was not to be denied. He seized me and bore me off in triumph. When we got into the water I felt an ominous totter and told him to return. But I entreated in vain; he paid no heed. More staggering about, and entreaties, but all to no purpose, on he pressed. Swaying to and fro like a bullrush in a gale of wind, I clenched my teeth and held my breath. They shouted from the bank for Johar to return, but it had not the slightest effect; he felt that his only chance now was to dash right on. We were now in mid-stream, and my hopes revived. I thought, perhaps———. But the water grew deeper, the rocks at the bottom became more slippery, the stream grew stronger. A frantic struggle, and down we went flat, Johar collapsing like an indiarubber ball punctured by a pin. Far better would it have been for me had I walked through, for then I should have been wet merely to the knees, whereas now I was soaked from head to foot. Happily I did not get fever, though I had some symptoms of it shortly after."

The following day gave them a taste of the kind of adventures for which they must prepare in Africa. It was Sunday, and they were resting after the services of the day, when Hannington, who was busy with some sick folk, noticed smoke, and soon saw that the high grass around the camp was in a blaze. Not a moment was to be lost. The grass was as dry as tinder and the encampment was in the utmost danger. All hands were called up, some were set to work to beat down the flames, while others struck the tents and took the baggage to a place of safety. "It was splendid to see the flames and to hear the crackling of leaves and grass, and the shouting and screaming of the excited men." After some trouble the fire was beaten out and the men returned to camp to rest themselves after their exertions, or *seemed* to do so, but in reality they nurtured quite other designs. They had discovered that the grass had been maliciously fired by the inhabitants of a neighbouring village. So each man quietly got possession of his weapon—gun, spear, or bow and arrows—and stole away to take vengeance and burn that village to the ground !

A whisper of this reached Mr. Stokes' ears, and at once "he ran off as if he were shot, crying out excitedly in the strongest Irish brogue, 'Write it down in ye diaries, gintlemin; me min have gone to burrn the village, and I can't stop thim.' I did not wait," says Hannington, "to get out my notebook to jot this down at the time, but tore after him as fast as I could, and we, with the assistance of the headmen, many of whom are chiefs, succeeded in stopping them. Only one man had been wounded with a war club in the head. I took him back to my own tent and bound up his head, and, better still, gave him a dollar. So all was over for that time. Congratulating ourselves that all had ended so well, we sat down to dinner. But we had more in store for us. We were discussing some of the never-changing goat soup, when the cry of fire was again raised. Off we dashed. This time the fire was simply terrific. The grass grew far over one's head, and there were, too, a number of palm trees with dead leaves attached to their trunks, which carried the flames high into the air. These conflagrations can only be got under by following them up from behind, and beating them with green boughs down the wind. It was enough to make one shrink and quail to dash through the raging furnace to reach its rear. But through we went, and the next moment the battle began. It was simply glorious. The naked figures of the men, leaping, yelling, and dashing about like so many hundred demons ; the roar of the fire almost drowning the cries of ' Piga moto ' (Beat down the fire) ; the lambent flames and the dense rolling volumes of smoke formed a wonderful plutonic picture. In the midst of it all the white men, scorched and dripping with perspiration, urged on the workers with all their lung power. While the confusion was at its height, I came across Stokes, who had attacked the enemy from another flank. He had fallen into a hole and was rather badly shaken, and did not get over it for some time afterwards. At last we conquered."

The London Missionary Society party were close at hand, as the two caravans journeyed together as far as Uyui. This was not always an advantage to either, since it was hard to supply so large a body of men with food on the route ; but on the present occasion the conjunction was a happy one, and the united forces, amounting to some five hundred men, were brought to bear, all together, upon the common enemy.

On July 17th, almost all the party were visited by a worse enemy than fire. All except Mr. Edmonds were laid low by the dreaded fever, that scourge of African travellers. The attacks were slight, but, in Hannington's case, often repeated. He was soon to make a closer acquaintance with this and other of the horrors that beset the southern route to the great Lake.

On the 21st they reached Mamboia, a C. M. Station, where they were heartily welcomed by Mr. and Mrs. Last. Hannington describes the station as well situated :—

"The house, or bungalow, is prettily placed on the side of the mountain, at about 3000 feet above sea-level, and commands most extensive and beautiful views. Immediately on the west side rises a precipitous cliff, in which a grand old eagle has its eyrie; to the east the mountains form an amphitheatre, and bold jutting crags add a wildness to the scene; all that it lacks to make it surpassingly beautiful is water.

"The soil is most productive, and the climate sub-Alpine, so that our English vegetables grow to great perfection. The flower-garden in front of the house was a mass of geraniums, nasturtiums, petunias, etc. Next to the house stood the Church—a very original structure. Circular mud walls had been built to the height of about six feet, which were covered by a deep sloping roof, open in the centre, from which rose wooden stancheons, which again supported a cap-roof—thus an open space was left between the two roofs for ventilation. Pews were not required. The congregation preferred to sit on the ground, and two chairs sufficed for the Europeans. The people are attentive to hear, and send their children to the school.

"On the 25th we were fain to proceed, our friends going with us some little distance. But at length a river sent them back. With many heart achings, for partings here seem hard to make, we said farewell. With one, Mrs. Last, we were to meet no more on this side the stream of death."

The next station was Mpwapwa.

On the way thither, Hannington had a very narrow escape of losing his life. He fell into one of those treacherous pitfalls which the natives set so cleverly for game. His gun was in his hand, and at full cock, but he had the presence of mind to let himself go, and think chiefly of his rifle, which, happily, did not explode. His terrified boy peered over the edge with dreadful anticipations, as there are often spears at the bottom of such traps, so set that any animal falling in is impaled. He was relieved by hearing, "There are no spears," and helped his shaken and bruised, but, providentially, unbroken master out. This pitfall was not less than ten feet deep.

There was also an alarm of Ruga-ruga (robbers), which excited everybody, but when they saw the impetuous white man rushing to the front, the marauders fled, and left him master of the field. As they drew near to Mpwapwa, Hannington went ahead of the caravan, and pushed forward with only a few attendants, as he was very desirous to have a long conversation with Dr. Baxter, who was residing there, and to avail himself of his knowledge of certain facts of which he desired to inform himself accurately. He says :—

" The others did not reach the station until the 29th, but I made a double march, and arrived there on the 28th, as I wished to have as much time as possible with Dr. Baxter. I have had much conversation with him on the subject of ———, but have not received any very definite advice. Should I live to reach my destination, the Lord will provide. We received news from Copplestone of the sad accident to Dr. Southon,* and of his amputating his arm. The brethren at Rubaga were well up to Feb. 19th."

At Kisokwe, near Mpwapwa, Mr. and Mrs. Cole had

---

* Dr. Southon, of the L. M. S., had been shot accidentally by his gun-bearer, and his arm shattered above the elbow. Mr. Copplestone, after many days, reached him, and received instructions how to amputate the limb. Dr. Southon then gave himself chloroform, and the operation was performed. Though he had never attempted such a thing before, Mr. Copplestone carried out his instructions very skilfully ; but the operation was performed too late, and his patient, to the great loss of the Mission, died.

established themselves, with their little baby—the latter an object of wonder and delight to all the people around, who had never seen a white baby before. Hannington says in one of his diaries :—

"Both Mr. and Mrs. Cole are earnest and devoted Missionaries. Mrs. Cole has a large Sunday School Class. Its members form such a quaint group ! I should like my friends at home to look in upon them some Sunday afternoon. Some were very gaudily clothed in all sorts of bright colours, some merely in goat skins. Others, again, were red with war-paint, and carried bows and arrows or spears. Altogether, it would be difficult to imagine a more queer yet picturesque group of children; and yet, for all this funny appearance, they were very respectful and orderly, and tried to learn the great lessons which Mrs. Cole endeavours to teach them about the Saviour of the world."

Writing to the C. M. S. Committee, he says : "We are resting to-day, Aug. 1st, at Khambe, a day's march from Mpwapwa. The reason for these rests is that we are waiting for the boat to gain upon us, and catch us up, in order to save hongo (tribute). But I do not personally believe in rests, either for masters or men." (The boat had been, perforce, left behind, through lack of porters to carry it.) "We have now some very hard work before us ; nearly twenty-four hours' march to-morrow."

"I am very happy. Fever is trying, but it does not take away the joy of the Lord, and keeps one low *in the right place.*"

CHAPTER XIV.

MPWAPWA TO UYUI.

(1882.)

"It grieves me, too, Lord! that so many should wander,
  Should see nought before them but desolate night,
That men should be walled in with darkness around them,
  When within and without there is nothing but light."
                                                    FABER.

DURING the march the African traveller has little time or
opportunity to indulge his taste for collecting. All through
the weary day he plods steadily on, nor dares to loiter, lest
he should fail to reach his camp and watering place by
nightfall. When at length tents are pitched, and camp-
fires lighted, he has scarce energy to write up his journal,
but flings himself down to snatch what brief rest he can
before the inevitable *reveillé* of the next sun or moon.*

Hannington made the best of his time during the short
halt near Mpwapwa. He scoured the district to make a
collection of its flora and fauna, specimens of which he preserved and packed to be sent home. Much of this, and
what follows, he describes in the interesting articles which
he wrote for the *Churchman* in 1883—4. We shall not
attempt to catalogue the results of his research, or our space
would wholly fail. It is enough to say that he brought back

---

* This when crossing desert districts. Even on days when
tents are pitched at 10 or 11 a.m. little energy is left to brave the
sun's rays after a long march through the night and early morning
hours.

with him, and sent to the British Museum, a large collection
of birds and insects, and that a valuable selection of mosses
and plants were forwarded to Mr. Mitten, of Hurstpierpoint,
for classification.

While hunting for specimens at Mpwapwa, with Dr.
Baxter, he says : " We suddenly came into the midst of an
enormous caravan of black ants, and although we fled as
fast as our legs would carry us, we suffered severely. The
noise these ants made on the march, as they went by in
their countless myriads, was like a kind of hissing roar, and
the dry bed of the stream in which we were was covered
with them as far as the eye could reach."

Hannington was well bitten on this and many subsequent
occasions, but his zeal for collecting was not to be damped
by any such trifling misadventures. While botanizing on
the Usagara mountains, he encountered a beautiful but most
malignant bean, the pod of which is densely covered with
short red hairs, which enter the skin and cause the acutest
agony. He says : " When I first seized the tempting bait
I was nearly driven mad with pain, and was a long time
discovering the source of the mischief ; for, unlike the nettle,
which stings at once, this venemous pod does not develop
its evil effects until some time afterwards." *

He described to me an ant which was in the habit of
crawling as far as possible up the leg of its victim before
biting him, when suddenly the unfortunate who was thus
outraged appeared to his friends as though he were attacked
by some violent and uncontrollable internal pain, as he
clapped his hand to the part affected and rushed off to un-
dress and dislodge the fiery little assailant. Truly the
naturalist in Africa needs to be a man of courage !

The road to Khambe lies through dense forest of the

---

* This pod used to be employed—perhaps still is—in tormenting
criminals. Its application soon produces raving madness.

shadeless order, and over very stony ground. All were
thoroughly tired out, and looked forward to rest when they
reached their camping ground. When they had climbed
to the summit of the Pass above Khambe they looked
eagerly down and searched with their eyes for the tents, but
no camp was to be seen. A tempestuous wind was raging
below, whirling before it clouds of dust. The camp fires
had all been scattered and extinguished ; the men had taken
refuge in a deep trench which formed the course of a
mountain torrent ; nothing was to be seen but the long
driving of the dusty winds. Hannington says : " Two of
the tents were already down, while the others were fast getting adrift. Volumes of dust were swamping beds, blankets,
boxes, buckets—everything ; a more miserable scene could
scarcely be beheld by a band of benighted pilgrims. There
was no use in staring at it. As for myself, I seized a
hammer, and set to work on the tent pegs, and soon forgot
that I was tired. By and by we got things to rights, but
that night we slept in a dust heap. This is the kind of
thing all the way through U-Gogo. It is bad enough in a
hot climate to have dust in your hair and down your neck ;
but when every mouthful of food grates your teeth, I leave
you to imagine the amenities of tent-life in a sandy plain."

From Khambe a very trying march of forty miles lay
before them across the desert of Marenga Mkali to the next
halting place at Pero, the frontier town of U-Gogo. Darkness fell shortly after five o'clock with that suddenness
peculiar to the tropics, and which Coleridge has so vividly
described :

> " The sun's rim dips ; the stars rush out ;
> At one stride comes the dark."

They were in the midst of dense tangle overhead, with
rough stony ground below. For three miserable hours they
stumbled onward, not without many cuts and bruises, until

eight o'clock, when a halt was called, huge camp fires
lighted, and a few hours' sleep obtained.   At 1 a.m. the
drum summoned the sleepers, and the yawning caravan was
again put in motion.   The diary continues : " We were
not alone in this desert place.   I thought that I heard
voices.   This was doubted at the time, but when we
resumed our march we came upon smouldering fires scarce
a hundred yards distant.   When we numbered our men at
the journey's end one of them was missing, and the search
party discovered a pool of blood where he had evidently been
killed.   He must have straggled behind, and been set upon
and robbed of his load."

Their adventures were not yet over.   " When the sun
rose, and the heat began to increase, we found ourselves
very weary.   Presently three shots were heard, and the cry
of ' Ruga-Ruga ! ' (robbers) ran down the line like wildfire.
The men, especially the warlike Wa-Sukuma, roused
themselves in a moment ; their headman begged me to see
to the piling up of the loads while he and his chief men ran
to the battle.   What a transformation !   Mild-eyed, gentle-
looking blacks appeared as altered men ; their nostrils were
dilated, their eyes flashed fire, and every muscle quivered
with excitement as they dashed past eager for the fray.
It was more than I could stand.   I deputed the care of the
baggage to more peaceful brethren, seized my gun, and advanced toward the scene of action.   After all it turned out
to be a false alarm.   A disappointment to the Wa-Sukuma !
We found out afterwards that it was a got-up thing by the
wily Stokes.   Seeing that the men flagged, and were nearly
worn out, he thought that a little excitement might have a
good effect ; and so it had.   Not knowing the imposture,
we all revived and marched on with a will, and at 11.30 a.m.
reached Pero."

From Pero the men were hard to move.   Much persuasion, and the promise of a short march, got them as far as the next camp. Here " the water was desperately bad. A deep well was the only resource, and this was full of dead toads and rats, which putrified there. No filtering or boiling availed to make it drinkable. It smelt abominably; all food cooked in it was flavoured by it." It is not surprising that on the following Sunday, August the 6th, Hannington developed symptoms of fever. He determined to try and walk it off. On the previous day he had seen three lions, and had followed them into some dense bush, where they were lost; he now, though without his rifle, turned his steps in that direction, taking Mr. Gordon, his nephew, with him. He had not gone far when the fever laid hold upon him, and he staggered back with difficulty to his tent. That evening his temperature reached 110°, and he was seized with violent rigors, and then with alarming fainting fits. The others were most kind and attentive, and the hospital donkey was made ready for him next day. However, he insisted that he was able to walk, and, with that wonderful unselfishness of his, in a land where every selfish characteristic of the traveller seems called into active play, placed a weary companion upon the beast instead.

The next camp was little better. A frightful stench pervaded the air, as of animal putrefaction. They named it " Dead Man's Camp." Here Hannington was again put on the rack by another terrible attack of fever. He says : " Fever is not always agonizing, but sometimes, as on the present occasion, it is accompanied by violent sickness, intense pain in every limb, and burning thirst. I had nothing to drink, and my tongue was so hard and dry, that when I touched it with my finger, it made a noise like scraping a file." As he could not be allowed to remain there, and was now too feeble to stand, he was placed in a hammock and carried by two men.

Even in the midst of intense suffering he never lost his sense of the humorous.

He says : " The curiosity of the natives in these parts was unbounded ; they swarmed round our tents from morning to night. The men were quite naked, but for a short cloak of goat skin, which reached to the waist, and their bodies besmeared with red ochre. The women were clothed, and covered with copper and iron chains, which were quite becoming. The lobes of their ears were distended, and made to hold all sorts of things, from an old

cartridge case to a block of wood as large as the cork of a gooseberry bottle. Sometimes the lobes break down, so that, to their immense regret, they can wear nothing in them. I have often been asked to mend their ears ; but, although I could easily have done it by nipping off the ends where they were broken and binding them together, I always refused to encourage their vanity.

" The inquisitive Wa-Gogo followed us in swarms as we marched, like the people at home running after a drum-and-fife band. The vexing part of it was that they seemed to think us far more curious than they were and not nearly so enlightened, or civilized, or fashionably dressed. Nor, indeed, were we in those parts. But that was not easy to recollect."

The sketch represents his tent. One native, who cannot get a view, is supposed to be saying: "I shall abide my time; I daresay he isn't worth much;" while from the crowd issue cries of "Did you ever see such a creature?" "No, we never did!!!" "What are those things on his eyes? are they horns growing?" To his young friends at home he wrote: "Fancy a set of hideous savages regarding your uncle as a strange, outlandish creature, frightful to behold! 'Are those your feet, Whiteman?' 'No, gentlemen, they are not. They are my sandals.' 'But, do they grow to your feet?' 'No, gentlemen, they do not; I will show you.' So I would unlace a boot. A roar of astonishment followed when they saw my blue sock, as they thought my feet must be blue and toeless. I pulled off the sock, and they were dumbfounded at the sight of my white, five-toed foot. They used to think that only my face and hands were white, and the rest of me black like themselves. My watch, too, was an unfailing attraction. 'There is a man in it.' 'It is Lubari; it is witchcraft,' they would cry. 'He talks; he says Teek, teek, teek.' My nose they would compare with a spear, it struck them as so sharp and thin as compared with their own. Often one would give my hair a smart pull to try whether it were a wig, and would come off."

The Wa-Gogo have an ill repute for their treatment of travellers, but Hannington took a decided fancy to them, and thought that he saw in them certain manly characteristics which might be won to the service of his Lord. He noted, however, that as yet, though they watched the white men at worship, they themselves showed little or no interest in the Gospel message.

He writes : " By the 21st of August we had passed through U-Gogo without having paid hongo (tribute), a triumph of African travel." The system of blackmailing is one of the great hindrances to travel in the interior, and is a heavy tax upon both the time and resources of a caravan. On this occasion Mr. Stokes tried a new route, and they escaped without the usual trouble.

By the commencement of September the caravan was within a short distance of Uyui, where there is a C. M. Station. During the whole time Hannington had never been free from fever, but he had marched resolutely on, and kept determinedly to his own feet so long as they would carry him. He was the life and soul of the party, and never let his companions' spirits flag. This is how he describes the incidents of a march :

" Take it as a rule you start at sunrise, which is often so gorgeous that it defies description. During the early hours herds of antelope bound into the thicket at your approach. Wild boar, giraffe, fresh tracks of elephants, but never elephants themselves, are met with.

" Presently you enter dense tangle, so thick that it seems to defy even the wild beasts to penetrate it. No view is to be had. The pathway itself is, at times, quite hidden ; and yet, in the dry season, the leafless boughs form no protection against the burning rays of the sun. Now we come upon the dry bed of a pool, and I discover a shell that I have never seen before. It considerably enlivens me, and the next mile passes without a murmur.

" Then a shriek of joy. ' Elephants ? ' ' No, or I should not have made a noise ! ' ' Giraffe ? ' ' No.' ' Water ? ' ' No.' ' Well, *what ?* ' ' A Tortula.' ' What's that ? A snake ? ' ' No ; a moss ; haven't seen a vestige of moss for a hundred miles.' ' *Oh !* ' with an emphasis that no explanation will exactly convey. Afterwards, 'Ona Bwana, mbuzu!' ('See, master, a baobab tree.') | Ah, yes, sure enough, standing out in solitary grandeur, there it is, and that means water, and a halt for the night."

On August 26th he writes : "Gordon and I started early to take advantage of the cool hours. We saw many nice sights which we should otherwise have missed, as the beasts were still moving. More than once hyænas of the yellow variety crossed our path, nor did they appear to notice us. By and by we came upon skulls, broken boxes, and other signs of a fight with robbers. An eagle flapped lazily across the path. He, too, had had his share of the spoil ; and of the fight also—for he would have to battle for his portion with the jackals and hyænas. It was a ghastly sight, and inclined us for a moment to think that it might be wise to wait until the caravan came up."

On the 30th, they rested for a day at Itura. The Wa-Nyamwezi women determined to honour them with a national dance, and as Hannington was Bwana Mkubwa (great master), they arranged themselves in ranks before his tent for the purpose. They danced him nearly to death. No remonstrances availed. They never seemed to tire, but the chanting and drumming went on incessantly, hour after hour, till he says, "one grew pale with the ceaseless thudding of the drums."

When at length the dance was over, Hannington solemnly displayed to the assembled women a doll which a friend had sent him, and undressed it before their delighted eyes. They were charmed to see thus practically illustrated the manner in which English ladies clothe themselves, and the multitude and variety of their white sisters' habiliments.

On the 31st, another Pori, or forest desert, of about eighty miles, lay before them. As far as the eye could

CURIOUS ROCKS IN THE MSALALA COUNTRY

see were tall, thin, and shadeless acacia trees, and hard-
baked soil which threw back the rays of the sun with terrific
force.   On Sept. 2nd, while still painfully plodding through
this Pori, as there was a full moon, a start was made at
midnight to avoid the intense heat.   Hannington brought
up the rear, to keep the men from straggling.   "At last,"
he says, "they got a little troublesome.   I said to a man
who persisted in loitering, 'Very well; then I shall leave
you to be eaten by lions.'   A moment or two after I heard
a shot, and then another, with yells and shouts.   Of course,
I thought that the dreaded Ruga-Ruga were upon us, and so
rushed forward, forgetting my gun, which my boy was carrying behind me.   The firing and yelling increased as I neared
the front, and I seized a gun from the retreating form of
Duta, and pressed on.   Then I found that the commotion
was caused by a lion who was enjoying his supper in the
bushes before us, close to the path, and who, in spite of the
uproar and firing, refused to budge an inch.   I begged the
men to be calm, and taking my own gun, advanced for a
shot; but they danced round me, shouted to me to come
back, and one even seized my coat-tails.   I turned quite
rusty at this, and pushed the stupid man aside.   Two of the
white men now took to the trees, when they saw that I
was in earnest, and most of the black men followed them.
The other two white men, Ashe and Gordon, determined
to abide with me and share my fate; the former armed with
a revolver, the latter with his umbrella!   Of all lion-
adventures that I have heard of, this was about the most
laughable.   There was the lion, very wroth, like a dog
with his bone.   There was I, with my valiant body-guard
in line behind me.   There were the others, thickly clustered
upon the trees, like so many crows.   I was preparing to fire
when in rushed a black boy, and discharged his gun wildly
in the lion's direction.   Happily he missed, though the

bullet went close to where the lion lay. I saw him move and drag his prey further into the jungle, where we lost sight of him, though we could still hear his deep growlings. My two friends refused to leave me. I felt competent to avoid the charge of the beast myself if he were wounded, but could not look out for them; so I sorrowfully turned away, feeling that a grand opportunity had been lost. After this there was no difficulty in keeping the stragglers together. Their fatigue suddenly disappeared, and they packed together like a flock of sheep."

After a long and painful march which taxed their powers of endurance to the utmost, they reached the Mission Station of Uyui on the 4th of September. Here Hannington was seized with dysentery, and during the next ten days was brought to the very door of death. The Jesuit priests at Unyanyembe (the spot where Livingstone and Stanley parted) prescribed an injection of carbolic acid, which for a time relieved the most distressing symptoms, but nothing seemed to avail permanently.

On the evening of the 13th the other members of the Mission met in council. Hannington lay in his bed, anxiously and prayerfully awaiting their decision with regard to him. He hoped against hope that he might still be able to proceed to the Lake. After long deliberation, they announced to him the result of their consultation. He was to be left behind at Uyui whilst the others went forward without him. He says: "This decision came as a tremendous disappointment; but I had expected it, and received it as an oracle from heaven." On the 15th they left, and he remained in the brotherly hands of Mr. Copplestone, and under the special charge of his nephew, Cyril Gordon.

During his sickness, Ngembi, the chief of the district, called. Hannington made a great effort to sit up and receive him. He made him a present of a dressing-gown in the

name of the Society, as the chief had heard that both
Mirambo and Mtèsa had been officially recognized by the
Europeans, whereas he had been neglected. Hannington
writes : " He is chief of a large and important district, but
is a great drunkard, and difficult to get on with, yet wonderfully improved of late. He is very frightened at the comet ;
and a conversation about this gave Copplestone an opening
again to put the Gospel before him."

During the interview, however, Hannington sat in a
draught, and the consequence was that an old enemy of his,
acute rheumatism, set in, which in a few days turned to
rheumatic fever. This, on top of his fever and dysentery,
reduced him to the lowest ebb ; it seemed impossible that
he could recover. He says :

" Let me bear witness to Gordon's extreme attention
and kindness, in nursing me night and day. He would
not let me die. On Oct. 15th dysentery returned ; I was
desperately ill, and in such agony that I had to ask all to
leave me and let me scream, as it seemed slightly to relieve
the intense pain. In this state, I said to Gordon, 'Can it
be long before I die ?' His answer was, ' No ; nor can
you desire that it should be so.' "

I have received a most interesting letter from Mr.
Copplestone which refers to this period. He writes :

" Mr. Stokes had been loud in his praises of our friend,
so that I was in some measure predisposed in his favour,
and an openness and freeness sprang up at once between us.
The day after his arrival he went to my well and drank two
glassfuls of the water, which he found very cold and refreshing.
But we had not the slightest doubt afterwards but that that
water, delicious as it was, was the cause of that long and
protracted illness which took so many painful forms, and
eventually necessitated his reluctant return to England.

His illness came on so suddenly and was so severe that, for days, we thought that he could not recover. We placed him in a comfortable room which I had built for a school. On the departure of Stokes, Ashe, and Wise for the Lake, he was removed to my house, occupying the guest room, and thus conferring upon me the honour and privilege of having him and dear Gordon as guests for six weeks.

" I did not, however, get to understand him properly. There was a something in his character which I could not get to the bottom of. I did not then hold the key to his life. Although so weak and ill, he was very seldom still and never idle. I often wondered why he did not rest more. When compelled to keep to bed he did his best to paint what flowers Gordon might bring in to him from our rambles. As often as he could he would sit up, always at work at writing or painting. One thing he did was to draw up a small book of information for the guidance of men who should leave home for Africa, and for the Committee. From the very commencement he was bent upon making the best possible use of the knowledge and experience which he had gained.

" I have a distinct remembrance of one of the few walks which he was able to take with myself. ' Copplestone,' he said, ' I do not think that I can recover from this illness. Let us go, that we may choose a place for my grave.' So we went, and he selected a spot where he said we were to bury him. He did not expect that he could live long in such a state as that in which he then was.

" His stay with me was a real blessing. His spirituality was very deep. Oftentimes he would say, ' Come, Copplestone, sing me one of your consecration hymns.' His favourite was, ' I am coming to the Cross.' Nearly every night we would have a special time of prayer together before retiring to rest. Yes, those were hallowed times, never to be forgotten.

" The return of Stokes to Uyui, after his unsuccessful
attempt to reach the Lake by the old route, and his departure
again *viâ* Urambo, took away my friend, for he insisted that
he should go forward, though he should be carried the whole
way.   I accompanied them as far as Urambo, to see
Mirambo, the chief, about securing a road through his
newly-acquired country, to the South end of the Lake.   I
spent a night at their camp at Kwandi, and went some
distance into the jungle, and bade him good-bye in the
best of spirits, though very weak in body.   He was then
being carried.

" I did not again meet him until after his return to
England, and found in him an irresistible desire to return to
Africa.   At this I was not surprised, and not very much
so when I heard the report that there was a probability of
his being consecrated Bishop of Central Equatorial Africa.

" I have said above that I could not understand much
of what I saw in the Bishop when at Uyui, and that
because I had not then the key to his life.   This, however,
was given me in some measure, when on a visit to Hurst ;
but more definitely during a week I spent with him at
Martinhoe after his consecration.

" He appeared to have such an open, frank carelessness ;
and when I saw him at Hurst, and the way in which he
went about there, it was clear to me that there was something more than ordinary in him, and an amount of
originality about him that made him different from many
other men.   The earnestness with which he carried on the
work of his parish corresponded with the longing desire
after the welfare of his people which I had seen in him
when in Africa.

" The young men appeared devoted to him.   He was
one who could come down to their level, and make himself
one with them, and from his influence over them I could

see clearly that, like David, he bowed their hearts like one man.

" He invited me to spend a few days at Martinhoe. On the appointed day we met at Exeter. There were with him Mr. Ireland and Cecil M'Gillivray, a native teacher of the Universities' Mission at Zanzibar, of whom the Bishop was very fond. Among our many rambles over the cliffs and by the shore, he took us one day to visit the caves which he had discovered in former days, when he was a pupil with Mr. Scriven. We were caught by the tide. It was delightful to watch the dear Bishop springing over the rocks and through the pools, and finally he had to take off his coat as well as ourselves, and almost swim in order to reach his ' Jacob's Ladder.'

" Wherever he went he always had a warm welcome from old friends, and the poor people were continually showering grateful blessings upon him as he passed. The secret was, I am sure, his true sympathy and endeavour to make himself one with them ; and grandly he succeeded. I think it was the day before we left that he invited about a dozen of the old women to a sumptuous farewell tea. And before they left he had readings of the Word and gave them a homely address."

I have quoted this letter farther than its immediate reference to Uyui, because it throws light upon Hannington's character and goes to prove how essential an intimate acquaintance with him was to the right understanding of his rare nature.

The caravan in the charge of Mr. Stokes had, in the meanwhile, gone some distance along the old road to the Lake, when the natives endeavoured to extract an extortionate hongo, and to enforce its payment by arms. Mr. Stokes paid their demand, but very wisely refused to pro-

ceed, and returned to the chief of the district with a complaint of their breach of faith.   The chief, who had received
his tribute, and was responsible for their safe conduct, was
very angry, and demanded the return of the hongo from the
tribesmen.   While this dispute was pending, Mr. Stokes
brought the caravan back to Uyui, and determined to
approach the Lake by a different route.*

In Hannington's diary is the following entry :

"*Oct. 6th.*—Slightly better, but still in very great pain.
To our immense surprise Stokes turned up early this morning.   When I heard his voice I exclaimed, 'I shall live and
not die.'   It inspired me with new life.   I felt that they
had returned that I might go with them."

Again a consultation was held.   This time the members
of the Mission were divided in opinion.   The majority,
however, held that their leader was different to other people,
and that his iron will might possibly pull him through,
where a man of less strength of purpose would be doomed
to failure.   A hammock was prepared, and it was decided
that he should accompany them to the Lake.

---

* It appears also that hongo was demanded in guns and
powder, which is a kind of tribute which the agents of the C. M. S.
always consistently refuse to pay.

CHAPTER XV.

(1882.)

"His soul is too fresh with heaven to take the world's point of view about anything."—*Letter from Mrs. Nathaniel Hawthorne.*

WRITING to Mr. Wigram from Uyui just before his departure, Hannington says :

"Do, my dear sir, forgive me for writing so much about myself and so little about the others. My severe and repeated illnesses have made me think too much of myself, I fear, as if I were the centre of interest instead of those who are strong and healthy, and likely to carry on the work. *They* are the centre of our hopes, and it is they whose movements should be described. An empty bottle on the shelf requires no description. . . . I have decided to go on the day after to·morrow, . . . but I am prepared to be careful and to go, as we say out here, 'Pole pole' (gently). . . I close with words of hope. I am better ; full of joy, and, I hope, of praise to my God."

On Oct. 14th the messenger sent to recover the hongo which had been extorted from the caravan returned, bringing with him all the bales of cloth, except one which had been opened. The people, under pressure from their suzerain, offered eight cows in place of the missing bale, and thus the dispute was most happily arranged.

On the 16th all was ready for a start. Hannington

says : " I had stipulated that I was to have six porters exclusively to myself, to carry me, for I had already had very
disagreeable experience of a scratch crew ; and I further
offered to pay for them myself. On arriving in camp I
found all confusion. Fifty men had run away. They had
deserted, panic-stricken at the idea of crossing Mirambo's
country. We, however, determined not to wait, but to
proceed with as many loads as we could, and leave headmen
to gather porters and bring on the rest. The next thing to
be arranged was, what was to remain and what was to go.
During the turmoil I crept out of the way and remained, I
will not say rested, on the ground under a tree for two hours
and a half. At length, at half-past four, the drum sounded
and my men came up. I was too ill to scrutinize them, or
think who they were, or how many of them had been told
off for hammock duty ; so we started. Presently I discovered that I had only four bearers, and these, with one
exception, were the very dregs of the caravan. . . . By
and by my men began to totter, and finally let me drop.
Fortunately I expected it and was prepared, and caught myself, thus saving an ugly fall ; it is a most dangerous thing to
be dropped suddenly from a hammock, as one falls first on
the small of his back and is likely to injure his spine. I
gave them a long rest, but it was not of the slightest use,
and finally, for safety's sake, I was compelled to abandon the
hammock and walk for two hours. I had been in bed for
nearly six weeks before. It only proves what one can do
when one must. . . . The next day I got fresh carriers,
but they were not used to the work, and I was worse off
than before. The scenes of the past afternoon were painfully repeated ; so the day following I declined to stir an
inch until I had six good men allotted to me, for my life
absolutely depended upon it."

On the 20th, Mr. Copplestone and Mr. Stokes went

to Mirambo's village to interview that renowned African monarch, so the following day the porters took advantage of the absence of their caravan leader to be troublesome. When they arrived at a certain village where no halt ought to have been made they insisted they would remain there. Hannington says : " The men made a great row, and vowed they would go no further. I sat perfectly still until they had shouted themselves out, and then ordered my hammock and said that I was going on. The last shout that I heard was ' We won't come ; ' but about five minutes later I perceived that they were on the road, and on arriving very shortly at a better camping ground, they were in excellent spirits, and said that they were glad that I had made them go on."

On the 22nd they arrived at the Pero (the frontier tow...) of Urambo, and received a message assuring them of Mirambo's friendship. Hannington and Mr. Wise were too ill to leave the camp, but all the others went to the capital to pay their respects to the king.

On the 25th they started for the comparatively new country of Msalala. The only white man who had passed that way before was Speke, and he had only touched the route at one or two places. They thus looked forward to the journey with much interest.

In spite of his weakness, Hannington enjoyed this changeful life. Drenching rain succeeding furnace-like heat ; soaked clothes by day and wet bed-clothes by night could not damp his spirits. He says : " I can now just sit up for meals ; the rheumatism in my right leg and back is still rather relentless ; if I were at home the doctor would be wrapping me up in cotton wool, but this life is thoroughly agreeable to me. If I had good health I should be too happy. What wonderful mercy surrounds us. Truly, underneath are the Everlasting Arms ! "

On Nov. 1st they encamped near the village of a chief

A VILLAGE IN CENTRAL AFRICA.

called Shimami, " a great chief—great in possessions, stature, and power. A man of remarkably fine points." After exchange of presents, Shimami took Hannington for a tour of exploration through his village. They set off in single file, Shimami—wearing one of the presents, a pair of blue spectacles—leading the way, his guest second, and the court officials following in order of rank. When near the village, Hannington bestowed upon him a wide-awake hat. " His delight knew no bounds. He put it on, and, spectacles and all, strutted off as proud as a peacock. His chief minister discovered that the crown of the hat was flattened a little, in the fashion we generally wear our wide-awakes. So it was taken off and erected in a sharp peak; then its rim was bent up *au brigand*, and altered again and yet again. I was immensely amused, but my mirth only caused greater delight, for in Africa laughter is seldom expressive of ridicule."

" Nov. 4th brought us to the Sultan's, a minor of about 12 years old named Gargi. I can only speak of him as a delightful little black. He quite won my heart, and we were soon walking about hand in hand together, though followed by a large retinue to see that we did not get into mischief."

On the 6th Hannington was so much better that he attempted the ascent of a mountain. He went alone, ascending by creepers which hung from crevices in the iron-stone rock. Above the crags was dense jungle. He soon, however, struck a path which led to some deserted huts, which had the appearance of a robber's hold. This looked bad, but the hope of fresh botanical treasures urged him on. For some time he crept upward, often on hands and knees, through the thick undergrowth, till by and by he heard an ominous rustle. At first he thought of lions, and remembered that he was unarmed. Then as he peered into the tangle he heard a whisper that sounded very human, and his thoughts at once reverted to the abandoned huts and to murderous robbers. Soon appeared three men armed with a pistol and bows and arrows. There was not much hope of escape if they meant mischief, so he at once resolved to face them, and descending, called out " Wadela," which is Kinyamwezi for " good afternoon."

The reply was not, as he half expected, an arrow or a bullet ; those three had dogged his steps for some time, as in the " prospecting" regions of America men dog the steps of one whom they suspect to have discovered the secret of a new mine. They were in want of water, and believed that the white man had power to create it. In fact, that his business on the mountains was to form a new spring ! Hannington tried to explain that this was in the power of God alone, but in vain, for " What," says he, " could a man be doing who kept picking little pieces of moss and examining them through a magnifying glass, or cutting off bark from a tree, or turning over a stone for a beetle ? Even in the West of England two very eminent botanists were regarded as ' old herbalists,' and were not altogether beyond the suspicion of necromancy ; but here, where witchcraft is the religion of the country, no words of mine could persuade them that I was not a most powerful magician, though unwilling to exercise my power."

" *Nov. 8th.*—After a twenty miles' march we arrived at Kwa Sonda, in Msalala, the last village under Mirambo's jurisdiction. Here we were promised our first view of the mighty Victoria Nyanza, and here we hoped to found a new Station. The Lake was supposed to be but five miles distant. We struggled on. But what was our bitter disappointment to see nothing but a green expanse of rushes, looking like a cricket field, and stretching away for miles. We had expected to behold a grand stretch of blue water and luxuriant foliage when we reached Kwa Sonda. Instead of this, only a sandy plain, and in the midst of it a singularly unpicturesque village. After we had been introduced to the chief and been assured by him that the water was not far off, I crept silently away to explore, but was soon discovered and followed by the others. As to the natives, they could tell us nothing with certainty. The greater part seemed never to have travelled northward through fear of hostile tribes. Some cried one thing, some another, so we had to find out our whereabouts for ourselves. Soon a drenching shower overtook us, which would have damped the ardour of most men, but not of those who had tramped nigh a thousand miles to reach their sphere of work at the sources of the Nile. We crept beneath a glorious jessamine bush and there sheltered until the worst was over. Then on we went and yet onwards : but though the scenery had changed and become very beautiful, yet no lake was visible. By and by we saw, from the top of a high rock, a swamp of reeds and grass which, as I have said before, looked like a well-mown cricket field, but not a drop of water. Our hearts sank, and with weary tread we returned to the camp to answer the eager inquiries of the men with ' Maji Hapana' (There is no water).

" I implored the brethren to reserve all remarks until after we had been refreshed by food ; for not only had we had a very long march, but also a fatiguing search and a great disappointment. After dinner, just as we had opened the books for prayers, in came the chief, and asked what we were about. When we told him we were going to pray to God, he replied : ' Go on ; let me hear you.' Then when we had finished : ' You must teach me.' This seemed to come to us as an immense comfort when we were all depressed, for although we were generally asked to remain permanently and form a Station, yet nobody had yet directly requested us to teach him to pray."

Elsewhere he writes : " I do not place too much stress on this, and yet it seemed an earnest from heaven, and it set my heart praising, and filled me with assurance that our most loving Father has not forgotten us."

" We heard afterwards that we had not gone to the right place from which to see the water, so the next morning, before the sun was up, I started ; but was soon outdistanced by Stokes and a troop of men. Presently I heard firing, and thinking that they had overtaken a hippo., I seized my gun, and began to run, when I made the painful discovery that I was quite unable to do so. I was by this time strong enough to walk for a few miles, but not twenty yards could I run. I cannot describe my feelings as I handed the gun to my boy and told him to run. Nor was my mortification lessened by the way he dashed off. I watched him disappear, wishing heartily that he would occasionally move like that when I was in a hurry, and inwardly resolving that he should. By and by he returned, saying that the firing was not for Nyama (game), but for Furahi (joy). They had reached the Lake. I brisked up at once, and soon reached the mighty Nyanza, here like a duck-pond, or sluggish English river in the summer time. The Nullah cannot be in this place more than a mile across, for some natives came rushing down on the opposite bank to see what was the matter, and we could distinctly hear their voices. Only a very small portion of the intervening space was water ; the rest was reedy swamp. There were no canoes, and no communication seemed to be kept up with other parts."

They had reached the Lake at a point to the west of Kagei and Jordan's Nullah, marked Msalala with a blue underline on the map, but did not yet know their exact position. Writing to the Committee of the C. M. S., Han-

nington says : " I incline rather to our being on the west
side of the west channel of Jordan's Nullah. But time
will settle the question for us." In his diary he writes :
" A council of war was held. There seemed but one course
before us. There we were. Cloth short. A caravan still
behind us, nothing before us, what were we to do ? We
must stop where we are until Raschid comes with the
boat."

The rainy season was upon them, so they set to work
at once to build huts, and in the meanwhile sent letters by
Kagei to U-Ganda announcing their arrival, and telling the
brethren there to send canoes for them if their immediate
presence were required.

The ranks of the Mission party were now to be still
further thinned. Mr. Blackburn and Mr. Edmonds had
been left at Uyui to take the place of Mr. Copplestone, who
was about to return to England. Now Mr. Stokes returned
to the coast. So Hannington and Mr. Gordon sallied forth
to choose a good site for their tent at a place some miles from
the village. The journal says : " Gordon and I were quite
alone last night in the heart of the forest. Three or four
tarantulas were dashing wildly about the tent. Mosquitos
swarmed. Lions roared close to us during the greater part
of the night, four different kinds of ants made themselves at
home with us, and in the morning a whole stream of
Chunqu (bitter) ants, the largest and fiercest ants there are,
advanced as an army into our tent. There was nothing to
be done but light a fire and regularly fight them, and even
then we had great difficulty in getting rid of the enemy.
In spite of these trifling drawbacks we congratulated ourselves upon having pitched upon an exceedingly pleasant
spot, and determined as soon as possible to hedge ourselves
in with a fence of thorns, to prevent a buffalo or stray
rhinoceros from charging the tent, or a lion from slipping

his paw under the curtain and clawing one of us out of bed."

" *Nov.* 13*th.*—After we had enlisted a sufficient number of volunteers from the porters to remain with us, the rest returned with Stokes to the coast. We were very sorry to bid him farewell. His unceasing kindness had been a great comfort to us, and his ability in managing the men a great advantage. When he was gone a slight feeling of loneliness crept over us. We felt rather like men with empty pockets turned adrift in the wide world, not knowing exactly where we were, or what to do next. Our instructions, in rough outline, were as follows : ' Ashe and Wise to form a station somewhere at the end of the lake ; Gordon and myself to proceed as speedily as possible to U-Ganda.' Very good ; but the difficulty was that our supplies had run short, and the horrors of the rainy season were upon us.

" However, the next day I dug a well with my own hands, as Gordon was ill. Then, that no opportunity might be wasted, I persuaded the chief's brother to come to me to learn the alphabet. How I longed to be able to talk sufficiently well to teach the people the way of everlasting life!"

The traveller in Africa must always depend in a large measure upon his gun for a supply of fresh meat for himself and his men. However unwilling he may be to take life, he will find it necessary to avail himself of a halt to try and replenish the camp larder. Hannington was always chary about inflicting unnecessary slaughter. He had no sympathy with the ambition which consumes some men to make a large bag. Now and again, however, he would scour the country about the encampment in search of game, and his fearlessness often brought him strange adventures.

One day, as he and his boy Duta were trying to stalk some antelopes, and were worming themselves on hands and knees through the high grass, he saw something dark ahead. He whispered to Duta: " Is that a rhinoceros or a clump of bushes?" Just then the object moved, and they saw that it was a black rhinoceros. Hannington thus describes what followed : " Back we darted into the thicket, and took a large circuit, coming out again on the edge of the plain just in time to see a cow with her calf retiring slowly in the jungle. Quietly we crept back, and again emerged, this time about twenty yards from her. Her head was turned from us, and on her back were a number of yellow ' rhinoceros birds.' These flew up with a screech and apprised her of her enemy. Before she could spring round I fired. As the bullet struck her she uttered a fierce screaming grunt, and in a moment, about ten yards from where I stood there rushed from the jungle a bull and another cow rhinoceros bellowing most fiercely. Happily for us they did not see us, as the vision of the rhinoceros is very limited, and we were to leeward, so that they could not get our wind. But when about thirty yards distant some whiff of our wind must have reached them, for they wheeled round and charged furiously towards us. ' Fire, bwana, fire ! ' excitedly cried my boy ; and as he ceased speaking I could hear his heart thumping loudly. ' Be still,' I said. ' Stand perfectly still ; ' and the lad, to his honour be it said, was brave enough to obey. When about ten paces distant, seeing that we remained motionless, they came to a halt, and eyed us fiercely, pawing the ground and snorting defiance. It was an embarrassing situation. The eye wandered round for a tree up which to climb, but there was not one within reach. We were standing in dense mimosa tangle about chest high ; flight through this was impossible. I thought, Should I fire ? But I determined not to do so, for even if, by the greatest good fortune, I brought one to the ground, there were still the other two. They them-

selves at last took the initiative. The cow which I had
wounded stole away across the plain. I decided at once to
follow her and get another shot. The other two stood gazing
at us until they saw that she had out-distanced us, and then
they quietly turned round and disappeared in the jungle."

Like most other African travellers, Hannington has a
hunter's joke to tell against himself. As his is characteristic,
it is worth repeating. The tangle of an African " forest "
is so dense, that it is the easiest thing in the world to pass by
the largest game without seeing it, or even being aware of
its vicinity. The first warning of the neighbourhood of a
rhinoceros or buffalo is often a furious charge from some
cover a few yards distant. Instances have been known in
which a hunter has almost stumbled over a sleeping lion, or
has even run right up against an elephant ! *   Often the only
sign of the beast which he is diligently stalking, in order
that he may replenish his exhausted larder and feed his
hungry porters, is a certain thickening in the bush which
suggests some solid body. It is not, therefore, odd if a
hunter should occasionally send his bullet into the heart of a
log, or to the core of an ant-hill, or flatten it against a rock.

Here is Hannington's story. He says : " I had taken
my butterfly-net and accompanied Wise for a walk. We
had not gone far when we came to a beautiful flowering-
shrub, covered with insects ; and here I should have probably remained for the rest of the morning, had I not been
excitedly summoned by the others to come and hunt a
rhinoceros which they had just sighted. 'Well,' said I,
' rhino or no rhino, I have just seen a new butterfly, and I
do not leave this spot till I have secured it.' Could anyone
know me so little as to suppose that I would lose the opportunity of capturing a new butterfly for a chance shot at a

* Thomson, *Through Masai Land*, p. 550.

AN AWKWARD SITUATION.

rhinoceros ?　So I caught and boxed my fly, and then, with much elation, I seized my gun, and went in the direction pointed out.　Wise had not yet been face to face with big game, and was in a great state of excitement, trembling with combined hope and fear.　We marched in single file under cover of a tree; and Wise was in such a state of high pressure, that I momentarily expected the contents of his barrels to lodge themselves near my calves.

" We took a hasty glance round the bush, and there, sure enough, we saw a magnificent rhino, lazily eating the rich herbage, and taking no notice of our approach.　Back we darted into cover.　There was another bush about twenty yards ahead : my two companions were told off to crawl under its cover; then I was to suddenly emerge to the right, and they to the left, and all to take aim and fire.　If this produced a savage charge, there was the bush to serve as shelter.

" It was an anxious moment.　How would my companions conduct themselves ?　Would they dodge, if necessary ?　Would they stand firm, if need be ?　'Now, then, are you ready ?'　'Yes, quite.'　'Now for it '——

" We emerged with bated breath; and lo !—the rhinoceros had disappeared, and there before us stood, or rather lay, a fallen tree !　Who shall portray our looks of disappointed disgust and surprise !　Even my boy, a born son of the forest, had been taken in."

After reading an article which I had written in *The C. M. Intelligencer,* containing some Recollections of Bishop Hannington, one of his friends objected to a lion story there given, as an instance of his remarkable personal courage.　My friendly critic remarked that the story bore on the face of it an air of improbability.　If this be so, I can only regret it; but I gave the story almost word for word as I received it from his own lips.　I find reference to the incident in his diary, as occurring on the 16th of

December, and venture to repeat it here, as illustrating his dauntless nature. Hannington himself was always shy about telling this story to any stranger, lest it should be received with incredulity; but to those who knew him intimately it will not, I think, sound incredible.

Both Hannington and Gordon had been severely scourged by fever; but on Dec. 16th the former felt better, and he thought to take a short stroll and collect some botanical specimens. At about a mile from camp he saw some animal moving through the dense mimosa scrub, and firing, killed it. His prey proved to be a large lion's cub. The gun-bearer, seeing this, fled with every sign of terror, and shouted to him to do the same. It was time indeed to do so. The cries of " Run, bwana, run ! " were accentuated by a double roar, and, looking round, Hannington saw the bereaved parents, a fine lion and lioness, coming toward him with long, bounding leaps over the scrub. An ordinary man, encountering lions face to face in the open for almost the first time, would probably have lost all presence of mind, and, turning to run, have been inevitably destroyed. He deliberately faced round upon his enemy. The enraged lions were distant but a few paces, but they suddenly checked, and both stood, as though transfixed, glaring upon him. So they remained for some time, till Hannington, placing one foot behind the other, and still keeping his eyes fixed upon the yellow orbs before him, gradually increased his distance, and, having placed about a hundred yards between himself and the monsters, quietly walked away.

But the indomitable nature of the man comes out more strongly in what followed. Most men would have concluded that they had had enough of such an adventure, and have accepted their escape from the jaws of death, or at least would not have renewed the contest without assistance. Hannington was formed of quite another metal. Though the light was waning, he determined that he would return and secure the skin of the cub he had killed; so he retraced his steps. When near enough to observe their motions, he could see that the lion and lioness were walking round about their cub, licking its body and filling the air with low growlings. At this moment an unknown flower caught his eye. He plucked it, took out his note-book, pressed it between the leaves, and classified it as far as he was able; then, with coolness perfectly restored, he ran forward a few paces, threw up his arms and shouted! Was it that the lions had never encountered so strange an antagonist before? At all events, they looked up, then turned tail and bounded away. He dragged the cub for some distance, till having left the dangerous vicinity, he shouldered it and brought it into camp.

Acts such as these gave him unbounded influence over his men. They learned to regard him as invincible, and entertained a most wholesome dread of opposing his expressed will.

Matters were not going well at Kagei. All failed with fever, one after the other, and all at once. News, too, came that Raschid, who was in charge of the boat,* was delayed, through want of cloth, at Kwa Sonda.† Raschid

---

* The boat was carried in sections as far as Jordan's Nullah, where it remained until July, 1883, when Mr. Mackay came from U-Ganda. As the boat could not be launched from Msalala, where the Nullah is choked with weeds, and unnavigable, he took it to a village in Urima, where the fragments were united. The boat was launched on Dec. 3rd, 1884, and named the *Eleanor* (after Mr. Wigram's eldest daughter). She proved to be a great success, and took the Mission party safely to U-Ganda, where she received the additional *native* name of *Mirembi* or *Peace*.

† Marked on the map *Msalala*. The name changes according to the chief. It is now Kwa Chasama.

appears, from the account, to have been a scamp. The
unfortunates at Msalala had expected that he would bring to
them a fresh supply of stores, and now, to their dismay,
they learnt that he had either wasted or appropriated the
goods entrusted to him, to such an extent that they would
have to send him some of their own rapidly diminishing stock.
It was decided that Ashe and Gordon should go to meet
him, and bring on his caravan, while Hannington negociated
with Romwa, King of U-Zinza, with a view to his assistance in reaching the head of the lake. Romwa's capital is
on the shore of the lake, a few days' journey from Msalala.

In the meanwhile, the neighbouring chief was making
himself very disagreeable, and charging exorbitant prices
for all provisions, especially for milk. Hannington called
this " the milk war."

" *Dec.* 16*th.*—The milk war opened again early this
morning. The first thing was the arrival of the two headmen
who own the cows. They came into the boma (the fence
about the camp), and posted themselves down without any
especial remark. By and by the chief's mother, wives, and
sisters arrived, accompanied by ladies of the court bearing a
present of Indian corn, which they laid respectfully at my
feet. This I accepted, as coming from the ladies, and gave
them gilt buttons to the value of the corn—for that is the
way one accepts a present in these parts. By and by, while
these visitors were still with us, a present of milk arrived
from the chief, and, lastly, the chief himself and his retinue.
My yard was crowded. I at once announced that I did not
want a present of milk, but a supply of milk every day, and
that I was ready to pay a fair price for it. The chief then
asked for a red pocket-handkerchief in return for his milk.
I told him that I had not accepted it; that I should give
him no present, as we were not friends, and that he was

trying to drive the white man out of his country ; that if he persisted in his conduct he would gain his end, for we should all leave.   He then asked me what we should do with the huts which we were building.   To which I briefly replied, ' Moto ' (fire) ; then I expatiated upon our readiness to remain with him, and that we wanted to be friends if he would act fairly by us.   I then asked what they would arrange to supply us with milk for.   He replied that if we wanted milk daily, we must pay for it with red cloth. This exceeded any of his former demands, and I fairly broke out in wrath, and drove them all from my presence.   I then followed them over to Wise's as quickly as I could, but not in time enough, for he came out to meet me in great triumph, saying, ' I am flooded with milk to-day ; see, I have got this present from the chief.'   This really was too pro-voking.   I had sat with that milk under my nose for half an hour.   I had refused it because I was fighting for my friends, who are expecting to stop here long after I have left for U-Ganda, and now all that I had done and said was frus-trated.   I returned to my quarters rather crestfallen and worried, feeling that I had got the worst of it for the fifth or sixth time.   However, I think that, with a little persever-ance, I shall yet bring them to terms, and the battle must be fought out for the sake of the brethren who remain."

After the adventure with the lions narrated above, the people of the district treated the dauntless Englishman with greater respect.   He had managed to recal his terrified boy before he regained the camp, and after giving him a good scolding for leaving him to be killed while he fled to save his own bones, he made him drag the carcase of the cub for the remainder of the distance home.   " The boy Backit," he says, " walked in perfect terror, expecting every moment that the lions would hunt him down, especially as he was obliged to drag the cub along the ground. Nor could he sleep for two or three nights afterwards, feeling sure that they would come to find their offspring. The affair made a great stir in the village. They would scarcely believe that I had ventured to kill ' a child of the lion.' It was, they said, a far more hazardous thing to do than killing the lion himself. I almost think that now I shall get milk sent in regularly ! "

The skin of this cub, so dearly obtained, was unfortunately eaten by ants, but the tuft at the end of its tail is still preserved as a trophy of one of the coolest acts of deliberate hardihood ever performed by a man.

On Dec. 19th Gordon and Ashe returned with Raschid and his caravan. Both were very ill, as also was Wise. The whole burden for a while fell upon Hannington, who was himself again failing with fever. He describes the kind of work which falls to a camp leader from sunrise to sunset, in his half-humorous, half-pathetic style

" Moses : 'What am I to do with this ? ' Raschid : ' How am I to arrange that ? ' ' There is rain coming; how are we to manage ? ' etc., etc. Between the patients, the constant worry of the caravan, and my own vexing weakness, I was in the depth of despair. The boys, the men, the food, all required constant looking after. Natives ever coming and going, begging, buying, and selling. I got through the day, for grace was sufficient.

" The next morning found all slightly better ; but before I could get to Ashe, he had crept over to me full of perturbation and bad news. Raschid and his men had announced their intention of immediately leaving us. What did this mean ? Starvation. It would throw us on the exorbitant natives, to whom we would have to pay ready money, in the shape of cloth, instead of having the help of the coast-men, whom we could always pay with promissory notes upon our agent at Zanzibar. The men had been told that they might return when Raschid went back, but we had anticipated that he would remain with us until our winter huts were completed, and a temporary station formed. I pleaded with the men, and put the matter in every possible light before them, but all without avail. They thought that they had us in their power, and, in African fashion, they meant to use it. ' *Will you go ?* ' ' Yes.' Suddenly I bounded from my seat, and said, ' Then go—go at once— instantly leave my presence, and go; but you go *as runaways !* ' The afternoon brought messages that they did not exactly wish to leave us on those terms, and that they supposed they must stop."

An interview with the men settled the matter satisfactorily. They consented to remain without Raschid and the malcontents, so he and his ill-conditioned crew were suffered to depart. The same day brought a message from Romwa that he would assist the Mission party to the utmost of his power, and supply them with canoes for the voyage up the lake. His terms seemed to Hannington, who had grown wise by this time in the wily ways of African chiefs, too liberal to be altogether satisfactory ; however, it was decided that he and Mr. Gordon should visit Romwa's capital, leaving the others in charge of the station at Msalala.

CHAPTER XVI.

THE LAKE.

(1882—83.)

"He that hath so many causes of joy is very much in love with
sorrow and peevishness if he loses all these pleasures and chooses
to sit down on his own little handful of thorns."—JER. TAYLOR.

"*Christmas Day*, 1882.—Gordon very ill in bed. Ashe
and Wise tottering out of fever beds; I myself just about
to totter in again. In spite of our poor condition, we
determined to have our Christmas cheer. We had a happy
celebration of the Holy Communion at 8 a.m., and thought
much of the dear ones at home, praying for us and wishing
us true Christmas joy."

There, in the heart of the great wilderness, that little
band of fever-stricken men assembled together, and for a
while forgot their loneliness and their pains as they offered
up their Sacrifice of praise and thanksgiving. There in the
dark land, where the shadow of spiritual death hung like
a heavy pall which might be seen and felt, they drew near
with faith and took that Holy Sacrament to their comfort.
With angels and archangels, and with all the company of
heaven; with the Church of Christ scattered throughout
the world, they raised their weary voices to laud and
magnify His Holy Name, who had sent His dear Son, Jesus
Christ, that their bodies might be made clean by His Body,
and their souls washed through His most precious blood.
And as they ate and drank the holy symbols there, in the

tangled forest, amidst wild beasts and wilder men, they felt that neither time nor space could separate them from their fellow-worshippers who also on that day were making their Eucharistic Feast; but that they being many were one bread, and one body, for were they not all partakers of That One Bread!

"In spite of our poor plight," writes the leader of the expedition, "we determined to celebrate the day; so I killed a kid, and Ashe undertook the pudding. As to the pudding, I am sure that many a cottager had a better one, but I doubt if any enjoyed theirs much more than we did ours. Its drawbacks were certainly not few. The flour was both musty and full of beetles and their larvæ; the raisins had fermented; the pudding was underboiled, and yet boiled enough to have stuck to the bottom of the saucepan, whereby its lower vitals had suffered considerably; and yet a musty, fermented, underdone, and burnt mass of dough was such a real treat that day, that I cannot remember ever to have enjoyed a Christmas pudding half so much. We felt quite cruel in denying a slice to Gordon, who was not in a fit condition for such delicacies."

A move was made in the direction of Romwa's on the 30th of December. By this time the C. M. S. camp was in a sad state of destitution. Owing to the roguery of Raschid, they were now almost entirely without cloth; anglicé, they were almost penniless.

To be penniless in Africa is to be destitute indeed. In no country in the world is the rule of nothing for nothing more rigorously adhered to. Hannington was soon to have an illustration of this. When he reached Mkola's village with Gordon, the others following some distance behind, he found himself without cloth. He says: "It began to pour with rain, and we had no better refuge than a tree. I tried in vain to purchase something to eat, but could only succeed in getting one old woman to trust us with a little milk, which we shared." The rest of the party did not come up, and seemed to have lost themselves. " We were utterly bewildered and exhausted, for we had had no food for eighteen hours. Before following any decided course of action, I said I would take my bed under a distant tree and get a little rest, for my soul fainted within me. I had, however, scarcely composed myself, when my boy, Duta, came from Ashe, saying that they had mistaken the road and were some two or three miles ahead. At once we started. A rhinoceros charging across the path rather revived me ; and in about two hours we came up with Ashe, who was encamped by the edge of the water ; and soon we had our first boiling of anything like drinkable water since leaving Uyui last October. So we spent the rest of this the last day of 1882 in peace and happiness, praising our loving Father who had strengthened and protected us thus far."

The next day, New Year's Day, 1883, the canoe journey to Romwa's should have commenced, but as Mr. Wise was sick, and could not superintend the porters, they left half their loads behind them at the old camp, and had to be sent back several times before all was gathered up. The captain of the canoe also began to give proof that he was capable of making trouble. He demanded extra fare before he would consent to move.

" *Jan. 2nd.*—The things arrived early, but one load, the most important of all, was left behind, and yet again we had to send back. Again the old man of the sea refused to start, saying that his canoe leaked. I had an attack of dysentery, but as Ashe and Wise were both incapacitated by sickness, everything fell on me. I selected a few packages, and had them stored in the canoe, at the same time bidding the Mzee * remember that I had ten more to come. At 2 a.m. he called me up and said we must start. Well, unearthly as this hour was, I got up, saw to everything, cooked my brethren some food, had the tent taken down, and the things taken to the boat, when Mzee turned round and declared that he had no room for the luggage, and refused to start till daylight. This meant that my sick companions and I should sit about in dewy grass for some three hours. My patience now broke down, and I said that, Mzee or no Mzee, I *would* start. Hereupon he and his crew rushed to the boat and began tearing out the baggage. A fearful scrimmage ensued, during which I trod into a colony of ants, and got wofully punished. Everything was mixed up so that we could not tell what we had taken, and what we had left, and eventually many packages we could ill spare were left behind. However, we *did* get off about 4 a.m., a hippo blowing a salute as we started. We had not gone far when a loud bang startled us, and, looking up, I saw two legs of my only chair flying upwards. My stupid boy had placed his gun loaded and full cocked into the canoe. My best waterproof rug was cut in half, the side of the canoe broken, and my chair spoilt. Happily no one was hurt. I am very angry, and at once have all the guns secured, but forget the pistols.

" Our next escapade is to rob some natives. Our men spy a small canoe, to which they at once give chase, and hunt it down. A goat was handed over, and transferred to our boat. I thought that they were merely having a chat or friendly barter, for the thing was done as quietly as possible, and we went on our way. It was not until some

---

* "*Kiswahili* for ' old man.' The captain of the canoe was always called Mzee. I translated this somewhat freely ' the old man of the sea,' as he was so excessively troublesome."

time after that it came out that the goat had been forced from its owner. When I expressed my horror, I was informed that Mtesa's men are accustomed to act in this manner !

"The scenery now becomes very beautiful and varied. Cormorants, darters, belted kingfishers, and a very small blue kingfisher, with a bright red breast and dark blue back, constantly cross our track. Crocodiles and hippos float lazily on the surface. We land for lunch. Bananas and milk abound. The people all flock down to see the first white men who have ever passed that way. The greatest excitement prevails. They pull our hair and beards ; they want to know if my boots grow to my feet, etc., etc. Their chief wears an expression of delight beyond bounds at six needles with which I present him. At sunset we en- camped for the night. Gordon had to be lifted out of the boat. Ashe crept out and at once went to bed. There was no firewood. After an hour's search I found a little, and bought some more, and then superintended the cooking, for the boys were all worn out. Then came Mzee, and said that I must get the things out of the canoe, as it leaked. And so it did, and most of the cloth was wet through. It was very dark, we had but one candle, and the air was so thick with mosquitoes that one might almost have cut a slice from it with a knife. At last the bales were got out, and I sat down to enjoy a well-earned meal, when Duta came and called me from the tent and said that the men refused to go further unless they were paid extra cloth, and from what he had heard he thought they meant to desert us. I kept this from the brethren to spare them any extra anxiety, but slept little that night. However, daylight found the men still there. Three valuable hours were spent in haggling, and in the end I had to agree to pay them more cloth. At 11 a.m. we started. We had not gone far when

STRANGE HEADLAND, JORDAN'S NULLAH.

a storm gathered, and we put into port ; and only just in time, for a fearful hurricane burst upon us.   Great waves, like those of the sea, rose almost in an instant, and beat upon the shore, washing up weeds and shells.   By and by we went on.   We passed a rocky little island completely surrounded by crocodiles drifting about on the surface, and one huge monster, which had been basking in the sun, rolled lazily into the water and disappeared as we approached. By and by three hippos put their huge heads above water and snorted at us.   They followed the canoe for a consider-able distance.   The hippos of the lake are sometimes very savage and dangerous.   I felt no temptation to have a swim. The sun then sank into the west, and we were still at sea. I looked at the pale faces of the invalids, I looked at the luggage, the tent, my helpless boys, and the savage ruffians in the canoe, and my heart rather sank.   We did not reach the camping place which the boatmen had selected until 8 p.m.   It was so dark that it was some time before we could find a break in the reeds through which we might wade ashore, and when we landed the place was so rocky and wet that the tent could not be pitched.   We crept on about half a mile till we reached a hut.   We begged admit-tance, and the owner liberally said that we might occupy the goat-house.   'Impossible !' said I, as I beheld the thatched-in manure heap, ankle deep in mire, so we returned tottering and stumbling and down-hearted to the boat.   But here things were so hopeless that we again made request for admittance to the hut.   This time the native, seeing my companions' woeful faces, generously vacated his dwelling and we slept in the open air within his enclosure.

"At 2 a.m. rain came on, and the invalids took to the hut, but I preferred wrapping myself in my waterproof and facing it.   When daylight dawned, I found to my despair that the canoe had sunk during the night, and that almost everything we had was drenched. It was hard to think that notebooks, barometers, botanical specimens, etc., were all injured and some spoiled. But the man who goes to Central Africa must learn ' to take joyfully the spoiling of his goods.' The old man of the sea and his crew refused to bale the canoe out, so the boys and I set to work in pouring rain, and by eleven o'clock the weather broke and we started. Very soon the clouds reformed, though evidently only for soft rain, but the men turned the head of the canoe towards a deep bay, and stated their intention of landing us there and taking us no further. ' Should we find canoes there ? ' ' No.' ' Was it far from Romwa's ? ' ' Yes ; altogether out of the way.' ' Why, we shall die if we are left in this way.' ' Well, Mzee says he will not go on.' Then I said in a firm, clear voice, ' Give me my gun.' I deliberately proceeded to load it, and pointing at Mzee at about a yard distant from his chest, I said :

" ' *Now*, will you go on ? '

" ' Yes, Bwana, yes ; don't fire ! ' The effect was magical ; round flew the head of the canoe, once more we speeded over the waves ; and a few minutes later his own men were imitating my solemn gestures, and laughing at me, confessing that, after all, they were very glad that I had made them go on. But I had found out a secret—I was, from that moment, the master, and it is not too much to say that our lives were saved by that one prompt action. I could now afford to be generous, and so promised the men a goat when they landed if they behaved themselves well. The offer was received with joyous acclamations, and we paddled shoreward for lunch, thinking all trouble over. When lunch was finished and a start made, they coolly said that they would go no further than the next village, and then leave us. I made no comment, thinking that I would get there first. To our great delight, when we landed we found that the men whom

we had sent overland had hit upon this spot, so that now we
had a small army of men to dry our goods, pitch tent, and get
things in order.   We further learned that Romwa's capital
was close at hand.   A messenger from Romwa himself soon
arrived, and we thought that all trouble was past.   Alas !
. . . .   Well, first we were detained two days, during
which Romwa made medicine, and consulted oracles as to
whether the white men would harm him.   The Delphian
reply was, ' The white men are good for you and for your
people, but injurious to the medicine men.'   Then Romwa
was not content with his present.   Asked why I had sent
him such a rubbishing present.   He was a great Sultan ; he
wanted cloth and guns.   This was a bitter pill, but we
resolved not to yield.

   " On Sunday, the 7th, I failed with severe fever, but
could not give way to it, for somebody must see the matter
through.   I only remember suffering more pain.   Romwa
sent to ask the white men to come and visit him, and next
day a start was made.   No sooner had we got fairly off than
I perceived that there was a terrible leak in the canoe, and
that the canoemen were drunk.   We landed and repaired the
mischief, and the men plied themselves with more pombé
(native wine) which they had brought with them.   The
result was that when we resumed our way they were worse
than ever, and yelled and screamed until my poor comrades
were overcome by the fearful noise.   The captain then
stood up and executed a war dance upon a bale of goods,
ending by falling upon me.   This was more than I could
stand, so I gave him a needed warning and said that next
time he should have a cold bath.   In a rage he ordered his
men to land us at once.   This they refused to do, fearing
Romwa, and perhaps my wrath more than the captain's.
Then a free fight commenced, which ended in the captain
falling overboard.   He climbed in again, and furiously

seizing a paddle, aimed a heavy blow, as I thought, at Ashe, which happily just missed him, but shivered the paddle to pieces.

"Believe me, ill as I was, I bounded from my seat, seized him, pulled him down and dared him to move. I was proceeding to further measures when one of the men took me and gently forced me back into my seat, and then proceeded to pat me on the back and talk in this fashion : ' White man, be calm, be calm ; gently, gently ; don't disturb yourself. We will go on ; indeed we will. White man, be calm ; quietly, quietly, quietly.' With each word he administered a gentle pat, until at last I fairly burst out laughing, and the April shower of wrath fled before the sunshine of mirth."

"*Jan. 9th.*—Romwa sent word that he was coming to see us, so we made ready to receive his majesty suitably. Presently a great noise was heard, and, looking out, we saw a long procession of medicine men carrying horns full of rancid butter, probably mixed with blood ; then came Romwa himself, an immensely tall man, not much short of seven feet ; then wives, councillors, and medicine men *ad lib*. We were asked to place his chair in the centre of the tent, and as soon as he had seated himself, the horns were planted in the ground all round him to protect him from the white man's witcheries. Nor was this enough. As an additional safeguard, the monarch had anointed himself with castor oil from head to foot. Never had we been witness to such a scene of superstition, nor, I think I may add, smelt such a perfume.

"Romwa was anxious that we should stay and build, but he soon got upon the universal subject of GIVE. I told him that I had a very handsome robe for him, but no cloth and no guns, whereupon he rose in a passion and stalked off, saying he was a great chief and would have a great present.

We were betrayed.   Instead of the mild sage we had been led to suppose him, we saw the royal savage in his true colours.   And yet, in spite of his being one of the worst men we had to deal with, there was something in him that I loved.   When alone with me and free for a few minutes from the influence of his medicine men, he would grow kindly, would feel my pulse and pat my fevered brow."

Romwa continued to demand guns, which the Mission party steadily refused, though their lives were made a burden to them by the exactions of their host. Hannington, speaking of that first day, says : " The day ends.   Never, I think, did I pass through one much worse, for, in addition to the incessant worry, I was very seriously ill, having to speak constantly when utterly unfit to do so."

" 10*th.*—A terrible night of fever, and inclined to be delirious.   Romwa arrived early, and in rather a better temper than yesterday.   He gave permission for us to move up the hill, as our present situation is very low.   I had several semi-faints while moving, but managed to walk up the hill, only collapsing twice on the way up.   It was a most lovely spot.   We pitched our tents upon a rocky eminence clothed with beautiful foliage, from whence we gazed out upon the broad expanse of the mighty inland sea."

The next day Romwa repeated his demands for presents. He took a fancy to Duta's gun, and requested that it might be sent to him at once.   Hannington absolutely refused. He said that nothing should be taken by force from his servant.   Romwa, seeing that he was firm, offered Duta two inferior guns in exchange.   The frightened boy unwillingly consented, and Romwa appeared in the distance, afraid to expose himself to witchcraft, but shouting his orders from a neighbouring rock.   As soon as the gun was taken from Duta, Hannington ordered the tent to be struck, and stated that his party would at once leave the country.   Romwa

shouted back that, in that case, they would have to pay two
hundred cloths as hongo, as they would not leave as friends.
Hannington replied that, rather than be so treated, he would
pay and go. Romwa now perceived that he had gone too far,
and sent a more conciliatory message, but they told him that
they were fully determined not to remain unless they were
allowed perfect liberty to come and go as they liked, and
were guaranteed against extortion. To emphasize this, the

tent was struck. Romwa now gave in, and granted all they
asked, but for some time they were in a very awkward position, and felt that they were kept there as a kind of state
prisoners, and at his mercy. However, at last, the king
consented that Hannington should proceed by himself to
U-Ganda, upon condition that the others remained. On
Jan. 22nd, he accordingly started in a canoe with two of
his boys. The usual procrastination delayed the start, and
by midnight the canoe and its occupants had not made much
way. Hannington says: " We crept quietly ashore, un-

certain whether the people were friendly or not.   A storm
on the lake had drenched all our things.   I had my wet bed
and blankets carried up a little way from the swamp-belt of
the lake.   The boys and men were afraid to remain with
me so far from the canoe, so I laid my weary frame to rest
under my umbrella, for it was raining, and unmindful of
natives or beasts of prey, I commended myself to the care of
the Almighty and fell asleep.   Soon a tremendous roar close
to my head caused me to start wide awake.   What could it
be—a lion?   No; lions are not so noisy.   It was only a
hippopotamus.   He had, no doubt, come up to feed, and
stumbled nearly on top of this strange object, a sleeping
white man with an umbrella over his head; so bellowing
out his surprise he made off for the lake."

Hannington's sketch, of which the subjoined is a not un-
faithful reproduction, does not altogether give the idea of a
night scene, but is otherwise very graphic, and illustrates not
only the incident, but the humorous good temper with
which he was accustomed to regard the discomforts and
perils of a missionary life.

"Before daybreak we were off, and soon reached Kagei.
I was welcomed by the Arab chief, Sayed bin Saif—'the
white man's friend'—and as I was seated, sipping some
delicious coffee, a strange white man stood before me.   I
sprang to my feet, only to hear, 'Bon jour, Monsieur.   C'est
M. Hannington, n'est-ce pas?' and then I knew that I was
in the presence of one of the French Jesuits.   They had
recently left U-Ganda, and had much to tell me of our
party at Rubaga, who were anxiously expecting my arrival.

"*24th.*—I had no sooner finished my usual cup of
milk and porridge, than one of the priests arrived and bade
me to breakfast.   I expected a cup of coffee, but found
déjeûner à la fourchette, and at six o'clock the hospitable

priests again provided for me a sumptuous dinner. They were very brotherly and kind."

Sayed bin Saif also treated Hannington right royally during his short stay at Kagei, and kept his table supplied with delicacies.

He says : " To-day being Sunday, he sent me an extra grand spread. A chicken stuffed with almonds and raisins ; a rich cake beautifully prepared with honey, and I have no doubt he would have sent me a second edition at night, but when he called to see how I was, I begged him to send no more to-day, as I had had enough for both meals."

When Mr. Gordon arrived, the large-hearted Arab sent him a special dish of curried beef, with rice banked up on it, mixed with raisins and all manner of curious spices. Hannington says: " This change of food has benefited us ; we have scarcely tasted meat for three months."

" I now began," he writes, " to prepare for the journey onward to Rubaga. Resolving not to return to Romwa's, I sent canoes to try and bring off Gordon and Ashe, if necessary, even by stealth. However, in a favourable mood, Romwa consented to their departure ; so Ashe returned to Msalala, and Gordon joined me at Kagei. We then agreed that I should go round by land to Msalala and bring the remainder of our goods to Kagei; after which we hoped, both of us, to be able to proceed to Buganda.

" *Jan.* 30*th.*—Took leave of the French priests and Sayed bin Saif. The latter was suffering from headache, and was greatly delighted with some ' sherbet' (Eno's Fruit Salt) which I gave him. I also presented him with our barometer, an article which I knew he was most ambitious to possess. 1.30, started with six men, a slave of the Arab's, and a guide, with my faithful Duta and Ibrahim. Walked till 4, and camped in a very pretty village in U-Sukuma."

"I had to cross U-Rima, in parts of which they had never seen a white man before. I had no reason to suppose that they would molest me. However, on Feb. 4th, a number of warriors, almost two hundred, turned out and surrounded me. The least show of resistance or of fear on our part might easily have been fatal. They peremptorily ordered me to stop and pitch my tent, and then they surrounded me with a cordon of armed men to prevent my escape. In the meanwhile they despatched runners to the chief of U-Rima, to tell him that they had captured a white man, and to ask what they should do with him. I was kept in this durance vile for the whole day, but I punished the rough soldiers around me, and myself not a little, by sulking within my closed tent, so that they were unable to inspect either me or my things. Just about sunset an ambassador arrived from the chief, demanding a present. I assured him that I had nothing suitable with me, whereupon he replied that he must be convinced that I spoke the truth. So, accordingly, I had to show him all I possessed. At my blanket—you know my blanket, it has been my companion for fifteen years—he paused. 'He must have that blanket, Bwana Mkubwa (great master).' I said, 'The white man is cold; he wants much clothes. If you take his blanket he will die. When the sun is gone to rest the white man grows chill. Leave him his blanket.' The earnestness of my eloquence prevailed, and the next day I was permitted to depart on condition that a messenger should accompany me to receive a present when we reached Msalala.

"Then arose a question about canoes to cross the Nullah. At first they were denied, but after a great deal of palaver, my arguments again prevailed. A council of war on an occasion of this kind was really a fine sight. I would sit on my bed in the tent and have the curtains at both ends flung aside. Then the ambassador would take the seat of honour next to me, his chief attendants near him, while close to me would be my men and boys. All around the tent without would crowd a throng of breathless listeners. I would tell my head man in Kiswahili what I wanted, and this he would translate in Kirima to the ambassador. He would say three or four words only at a time, snapping his fingers between each sentence, and further pausing for the audience to exclaim 'Baba.' As for example : 'The great white man' ('Baba!') 'has come a long distance' ('Baba!') 'He has come to teach the black man' ('Baba! Baba! Baba!'). 'He asks the black man to be kind' ('Baba!' rather feebly) ; and so on ; and if he spoke for an hour, no one would move, or interrupt, or object until he had concluded. Then all eyes would be turned to the ambassador, who in the same solemn way would state his objections. The first council of this kind is amusing enough, but when they come to be repeated two or three times a day, one's patience is most sorely taxed. The patience required in dealing with Africans is almost superhuman."

All this time Hannington was in great distress of body. The very day after he left Kagei he wrote in his diary : "Very ill with dysentery and violent internal pain. My liver, too, is in such a state that I have to walk with my hands tied to my neck to prevent my arms moving, as their least motion gives me intense pain." And so on, from day to day, ever from bad to worse, till, fainting and exhausted with cruel suffering, he barely crawled to his friend's tent at Msalala. He had struggled long and gamely, but his weakness now came upon him suddenly like an armed man ; he could no longer hide from himself the bitter truth ; and the brave heart which had so long supported him at last gave way. He confessed that he was "done."

VILLAGE IN URIMA WHERE I WAS DETAINED BY NATIVES, FEB. 3-5, 1883.

CHAPTER XVII.

BEATEN BACK.

(1883.)

"In la sua voluntade è nostra pace."
In His will is our peace.   DANTE.

"Joie, pleurs de joie; renonciation totale et douce."
PASCAL.

WHEN Hannington bade farewell to his friends at Kagei and started for Msalala, no one would have been more incredulous than himself had it been suggested that he was also bidding farewell to Africa. But it was even so. His struggles against those increasing symptoms by which an over-wrought nature was giving him notice of her inability longer to endure the strain put upon her, had been heroic. He had refused to believe that he was to be stopped before he reached his destination, and had set his face desperately toward the goal at the head of the lake. But it began now to dawn upon his reluctant mind that he was beaten.

Racked with fever ; torn by dysentery, scarce able to stand upright under the grip of its gnawing agony ; with his arms lashed to his neck lest their least movement should cause intolerable anguish to his diseased and swollen liver— the bright and buoyant figure which had so often led the caravan with that swinging stride of his, or which had forgotten fatigue at the close of a long march, and dashed off in pursuit of some rare insect—

"His beard a foot before him, and his hair a yard behind,"

was now bent and feeble, like that of a very old man.

Very pitiful is it to read the following—the words sound like a groan: " I am, I regret to say, beginning to look backwards. My life has become a burden to me. Oh, it should not be." When at last he reached Msalala, after a week's painful travel, he unburdened his heart to Mr. Ashe.

" The reply was, ' Listen to a letter which I have written to the Committee about you.' It ran somewhat as follows : ' Hannington is pressing on against all our advice : if he still lives, I look upon it as your duty to recal him.' "

There can be no doubt that Mr. Ashe was right. To have persisted under such circumstances would have been little short of suicide. " So," writes Hannington, " with a heart bowed with disappointment, I consented to leave those brave men to bear the burden and heat of the day by themselves. Yet, though deeply thankful for a spared life, I have never ceased to regret that, in a weak moment, I looked back."

To Mr. Wigram he wrote in a very broken-hearted way : " I dread to write to you, because my letter is one of the keenest disappointment, and contains no good news. . . . I am not dull at my broken health and the constant pain I suffer. I am not dull at the very slight prospect, from a human point of view, that I shall ever reach home. I am dull that I have been permitted to do so little for the Society. I am dull because I think that a few pounds extra in outfit would have made an immense difference to me. If I live a little longer I will write a short list of things that I have personally suffered much from not having. £10 will, I think, cover them all. I blame no one. It was simply a matter of want of experience. But, alas ! it costs both myself and the Society much, for I am a practical failure, and I have suffered terribly. Forgive me. . . . I hope my heart is full of praise for the tender mercies of the Lord. Even to-day I have experienced *that*."

Hannington now made arrangements, with a sad heart enough, for his departure. He arranged that Mr. Ashe should take his place, and accompany Mr. Gordon to Rubaga. He established Mr. Wise at Kagei. He received a deputation from the wily Romwa, who, " like Pharaoh, regretted that he had let the people go." Then, having put everything in as good order as he was able, and committed his fellow-workers and their Holy Cause to the keeping of his God, he threw himself into the same strong Hands, and, turning his face away from the great lake, commenced the long and weary journey to the distant coast. Alas ! how different was the aspect of that wild country to him *now* to the seeming of the land when he had entered it seven months before. *Then* it was the land of hope, and every step of the march over that seven or eight hundred miles of forest, morass, and desert—from the moment when he leapt into the water and waded ashore at Saadani, to that in which he gazed upon the waters of the Victoria Nyanza—had been lighted up by the gladness of his own heart, and the thought that every stage of the journey was one march nearer the sphere of his work. Now, he was returning, a disappointed man—in his own opinion, and that of his friends, appointed to die. He writes to Mr. Wigram from Uyui: " The rainy season is just at its worst. Blackburn is going to see me on my way. Perhaps it won't be far. I am going on and on, but against hope ; I am now a complete wreck. Do not make this public, for I do not wish my wife to see this mail. I have much want to write but can't." So he writes in disjointed sentences ; and, from the quavering formation of the characters and the straggling trend of the lines, the reader of that letter can easily surmise his extreme weakness and exhaustion. It is wonderful to note how, under such circumstances, he still continued to look at things from their bright side, and to take advantage of every happy or humorous

incident of the journey for future description and delinea-
tion. In him the old proverb, " There is life for a living
one," found its most literal illustration.

But we must give a few extracts from his own journal.

" *Feb.* 9*th.*—I have arranged to start to-day from
Msalala. It was a sad moment saying good-bye to Ashe
and Duta."

As we have seen, Hannington possessed a wonderful
gift of attracting to himself the devoted attachment of
young men. His English servant had thrown his arms
about his neck and wept passionately when he left Hurstpierpoint; his black boys, also, felt and owned his influence. Duta was no exception. When left alone with
him upon one occasion, Hannington wrote of him in the
following terms : " I am now under the most tender care
of my faithful boy. However ill, I should be content to
be in his hands. The Lord has indeed blessed me in this
respect, for none of the others have been able to get on
with their boys."

" 11*th, Sunday.*—I had the Service to myself, and was
refreshed by it and the pleasant rest. I have tried to hire
men to carry me, but cannot conscientiously afford their
price.

" 12*th.*—Started at daybreak, and soon entered the
plain. It was covered with thick grass, wringing wet with
dew and higher than one's head, and there was water in
most places up to the ankles ; elsewhere mud of the most
horrible consistence. No Sussex fallow ever bound more
tenaciously. The detonations were as loud sometimes as
pistol-pops as the foot was drawn out and the air rushed
into the deep hole in which it had been imbedded. Several
times I thought I must give up before the three hours'
march was over. Then came a second plain, with even

worse ground and more water. One of those tropical showers came on, accompanied by thunder and lightning, and we took refuge in a native hut, while the ground literally ran with water.

" 13*th.*—I was so exhausted yesterday that I thought it advisable to try to get carried to-day, but could not succeed in making an arrangement, so walked as far as the little Sultan's. They were at war. Two corpses lay in the path, evidently only just killed. One was headless. On arriving at the village, I found the people in the most turbulent and excited state, just starting upon another raid. One old man, of disgusting and truculent aspect, and with a piece of the brain of the beheaded man tied to his hair and hanging down upon his forehead, was addressing a wild mob. I am failing with fever, and have a splitting headache. The drums are beating and the people incessantly yelling. The little Sultan took up his abode in my tent, and wanted everything. Fortunately, he was sufficiently amused to let me go on with my writing. While I am writing these words he has got hold of my breechloader in one hand, and is making a raid upon the arrowroot box with the other. To my great terror, my gold spectacles are next on his nose, and he is asking to go for a walk in them, and to be allowed to carry the gun. I can't very well refuse, so I follow him and see him, so caparisoned, join in the war-dance of his warriors. The war-dance was most ferocious. The warriors, all armed to the teeth, make a sham attack, then they retire, and the women rush in and encourage them, yelling with their shrill voices like demons. The drums beat with incessant fury, while guns are discharged and bullets whizz past in the most promiscuous manner. It was no small satisfaction to me when, at last, the warriors retired to the proper field of battle, and left the village in comparative peace.

" 14*th*.—Dysentery and extreme exhaustion. I hired men who carried me. Met Edmonds, who was on the march to Msalala. He returned with me, sending the caravan and cloth in charge of Bunduki to Ashe.

" 15*th*.—Had been told that a midnight attack upon the village might be expected—rather, I think, with the view of finding out whether I could be relied upon to help in such an emergency. Towards the small hours I was awaked by a shot, and heard the whizz of a bullet; then some twenty shots or more. 'Am I to fight,' said I to myself, 'or not?' 'Am I to see this village burnt to the ground, my men killed, myself——?' Then I heard a laugh. 'It is not war,' thought I; 'I will answer that question another time.' So I turned over and went to sleep. The next morning we heard that it was a lion which had sprung over the stockade into the cattle-pen. Lions are dangerous sometimes. At Uyui there was no door to the room in which I slept, and the very day after I left it I was told that a lion had seized and killed a woman in broad daylight, close by.

" 17*th*.—Tooth extracted by one of the French priests whom we met just past Shimami's. To my despair, he produced a very rough hawk's-bill instrument, had one or two tries to adjust it, and finally broke the tooth off; however, he relieved the pain.

" 18*th*, *Sunday*.—We invited the priests to meals. Had our morning Service. Both touched with fever. I was very ill during the night, but got some valuable hints from the priests.

" 19*th*.—The French priests took leave of us, and one of them presented me with a very curious pair of U-Ganda shoes, which I gladly accepted to add to my collection.

" As we marched we fell in with many rivers and morasses, and the rains became so heavy that I doubted

NEAR MAKOLA'S VILLAGE, JORDAN'S NULLAH.

whether we could go much further.   There was an immense deal of water on the road, sometimes ankle-, sometimes knee-deep, and sometimes I have been carried for the
best part of an hour with the water up to the men's chins.
In cases of this kind I used to cling round the pole of my

Crossing a lake

hammock, and six men would carry me on their heads, as if
I were a log of wood.   I have often thought of poor Dr.
Livingstone's trials, and realized what he went through,
for my own experience very closely resembled his.   If the
picture on the cover of 'His Last Journals' is correct, my
mode of being carried across deep streams is, I think, better
than his.   If you glance at the illustration you will see that

I knelt on the shoulders of a tall, powerful man, and held
the uplifted hands of another in front, while a third behind
grasped my feet and kept us steady.   In very swift streams,
sometimes six or eight men were required to keep the three
bearers, with their burden, from being swept away.

   " These floods kept me in constant suspense lest, in my

The above and succeeding sketches are all reduced fac-similes
from the Bishop's note-book.

weak state, I should be plunged into the water; but far worse are the morasses. For a mile together I have been borne through the most horrible black mud, often above the knee. This was exceedingly fatiguing for the men and trying to me, the more so as I knew that I was inhaling malarious poison of the worst description.

"23*rd*.—My men again ran away, and I had to walk, or rather crawl, for fifteen miles, which tired greatly my poor little strength. We crossed a picturesque bridge over a very wide river, and reached our friends at Urambo at about 12 o'clock, and received a very kind welcome." (This is a station of the L. M. S.)

"Shaw kindly received me, and Willoughby entertained

Through black mud.

Edmonds, who had joined me a few days before. Willoughby was not in when I arrived. He has since told me that Shaw came outside the house to tell him that he would find me very altered—dying, in fact—but he must not appear to notice the change, lest it should alarm me. He asked my black men about me. They replied, 'Master must die; he is sure to die; but how is it master is always so happy? Black man would lie down by the side of the road and die like a sheep.' *

---

* On two occasions the bearers laid what they believed to be his lifeless body on the ground, and left it, saying that it was useless to concern themselves further about a corpse. Each time consciousness returned, and he crawled painfully after the caravan till he was discovered. But through all, his patience and cheerfulness never forsook him.

" Penry, one of the L. M. S. men, who had also been ill and was returning home, wished to join me. This delayed me a few days, during which time I had an interview with the celebrated King Mirambo. Mirambo's history is too long for me to attempt to give it here. He was first called Mtelya, but in consequence of his many victories he assumed the name of Mirambo, which seems to mean 'Killing many men.' He is further surnamed Nzige, or Locust, because they say he eats up all before him; and lately he has added the name of Malomo-Maliu, or Five Lamps, being the number of important places around, in all of which, as he says, 'he is able to discern between friends and foes.'

" Before Mirambo came to the throne he used to get drunk on pombé just as others; when, however, he was made king, he at once became a total abstainer, for he said, 'I could not do all my business and govern my people well if I drank pombé.' He was formerly a most blood-thirsty tyrant, inspiring terror for miles round; but now, though not yet a Christian, he has been strongly influenced by Christianity, and is very favourable to Missionaries.

" Justice in Urambo is swift and sudden. A short time before our arrival the king had ordered a levy of men to be made in the surrounding villages. Three men in a distant village made excuse, saying they were ill. The next day, Mirambo, without any warning, arrived in that village, and found them busily engaged with their own work. He immediately ordered their heads to be struck off. The resident Missionary said to him, 'Mirambo, our Queen is a great Sovereign; she never does things of this sort;' and then he proceeded to explain to him the judge and jury system.

" 'Yes,' replied Mirambo, 'that is very good for your Queen; she is, no doubt, surrounded by clever gentlemen;

but it would not do for me. My people are so foolish, I can only govern them in this way.'

"When Captain Hore of the L. M. S. passed through, Mirambo gave special instructions that no one should raise a finger against his white friend. The night before he left the capital, one of Mirambo's pages was caught stealing, and, as a slight punishment, was tied to a post. It happened that Mirambo, visiting the white man's camp in the early morning, before the rest were awake, spied his own page in durance vile. He hastily retired, and by and by sent down privately to inquire how this came about. He heard, and held his peace until Captain Hore had departed ; he then sent for his page, who had returned to the palace.

"'Where were you last night?' 'Thy servant went no whither,' was the unblushing lie. 'Then I will tell you where you went;' and so he recounted all. 'Now,' said he, 'I will teach my people not to disobey orders, and molest my white friends.' So he took a bow and arrow and shot him through the heart, and then, as he did not die instantly, took his bow and bowstrung him. The act was cruel and severe, but the circumstances of the case must be remembered. It is a noted fact that he is not accustomed to put anybody to death with his own hand, but always employs an executioner. In this case he made a special exception, in order to let his people know that he had had nothing to do with the theft, and that he meant to stand by the white man and protect him from molestation.

"One of his medicine men came to examine me. This man was of vastly superior morality to the majority of his fellows. His method was to use a pair of lazytongs, with a little figure at the end, over which he appeared to breathe a prayer. When the doll had peered into my chest, by an almost imperceptible turn of the wrist it returned to its master to deliver its message. This was thrice repeated,

and then I was told that I had a cold, which, considering
that I had been coughing and sneezing ever since I had
been in the hut, was easy to guess and impossible to deny.
I questioned him about his medicine, and asked if he
thought that putting a little bottle in the earth, and saying
a few words over it, could make rain. He replied : ' Certainly not! only God could make rain ; but how can we
expect Him to do so unless we pray and make right offerings ? ' He always went into the forest to pray, so we
asked him if God was only in the forest ? ' No ; but the
forest is retired and quiet. There is only one God.' Here,
of course, was a great opening for Gospel teaching, which
he was quite ready to listen to.

" Now, lest any should think that this man was sufficiently enlightened, and stood in no need of our teaching,
hear the following tale. His son was dying, and he sent a
message to Mirambo to accuse a man of bewitching him.
The answer was : ' You know the punishment for witchcraft ; apply it.' The accused, however, was a desperate
character, and nobody dared to carry out the sentence, so
word was sent to the king, who asked which of his warriors
would undertake the business. All shrank back but one
man, whom I knew well, and who expressed himself as
willing to do it. The supposed wizard was asked to meet
him at supper. This he refused, so he went to the man's
house, and stood near his door till he could shoot at him and
wound him. The men round then rushed in, and speared
him to death !

" *February* 27*th.*—As Penry is unable to get men, we
have asked Edmonds to go round to Unyanyembe alone,
and let us cut across to Uyui direct.

" *March* 5*th.*—Packed up and started with Penry for
Uyui at 10 a.m.

" *March* 7*th.*—I had a sharp attack of fever, and ought

to have stopped ; but onward was the word, and this I
heartily endorsed, as, when in fever, I was generally better
on the road ; so, sometimes walking, sometimes carried, I
went forward till about three o'clock, when I became worse,
fainted, and seemed to be dying. However, by the mercy
of God, I rallied, and the next day we resumed our
journey.

"*March 9th.*—Off before daybreak, and was carried
until one o'clock, when I was taken desperately ill in the
desert, and had another fainting fit. We were near no
camping ground or any shelter. At four o'clock I endeavoured to stand, but was unable, so I had the tent pitched
close to where I lay. Then I begged them to carry me to
it, about ten yards off. The trouble would not have been
great, but my headman refused, and two of them led me by
the arms. The consequence was I again fainted.

"*March 10th.*—At one a.m. woke, very ill. Suffocat-
ing action of the heart. Took stimulant, but for an hour
I appeared to be sinking. Scarcely able to whisper, I sent
for Penry, and took leave of him. But when day dawned
I revived slightly, and, although I could not stand, and
scarcely move hand or foot, I allowed myself to be
lifted into the hammock and be carried on. The air
refreshed me, but when we reached Uyui, at about nine
o'clock, I was again apparently in a dying condition.
Blackburn, who had come to meet me, seeing how I was,
ran to the house, prepared a bed, and revived me with
strong stimulants. Humanly speaking, I owe my life to his
assiduous attention. I was then moved into the school-
room where I had lain so long on the way up, and felt as
happy as possible, though utterly prostrate. All agreed that
my only chance of recovery was that the fever should not
recur. Before sunset, however, it set in heavily with
delirium.

" *March* 11*th, Sunday.*—As soon as the fever passed my temperature sank very low, and the cold sweat of death seemed to stand on my brow. I asked them to have the Service in my room, and none of us thought that I should see another Sunday. In the afternoon the fever returned, and my dear boy, Backit, stayed by my side for twenty-four hours, while I was delirious, without leaving to eat a mouthful. I remained in this critical state for five days; Blackburn very kind, and watching by my bedside. At times I could not help smiling at his intense desire to save my life —it seemed such a hopeless struggle.

" *March* 15*th.*—Called two of my boys, got up, and, leaning on their arms, went out of doors, and, to the utter amazement of everybody, walked about a hundred yards. On the 17th I was weighed—8 stone 6 pounds. That is to say, I had lost four stone since leaving England.

" On the 17th we made preparation for departure. I feel that I must proceed for life or death. Either will be welcome, though I confess to a longing to live. Blackburn insists that he will come with us as far as Mpwapwa. From this time," he adds, " I began slowly to mend."

Writing for the children at home, Hannington described his experiences of life in a hammock in a serio-comic vein. He says :

" It sounds very luxurious to be transported from place to place in a hammock. Well, all I can say is, let those who think they would like it try it. I am sure I could write a book on the subject; I have had such an experience of the excitements, monotonies, and discomforts of the hammock. I will give you just one illustration. Sometimes the man in front falls down, and I fall forward. On one such occasion the bearer was, by some miraculous means, pinned to the ground by the hammock-pole; nor

could he move until a companion released him.   Sometimes
the man behind would trip up ; in which case I fell on the

Fall forwards and catch my porter

back of my head.   At another time he would glide on to
his knees, and let me down in several inches of black mud.

Fall backwards

Yet, again, *both* bearers would trip simultaneously, and a
complete downfall would take place.

Smash

"Then boughs would whip one in the face ; or the men
would bang one against sharp-pointed stumps of trees ; or
stepping unequally, jump one up and down like a pea on
a drum.   One good man who carried me had a kind of

spring-halt which was particularly unpleasant, especially
after a meal.   As for being lifted over and under fallen
trees; being handed down
deep ravines and up the other
side, with one's feet far above
one's head; why, that happened so often that I grew
accustomed to have my heels
high in the air."

After a time Hannington
discharged his Wa-Nguana carriers, and hired Wa-Nyamwezi.
He says, " The Wa-Nguana
are bad travellers in regard to
weight, good good in respect of not caring about the
shape of the load.   They have learnt, too, the white man's
ways.   They know that he must have clean camping
ground and good water.
They are very handy about
the camp and tent.   Wa-
Nyamwezi, on the other hand,
are very stupid about camp
but they are splendid load
carriers, and, as travellers,
are up to anything, so long
as you do not ask them to
venture out at night."

On March 27, a dispute
arose with the Wa-Nyamwezi porters which might
have turned out very awkwardly.   One of them was slightly
punished for having insulted Mr. Blackburn, whereupon his
companions threatened to desert in a body unless he were

compensated by a present of cloth. This would have left the white men helpless in the midst of a pori (desert). Matters looked serious, as the men would not give way, and their masters could not overlook the breach of discipline. They met together in Hannington's tent, and laid the matter before the Lord. Prayer was scarcely finished, when they heard the headman of the Wa-Nyamwezi making a speech, followed by a sign of assent from the multitude, and a messenger was sent to them to say that the Wa-Nyamwezi acknowledged themselves to be in the wrong, and that the white men were right. So they praised God, and continued on their way.

Result of leaving my hammock
I fail to punish a transgressor

On April the 19th, after the usual trials with porters, and discomforts attendant upon travelling in the rainy season, they reached Kisokwe, where a hearty welcome awaited them from Mr. and Mrs. Cole. Hannington writes : " When we approached Kisokwe (near Mpwapwa), I saw that, even since my last visit, the population had considerably increased, and that fresh tembes had been built. Indeed, it is not necessary that a white man should fix himself in an unhealthy situation merely because it has a large population. Let him choose a healthy and convenient site, and the people will soon swarm around him. This, of course, does not apply to towns like Rubaga, and those on the west coast, but to intermediate stations and districts.

On the way I was greatly upset to hear of Mrs. Last's death. This is, indeed, sad for poor Last. They were so happy and comfortable at Mamboia, and seemed likely to do a great work.*· On arriving at the Coles's house I was greatly affected at the sight of the baby. The thought of my own sweet children filled my heart, and the slight hope I have had, and still have of ever seeing them again all came before me so vividly that I must confess to crying like a child. I rushed at the baby, and begged to be allowed to hold and kiss it. Ah! what changes are wrought in one out here in the wilderness. I am not one bit ashamed to own this, though, but a short time ago, I should have looked upon it as the most intense weakness."

" Penry seems very sleepy and strange to-day. We all think that he has taken too large a dose of opium to ward off the dysentery from which he is suffering. He has slept nearly all the day and eats nothing." Mr. Penry had been for some time in a very weak state, but had given his friends no serious alarm. He, however, had not Hannington's recuperative powers, and at Kisokwe quite suddenly sank and died. The following entry describes the end :

" At about one p.m. we were summoned to his bedside, and he seemed to be dying. I treated him as I had had myself treated over and over again, and toward daybreak he seemed better. However, he grew weaker during the day, and on the day following he quietly fell asleep in Jesus. We made the coffin, and with our own hands lifted him gently into it, and buried him that same night by the grave of Dr. Mullens, at Mpwapwa."

The above extract from the diary must be sufficient, as we cannot here repeat all that he writes of the terrible and

---

* Not long after this. Mrs. Cole also died.

repulsive details of a death by dysentery. " Monsr. * and I performed the last offices, and very terrible they were. Monsr., who had worked many years in a hospital, was at the time even more upset than I was."

This death was a great shock to Hannington ; he says : " Shall I, who have been always looked upon as the worse of the two—and especially by Penry himself—be the next prey that death will seize ? "

Sunday, the 22nd, was spent quietly at Kisokwe with the Coles. " These kind people having insisted that I should stay with them, I have to-day had an opportunity of witness- ing their Sunday work, though, with them, every day is a Sunday, and spent in Missionary endeavour. To-day there was a Service at about 11 for natives. The church was well filled by Wa-Gogo and Wa-Nguana, and the Service was accordingly divided into parts, and made to suit both sections. Short addresses and catechisms were given in both tongues. They joined in the hymns very fairly, and are fond of singing, but the Africans here have not good voices ; they can chant monotonously, but I have not heard one really good voice among them, even among the boys in Zanzibar Cathedral. At 3 p.m. there was another Service in the vernacular, and an even better attendance. I tell Cole that he will soon have to build a new church." (Mrs. Cole's remarkable Sunday School Class has already been described on page 217.) " The Mpwapwa work is very similar to this, and is being energetically carried on by Mr. Price. He and Blackburn walked over to Kisokwe, and I administered the Holy Communion to the little gathering, and a very solemn and devoted time we had together."

" 23rd.—As some of Penry's things have to be disposed

---

* One of the Jesuit band who accompanied the caravan to the coast.

of here, in accordance with his instructions, I have another
day in this pleasant spot with these agreeable people,
and my friend the baby, who is a wonder for size, and is
healthy and strong, and very good tempered. The natives
delight in him, and call him a Mgogo, one of themselves,
born in their country, and so quite different to other
Wazungu (white men) who were born in Ulia (Europe).
The day passed only too quickly, and, in spite of a good
deal of pain—for I have been poisoned by the terrible
stench in attending upon the dying man, and have a slight
attack of dysentery—I enjoyed myself greatly, spending
a portion of the day in pursuit of my favourite study of
botany. I ascended one of the surrounding hills for a
short distance. The panorama is magnificent. The distant
hills of U-Sagara are visible, range after range rising in the
far distance, and gradually fading in colouring until they
are quite blended with the clouds."

The next morning they were off again, and, after a
night at Mpwapwa, took the path for the coast. Hannington says : " I find an immense advantage in having
everything placed in exactly the same spot every time
that the tent is pitched, and insisting upon it. After a
little trouble at first, the boys soon learn to know what you
want, and do it without being told, so that when you step
into your tent at the end of a march, though all is fresh
outside, yet within it looks as though the tent had not been
moved ; and what is more, you know where to find everything even in the dark."

" *April* 25*th*.—One of the up country mails passed us,
and say that our letters are a day or two behind them, so it
will not be long before we get more news of dear home.
How I delight in the thought ! "

" 26*th*.—Onwards, ever onwards ; pori and plain to pass.

Beautiful weather and good-tempered men, though always inclined to be troublesome. Camped 5000 feet above sea level. Air so cold that I quite shivered.

"27*th.*—Mamboia. Keen disappointment. Last gone away for six days. Our messengers had loitered, and did not arrive till too late. So no welcome and no rest."

On the 29th, Mr. Last, who had heard of the visit, caught up Hannington's party, and accompanied him on his journey for a day or two. In the keen and bracing air of the mountains near Kwa Chiropa, Hannington recovered his strength rapidly, and he ascended to some height with Mr. Last, making botanical collections. "On our way down we saw an abandoned village, the inhabitants of which had all died of small-pox. The havoc which this disease makes is terrible. It is computed that during the epidemic in Zanzibar which lasted about four months, 30,000 deaths occurred. When we returned, we found that one of Mr. Last's men had run away, taking with him his gun, sextant, and prismatic compass!"

"28*th.*—Took leave of Last. For an hour or so we waded through the most horrible black mud, knee-deep, and smelling beyond description, densely overhung with grass and reeds to the height of 10 to 20 feet. So, more or less, all day till we reached camp.

"Soon after arriving, a message came from Dr. Baxter that he had heard that Penry and I were very ill, and that he was returning to meet us. Happily I now require no doctoring, and Penry has gone, but I cannot imagine a nobler act than that a man should return from the coast at this season of the year, with heavy rain still threatening. The moment we stepped out of the village on May 3rd we were in black mud and water knee-deep, and this continued till we reached a branch of the River Wami. The same

fearful swamp till the next river, and so on.   One river was
crossed by a loose bridge of creepers and poles partly knee-
deep in water.   Here we had more difficulty than anywhere.
It was not until I drove away the men and made them swim
for it that we were able to get at all into order.   I then
posted men all across the bridge, and had the loads handed
from one to the other ; and thus, as a load, was I handed
across myself.   Two hours were occupied in getting over
about 80 loads.   Then deep mud for the rest of the journey ;
and then Kidudwa and the cheering sight of the good
doctor.   It was in one way a great satisfaction to me to
hear the doctor say, after he had gone into my case, that I
had done right to return, and that I could not have done
anything else.   For the last day or two I have recovered so
fast that I have had serious questionings with myself
whether I should not now return to the lake.   This Dr.
Baxter entirely forbids.   He says that I should be mad were
I to think of returning."

The next day, in crossing a river, they got separated
from their men and then from each other, and finally did not
reunite their forces until after a long and tedious time.
" Did not get into camp until night.   No cooked food all
day.   I was utterly done up, and, I am sorry to say, very
tart with everybody.   Blackburn, however, quite won my
heart ; for, seeing how matters stood, and how knocked up
I was, he did all he could to make me comfortable, without
appearing to notice how irritable I was.   We are travelling
too fast for a sick man, but it is entirely my own doing, as
I am very anxious to catch the Sultan's steamer."

" *May 6th.*—Our last Sunday on the main land ; perhaps
in Africa.   This day week I hope to be at sea !   As this
was the first place at which we have stopped where the
coast language is spoken or understood, Dr. Baxter held a

Kiswahili Service in the open air. Quite a crowd or people gathered round, and listened to what he had to say.

" *May 8th.*—Arrived at Saadani at about 10 a.m.

" *May 9th.*—Called at 2 a.m. to the boat. As usual, everything in confusion and excitement. The Wa-Nyamwezi who were travelling with us had taken possession of the second boat, and our men were stuffing themselves into our boat, and were quarrelling and shouting for places in a dreadful manner. We were able, after a time, to hire another boat. Let me warn travellers against allowing another party of natives to attach itself to their caravan. I held out against it from the very first. However, all's well that ends well. We started at about 4 a.m., and had a speedy run across to Zanzibar, arriving at about 10 o'clock. A good bit of trouble at the Custom-house, chiefly through those horrid Wa-Nyamwezi, who tried to smuggle their own goods through, on pretence that they were ours. Went to the French Hotel. Heard that the steamer starts on Saturday, at about 12 noon. This is good news, as far as getting away from Zanzibar is concerned, but it gives us very little time.

" *11th.*—Yesterday and to-day I have been hard at work getting my things packed, and making the necessary arrangements for the start. I have been exceedingly well. Called at the Universities' Mission, and some of them called upon me ; but I have very little to enter in my diary, as the details of packing are not interesting.

" *12th.*—I concluded all my own arrangements, and was ready by 12.45 ; but where was ———— ? He had overslept himself, and then forgotten the time, and was not ready. I had the greatest difficulty in getting him off, and in the end the steamer started without him, when an umbrella was seen waving in the distance, and they stopped and took him in; however, he had to leave the greater part of his luggage behind. All I say about it is to ask, How men can systematically do such things, and get through the world at all? One result was, that the cabins which had been chosen for us had been given to other people, and we were obliged to share one between us."

So the long and perilous journey was at length completed. The sick man whose life had been so often despaired of stood upon the deck of the homeward-bound steamer, and felt that every revolution of the screw was bearing him nearer to those friendly faces and voices which he had thought never again to see or hear.

Already the project was forming within his heart to revisit the dark land from which he had been compelled to flee. He would not be content now until he had retrieved his defeat, and planted the banner of Christ in the centre of the Great Continent. He had seen that the most savage and degraded people were amenable to Christian influence, and he meant, at no distant time, God helping him, to make another attempt to carry the Gospel to them. He wrote, after his arrival in England: " I am thankful for experience gained, and that I have lived to plead a cause which is nearer than ever to my heart; for I have seen the need of the Africans, and have realized the sufferings of their spiritual teachers. As for the former, though they are ofttimes ' hateful and hating,' yet there is much in them both to admire and to love. Even men who, like Romwa, or ' the old man of the sea,' lied, cheated, and extorted to the utmost of their power, touched a tender spot in our hearts. With all their depravity and darkness, I fully endorse Livingstone's words, that there are excellent traits in their character; that they compare favourably with the early history of now civilized nations, and are capable of a high degree of culture."

He adds : " Forgive the one that turned back." But though that " turning back " was only a retreat before overwhelming necessity, he could never forgive himself until his foot was once more planted upon African soil.

CHAPTER XVIII.

THE SECOND MISSIONARY JOURNEY.

(1883—4.)

"O bona Patria, lumina sobria te speculantur :
   Ad tua nomina, sobria lumina collacrymantur :
   Est tua mentio pectoris unctio, cura doloris,
   Concipientibus œthera mentibus ignis amoris."

BERNARD DE MORLAIX.

"For thee, O dear, dear Country !
   Mine eyes their vigils keep ;
For very love beholding
   Thy happy name, they weep :
The mention of thy glory
   Is unction to the breast,
And medicine in sickness,
   And love and life and rest."

Trans. by DR. NEALE.

ON June 10th, 1883, Hannington was again among his friends in England. They had anxiously followed his course homeward during his terrible journey from the Lake, and the infrequent letters which he had written when he was able to hold the pen had all been treasured up. He was received as one alive from the dead. Both in the Committee Room of the C. M. S., in Salisbury Square, and from his people at Hurst, he met with the warmest welcome. What passed between the husband and wife thus given back to each other may be better surmised than described. Once more the "little dear face" of his own baby was taken between his hands and kissed; and the other little ones whom, three months before, he thought he " would never see again," were gathered up into his arms. He settled down to his work at Hurst as though he had never left it, and his young men once again rallied round him.

But with returning health the desire to assail once more the fortress from which he had been driven back came strongly upon him. He never for a moment lost the idea that he was to renew his labours in Africa. He was saturated through and through with the Missionary spirit, and he counted the days when he should have sufficiently recovered his wasted strength to again face the Medical Board, and retrieve his first repulse. In the meantime, since he could not persuade anybody that he was well enough for work in the tropics, he placed himself at the disposal of the C. M. S. Committee for deputation work at home. During the next twelve months he both preached and spoke upon platforms many times in behalf of the Society. His graphic descriptions of the life and labours of an African Missionary, and his earnest appeals in behalf of the Mission cause, will be long remembered in many an English town and village. The " C. M. S. Report " for 1884 thus alludes to him: " The health mercifully given back to him by the Great Healer has been employed without stint in service at home, as the Society's friends all over the country well know; and the Committee trust that the desire of their dear brother's heart may be granted to him, and that he may be enabled to go forth again into the field." So runs the Report; and well did the Secretaries know the " desire of his heart," for there was no available occasion when he did not present himself at the " House," to see whether the doctors might not be prevailed upon to take a more favourable view of his state. On Oct. 8th, 1883, he writes to his wife :

" I saw the Board to-day, and the verdict was ' Africa NEVER.' And so I say, The will of the Lord be done. Any question about other climates and countries must be left for the present. I am very melancholy about Africa. But I ought not to be."

His state of mind may be somewhat realized from the following intensely characteristic letter, dated Dec. 5th :

" MY DEAR,—

      " Hallelujah, Amen.
      Hallelujah, Amen.
      Hallelujah, Amen.
    HALLELUJAH ! ! !
     HALLELUJAH !
   And again I cry, Hallelujah !

" And now quietly to begin my tale.

" What a wonderful thing ! I was feeling so fagged on Monday that I thought I would not go up to town until Tuesday, and almost made up my mind not to start, but was overruled. On arriving at the Square, I found that there was a Medical Board sitting, and asked how many were to be seen. I was told, Only one. So I said to B——, more than half in fun, I wish you would ask them to see me. I scarcely thought he would say anything about it, but lo ! he went and put my name down to be interviewed. I was quite frightened when he told me, as I thought they would be in an awful rage, as I had been told not to come up before April.

" I went in, and, after a long interview, the verdict was, ' *May go anywhere except Africa and Ceylon.*'

" Hallelujah, Hallelujah, Hallelujah ! ! !

" But this was not all (drowning men catch at a straw). At first I was not encouraged by it ; but I presently learnt that Mr. Wigram had slipped into the Committee, and told the news to Mr. Stock. I took that to be a good sign. But when, the next morning, Mr. Wigram shook hands with me and said, ' I am so thankful to hear the verdict,' I was not able to speak much, but my heart said Hallelujah, Amen; and I am quite certain that you will be able to join in the cry. Of course, nothing is settled. I am to see the Board again in April, so that really we are only one step further advanced; but there are signs enough to make any Missionary heart rejoice. Once more judged worthy to anticipate.

" Fly in and tell my brother to rejoice together with us."

Such a letter was the safety-valve of a bursting heart. It reveals in a wonderful manner the intensity of the fires which were burning within him. At this time he had no thought of the Bishopric. It had not occurred to his mind that he might be sent out again in any other capacity than that in which he had sailed eighteen months before. Those who knew him best can testify that at this time it was impossible that ambition should have had any part in lighting those flames by which he was inwardly consumed. His friends thought that he had done enough; but it was borne in upon his mind with ever-increasing insistency that a dispensation of the Gospel had been committed to him, and that he must return to the Mission-field; his heart made request that it might be to Africa; but, if that were forbidden, then—somewhere else.

> " He saw a Hand they could not see
>   Which beckoned him away;
> He heard a Voice they could not hear
>   Which would not let him stay."

When health had fully returned, and the Bishopric was offered to him, he took it as a sign from God that he had a work to do for Christ in Africa. About accepting the Bishopric he had his doubts and fears; about returning to

Africa, none. When I wrote to congratulate him and wish him God-speed, he replied : ' I feel that I could no more say No than did Gordon when he went to Khartoum."

When Hannington visited Edinburgh in January, 1884, we noticed a great change in him. His old exuberance of spirits was gone. We were almost inclined to say to him, " Is all laughter gone dead out of thee ? " It was evident that he had passed through a heavy strain, which had taxed his constitution to the utmost. By and by flashes of the old wit somewhat reassured us ; but it was plain that the rough chastening of those terrible months of sickness in Africa would leave scourge marks not readily to be healed or forgotten. At the same time, that " chastisement " had not been without its distinct benefit. He was in every way softened and mellowed. While his sense of the humorous was as keen as ever, his consideration for the feelings of others was much greater than formerly. He was gentler and more tender, quieter, and more outwardly affectionate in his manner than of yore. The current of his life seemed to run more stilly and more deep.

Just now and again the old " Jim " would leap into life and almost make me forget that we were not still undergraduates together. As, when we were spending the two hours which intervened between the morning and afternoon Services in the vestry, he suddenly declared that his legs were so stiff with sitting still that he was sure he should not be able to ascend the pulpit steps, and so, placing two chairs close to each other, he leapt backwards and forwards over them till he was tired with the exercise and I with laughing. What a sight—had some " grave and reverend signor," some austere father of the Church, looked in at that moment ! Ah me, would he not have concluded that the " deputation " who had so edified him in the morning had suddenly gone mad ! But we knew better.

He remained with us rather more than a week. We found his society very helpful. His attitude of mind was deeply spiritual, and there was nothing which he loved more than to talk over some passage from Scripture, often throwing the most vivid light upon its inner meaning.

He was very full of his African work, and all the time he was with us was busy preparing those sketches of his adventures, many of which appeared in the *Graphic* and other illustrated papers, and a few of which have been reproduced in this work. Seated in a low chair in a corner of the study, with a box of water-colours and a sheet of drawing paper, he would fight his battles over again, and narrate every incident with the keenest zest. I had the great advantage of hearing from his own lips most of those exploits which have been chronicled in these pages. He was full of hope after his last interview with the Medical Board, and was looking forward eagerly to the time when he should be again examined; for he firmly believed that he would in the end be permitted to return to the Dark Continent.

There was one change in him which, at the time, I failed to understand, but the cause of which has since been made clear to me. In former days Hannington had been the most generous of men. He did not seem to consider money, but rather rejoiced in spending it upon any object which took his fancy. Now, though he did not specially allude to the subject, I could not help seeing that he was careful in his expenditure, and weighed the cost of everything. I should not perhaps have noticed this, had I not been so familiar with his character; but, knowing his former habits, and that his income was not diminished, it did occur to me once or twice to ask myself whether this new phase implied that my friend was becoming " near." It was not until after his death that this was explained, and I discovered that he had been giving a FIFTH of his strictly-limited income to *one* society alone, irrespective of his other charities. O thou noble soul ; thy gifts did not stop short of self-sacrifice, nor didst thou offer to the Lord what cost thee nothing !

Shortly after this the Committee of the C. M. S. began to reconsider a scheme which had been first mooted in the life-time of the Rev. Henry Wright, that the Mission Churches of Eastern Equatorial Africa should be placed under the supervision of a Bishop. The Universities' Mission, over which Bishops Mackenzie, Steere, and Smythies have been successively placed, has its own sphere of work, but does not extend so far into the interior as the stations of the C. M. S., which had been hitherto without episcopal supervision. Mr. Wright had corresponded with Bishop Steere as early as 1880 on the subject of a division of territory, and the formation of a new See, and had received assurances of his cordial sympathy and cooperation. No further steps, however, were taken until the scheme was revived in this year 1884. It was now felt that the increasing number of stations in Central Africa demanded supervision. That the Mission having been placed upon a sound basis, what it now required was that the widely-scattered Churches should be bound together by the personal influence of one who would have authority to command, wisdom to organize, and character to ensure that his commands should be obeyed. The Committee, therefore, began to seek for some man who united in himself, with unfeigned Missionary ardour, a somewhat rare combination of gifts.

The post demanded a man of dauntless personal courage, tact, spirituality of mind, and prompt, business-like habits— a man who coupled gentleness with a strong personality. Hannington had proved that he combined these opposite characteristics in himself to a very remarkable extent. The eyes of the Committee naturally turned to him. His health had so rapidly improved during the past six months that Sir Joseph Fayrer, the climatologist, gave it as his unqualified opinion that he might now return to Africa with a good prospect of being able to live and labour there for many years. This being so, the matter was laid before him, and he, after much searching of heart, but with deep gratitude to God as for the answer to his constant prayer, accepted the responsibility. The consent of the Archbishop had been already obtained, and the consecration took place on St. John the Baptist's Day, June 24th, in the Parish Church of Lambeth.

On that day two Missionary Bishops were consecrated for foreign work, the other being the Hon. and Rev. A. J. R. Anson, who was appointed to the diocese of Assiniboia.

Shortly before eleven o'clock, the two Bishops-Designate met the Archbishop, together with the Bishops of London, St. Albans, Rochester, Lichfield, Dover, Ohio, and Saskatchewan, in the library of Lambeth Palace. Thence they proceeded to the Church. As the procession entered the sacred building, the choir chanted the *Magnus Dominus*, Psalm xlviii., the concluding words of which came to the two new Bishops as a message from heaven—to Hannington almost as an omen—"This God is our God for ever and ever; He shall be our Guide unto death."

In due course the two Bishops-Designate are kneeling before the Archbishop, and the Veni Creator is sung:

> "Come, Holy Ghost, our souls inspire,
> And lighten with celestial fire."

And when they rise it is with the injunction that they so care for the flock entrusted to them, that when the Chief Shepherd shall appear, they may receive the never-fading crown of glory, through Jesus Christ their Lord.

It was under the influence of no shallow self-confidence

that Hannington undertook this great responsibility. He was fully aware of the special difficulties of the charge committed to him. He knew that not merely energy and courage, but tact, wisdom, and patient endurance, not only of toil, but, what is far harder to bear, of contradiction, would be required of him. He was about to shepherd no ideal flock in some pastoral Arcadia where he might decorate his crook with ribands, and pipe strains of gentle music, surrounded by happy shepherds and shepherdesses. He knew that in the fierce tropic climate of that fell land in which his work was to be done, not only the wild flock, but the under-shepherds themselves would need more than ordinary skill to guide them aright ; and that his crook must be held with a hand both gentle and strong. By no one need the *suaviter in modo, fortiter in re*—the art of concealing the hand of steel in the velvet glove—be more diligently practised than by an African Missionary Bishop.* It was with the full consciousness that his path would not be strewn with roses that Hannington accepted the Bishopric ; but he was ready to " endure hardness as a good soldier of Jesus Christ," and was, moreover, strong in the confidence that the Lord would " deliver him from every evil work, and would preserve him unto His Heavenly Kingdom."

The following anecdote was related to me by one of the Secretaries of the C. M. S. The day after his consecration he had occasion to call at the House in Salisbury Square. A well-known member of the Committee met him on the staircase, and greeted him with, " I must *congratulate* you, Bishop Hannington ; " to whom he replied half-humorously, yet not without serious meaning, " *Commiserate* me, you mean."

---

* " He was beloved by every Missionary. There never was a Bishop who could be so firm, and, at the same time, so kind and considerate."—*Letter from the Rev. E. A. Fitch.*

The four months which he spent in England after his consecration were employed in organizing his new diocese, in commencing a Diocesan Fund, and in making additions to his working staff. His departure was somewhat delayed by the expectation of a domestic event which added a fourth child to his household. But he was not idle during the interim. To myself he wrote, " I want you to look about and see if you cannot secure me a doctor or two." No doubt many others received similar communications. He searched the ranks of his friends for suitable men who would be willing to accompany him to the post of honour and danger at the front.

Amongst others he corresponded with the Rev. E. A. Fitch, of Pem. Coll., Cambridge, whom he eventually decided to take with him as his Chaplain.

In a letter to Mr. Fitch's father, the Vicar of Cromer, he says :

" My Dear Sir,—I am afraid that you will look upon me as a wolf and a robber ; though I hope not.

" From the moment that you mentioned your son, I could not divest myself of the feeling that I must see him, and everything then seemed to lead that way. Most earnestly have I prayed that I might not act contrary to the Mind of the Spirit. It is a great question, both for you and for him ; but I am sure you will be blessed, aye, greatly blessed, in making the sacrifice. I am giving up three children to go out, for they cannot go with us,* and nobody can tell how at times my heart bleeds. It is agony. But I can do it for Christ's sake, and I believe that He asks it of me.

" If it is finally settled that your son goes out, I will

---

* At that time it had been planned that Mrs. Hannington and her baby should follow the Bishop to Africa, and reside at Mombasa.

endeavour to be a brother to him and a firm friend. Even yet the Lord may show that He has appointed us to run some different course.

> " I remain, yours sincerely,
> " JAMES HANNINGTON,
> " Bishop in E. Eq. Africa."

He was in much request during his short stay at home, and was invited to many places. Amongst others I find reference in a letter to his wife to an Undenominational Conference which had been arranged by Canon Basil Wilberforce to meet at Southampton. He says :

" Well, we had a curious gathering down here. On arrival, I found myself forming one of a select party—the Canon, Mr. Spurgeon, Lord Radstock, and the Earl of Lichfield. Every word of the conversation (after they had got to the end of cross-questioning me, which took about an hour) seemed worth listening to. On Thursday we commenced with prayer at 8, Conference at 11, at which Mr. Spurgeon first spoke, then the Bishop, then Lord Radstock. Afterwards Lord and Lady Ailsa, and Lord and Lady Mt. Edgecombe came to lunch, and spent the day. They all seemed bright Christians. Spurgeon and I had a good time together, and I enjoyed his society immensely."

Writing to myself some short while later, he says :

" I have a commission from the Archbishop to visit Jerusalem, and confirm the Churches on the way out ; so I start (D.V.) on Nov. 5th for the Holy Land. . . . . My wife and the little one are going on most excellently well. . . . I am so overladen with work that I scarce know what to do. Warmest love to self and Lucy,"—while tucked into the corner of the letter are the words, " Pray for us."

In some form or other that request was seldom absent from his letters. He was never content unless he believed that all his friends were praying for him. In this respect he reminds one frequently of General Gordon. Lord Tennyson surely conceived well the attitude of a truly great and simple mind when he put into the lips of his Arthur :

> " More things are wrought by prayer
> Than this world dreams of. Wherefore, let thy voice
> Rise like a fountain for me night and day. . . .
> For so the whole round earth is every way
> Bound by gold chains about the feet of God."

The word *prayer*, often as it is alluded to in his letters, never fell from his pen as a conventional platitude. Prayer was to him, in the most real sense, "the rope which pulls the bell in heaven." Here is a letter written at about this time to the Hon. Secretary of the C. M. S., when some important subject, upon which there were likely to be differences of opinion, was about to be discussed :—

" MY DEAR MR. WIGRAM,—I must send a word to say how fully I realize that you will be helped and guided by the tenderest of Fathers, the God of all Grace, on Monday. I gathered that possibly a few bitter things might be given utterance to, though I hope not. At all events, 'tis a trying time and a crisis ; and we who cannot speak much are going to pray for your guidance. The wisdom of the serpent would suggest that —— —— should be received with warmth and extra courtesy.

" Yours in something more than affection,

" J. H., Bp."

Having received the aforesaid Commission from the Archbishop of Canterbury, Bishop Hannington sailed on November 5th, making his passage in the *Nepaul*. They had troops on board, two hundred of whom were to be

transferred to another vessel at Gibraltar ; them, on the first
Sunday, the Bishop addressed in a vigorous ten minutes'
exposition on "the command of the King to repent."
This was a thing he could do well and effectively, and the
men heard him with marked attention. To his wife he
wrote by the next mail : "To realize more of the wonderful
love of the Lord is what we want, and we can then endure
separation and any other hardships for His sake. . . .
I hope Meppy liked his letter. I must send Carry the next
one, and then I suppose that Paul must not be left out in
the cold." On the following Sunday the Bishop was again
hard at work, first conducting Service and preaching to the
soldiers, then hurrying to the other end of the ship and
addressing the saloon passengers ; and finally giving a Missionary address in the evening, in consequence of which one
of his hearers gave him £5 for his Diocese. There were
some Sussex people on board, who soon told everybody all
about him, and he was made a great deal of.

At Port Said the Bishop and his Chaplain were transferred to the *Clio*, in which they sailed to Beirut. Then
followed five tedious days of quarantine ; but our Bishop
was not the man to gnaw his nails and look glum upon
such an occasion. Out came his note-books, paint-box,
grammar, and writing-desk ; and what with his endless
correspondence, languages, and water-colours, the time
passed rapidly enough. He says : "It has given me the
opportunity of writing up many of my African letters and a
few home to odd friends. I am, as usual, full of various
little items—reading, painting, writing, etc.—so that I find
very little spare time."

At Beirut and other places he confirmed many Europeans
and natives, and visited Christian Missions of every deno-
mination, being everywhere well received. From Tiberias
he writes to his wife : "What is more, I have been able to

stick to my flying colours, and shall finish up, God willing, in a month instead of two ; though I would willingly have trodden those sacred spots for another month."

From Damascus he visited Bashan and the " giant cities," and so to Tiberias.* He continues : " Mr. Connor,† the Hauran Missionary, accompanied us, and added greatly to the interest of the journey, as he knows many of the great Druse chiefs, and speaks Arabic very fluently, so that we were not only able to hear all that was passing, but also to see into the home life of these chiefs. We were entertained in a ' tent of Kedar.' I visited all the schools near Damascus but one which had been visited by Mr. Allan. I was greatly pleased with what I saw, and encouraged by the work. I am thankful to have been not only the first Bishop, but also the first visitor to inspect this work. Very few travellers venture through the Hauran, on account of the danger from Bedawin ; but, as you know, that was not likely to prevent your husband."

At Jerusalem he was in great request, and got through an immense amount of work, confirming, preaching, and inspecting ; notwithstanding, he found time to visit nearly all the traditional sites of interest. With modern Jerusalem he was not favourably impressed. He writes : " The town is vile, and the sites are chiefly fictions. The Mosque of Omar, however, is a magnificent building, and the whole of a morning was soon swallowed up inspecting it, as I had the benefit of the architect who is superintending the repairs, and who accompanied me and pointed out all the noticeable features and the few discoveries which have been lately made."

---

* " The Bishop would often dismount and walk to keep himself in trim for his African marches."—*Letter from the Rev. E. A. Fitch.*

† The Bishop while in Palestine ordained Mr. W. F. Connor, together with two native agents, Messrs. Ibraham Baz and Murad el Haddad, all admitted to Deacons' Orders.

He was much amused to find how great a personage he had suddenly become, and what a vast difference there was in the estimation of some people between Mr. Hannington and the Bishop of Eastern Equatorial Africa. He writes to his wife, with a pen that reveals a quiet smile, " I find that people stand rather in awe of your poor husband ; but I am sure that they need not, for I am an exceedingly meek and unpretentious individual."

Had they seen him leaping through the pools at Martinhoe in his episcopal apron and gaiters, would they any longer have stood in awe of him ? Perhaps not ; but they would have loved him none the less.

New Year's Day, 1885, the commencement of the last year of his short life, was the last day of his sojourn in Palestine. It was spent at Jaffa, which he describes as " a complete sea of oranges." While there he inspected Miss Arnott's school, of which he jots down the following appreciatory note : " Much pleased, the singing being especially good. I wrote in the book to the effect that this was the best school I had inspected."

Mr. Fitch, writing of the time which he spent with his Bishop in Palestine, says : " How kind and gentle he was to all ; how considerate for others, and anxious not to give an offence, even where a rebuke was necessary ; and so spiritually-minded, walking so closely with God. I shall never forget our journey together. Every morning, often in the early dusk, we would have prayers together, and always the Hundred-and-twenty-first Psalm, which I had to read. If the books had been packed away, the Bishop himself would say the psalm by heart. He was so kind and genial ; everybody loved him. Wherever he went there was a brightness. On board ship all loved him. Wherever we went in Palestine the people complained that their time with him was too short."

On January 2nd the African party embarked on board the *Ettore*, from which, in due course, after visiting Cairo and the Pyramids, and holding out the right hand of fellowship to all the Christian workers whom they were able to reach, they exchanged to the *Surat* at Suez. A less profitable exchange was again made at Aden, into the *Baghdad*, bound for Mombasa. The Bishop writes in his pocketbook : " My heart sank as I smelt the cockroaches and bilge-water." A polite and obliging captain, however, made up for many discomforts, and the weather being propitious, the voyage was concluded pleasantly enough.

" The Chaplain most indignant with me for betraying that he had not crossed the line, not knowing that there is not a sufficient staff on board to enact the part of Neptune and his crew. Mr. Gordon, the ship's purser, and the Chaplain, are getting wrought up to a tremendous pitch about Neptune ; alas ! that he cannot come on board ! " There is little doubt that these fears would not be calmed by that old and accomplished hand at teasing.

Next, the father's voice is heard in the little pocketbook : " To-day we get into the latitude of flying-fish. They completely swarm ; flying out of the vessel's way by shoals. Two flew on board. I wish the children could see them !

" Onward we go, winds and waves helping us ; and to-day, Jan. 21st, we cross the line, nobody knows exactly when and no Neptune. And now we must find a new string to the teasing bow, or fall back upon Taylor's ' theories.' "

Onward he went, winds and waves helping him. No contrary gales this time ; all things were made easy for that last voyage which was to conduct him to his death. The vessel cut her way steadily through smiling seas, leaving a long track of foam behind upon the blue water, and scattering the glittering shoals of flying-fish from her prow. On board all were full of life and hope. The Bishop sparkled with kindly fun, and communicated his cheerful spirits to all the company. How could they foresee what nine months might bring forth ? The shadow of that great sorrow which has fallen upon the Church on his account was creeping upon them, and those events which were to consummate his death were already combining; but of that shadow they, as yet, felt not the chill.

Thursday, Jan. 22nd.—"Smell of the shore came off to our salt-washed nostrils."

As they entered Lamoo Creek, the first sight that met their eyes was a sort of symbol of the contest in which they, as emissaries of the Lord's Host, were about to engage. "On the shore we could see a battle-field, with numbers of bones lying about."

On Saturday, the 24th, they steamed into the sheltered harbour of Mombasa. The Bishop was not expected. No one knew exactly when he might arrive. "No stir in either place. Frere Town might have been in bed.

"Presently a small dingy pulled leisurely past, and learned the news. The dingy flew back to Frere Town. There the crew dashed out and ran up the bank, and in two minutes the whole place seemed alive. In a trice two boats came racing down upon us and carried me off. A thousand people came to the shore; guns fired, horns blew, women shrieked, I laughed and cried. Altogether, there was a grand welcome, and the moment we could get a little quiet we knelt down and thanked God'

CHAPTER XIX.

FRERE TOWN.

(1885.)

> " To use force first, before people are fairly taught the truth, is
> to knock a nail into a board without wimbling a hole for it, which
> then either not enters, or turns crooked, or splits the wood it
> pierceth."   FULLER: " *The Good Bishop.*"

As may be seen by reference to the map, Frere Town is
situated on the mainland, four degrees south of the Equator.
The size of the map does not permit it to be made equally
clear that Mombasa is an island separated from Frere Town
by a narrow channel, about a quarter of a mile in width.
When Sir Bartle Frere returned from his special Mission to
Zanzibar in 1873, to endeavour to put down the slave
trade, he strongly urged the Church Missionary Society to
establish a settlement for liberated slaves at Mombasa.
Tidings of the death of Livingstone, which reached home
early in 1874, had caused the ears of Englishmen to tingle,
every one was interested in the suppression of the horrible
slave traffic, and a special fund was speedily provided for the
purchase of the necessary site. Ground was bought upon
the mainland opposite to Mombasa; houses were built, and
the settlement was named Frere Town in honour of its
originator. In the following year nearly 500 slaves rescued
by British cruisers were received. Gradually, also, a multitude of the neighbouring Wa-Nyika attached themselves to
the settlement, and Frere Town may now be termed the

head-quarters of the Church Missionary Society's work on
the East Coast of Africa.

Frere Town is pleasantly situated. Mr. Joseph Thomson thus describes it : " The view of the station across the
apparently land-locked creek was most inviting. On the
left, from a dense grove of magnificent mangoes, could be
seen a snow-white house, with iron roofing, well set off by
the dense shade around. Further, to the right, lay another
white house with flat roof, situated among more airy trees
and waving palms. Several edifices of smaller size gave the
idea of a charming European settlement." *

Behind Frere Town the creek extends for some twenty
miles inland toward Kisulutini, or Rabai, as it is more commonly called, and as we will henceforth term it, where there
is also a C. M. S. station.

The church in Frere Town was at that time in charge
of the Rev. J. W. Handford. The Rev. W. E. Taylor
was located at Rabai. The whole of the new Bishop's
working staff in Central Africa consisted of twelve clergy,
priests and deacons, eleven laymen, and four ladies, wives
of missionaries ; twenty-seven in all. These, as will be seen
by reference to the map, where all the Stations of the
Diocese are marked with blue ink, were scattered over an
enormous extent of country.†

The Bishop's first care was to make himself thoroughly
acquainted with all the details of the work which was being
carried on in the district. He began at once with Frere
Town ; visited the schools, and was present at the Services in
church. With these he was more than pleased. The voices
here were far better in quality than those of the tribes
further south, and the singing was delightfully hearty. The

---

* *Through Masai Land*, p. 39.
† The stations of the Universities' Mission are marked U.

church, too, was crammed with a very well-behaved body of worshippers, who seemed to realize the purpose for which they were gathered together.

It is true that all things did not equally meet with his approval, but the letters which follow must be read by one who either knew the Bishop in life, or may have learned to know him in the preceding pages. It is exceedingly difficult to convey an accurate impression of his feelings by a mere reproduction of his letters. To a stranger they might even suggest an entirely different meaning to that which the writer intended, or which his correspondents understood. The golden rule to be observed in reading his private letters is to remember that his emphatic diction *must not be taken too literally.* By this it is not meant that he was given to exaggeration. That is the last crime that could be laid to his charge. He was perfectly well aware that his friends understood him. To strangers he could write staidly and formally enough. When he styles himself to a friend as " in grief, sorrow, and amazement," another person would probably have merely written a note of exclamation after his statement. When he assures his correspondent that he was " frightened out of his wits," he merely intends to remind him that the situation was an awkward one. He loved to describe himself as " boiling over with rage," " frantic," etc., etc., but his real anger, upon the rare occasions on which it was displayed, was expressed very differently.

There is a very characteristic letter of his in which his disapprobation is shown by a number of deep pen-strokes or sputters driven through the paper, and described as " marks of wrath " !

The following letters, then, must be read, in the first place, as written *by Bishop Hannington* ; and, secondly, it must be remembered that they were written to those who, as he well knew, thoroughly understood him. It is a very remarkable testimony to the complete concord which existed between himself and the Committee of the Society whose Missionary Bishop he was, that he should have allowed his letters, even when addressed to them as a body, to be characterized by so much freedom of expression. But, indeed, he was both loved and esteemed at Salisbury Square, where the greatest confidence was felt in his judgment, and where his schemes and reforms met with the heartiest encouragement.

The following letter was addressed to Mr. Lang :

"Greetings and good wishes very many, with fervent prayer for blessing on your work. . . . . And now for first impressions. Frere Town struck me as one of the most lovely spots I have seen. It is laid out with the care and precision of those advertisements you see hanging up at railway stations ! But—one shudders slightly (a kind of half-gratified shudder, as we reap the benefit) to see such palatial residences. . . . . Then followed grief, sorrow, amazement, which increases, to find the Missionaries dwelling in houses of cedar, and the ark scarce resting in curtains. . . . This must strike most painfully on all comers. . . . The opinion of the world is not what we should care about, but this cannot be right. And I mean to stick to my opinion."

Others than Bishop Hannington had, indeed, noticed this fact. Mr. Joseph Thomson, for example, writes, rather sarcastically : "This charming European settlement suggested the mental ejaculation that, however dark and dreary might be the moral and religious outlook, temporally the lines of the Missionaries had fallen in pleasant places."

The Bishop felt most strongly that this ought not so to be. And one of his earliest cares was to remove this reproach, and arrange for the building of a church which should be worthy of the head-quarters of the Mission. Writing to Mr. Wigram, he says :

" And now, be frightened, and talk about 'new brooms;' but we have quite decided to appeal for a new church. I won't fulminate by this mail, but we must have a decent church. Not a tin ark, or a cocoa-nut barn, but a proper stone church, a church to the glory of God ; and so, in spite of famine and other difficulties, let us strike for it now."*

One of the first aims of the Bishop was to stir up in his diocese a keen desire for souls, which should not be satisfied by merely external improvement in the moral and social state of the natives. He knew that personal holiness among the workers was the only surety for work of this kind. Both by example, and by his stirring addresses, he inculcated a high standard of Christian life.

In no place more than in Africa are George Herbert's quaintly-sounding words verified :

" Who keeps no guard upon himself is slack,
　And rots to nothing at the next great thaw.
　Man is a shop of rules ; a well trussed pack,
　Whose every parcel underwrites a law.
　Lose not thyself, nor give thy humours way ;
　God gave them to thee under lock and key."

---

* It is right to state that, about ten years before, a sum of £1000 was provided for the erection of a church at Frere Town. Owing, however, to the wreck of a dhow which contained a considerable portion of the materials purchased at Bombay, and to other causes, only sufficient reached Frere Town wherewith to build a school-room. The C. M. S. very properly does not hold itself responsible for the building of permanent churches. When a community of native Christians has been formed, and the preaching chapels no longer suffice for their wants, the building of a suitable church is left to their own individual effort, aided by a special grant and such appeals to the Church at home as Bishop Hannington proposed on this occasion to make.

Both men and institutions are apt to grow " slack " when long removed from the wholesome stimulus of public opinion.

The man who is long separated from the elevating and stirring influence of his equals and betters needs to maintain a high level of spirituality lest he should sink to the low level of those by whom he is constantly surrounded; with whose customs he becomes daily more familiarized, and of whose frailties he almost insensibly becomes more and more tolerant. There have been terrible falls in Africa. Hannington felt that if his diocese was to shine as a City of God, it must be occupied by a body of men who were united together by the consciousness that each one was himself united to the Lord of the Church. During his short episcopate he did much to infuse spiritual life and vigour into every man, and every branch of every department of the work.

He found an excellent organization, good schools, and a crowded church.* Into this well-ordered community he came as a spiritual impetus, and as one who was well fitted to supply the one crying need of that time—the leadership of a master mind, whose authority was properly constituted and generally acknowledged, to bind together the individual workers, and give them the impulse of a body united under one head. A flock of shepherds is well nigh as helpless without a head shepherd, as without them is a flock of scattered sheep.

The Bishop set about altering such few things as needed reformation with consummate tact. Take the case of the Mission steamer as an example. He is writing to the Secretary of the C. M. S. to ascertain exactly what amount

---

* At the *daily* Morning Service at 6.30 a.m., Hannington noticed on one occasion about 500 present.

of authority they will authorize him to exercise over their lay agents :

"I feel that I may without hesitation speak in the highest terms of the seagoing qualities and the pace of the *Henry Wright*. I am more than gratified and surprised. Of course, I am comparing her with other vessels and yachts of her own size. Some who have spoken of her discomforts only remember P. and O. boats, and I might thus appear to contradict them, and make Salisbury Square wonder which to believe. As to the condition in which she is, I find that terrible ; and the tale of the West Coast will soon be repeated unless attention is paid to this. I at once spoke my mind, but at present have met with little response and plenty of excuses and objections.

"I find that I don't really know what authority I have, and what arrangements you have made with the captain. You must let me know fully about this, and let him (and others) know whether I am to act as your representative. I find him a very nice and kind man, most attentive to all my wants, and I think that I have gained his estimation by being capable of taking a spell at the wheel, and turning out at about 2 a.m. to see that things were proceeding comfortably. At the same time, there is very little recognition of the fact that the ship must be kept differently, otherwise decay, moth, rust, etc., will do their work. The difficulty is, that the sailors would strike for higher wages. I offer a solution, namely, that the best man be raised a little, and made a petty (very petty) officer. That No. 2 be discharged if he will not do more work, and another be engaged at a lower rate. That every day when the *Henry Wright* is in harbour, three or four of the schoolboys be sent off to be trained in cleaning the ship. These boys could then, after a time, easily get berths as officer's ser-

vants on the steamer, or would come in for house boys. I
do not know how you, or Handford, or the captain will
receive this; but of one thing I am certain—something
must be done. If you can give me no autocracy,* you will
not inform the captain of this. . . . I have gently
assumed that I am to act for you, taking care not to place
myself in a false position, or rather lay myself open to a
refusal before I could meet it."

He determined that he would not rest until he had put
all things in order; but as it had been at Hurstpierpoint, so
it would be in Africa, his suggestions would be so gently
and seasonably made that the reformed would probably look
upon themselves as the reformers. In the meanwhile he
roused up everybody by his own indefatigable energy.
None could settle with any comfort upon their lees while the
Bishop stirred about so briskly, and displayed such boundless
powers of locomotion. To-day in Mombasa, to-morrow at
Zanzibar, a few days later at Taita, again prospecting around
Kilima-njaro, and, suddenly, while all thought him far away
in the interior, reappearing in the streets of Frere Town.
No one knew where next to expect their Bishop. He carried with him an atmosphere which annihilated stagnation.
All were kept in expectation and movement, and while he
thus set the example of unsparing application to the work of
the Mission, he also in the most quietly practical manner
demonstrated what in Africa is not always easy to put into
practice—is it easy anywhere?—the duty of considering
others' comfort before one's own.

Mr. Copplestone has communicated to me one example
of this among many such which is very characteristic of

---

* The Bishop afterwards learned that he was regarded as the
Head of the Mission, and that the Committee had given him full
authority to do all that was necessary.

Hannington's way of life. He says: " On our arrival at Frere Town we had another exhibition of his grand unselfishness. He made us put up at his own house, the palace, and, out of the two bedrooms, he gave one to Mr. Hooper and the other to myself, while he himself occupied a small place close under the roof; and, do what we would, we could not persuade him to change his purpose." That was his notion of the manner in which "humanity" should be showed to strangers.*

Acts of this kind which call forth no heroic self-sacrifice, but which merely entail personal discomfort on behalf of others, are ever the hardest to perform graciously, and the rarest. But by such the memory of a man lingers longer in the hearts of his friends than if, on some supreme occasion, he had ventured his life for them.

One of the Bishop's first acts was, of course, to pay a complimentary visit to the Arab Governor of Mombasa. The Governor, whom Mr. Thomson mentions as not being on a very friendly footing with the Missionaries, had been superseded by another, of whom Hannington says that he was " a very nice man." It is amusing to note in the day's brief entry in the tiny pocket-book the words : " Weather less warm ; in spite of Bp.'s clothes, felt cool." Our traveller, who would, if he could, have willingly imitated Fox, and donned a " perennial suit " of some ever-enduring substance, was evidently rather impatient of his episcopal apron and gaiters. He would not be quite comfortable until he could once more thrust himself into that old coat of rusty brown tweed, in which he had botanized on Lundy, scaled the Alps at Zermatt, and walked nearly a thousand miles to and from the great Nyanza.

---

* " Vidi necesse esse habere episcopum exhibere humanitatem quiscunque venientibus sive transeuntibus."—S. AUGUST.

A few days after his arrival he gave a great feast to the inhabitants, at which 800 sat down to curry and rice. Afterwards, he says, "they beat the drum and danced; one or two of the different tribal dances were very curious."

"*Sunday, Feb.* 1.—Handford has had a kind of throne made for me outside the chancel rails, and to-day I was enthroned. Administered the Holy Communion. About 60 present."

The next day he left in the *Henry Wright* for Zanzibar to visit the Sultan and Sir John Kirk. He was also anxious to have a talk with Bishop Smythies. The Consul, however, was away from home, and Bishop Smythies was on the mainland, at Magila. Hannington at once made up his mind to cross to Pangani and walk to the Station of the Universities' Mission. The heat on the road was frightful. Hannington was not yet "in training," and he found that the twenty-five mile walk along the waterless track taxed his strength to the utmost. Indeed, he got a touch of the sun, and fell, half-fainting, in the path. A donkey was sent to meet him from Mkuzi, and he remained there for the night, hospitably entertained by Mr. Wallis, the clergyman in charge. The diary continues:

"Too much exhausted to talk or do anything. Managed, however, to attend Evening Service. An alarm of an attack by Wadigo, a savage tribe, before going to bed. Couldn't sleep for heat, fleas, mosquitoes, and extreme exhaustion. Very poorly in morning. Attended Morning Service, but had great difficulty in sitting up to breakfast. After mid-day, however, the heat, 90° in the shade, fell rapidly. I revived, and started on the donkey. After riding about eight miles, the Bishop met me with a hearty welcome.

"Next day, Sunday, 6.30 a.m., the Bishop held a

Confirmation. Mitre and Cope. Address very good. After the Services of the day, in the cool of the afternoon, I had a long talk with the Bishop; with all his ritualism he is strong on the point of conversion, and is very particular about Baptism and Communion not being administered before conversion, either to heathen or professing Christians. Monday, 4.30, left on donkey, the Bishop accompanying me a long distance on the road."

Three days later he called on Sir John Kirk, who strongly advised him to advance the Mission to Taveta and Chagga, and after an interview with the Sultan and his commander-in-chief, Gen. Matthews, he once more steamed northward in his own vessel, the *Henry Wright*. He says: " No one who has not experienced the horrors of a voyage in an African dhow can appreciate what a comfort this little steamer is to us."

They did not reach Frere Town until Sunday morning, as the engines of the boat were rather out of order. " Very surprised to find that a new aisle to the church had been commenced without my hearing a word about it. To-morrow I must speak, not to-day."

Mr. Handford had evidently not yet accustomed himself to the idea that he was no longer commander-in-chief at the Station. On the following day a Committee Meeting was held of all the workers, to discuss the affairs of the Mission The following brief entry in the pocket-book refers to it : " We discussed some disagreeable questions, but all passed off well, and I feel that matters will in future be less difficult for me."

It was clear that the new Bishop would require all his tact to maintain his just authority without causing an uncomfortable amount of friction. But if friendship and general hearty good-will were to be preserved together with discipline and obedience, this was surely the man to effect it.

A day or two later he writes : " All I can do is letters, letters, letters, with just a little exercise and a good many interruptions. Things going smoothly, and *much more comfortable for me than before.* The Lord be praised."

Bishop Hannington wrote a great number of important and valuable letters from Frere Town, which throw light on everything of which they treat, and help to disentangle some knotty questions. Though his own supervision of the diocese was so brief, it will be found that he has done much to clear the way for his successor, and to make his position a plain and simple one. We may here give quotations from some of these letters, without placing them in their chronological order.

It was not long before the vexed question, whether Missionaries should take their wives with them to unhealthy and perilous posts, came up for discussion. On this subject the Bishop's experience led him to form a very strong opinion. He was not aware at the time that the Sub-Committee on African Missions quite agreed with him, and took his view of the matter. The letter is given as eminently characteristic.

" With regard to the Marriage Question, I have already spoken strongly, for I feel strongly, and am therefore prepared to act somewhat strongly if I am constrained to do so.

" Granted that the help of ladies in every station would be of very great advantage, I am certain that we are not yet sufficiently advanced for ladies, especially young married women, to enter upon the work. It is little short of homicide to permit them to go beyond the neighbourhood of the coast. However, if, in spite of your recent terrible experience, you feel differently, I will most reluctantly consent that the region of Usagara—*i.e.*, Mpwapwa or Mamboia—be again tried; but *nothing shall induce me* to give my consent that ladies should attempt to cross the Wanyamwezi deserts in the present state of the country. As a hardy, even somewhat reckless, traveller, I shudder at the idea of attempting these, by and by, myself. With regard to *laymen*, as ——, I have no legal jurisdiction, and the matter rests with you; but I refuse in any way to correspond or work with such, deeply as I should regret it, if he is permitted to take a young wife beyond Mpwapwa.

"With regard to ——, I have jurisdiction; and I refuse to have him located beyond Mpwapwa, or in any other spot, until my sanction has been obtained. And what I have said about these two individual cases will apply to all others; that is, until the present state of things is changed, and medical men can be placed at the various stations. Personally I have no objection to —— obtaining leave of absence, returning to England and marrying, then leaving his wife and proceeding to Uyui; nor to —— marrying now and doing the same, letting their wives remain in England until after their first confinement; then I would, if I am still alive, reluctantly consent to their attempting to reach so far. But to send young married women like —— up country, where there is no medical aid at hand, is, if you will forgive me for saying so, a rash folly, to which I will never consent.

"Had we time to write backwards and forwards on this subject, I would not have written in this very dogmatic and perhaps irritating strain; but as there is no time for correspondence, I think it better to let you know exactly how I feel, and how I am prepared to act."

By all which it will be seen that the good Bishop knew

how to think and act with decision, and that he had the
courage of his opinions.   He continues this subject in
another letter as follows :

"——'s recent very severe illness in her confinement,
and ——'s case, which appears to have been greatly aggra-
vated by nursing, and the probable return of both makes
me feel that it is my duty once more to bring the marriage
question before you.

"In addition to these two, I feel that I cannot but revert
to what I hear of the late Mrs. —— here in Zanzibar ;
namely, that without a proper nurse, without either of them
understanding about such cases, she was treated from a few
rules laid down in an old-fashioned book.   She dies, and we
talk about 'the mysteries of Providence'!   It would surely
be a greater mystery if in such a case she had lived.   In
the face of this and the other deaths, I was quite shocked
to hear of ————'s proposed marriage.   I hear also of
another married couple wishing to go to Mamboia . . .
and you will remind me that I . . . consented that such
should go so far.   Now, however, after further experience,
I feel that I have done wrong even in consenting to this.
I therefore wish to withdraw my acquiescence, and to send
you my more developed views.   Again I acknowledge the
great help that Christian ladies are in all the stations ; also
the immense comfort of their society to our isolated Missionaries, and that their presence would often hush scan-
dalous whispers ; notwithstanding, seeing how difficult
African travel is—how inexperienced the newly-married
are—the entire absence of nurses qualified to wait upon
Europeans—the almost entire absence of medical aid—and,
above all, reading in the cases we have had before us the
unmistakable voice of God—I feel in conscience bound to
protest against any newly-married ladies being sent to any

of our stations beyond Frere Town, Rabai, and their immediate neighbourhood."

In a succeeding letter he deals with the matter in a lighter strain, and says :

" With regard to your suggestion about a lady-helper— that is, I quite believe, what we want here; and the right person would be of the greatest assistance.

" A dash of the obstetrix would be exceedingly useful, and would relieve my mind very greatly. If she has had no experience in such matters, could not a little be gained before coming out ?

" P.S.—While I shudder at the thought of young married women coming out, I should gladly welcome a few strapping old maids, who could go about by twos even to U-Ganda. Send out a dozen to try."

Another important letter deals with the question of the Baptism of Children of Slaves :

" I find that the custom has been to baptize children up to the age of eight years, who have been received from slave dhows, etc. Hence they get Christian names, and are, of course, educated as far as is possible as Christians, and go out into the world as such. The education they receive, good as it is, in too many cases does not seem to lead to conversion ; and so these go forth, some of them with very bad characters, yet bearing the name of Frere Town converts and Christians. This is, of course, the history of the Church at home, and its bane, but might surely be prevented here without our being accused of being Baptists. Bp. Smythies, I rejoice to find, feels very strongly as I do, and insists that in the churches of the interior there shall be no baptism till after conversion.

" You will understand, of course, that I am *not now speaking of the children of Christian parents.* As to the others, the present system allows a number to go forth into the world as baptized, while in a most unsatisfactory state, and who would never have been admitted to baptism had they been kept in the school some few years previously.

" The argument in favour of the baptism of these orphan children is that we Christians then become their foster-parents. Yes,—but then they come to us not as infants, but as children who have from their earliest years grown up in all possible wickedness."

This letter is very interesting, as throwing light upon such complaints as those so freely made by Mr. Johnston and other travellers as to the worthlessness of many of the " Mission boys." The question propounded is a knotty one, but no doubt some practical solution will in time be found.

Another letter deals with the Ordination and Licensing of Catechists :

" With regard to the Ordination of the two natives, William Jones and Ishmael Sember, they both express a wish to delay for another year, and far be it from me to thrust them into office. However, as far as I can discover, their only reasons appear to be the examination. They dread to be examined.

" I find these two men in particular holding services, preaching on week days and Sundays, and preaching at Frere Town when there have been as many as four white teachers present. William Jones has also had entire spiritual charge of Rabai for some months; I feel, therefore, that if it is simply a matter of shirking examination I cannot give way to it.

" I feel strongly, too, that all these men who preach in

the regular Church Services ought to be examined by me, that I may judge whether they are really fit to teach.

"I am, therefore, proposing to examine all the *preachers* in the Old and New Testaments, and in the rudiments of the Gospel of Christ. If I find them satisfactory, I will give them a licence as lay readers and helpers. This examination will include Jones and Ishmael. If they pass this satisfactorily, I shall, if we really find that this is the only obstacle, be ready to extend their licence to Deacon's Orders. At all events, I will sound them on the subject."

The Bishop had a high opinion of native capacity. In a private letter he writes : "I do not at present think that U-Ganda itself wants ' the flood of Europeans ' about which our brethren talk. ' Not by might nor by power, but by My Spirit.' I believe (between ourselves—whisper it not) —I believe that with the present staff of natives, Frere Town and Rabai could be worked by one European effectively. I am sure, however, unsatisfactory as natives often are, that not enough is done to develop any of their powers, except those which relate to laying a cloth. However, you must take what I say *cum grano*—I am a fresh comer."

The following extract is interesting, as throwing some light upon the special difficulties of a *first* Bishop in a Mission district. Also as displaying his own spiritual thoroughness, and discontent with any reform that stopped short of the actual conversion of souls to God.

"I am almost afraid to discourse on Frere Town, lest I should seem to throw any reflection upon the work which is being done. We have an admirable secretary in the Rev. —— ; still, I am sure that there is an economy which may suit the lay department, but will not pay in the end. I want to hear more about saving souls than saving pice. I want to see far more Church order. I should like to know that the weeds are being pulled out of the hearts, while those in the shambas are not permitted to run wild. I pray that Mr. England * may be just the man to reach the souls of the boys in the school, for I do not see so many signs of their being reached now as I could wish. I do not want to be extravagant, but too much time can be spent saving pence, even in the Mission field ; so beware of over-economy. I have failed, at present, to get anything done for the first-class boys to bring them on to a higher grade of education, and prepare them for the Ministry, and for school teaching, or the medical profession. Surely, if a native Ministry is to be raised up, something of this kind should be done. At present, even the best teachers are kept at table dusting, etc. ; which, however good for their morals, is not, I think, the education to aim at. Economy in this direction will never pay in the end. I shall point out these things to Mr. England, if I see him when he arrives."

The Bishop concludes his letter as follows :

" I do hope you will not think that I am writing in the spirit of bitterness. These men that I have written about in an apparent spirit of complaint have far more excellencies than shortcomings. I only wish that your poor little bishop possessed many of their good qualities."

The following letter to Mr. Eugene Stock is full of specimens of Hannington's own style when writing to his intimate friends. But beneath his comic descriptions of himself as boiling over with passion while he brandishes his

---

* A lay schoolmaster then being sent from home.

"rancorous pen," one can read his intense love for the country of his adoption, and his devotion to his work.*

"MY DEAR STOCK,—I am not certain whether you have thrown me overboard altogether, on account of my perverse signature.† I give you credit, however, for being nearly driven to death during the last month or two, and so have had to pass me by. I wish friends would give me credit for being overdriven sometimes. They won't, however. But now, before I take another plunge into the interior, let me give you an account of the proceedings of the last three weeks, and if you don't doctor it up and use it, at least get it into something for me, for we must keep ourselves before the public.‡ I am simply boiling over with passion at the gross neglect of East Africa at the May Meeting. Does such a place exist in the mind of the Committee? If it ever had entered my head that no representation was to be made, I believe I should have slipped home the night before, and back again the following day, had it only been to have shouted, '*East Equatorial Africa needs your prayers!*' I don't regard a stupid little notice in the Report about myself as anything at all. Men in England do not realize how desperately hard the battle has to be fought out here.

"I am in a capital temper with Lang's last letters to Handford and myself. Things have been going on very nicely between us lately. May the brethren who are coming out

---

* See page 310.

† He had adopted the signature James, Bishop of East Equatorial Africa (or as he usually wrote it, Bp. E. Eq. Af.), omitting the "Hannington," as he thought that his own individuality would be thereby merged and lost in his Office, and in his work.

‡ This was accompanied by a long MS., containing an account of a missionary journey.

impart to us many rich spiritual blessings. I hope dear sister Maria and her boys are progressing? Just as I write, the girls in the school have struck up the Vesper Hymn, and warmed my soul, when I think that here, too, we are fellow-labourers with her and other dear Christians. Striving together for the Faith.

" One more thrust from my rancorous pen and I have done. Letters from Salisbury Square are so awfully official and full of business, that we are all complaining we find no spiritual lozenges to revive us. Would not some dear Christian soul in the Committee undertake to write us religious letters, and enclose little leaflets and choice crumbs —enquire after our souls, and draw out the depths of our heart. Ask for a volunteer for E. Eq. Africa, and I am certain he will be greatly appreciated. If business expels religious intercourse in letters between father and son (Cust says the relationship is parental, as you provide us with false teeth) woe, woe! death in the pot.

" I do not know that I have much more to say on paper : should I not like an hour or two with you in the little study in Milner Square! Did I tell you that the Sultan, through Sir John, had offered Mbaruk 400 dollars a year and a shamba in Zanzibar. This he declined. I have other terms to suggest, and I hope that I may be the means of getting him out of Fulladoyo and occupying the land.* I am rather expecting a fearful rebuke from Salisbury Square, and a warning not to meddle with other men's matters, and not to rush hither and thither, but to settle into a confirm-ing machine. But Africa must be won for Christ.

" Yea, I believe at this time ' *shall the present be brought unto the Lord of a people scattered and peeled, and from a people terrible from their beginning hitherto.*' And

* See page 360.

so I go forward, the Lord being my helper, to endeavour to
open up the country of the Masai.—Affectly yours,

"JAMES, Bp. E. Eq. Afr.

" ' Watchman, what of the night ? ' " *

Thus many matters are discussed with the Committee
of the Church Missionary Society, and various members of
it—some lightly, some gravely, but all with a good-humoured
insistance, which reveals at the same time the loving nature
of the man, and the hold which his work had taken upon
his heart.   Writing to a friend, he says :—

" I feel daily my own awful imperfections and shortcomings.   Why did they make me a Bishop ?   Have they
not—are they not, bitterly repenting it ? "   But immediately his heart is lifted up, and he cries, " Has not our
loving Father been gracious to me !   Oh, for a heart to
praise my God ! "

---

* He almost always wrote a motto, or watchword, at the foot of
his letters.

CHAPTER XX.

THE KILIMA-NJARO EXPEDITION.—VISIT TO CHAGGA.

(1885. MARCH, APRIL.)

"The tartarous moods of common men."
                                        BEN JONSON.

"I am being taught never to be disappointed, but to Praise."
                                        BISHOP HANNINGTON.

"But ever at each period
He stopped and sang 'Praise God!'
Then back again his curls he threw,
And cheerful turned to work anew."
                                        ROBT. BROWNING.

BISHOP HANNINGTON had not been long at Frere Town before he was called upon to consider the condition of Taita, which was then his furthest advanced post along that route westward. The Mission Station at Taita is planted upon the lofty mountain Ndara, and is separated from the coast by some two hundred miles* of difficult and dangerous desert. Mr. Wray, who had the honour of being the pioneer thus far into the wilderness, had gathered around him a number of learners; but his position had lately become very critical, owing to a prolonged famine which was

---

* Comp. Mr. Thomson's estimate of the distance which is added to the absolute mileage in a straight line from Mombasa by the windings of the desert path.—*Through Masai Land*, p. 188.

devastating the whole surrounding country, and had brought
down the anger of the tribes upon his head, as the possible
cause of it.   Mr. Wray's little flock in Ndara suffered terribly from the general want.   Great efforts were made to
send up supplies of food from Frere Town, and many lives
were thus saved ; but, owing to the distance and the necessity of crossing the horrible, waterless desert of Taro, the
difficulty of sending caravans was immense.

Bishop Hannington determined that he would himself
go to the front, and be guided in his future action by what
he saw there.   He therefore lost no time, but made up a
caravan of porters, and sending them forward to Bandera,
at the head of the creek, joined them on February
25th.   From Bandera a steep ascent of an hour and a half
brought them to the pretty Mission Station of Rabai.   Here
the people were expecting the Bishop, and a tumultuous
welcome awaited him.   The firing of guns, and the dancing
and shouting of the excited natives, continued without intermission from six o'clock until ten.   The Bishop says :—" I
joined in one of the dances—a kind of puss-in-the-corner-
drop-handkerchief—to the intense delight of the natives.
Henceforth we are friends."

The next morning, Thursday, the native catechist, Mr.
Jones, whom he afterwards ordained, preached to a densely
crowded congregation.   We may quote here a passage from
Mr. Thomson :—" I arrived while service was being conducted by Mr. Jones, the native teacher.   Not to disturb
the meeting, I stepped in behind the gathering, and was
greatly struck by the appearance of the well-filled church,
the strict attention of the audience (who were all dressed in
the height of Rabai fashion), and the fluency of the
preacher."   The Bishop was also most favourably impressed
by the appearance of everything at Rabai   He spent his
time there very busily in completing his preparations for the

march into the interior. The following jottings appear
in his pocket-book :—" Made my boys, Robert Livingstone and Legh Richmond, wash, giving them a lesson in
the art. . . . . . . Grand cooking preparations. I give a
feast to-day, at which I expect about six hundred guests.
. . . . . Our boys, to my bitter disappointment, caught
stealing. I tied up all four to separate posts, in sight of the
feast, for the rest of the day ; but it pained me more than it
did them. About twelve the feast began in earnest, and at
about five o'clock the dances and drums. I joined a little in
most of the dances, some of which are very grotesque, and
it gave the people more satisfaction than anything else.
The boys were released earlier than I had at first intended,
my heart relenting—and the next morning they stole the
sugar. One whom I believe to be at the bottom of all this
mischief is to be left behind. He is not my own boy, but
was brought at Handford's request.

" *Sunday, March 1st.* — I preached from the text,
' What must I do to be saved ? ' Jones interpreting. The
church was quite full, many sitting outside. Holy Communion afterwards to thirty-four. Fifty candidates are being
prepared for Confirmation.

" At the afternoon Service Jones preached from the
121st Psalm. It being my travelling Psalm, I take it as a
good omen."

" *March 2nd.*—Just off in excellent health and spirits.
' I will go in the strength of the Lord.' "

The Bishop continues :—" By two o'clock all was ready,
so we knelt all together in prayer, and then, with no slight
emotion, forced our way through the little knots of friends
and wives who had come to bid us and our porters—their
relatives and husbands—good-bye. We mustered about a
hundred, as we had to carry with us a month's food for the

starving Wa-Taita, in addition to our own goods. The heat
was intense, and nearly made me sick ; the sun almost
seemed to bake one alive."

Mr. Handford went with the Bishop. Soon they left
behind them " the cocoa-crowned heights, the verdant
ridges—with their stern, sentinel-like fan-palms—and the
cultivated outer slopes, and plunged into the Nyika, or
wilderness, beyond." Soon all verdure vanished, and their
route lay through a land of desolation and sterility ; an hour
or so more, and the glaring red sands of the coast hills were
passed, and they entered a more promising region, a grazing
country, where were " dense masses of evergreen trees, fes-
tooned with creepers, and intersected by green, grassy glades,
made gay with beautiful orchids." The Bishop makes no
special complaint, but during this first day's march the
porters are usually very troublesome.＊ Mr. Thomson says
that the experience of this first day " lowered the level of
his enthusiasm more than anything that had yet occurred."
No doubt the Mission party had their troubles. However,
Hannington says :—" After marching till sunset, we suddenly came upon an open glade in the forest, and camped.
The first time nothing goes right ; nobody seems to know
what to do, or where to go, so someone has to show them.
Gaiters, shovel-hat, and apron have all been laid aside for
the journey, and so, unmindful of dignity, we rush hither
and thither for firewood, and light the fire ; then with a
mallet, not without much shouting, we manage to erect the
tent ; next the bed, a mysterious puzzle which entirely
defies an African head ; and so, pushing one boy in one
direction, one in another, we do the thing for ourself, and
by eleven o'clock are ready to lie down and get some rest.

" Soon after 2 a.m. next morning we began to get under

＊ Thomson, p. 63 ; Johnston, p. 48.

weigh, and started at 4 a.m. It looks well for us that we passed the spot where we meant to halt for breakfast without knowing it. At about 9 a.m. we arrived at a good big muddy pool, and halted for the day to reorganize. It was a merciful providence that we were led to do so, for the heat was most intense—the men simply lay about under the bushes and groaned. As for myself, I had not even the energy to get out my thermometer until the cool of the evening. Even then it marked 100° Fahrenheit.

" We had here a good example of the fact that Africans can be plucky sometimes, and will endure great hardships for the sake of wives and children. We were overhauling the men, that we might send back those who were proving themselves unfit for the march through weakness or sickness. One man, Dudu (the " Insect "), was reported as suffering from dysentery rather seriously.

" Said Handford, ' You too will return, Dudu.'

" ' I don't want to, Bwana ; I want to go on.'

" ' You cannot, you are not able ; you must go back.'

" He still pleaded, ' I don't want to.'

" ' Not another word ; if you come with us you will die. Go ! ' "

" ' Then I won't.'

" Handford sprang to his feet at such an unusual occurrence, and the men standing round raised an astonished cry of shame against Dudu's rebellion ; when I stepped to the front and said, ' Let him come ; he has got some *go* in him.

" From that moment Dudu and I became friends ; but," adds the Bishop, very characteristically, " I must confess that he buzzed about me afterwards rather more than I liked."

Their march now lay through the sterile land of Duruma, where a tribe of Wa-Nyika do their best to maintain themselves in their thorny jungles against famine on the one hand and Masai raiders on the other. Passing through this region of spiny aloes and cacti, they pressed on through a sandy desert, and halted at the rock pools, or "Ungurungas," of Mount Taro. Hannington writes:

"Arrived at Taro at 7 a.m. A beautiful spot—an oasis in the desert, with plenty of water, if you don't mind toads and tadpoles and such-like denizens of stagnant pools. We had not been long in camp before a native of a small neighbouring village, somewhere in the heart of an impenetrable jungle, crept out and made his way to my tent, and implored me to send his people a teacher and form a Station there. If we did, they could live in peace and cultivate the ground. Now they dared accumulate no possessions, lest they should excite the cupidity of the raiding Wa-Kama. These poor creatures have to eke out a miserable existence on berries, roots, and such game as they can kill with poisoned arrows. I gave him a small present, which he received with great suspicion.

"Shortly after this our porters brought two Swahilis to Handford, asserting that they were sure there were slaves close at hand.

"Some hours later, a cry of ' Slaves, slaves !' was raised, and off dashed most of the men in the direction of the cry. It appears that one of the porters, searching for firewood, suddenly came upon a caravan, and fearing they would kill him, raised this shout. Expecting a hand-to-hand fight, away we dashed after the men. Away, too, went I, in shirt sleeves and slippers, clutching my gun. The slippers kept coming off, and I was soon outdistanced by Handford. But it did not much matter, as there was no fight. The owners of the caravan decamped when they saw us coming, and left their slaves, one woman and seven children, in the bush. So we found ourselves with eight poor, wretched slaves upon our hands. Such pitiable objects they were, more than half-starved. We decided to send them straight to the coast, in charge of some men. There the Consul freed them, and they were received by the Mission. It was, however, too late ; they never recovered from the cruel treatment they had received, and all died but one. Since this our caravans have liberated two more gangs The Swahilis are so frightened of being caught and handed over to the authorities, that they simply flee and leave the slaves behind, so that, as Sir John Kirk says, under such circumstances you cannot help yourself ; you must take possession of them. We are quite aware that we are not military authorities authorized to enforce the Sultan's laws, and, moreover, that it is not our part as Missionaries to employ force ; and we try as much as possible to avoid interference with any passing caravan. Interference, however, is sometimes thrust upon us. Would to God that we could overthrow this stronghold of Satan with the Sword of the Spirit ! "

The next march was through the dreaded Taro plain, which stretches almost waterless as far as Taita. For the first few hours after leaving Taro the country is pleasant enough—an undulating, fertile region, well wooded, and not without shade. There is a pool, too, called Ziwani, where a mouthful of dirty water may occasionally be obtained. After this an abrupt change takes place in the features of the landscape. Mr. Thomson says : " The agreeable alternation of ridge and hollow is exchanged for an apparently dead level plain, parched and waterless, as if no drop of life-giving rain refreshed the iron-bound soil. The dense jungle, the grassy glades, the open forest, disappear, and their place is taken by what may be called a skeleton forest."

Such trees as there are are almost wholly leafless ; stern, grey, and shadeless, they present rigid arms or formidable thorns instead of twigs and foliage. All green has vanished. Every sign of life is left behind, a dreary silence reigns supreme throughout this dreadful wilderness. Mr. Johnston, too, speaks of this part of his march as " that terrible journey," and tells how, in the fierce heat of that awful furnace, he and his men scarcely reached Mount Maungu alive.

Let us see how the Bishop and his party crossed this land of death.

" On the morrow we started for the dreaded Taro plain ; nor did we make a very happy commencement, for, soon after leaving camp, down came the rain in a perfect deluge, so that in a short time the ground was covered with an inch or two of water. Cloth, rice, and other loads were soaked, and their weight much increased for the poor men. We did not find the right track until nightfall. We then halted to wait for the moon, and meanwhile lighted a huge fire, at which we soon dried most of our things ; then, without pitching tents, we snatched an hour or two of sleep in the open. At 1 a.m. we made a move, and in about two hours Handford and I reached water. But where were the men ? They had, it appeared, allowed us to go on, and then had lighted fires and laid them down to sleep again. Finding that they were not coming, I rolled myself up in a canvas cover, and withdrew a little apart from the others, who were talking, in order to get a nap. Presently, just before I fell asleep, I was roused by the loud growl of a lion quite close at hand, so I took up my bed and went closer to the fire. At 11 a.m. we started again and walked till nightfall. Had to camp without water. Off again at 2 a.m., and by 9 a.m. we reached Maungu, after one of the most trying marches I ever remember. The road is most dismal. It passes through closely-packed thorn bushes, under, over, or through which you have to go. They tear your clothes and flesh, without affording a particle of shade. You can only see a few yards ahead, and the dead-looking forest is so monotonous that I can recall scarcely any special spot or feature as a way mark. I retched with the intense heat. The sun literally seemed to bake one through. At Maungu the men had to climb nearly 2000 feet before they reached the water. I had a slight touch of sun fever, but on we must go, so at 4 p.m. we started again and walked till sunset. Again we camped without water. How little we appreciate our comforts at home—the blessing of a wash, for instance. No water means almost no wash. Being an old traveller I meet the difficulty by filling my sponge before starting, and tying it tightly in its bag. If we have two days without water, the first day I have what a schoolboy would call a 'lick and a promise'; then the second day I wring out the water, and get quite a brave wash, the water afterwards coming in for the dog and the donkey.

"Another night's march brought us to the foot of Taita Hill. But what a climb! Three thousand feet of steep, rugged road has to be dealt with as best one can, on hands and knees sometimes. The gneiss rocks which jutted out gave a very poor hold. How tired I was! The natives choose these fastnesses for a double reason. They are excellent places from which to pounce down upon the weak, while, on the other hand, they are a natural fortress against the strong. After about a thousand feet of climbing we came upon villages, but everywhere deserted. What had once been banana groves and plantations are now patches of rank grass and ill weeds.

"We found Mr. Wray in a state of semi-siege. The Wa-Kamba had attacked and burned villages in sight of him, and for two days he and his people had been on guard, fearing, I think needlessly, that they might be stormed. Our arrival was a great relief to him, the more so as we brought the much needed food."

The mountains of Taita rise to between five and six thousand feet above the plain. Mr. Thomson says : " The whole appearance of the Taita highlands is strikingly suggestive of an archipelago of islands, rising with great abruptness from a greyish green sea, as the great weird plain, already described, surrounds it on all sides." About two thousand five hundred feet up the side of Mount Ndara is the Mission Station. There Mr. Wray was bravely holding the fort in spite of the difficulties which beset him. The people were dying of starvation, and inclined to curse him as the evil author of their troubles ; but he had, nevertheless, won the confidence and affection of those with whom he was able to come into contact. The Bishop writes of him :

" Corn in the ear he cannot point to, but I found that he had broken up an unusually hard fallow, and sown the seed of which the blade already begins to appear. He is much attached to the people. This being the case, and the station being a valuable link in a line of stations, one would make every effort to keep it going. Yet the famine presses hard. In spite of our supplies of food, many have died, many have left, and many have been killed or captured and sold for slaves. Thus, all the villages, except those immediately under Mr. Wray's wing, are utterly abandoned. The people around him number less than a hundred. These I assembled to hear their opinion upon the situation. They were most decided. ' We do not wish to desert Bwana, but we cannot stop here. Sometimes you feed us, some-

THE TWO TAITAS, FROM MAUNGU.

times you do not, and then we have to return to eating grass and insects. Not one neighbour have we left. Even if you gave us seed to-morrow, it would be four months before we could get any food.' It seemed then to all of us that, in the face of this, the station could not be continued. With so many demands for missionaries from populous districts, and when, too, these few families could be better and at far less expense cared for at Rabai, it appeared a waste of men and means to let Mr. Wray continue here. I therefore arranged that they should be received at Rabai, and the native catechist, Cicil Mabaruki, who has been under Mr. Wray, and of whom he speaks very highly, will be specially told off to look after them. If the mountain should again be populated, there will be nothing to prevent us from again taking possession of the same site at any time."

"Feb. 10th saw us on the move again, accompanied by Mr. Wray. The descent on the west side of Taita Hill we found to be much steeper, but shorter and less fatiguing than that on the east. At one part the track led over a smooth, steeply sloping rock, over which it was almost impossible to get the donkeys. One of them was rather badly hurt. When we reached the bottom, the arms of the great plain which thrusts itself in between the two Taitas had to be crossed, and on the morrow, after forcing our way through a terrible thicket, through which the men with great difficulty got their loads, we encamped near a Wa-Kamba village. We fired our guns, and the men rushed out. These are the people who have so cruelly ravaged Sagalla (Wray's mountain), but they were friendly enough to us, and here we spent our first 'money,' and for a little cloth bought some heads of Indian corn.

"*Feb. 12th.*—A day to be remembered. I must rank it among the red-letter days of my traveller's experience. I led the caravan out at 4.30, and got off clear, but Handford, who brought up the rear, met with some opposition and demands for hongo (here called ‘ fingo ’). One of the village elders blocked his path, and tried to extort a tribute. After a short climb over a steep and rugged track, we rounded the headland of the Bura Mountain, and crossed the beautiful pass of Kilima Kibomu. As we topped a rise, suddenly before our astonished gaze flashed Kilima-njaro in all his glory ! How lovely the great mountain looked—all radiant with the rays of the rising sun. We had, by the best fortune, arrived at this point of vantage just at the hour of sunrise, when the vast silver dome for a short time shakes aside the mist wreaths which during the rest of the day so frequently enswathe his snow-crowned summit. From where we stood, and at this distance, the two peaks— the dome-shaped Kibo and the needle-pointed Kimawenzi— were merged into one ; and only with the glass could I distinguish their different outlines. The sight was so surpassingly beautiful that it called forth long and loud exclamations from the stolid Africans around us, many of whom had accompanied Thomson or Johnston, some both, and who were well acquainted with the snow-giant. That an African should exclaim, or even take note of any natural scene, however grand, is something quite uncommon ; but now all, black and white alike, were in ecstacy at the magnificence and beauty of the sight. We at once called a halt, and, as long as time permitted, we feasted our eyes on snow under the burning sun of Africa.

“ Too soon we had to resume our weary march, and descending the pass we came to the dreaded hongo station of the Kilima. We met with a little braggadocio on the part of one gentleman, who even threatened to kill any stragglers we might leave behind ; but we told him that we did not mean to leave any, and very placidly wished him good-morning, and passed on, in spite of his war-cry and endeavour to raise the country against us. At the next village, Burra, passing a foot-track which led in the wrong direction, I, according to custom, drew a line across it with my stick, as a signal to those behind not to go that way. An old woman who happened to be standing on the path was seized with a paroxysm of terror. She was fully per-suaded that I had done this to bewitch her, and raised the most fearful shrieks, calling on all around to kill me. Through the woods and over the hills rang her shrill cries, so, as we could not in any way pacify her, and not knowing what might come of it, we left her screaming and hurriedly passed on.

" We were now on the verge of the vast and almost waterless plain which lies between Taita and Tiveta, and we were warned to expect no water for at least two days. So accordingly, we started, prepared for the worst. This plain exactly fulfils the idea which I had formed of an African plain from pictures and descriptions before I visited the country. It is covered with game of all kinds. Herds of inquisitive zebra came barking and galloping past to inspect the caravan ; hartebeeste, eland, springbuck, and other antelopes were to be seen everywhere. The long necks of giraffe issued, serpent-like, from the grass ; and in the dusk one could hear the deep roaring of lions over their meal. Thus the attention was always held occupied by some new or interesting sight, and minutes imperceptibly grew into hours, so that many an otherwise weary mile was passed swiftly by. Moreover, travelling was becoming far easier and more pleasant to me as I got into training. Here, too, at this altitude, the air was much cooler—even cold at night. At one spot we came upon a fire, round which was seated a group of starving Wa-Taita, endeavouring to struggle on to the more fertile districts that surround the mountain. They had already abandoned one woman and child. The mother was dead, but the child we enabled them to rescue by giving them food and encouraging them to return and search for it. Soon afterwards we came, quite unexpectedly, upon water. So the plain was passed without any difficulty. The men found the carcase of an antelope, upon half of which a lion had breakfasted ; over this they were soon quarrelling and feasting.

"On Saturday, Feb. 14, the dark green shades of Taveta began to be visible, and soon we entered a dense forest, through which we crept mysteriously, and on tiptoe, lest the inhabitants should hear us and shut the gates against us, refusing to open them until a heavy hongo had been paid. With bated breath we crept along ; so absorbed were we that I almost forgot to taste a new kind of fruit which hung overhead, and Handford forgot to look where he was treading, and so fell headlong over a stump ! (If we could have exchanged memories for the time, we should both have been better off.) Presently we arrived at the tunnel-like portal, so low that only on hands and knees can admission be gained, while some of the loads had to be coaxed through ; but to our joy the door was open, so we could easily afford to stoop. I found out afterwards that all our fuss was so much waste of energy. Confidence in the white man has been fully established here. I do not think they would keep one waiting outside for a single instant. The people received us in the most friendly manner.

"Next morning, on waking, we found ourselves in a magnificent forest, honeycombed with luxuriant gardens of maize, Indian corn, and broad-leaved banana trees. The people are peculiarly gentle and taking in manner and conversation. The description of Laish (Judges xviii.) seems to me exactly to suit them : ' *They dwelt careless, quiet, and secure ; and there was no magistrate in the land to put them to shame.'* Usually this would be a land of plenty, but this terrible famine has driven a large number of starving neighbours within their bounds, and they too are feeling the pinch.

" One thing we were all agreed upon—*this is not the place for a European Missionary.* Travellers who recommend it have probably not seen it as we did, in the depth of the rainy season, when the rich, black, vegetable soil constantly exudes poisonous vapours. The forest is so dense that it almost excludes the refreshing breezes, and so over shadows the open spaces and plantations that large parts of them are constantly wet. Both going and coming, Mr. Wray had attacks of fever here, and I had what might be called a loud warning ; so that, beautiful as the place is in many respects, we were uncommonly glad to be out of it, and to find ourselves, on March the 17th, *en route* for Chagga.* Martin, who was with Thomson, told me that Taveta was the only place where he was ill."

During the three days spent in Taveta, the Bishop lost no opportunity of inspecting the place with a view to future Missionary work. He also did some business in behalf of Mr. Johnston, leader of the recent Kilima-njaro expedition, and, in accordance with a request from the Consul, settled up Mr. Johnston's affairs, and paid off his men.

On the afternoon of the 17th, messengers arrived from Mandara with an ox as a present from the king. So they started. " Just as we approached our sleeping place, a rhinoceros strolled leisurely away, I suppose to make room for us, and I think he was wise."

The next morning they breasted the steep ascent to

* The whole highland district on the southern and eastern spurs of Kilima-njaro is called Chagga. It is occupied by several tribes, of which Mandara's is the most powerful.

Chagga. " Kilima-njaro, with his two peaks, Kibo and Kimawenzi, were magnificently in view in the early dawn, and remained so about long enough for me to sketch them ; then, as usual, they were again veiled in clouds. Herds of buffalo and large game appeared quite close to us, but we could not then stalk them. As we approached Moschi the men became very excited. We fired the royal salute which this august monarch rigidly exacts from his guests, and were answered by a salvo from his two cannon. It was quite night (8 p.m.) before we crossed the beautiful valley which separates the outer world from Moschi ; however, to my great surprise, we were ushered at once into Mandara's presence. If first impressions are to be trusted we shall get on. I was very favourably struck, not only with his general appearance, but also by his kindliness of manner and intelligence. The interview was a short one ; we craved no more than to be allowed to seek our respective couches.

" *March* 19*th.*—We had one of those drenching nights with which one sometimes meets in Africa. We could not pitch our tents till late, and then had no time to dig trenches round them. Consequently the water rushed through the tents in torrents. As the men and boys had no shelter of any kind, I invited as many as possible into my tent, which is a very small one. We managed to squeeze in, however, myself, two on the floor, another curled up on the foot of my camp-bed, and Pinto, my invaluable coolie, in the chair. Presently I heard an ominous sound and shouts for help. Handford's tent was laid flat. Thus, between one thing and another, our first night on the slopes of Kilima-njaro was not a pleasant one. However, I rose before daylight and made certain preparations, for I had my suspicions, which proved to be true, that dawn would bring the roseate Mandara (he wears a rosy-red robe). Sure enough there he was, with

KIBO AND KIMAWENZI, FROM NEAR TAVETA.

about twenty warriors, all stark naked, fine athletic young men of one of the Masai clans, and looking fierce enough to frighten one out of his wits. I presented Mandara with a box and uniform, which he received in a most satisfactory manner, nor did he ask to see a single thing in the tent, though I thought his one bright eye roved about in rather a restless manner. ' Wait,' said I, ' he will develop.'

" After breakfast we returned his visit, and received the present of a goat and cow. We then cautiously unfolded the objects of our visit. The same caution was strictly observed on his part. The sum of what he said is the echo of almost every chief's voice in Africa, ' I want guns and gunpowder, and if I can't have them, the next best thing is a white teacher to live in the land."

Those who have read Mr. Johnston's most interesting book on the Kilima-njaro expedition will scarcely be surprised to hear that Mandara did not appreciate the manner in which that explorer had taken leave of him. Mr. Johnston's subterfuge extricated him from a serious difficulty, but did not tend to make matters easy for any European who should come after him. Mandara's own provoking conduct, no doubt, made some exceptional measure on Mr. Johnston's part necessary, but he none the less resented the method of his escape. He complained bitterly to Bishop Hannington of the treatment to which he had been subjected, and said that after his recent experience of white men, he did not much wish to have another, though he would receive a *resident* teacher. The Bishop told him plainly that his present visit was merely one of inquiry, and that he would determine later whether a teacher should be sent. He writes :

" To the end Mandara maintained the same princely bearing and gentlemanly conduct. With the exception of

Mirambo, I have never met in the interior a shrewder or more enlightened chief.* I have but little doubt that the history of a Mission here, if properly maintained, would be the counterpart of most of our Missions : the reception of the white man with joy and gladness ; everything done for him for a week or two, then a cooling down of the first love, neglect, perhaps even persecution ; after which, if patiently endured, fresh overtures, a mutual understanding deepening into confidence and love ; then a gradual opening of the door, a breaking down of superstitions, a reception of the Gospel of Peace and of the sweet Saviour of men.

"May God give Chagga to His Son ! It is a lovely spot. I often exclaimed, ' Here is England ; England ! You see England here ! Yes, and that part of England which I love best, dear Devonshire.' "

" *Thursday, March* 19*th.*—Last night was too much for ————. He has determined to return. I am most anxious he should remain until Monday. He next to declines unless I command, which I am unwilling to do."

This determination on the part of one of his staff was most inopportune, as Mr. Wray was incapacitated by fever caught on the road, and the Bishop was left at a critical time to fall back upon his own resources. But, with his usual unselfishness and consideration for others, he did not insist upon retaining his follower for a single day longer than he was willing to remain. Happily, he was himself in good health and able to rise to the occasion.

" *March* 20*th.*—Writing as fast as I can, to send by the mail. ———— left about noon in pouring rain and

---

* It will be remembered that Bishop Hannington had not seen Mtèsa.

mist. Wet weather, very depressing. The chief visited
me again. I was drawing at the time, and drew him,
which rather wounded his feelings. Lovely view of Kilima-
njaro in the evening.

" *March* 21*st.*—A war party arrived to-day, about 500,
with immense droves of cattle, which Mandara distributed
throughout the various villages. Very little excitement,
and no tom-toming whatever. I was surprised at the order
kept. Went up to see Johnston's house; found that it
would be a nice place to pitch our tents, and so got leave
from the chief. Had Wray carried up, as he has fever, and
in the afternoon we were comfortably settled ; nearly 1000
feet higher than Moschi, and very private. These valleys
are very like Devonshire."

During his stay at Moschi, though all Hannington's
instincts prompted him to explore and collect, he set apart
but one day for that purpose. He never for a moment forgot the object of his journey, which was the establishment
of a chain of Mission Stations westward to the Lake. On
Monday, the 23rd, however, he determined to ascend the
mountain as far as he could in one day, and to make a
small collection of such of its flora and fauna as he could
manage in so short a time to secure.

He started from their camping place at Kitimbiriu,* early
in the morning, with his three boys. At first they ascended
through lanes of dracænas and gorgeous scarlet-flowered
aloes, and the track led past the clustering huts of the
friendly Wa-Chagga. These flocked out to see the Bwana
Mkubwa, who came of a race possessed of such a strange
love of wandering. A little higher than 5000 feet they
came out upon grassy downs which reminded the Bishop of

---

* Johnston, p. 142.

Devonshire.* Above this again began the tangled forest, with its dense and almost impenetrable undergrowth, which clings to the mountain to the height of about 9000 feet. The Bishop had no guide, and soon got into difficulties. He writes in one of his letters :

" I made one attempt to cross the savage country of Kibosho, not, as the last traveller, armed to the teeth, but with my three boys and umbrella.† We passed through some grand forest scenery, got into the region of heath and tree-ferns, failed to attain any great height (about 8800 feet), and finally got lost in a desperate tangle, out of which we had the utmost difficulty in finding our way."

His pocket-book journal is more graphic in its jottings :

" Started early with my three small boys, to try and pass the forest line on Kilima-njaro. Heavy dew and cloud was our lot, during a long ascent of some hours through a wonderful moss-and-fern-clad forest. At length we reached lovely tree-ferns and heath like a Devonshire moor, which made my heart beat quick. The path which we had ascended all the morning now divided, and the forest became so dense that we could form no idea as to where we were. So I decided to return. Missed the path, amongst the hundreds of elephant tracks, and got utterly lost. To

---

* Johnston, p. 230. " The surrounding scenery was now charmingly soft and pretty, so exactly like Devonshire hills and coombes in general aspect that I need not give it a more detailed description."

† Mr. Johnston had unfortunately for himself become entangled in Mandara's wars with his neighbours, and the Wa-Kibosho, in consequence, looked upon him as their enemy, and opposed his ascent of the mountain.

add to our misery, pouring rain set in, and I fell down an
elephant pit. Never had I felt more bewildered. The boys
were terrified.* At length one of them, a MTaita, roused
himself, and, with true native sagacity, discerned the elephant tracks from the path smoothed by human feet—no
easy matter—and brought us back to the right way. I only
got one peep of Kilima-njaro all day. Not over-tired, but
drenched through, and so wet my plants." Elsewhere the
Bishop says that he was so thoroughly wetted by the dripping undergrowth through which they passed that on their
way home he waded through a stream almost up to his neck
without getting any sensibly wetter. The following extract
from a letter to Mr. Mitten will explain the reference to the
plants :

"My dear Prof.,—I have to-day sent to the Brit.
Mus. a box of butterflies and a box of mosses from Kilima-
njaro. I have asked the Librarian to have them forwarded
to you. My plants all got spoilt with the intense rain,

---

* Mr. Johnston writes of this forest :—"The dull gloom was
very oppressive. The mists of the mountain permeated the foliage,
and a continual moisture dripped down on us. We were all
wetted through every covering. Our clothes were ponderous with
absorbed water—it was fatiguing to stagger under their weight.
Noises full of vague terror to my superstitious following broke the
stillness of the rank depths wherein we stumbled and crept along.
Each porter, as he clutched his load with one hand and with the
other pushed aside the interwoven boughs, turned his head un-
easily from side to side, dreading the sudden rising from the bush
of some terrible unimagined foe." No wonder that the Bishop's
boys became terrified as they tremblingly followed their master
ever upward toward the demon-haunted throne of the Spirit of
the Mountain. The traveller through these African forest wilds
begins to understand the feeling which originated those grim
and weird German legends, so full of the vague terrors of "the
Forest."

ferns and all, the mosses running a very narrow shave, and many are discoloured. I only got up about 8800 feet, but I am off there again if nothing prevent, and hope to get higher. I wanted to get to the snow-line for mosses, and made a desperate struggle, but the ascent is so gradual that it takes a very long time. I started at about 5000 ft., and walked from morning till 4 p.m. with scarce any stoppages, and then never got out of the dense forest tangle. Among the mosses I recognized several old acquaintances; in fact, I don't think you will get six new things out of the lot, as I swept pretty clean in U-Sagara last visit, and the same things seem to crop up here.* I have been wonderfully well and active, and have got over as much ground in a given time as anybody out here, and I believe that I could start with you to-day and run over the Alps better than ever I did before. This new road is perfectly healthy and very bracing, and travelling has been like in England or Wales. The rainfall here has been terrible, six inches in four days, so that I am expecting an unhealthy time very shortly. How I should like to show you round my garden and to see your's. Mine now is about the size of your's, and stored with the curious. The views from it are simply exquisite, as it runs down to the sea."†

An opportunity of re-ascending Kilima-njaro was again, somewhat unexpectedly, afforded, and this time the Bishop took Mr. Wray and eight men with him. It is, however, impossible to gain a great height without spending a night on the mountain, and they did not reach higher than 9000 ft.

On the 25th of March, Hannington paid his farewell visit to Mandara. He writes:

* Hannington's name is associated with an Asplenium, *A. Hanningtoni*, and a Passion Flower, *Tryphostemma Hanningtonianum*.
† This was written from the Bishop's House at Frere Town.

"This afternoon, he sent me a magnificent spear, a rhinoceros-horn knob-stick, and a beautifully worked chain, which latter I gave to Wray. I sent one or two extra presents to Mandara in my ecstacy over the spear.

"*Thursday, March 26th.*—Up at 4 a.m. Dreadful business with the men. Final visit to the chief; received an ox, a magnificent goat, an immense quantity of fresh milk, and a small elephant's tusk, for which latter he wants some soap and parafin. Mandara and I have hit it off very well, and we both express ourselves satisfied and pleased.

"The next day we arrived in Fumba's country. We were asked to halt and wait instructions, while the delighted people gathered round us in great curiosity, as this little territory is off the traveller's track; in fact, we only found ourselves there by having mistaken a turn. Presently the chief's father arrived, bringing with him a sheep. This had at once to be killed, though not before we and they had spit on its head. Then some strips of skin were cut off and made into rings, one of which was put on my finger, and another on Wray's; then we had in turn to put rings on two of them. After this, the liver was examined, and finally we were freely splashed with the entrails, and the ceremony which made us brothers was completed. We were now permitted to make a move towards the chief and to encamp. Then another sheep had to be killed, the same ceremony yet more elaborately performed, and the con_versation began. It was not interesting. It harped too much upon one string. The burden was the old African song, 'Give, give, give.' The next day we bade them farewell, and arrived in the truly lovely country of the young chief Miliali. He much wants a teacher; but, like the rest, wants gunpowder more.

"All these districts are on the eastern slope of the mountain, and comprise Chagga proper, the natives all appearing to speak the same tongue. I have seen no place in Africa so beautiful as this ; rapid torrents dash down the mountain sides, forming a succession of lovely cascades. There are grassy slopes, fern-clad rocks, even shady lanes, in which the blackberry abounds. Nooks entirely tropical, and snow-clad heights. You have, in fact, panoramic views of the scenery of the world.

"*March* 31*st.*—We left Miliali's at about 3 p.m., being rather delayed by the attempt of the natives to rob one of our men. We soon reached a river, and found an absolutely perpendicular precipice of some 50 feet, up which men can climb by roots and creepers ; but a sheer impossibility for Wray's donkey. We turned ; the guides vowed there was no other place, and defied us to try. We braved their wrath and found another, though the difficulties were scarcely less. Here, somehow or other, in the darkness we got separated, my tent and several loads taking an entirely different road from the one I had the misfortune to follow. Night came on, and with it torrents of rain. I waited, hoping it would clear, and expecting my tent. An hour passed and still I stood. Wray now made an effort and got his tent under weigh. It is a very small one, and with himself and six boxes there was scarcely room to stir. We tried to light a fire with oil and tallow and fat, but in vain ; for once we were entirely beaten, and, worse still, nearly blinded with evil-smelling smoke. Wray succeeded in getting a bed, but I had to face the mud on the wet ground, spreading a blanket over it. I had to lie down in my wet clothes, gaiters and boots, and I made two of my wet boys, both for their own sakes and mine, come and lie one on each side of me, as close as sardines, to prevent the chance of a chill. The rain killed one of the men—he died two

MOUNTAIN TORRENT, MARANGO, KILIMA-NJARO.

days after.*   How thankful we were when day broke !   In spite of being bespattered with mud, and wet through, it was delightful to be at least able to see what we were about. I had scarcely aroused myself when a shrill war cry rang through the forest, and a large body of armed men sprang from the bushes and bore down upon us.   Thank God, my old nerve remained.   I ran forward alone and unarmed to meet them, for the least false step on the part of our men would have caused a general massacre.   I must confess that my heart seemed to jump into my mouth as they charged up the hill, yelling and brandishing their spears.   I seized a bough, as a token of peace, and shouted, ' Jambo !   Good morning !   Do you want to kill a white man ? '   A sudden halt, and a dead pause ; at last, ' No, we don't ; but we thought you were Masai.'

"It appeared that a man living near had heard us talking in the dark, and thinking that the Masai were upon them, sent all round the country, and gathered a large force to annihilate us.   When they saw how matters stood, they at once made friends, and tried hard to persuade us to remain and visit Mambo, their chief.   But as I had no tent, I declined.   In revenge they made April fools of us poor dripping creatures, and sent us the wrong way through the forest, so that we had finally to cut a road with our axes for ourselves, until at last we joined the road at the top of the precipice which the donkey had been unable to climb. We then with swift steps fled from such dangerous quarters, but did not come up with our baggage, so we had again to sleep out without cover.   There had been no sun to dry our things, so we spent a miserable night.

"The next day I rose at 4 a.m. and doctored the sick

---

* Nothing seems to demoralize the coast porter more than continued, heavy rain.

man mentioned above. We then marched as well as our weary and stiff frames would let us along a heavy, wet road which led us to Taveta. Here we were made once more comfortable, and, by the great mercy of God, I escaped evil consequences from my two nights' exposure. The sick man, without my knowledge, asked to be washed in warm water, and a few minutes later I was called to see him, and found him dying. He was killed by the terrible rain, while I, in God's mercy, am spared without even a cold!

"Good Friday; up at daybreak to see about the grave of our poor porter. The men took great pains about it. He was not baptized, but had been under Christian instruction. We said some Collects over his grave. We then had the Service of the Day. I afterwards strolled in the forest, and, venturing to leave the path, had great work to return. On Saturday I had a good catch of butterflies. The place swarms with monkeys, vultures, and great quaint-looking hornbills.

"On Easter Day we had a Swahili Service for the men. We then celebrated the Holy Communion—our two selves and three of the men.

"Here I felt a near approach of fever, and only warded it off by an immediate application of remedies. Taveta is most beautiful and fascinating, with its groves and streams, and a kindly and hospitable people making the stranger welcome to their forest home; but it is most unhealthy, at least at this season. It is, in fact, the only unhealthy spot which we have visited on this route. Wray was also threatened with another attack of fever, and went straight to bed.

"On Monday we were off at daybreak; we had some difficulty in getting out, owing to the depth of black mud; but it was with no small satisfaction that I stood outside the forest and felt a blow of wind upon me once more.

" Giraffe, Koodoo and other antelopes all round, but they don't tempt me.

"*April* 7.—Fever threatening, but I won't give way." So he walked all day, as the best means of shaking it off. " Presently two guns ahead, and a man runs to meet me. He carries a letter.   Huzza !   Oh, the joy !—my mail, and all well.   Thank God !

" Game everywhere on the plain.   Saw many ostriches. Nearly picked up a snake, thinking it was a quail.

"*April* 8, 4 a.m.—Scotch mist, and very cold.   The men clung to their fires.   I had to dash at them and straw the fires out, and left camp hurling firebrands at some of the most obstinate.   Tedious march to Mgameni ; bad smell.   Wray gave in.   Terrible rain, but we were partly under cover.   On once more.   The hammock men went ahead, leaving me to walk through the river.   Very vexed, as it was thoughtless of them, and puts me in great danger of fever.   Wring my socks and get on as best I can.   Have to get all the men together to pass Kilima Kilomu, fearing hongo.   Escaped.   More rain ; tremen- dously long grass ; arrive in camp, 6 p.m., tired almost beyond endurance."

I quote these jottings as they are scribbled on the leaf of his pocket-book ; they seem to me to be more eloquent than many an elaborate description.   As we read them, the image of the weary and overdone man, who had given up his own hammock to his sick friend, stumbling through the sodden grass of the muddy plain, yet refusing to own himself beaten, and doggedly plodding forward, ever forward —stands out with the vraisemblance of an instantaneous photograph.

By the evening of the next day they reached Taita.   The Bishop expected to find here a caravan which Mr. Handford had been directed to send from the coast with food. Through a sequence of mischances this convoy had been delayed, and when the party arrived from Taveta with their own stores exhausted, they found no replenishment. The Bishop writes: " I was in despair. After waiting for a day or two on famine allowance, we were reduced to considerable straits. Barely eating enough to support life, it was difficult to eat that, for the poor starving Wa-Taita came round and watched every mouthful we took, like hungry dogs. I think I should go mad if this went on much longer."

After doing his best to inculcate patience among his followers, the Bishop relieved his feelings by a good butterfly hunt for the British Museum. But things were waxing desperate, when, late in the afternoon of the 11th, a gun announced the laggard caravan. He writes : " How full of joy I felt ! Food for the starving ! "

" On Sunday, April 12th, after Morning Service, we gathered together the remaining Wa-Taita, who were helpless against their enemies, and famishing, and arranged that some of them should go with me, the rest follow later on to the coast."

The next day the Bishop started, leaving Mr. Wray at the Mission House, and taking with him thirty of the half-starved people. He writes : " It was very nice to hear a little group of men praying round their fire as I laid me to sleep."

Happily the passage of this miscellaneous troop over the dreadful desert between Maungu and Taro was made on a comparatively cool day, so that they crossed the waterless region without any great suffering. In due time the Bishop brought his whole party safely through to Rabai. Here the Wa-Taita were left in good hands, and he himself, without stopping, went straight on to Frere Town.

Thus ended an eventful journey. The Bishop writes :

" I have to praise God for one of the most successful journeys, as a journey, that I ever took.   For myself, too, I have enjoyed most excellent health almost the whole way, during a tramp of four hundred miles.*   May its result be the PLANTING OF THE CROSS OF CHRIST ON KILIMA-NJARO ! " †

---

* This is a most modest estimate, and almost " as the crow flies."   The actual distance there and back, allowing for inevitable windings, would probably be more than five hundred miles.

† This has been the result.   A Mission Station is now esta-blished at Moschi in Chagga, where Messrs. Wray and Fitch do outpost duty.

CHAPTER XXI.

" THE WORK OF A BISHOP."

(1885. APRIL–JUNE.)

" Probably no one will deny that this . . . holiness has existed. Few will maintain that it has been exceedingly rare. Perhaps the truth is that there has scarcely been a town in any Christian country, since the time of Christ, where a century has passed without exhibiting a character of such elevation that his mere presence has shamed the bad, and made the good better, and has been felt at times like the presence of God Himself. And if this be so, has Christ failed? or can Christianity die?"—*Ecce Homo.*

SUNBURNT and shaggy, but glowing with health, the Bishop once more stood, surrounded by his friends, upon the threshold of his own house at Frere Town. He was overjoyed to think that upon this new route westward there were no difficulties which might not be overcome by courage, prudence, and experience. No ghastly malarial fevers ; no cruel dysenteric attacks, such as on the lower road reduced the strength of the strongest man, and neutralized his bravest efforts. When he compared his experiences upon this journey with those of his terrible march of death from Zanzibar to the Lake in the previous year, he was filled with a kind of triumph. What if it were possible to push straight through, as Thomson had done, to the North end of the Nyanza ! Might not many lives be saved, and incalculable suffering averted? Already the idea began to form itself definitely in his mind. The idea, once started, formulated itself rapidly. The more he thought about it, the more feasible did the new route appear. The way was shorter by a very considerable distance ; it was incontestably healthier ; it lay through a country which, in many places, possessed an English climate, and was thoroughly suitable for European residence ; there was at that time no reason to suppose that the Ba-ganda would offer any opposition to an approach from the North-East. The only serious difficulty appeared to be the lawless and irrepressible Masai. Well, Mr. Thomson had proved that it was quite possible to pass through the country of these truculent warriors without danger much greater than was incidental to all African travelling through unexplored regions. Jumba Kimameta and other traders were in the habit of taking caravans regularly backwards and forwards through the heart of the Masai country ; and, in fine, Hannington did not believe that there were any insurmountable obstacles to the establishment of a chain of Mission Stations which should extend from Mombasa, through Taita or Chagga by Lakes Naivasha and Baringo, to U-Ganda. But the weightiest chain of thought is, like other chains, no stronger than its weakest link ; and ignorance of a single detail may upset the conclusions of the most cogent reasoning ; and the Bishop and his friends were unfortunately ignorant of one fact of which we, who are wise after the event, are now aware. I mean the suspicion and fear with which all visitors from the North-East are regarded by the people of U-Ganda. But of this anon. The Bishop shall presently explain his own views in his own words. In the meanwhile, it is sufficient for us to note that his mind had already grasped the idea of a new and better route to the Lake, and that he was even now making inquiries with regard to it of every practical man with whom he was acquainted, and planning the details in his busy brain.

A few days after his return from Chagga he wrote to

Mr. Wigram : " You will be utterly frightened when you hear that I am consulting all whom I can, with a view to crossing the Masai country to the Lake ; but reserve your judgment until you hear from me by the next mail."

When the Bishop returned from his long tramp, he found a good deal of work awaiting him in Frere Town and the neighbourhood. He did not allow himself long to rest, but started again almost immediately to visit a station to the North, called Mwaiba (marked on the map Kamli-keni), in the Giriama country. He took with him his Chaplain, Mr. Fitch, and Jones, the catechist. On their way, they visited a station of the United Free Methodists at Ribè. Mr. and Mrs. Houghton, the missionaries there, are now well known by name, as they were both murdered by the Masai* in the spring of this year 1886, surviving Bishop Hannington by about six months. They gave him " a kind welcome "—which, no doubt, *he has since returned.*

Not far from Mwaiba Hill is the interesting settlement of Fulladoyo, where a number of runaway slaves have collected ; where also a chief named Mbaruk, who has been outlawed by the Sultan of Zanzibar, has taken up his abode. The C. M. S. has been compelled to eschew the neighbourhood of Fulladoyo, lest the Missionaries should be accused of leaguing themselves with the rebels.

The Bishop writes : " I determined to take a private peep at Fulladoyo, and, if possible, see this Mbaruk. Walked twenty-four miles ; arrived at F., 11 p.m. At first dawn the elders came to my tent. We were hardly seated, when about twenty of Mbaruk's soldiers marched up to my tent in a very imperious manner, and demanded why

---

* Mr. and Mrs. Houghton were not sent as missionaries to the Masai, but were located in the Galla Country, on the River Tana. They were killed during an attack by one of the raiding war parties which had penetrated Eastward from Masai Land.

I was there. Imperious not so much to me as to the Fulladoyo people, who I thought would have fired upon them
there and then. However, I sent a message by them to
Mbaruk, saying I wished to see him." At the interview
that followed, Mbaruk sought the Bishop's advice, confided
to him that he was weary of his present lawless life, and
wished to make peace with the Sultan. By the advice of
the Bishop, he then and there wrote to the Consul. Nego-
ciations have since been going on, which it is hoped may
terminate in putting an end to the brigandage of this robber
band. Bishop Hannington, ever on the alert to seize an
advantage for the Church, saw here an opportunity which
he did not lose, but made every arrangement to occupy
Fulladoyo as soon as Mbaruk should have evacuated it.
The large colony of escaped slaves had, many of them,
been for a short time under the influence of David Abe
Sidi,* a native Catechist, now dead, and would have welcomed a teacher. The Bishop says : " They still observe
the Sabbath, and, for the most part, have only one wife."

" *May 2nd.*—Again walked thirty miles with perfect
ease ; not even tired at the end of it. Since March, I have
walked about six hundred miles. To *Him* be the glory !
Amen ! "

On May the 13th the examination of catechists referred to in a former letter was held with a view to their
being licensed as lay-preachers ; and, on the last day of the
month, which was Trinity Sunday, there was an Ordination at Frere Town, when the first two natives of East
Africa, in connection with the C. M. S., were admitted to
the Diaconate. These were William Jones and Ishmael
Michael Semler, both of them rescued slaves, and men who

---

* David Abe Sidi founded the colony of Fulladoyo. When
war was made against his little flock of escaped slaves, he threw in
his lot with them, and perished in 1883.

had given for many years abundant proof of sincerity and zeal, and seemed to possess considerable spiritual gifts. The Bishop says : " Their examination, which also included D. Rosengrave, another native Catechist (a freed slave of 1875), was conducted by my Chaplain, and not only satisfied us, but surprised and rejoiced our hearts. Commencing on Thursday, we had every morning and evening special seasons set apart for prayer, and I then gave them brief charges on Christian life and the ministerial office. We all felt these seasons to be times of great spiritual refreshment."

The Rev. W. E. Taylor, B.A., was also admitted to Priests' Orders.

On Sunday, they assembled at Mr. Handford's for prayer, and then proceeded to the church. As the procession entered the building, the great congregation stood up and burst forth into the strains of that triumphant battle-hymn, " Onward, Christian soldiers ! "—and the church throbbed to the pulsations of Sullivan's martial tune, raised by hundreds of full-voiced natives, Christians and Catechumens, whose dark up-turned faces glowed with suppressed excitement. Mr. Handford preached in Kiswahili, from Matt. xiii. 52, and the well-known Ordination Service proceeded ; after which fifty-seven communicants knelt before the Table of the Lord. There were, it is true, some things in the conduct of public worship at Frere Town which did not commend themselves to the Bishop. [His diary of the Sunday previous to the Ordination has the following : " I have constantly to regret the dissenterish kind of Services they have here. A style of Service that has been handed down, I should think, from Rebmann. Why don't I have it altered ? Wait a bit ! "] But when he discerned the presence of the Divine Spirit, he could pardon many a minor detail ; and on that day the power of the Holy Ghost seemed to descend upon the people. All felt that One was present to bless. In the afternoon the Bishop preached from a favourite text of his, from which he was never tired of drawing inexhaustible stores of Christ-lore : " This is My beloved Son, in whom I am well pleased." " I can hardly tell you," he writes, " how greatly privileged I feel in thus having been permitted to ordain the first native ministers of our infant East African Church. The foundations of a native ministry have now been laid. I call most earnestly upon all the children of God to pray for these men, that they may be kept humble and zealous workers in God's vineyard, and that they may be made winners of souls."

On the first of June Bishop Hannington sailed in the *Henry Wright* to Zanzibar, to make preparations for a second journey to Chagga, where he proposed to establish Mr. Wray and Mr. Fitch, and to found a Station at Moschi. He had many interviews with Sir John Kirk, Consul Smith, and others, who all, together with the Sultan, were entirely in favour of his proposed expedition to the Lake through Masai Land. He left no stone unturned to gather up every possible scrap of information on the subject, and read with care all that Mr. Thomson has said in his remarkable book. The result was that he was more than ever confirmed in his opinion that this route ought to prove immensely superior in almost every respect to the old route through Uyui.

Nine days were spent in this manner, and in gathering together materials for the march to Chagga, and for the needs of the new Station to be opened at Mandara's capital.

His journal has the following entry on Sunday, the 7th : " Went with Fitch and Price to Early Communion in the Cathedral. I suppose we ought to have been shocked, but were not."

It will be perceived from the above and some previous entries, that Hannington's views upon Church order and outward forms of worship had undergone some slight modification since the early days of his ministry. A wider acquaintance with men and things had softened his prejudices and somewhat unbent his anti-ritualistic bow. He had never at any time been inclined to quarrel over the " non-necessaria," and was now less disposed than ever to adopt the repellant attitude of one who is always looking for something with which to find fault. He had seen and noted the dangers that lurk behind both excessive attention to ritual and its neglect; but he had learned to look within the shell of things, and had discovered that spirituality and fidelity may equally characterize men who commit either of these mistakes. As we have said before, when he thought that he discerned the Blessing of the Divine Spirit resting upon men and their deeds, he was not nervously apprehensive about sanctioning by his co-operation their modes and their methods. Even in his early days at Hurst, when a reaction from excessive formality had swung him to the opposite extreme, we have seen that he was as willing to preach in " one of the highest " churches in Brighton as in the lowest. And now, after some experience of both mistakes, he was rather inclined to avoid them himself than to be hypercritical of those who had not yet attained to the golden mean.

He thus journals the remainder of this Sunday : " Breakfast with the Bp. . 10 a.m., Swahili Service ; their singing does not nearly come up to ours.* 3.30, tea at the Univ. Mission. 4.30, preached in the Cathedral from the Transfiguration. I preached from the steps, and was in great liberty."

Shortly after this he returned to Frere Town, and on June 13th we find him holding his first African Confirmation. The Service was at 6.30 a.m. Thirty-three

---

* Comp. what is said on p. 284 about the singing in this part of Africa.

candidates assembled in the early grey of the morning, almost all grown men and women. He writes : " Many of them appear to be simple-minded, quiet Christians, desirous of anything that will bring them nearer to Christ."

At the celebration of the Holy Communion which followed, seventy, including the recently-confirmed, communicated.

The same day at noon a special meeting was summoned, and the Bishop and his party were dismissed with prayer for their second journey into the vast interior.

At Rabai a halt was called, and Sunday, the 14th, was spent at the Mission. Bishop Hannington writes :

" To-day I held my second Ordination in East Africa ; the Rev. J. C. Price, the missionary at Mpwapwa, was ordained priest. The Rev. W. E. Taylor preached the sermon, and Jones also assisted me. We took the whole in Kiswahili. It was a very primitive Service. We were unavoidably a surplice short, so we had to dress Taylor up in a sheet and a few other oddments ! Nevertheless the Service was impressive, and I was glad that the Rabai congregation should have an opportunity of witnessing the solemn setting apart of one for the office of presbyter."

The next day, after early Service, the party for the interior made a great effort to start, but failing to secure sufficient porters, they were obliged to remain and repack many of their loads. By leaving behind all their comforts, and many even of their barest necessaries, they were able to leave Rabai on Tuesday, the 16th. Hannington writes to his brother : " I never travelled so short before, nor—to be self-righteous—do I think that many would consent to do the like."

The Christians assembled for prayer. God's blessing was invoked and they were off. The route to Taita has already been described, and there was little to distinguish this march from that undertaken upon the former occasion. The only special incident that calls for mention is that the caravan narrowly escaped an encounter with a war party of Masai. These redoubtable warriors and inveterate raiders are the terror of the whole country over an area of many hundreds of miles. The young braves penetrate in every direction, seeking pastures new from which to uplift cattle and drive them to their distant kraals. The Duruma country is literally devastated by the Masai spear. The wretched inhabitants are driven to hide themselves in thorny tangles of impenetrable jungle in order to retain anything of their belongings. Mr. Thomson describes one spot not much more than a day's march from Rabai, where the ground for a long distance was "literally strewed with skulls," the scene of a battle with a Masai band.

It is of a place not far from here that Bishop Hannington writes : "The good Hand of God was markedly with us. Had it not been for what we naturally called the disappointments of the road, we should have fallen in with these dread warriors on the war trail. They passed our camp yesterday, and killed a man close at hand. I expected that the men would have been rather panic-stricken by the report, but no, they took the matter very sensibly."

General Matthews, the Sultan's commander-in-chief, was now at Chagga, the Sultan having acceded to Mandara's request that he should extend to him his protection, and fly his flag over Moschi. He and his detachment had had trouble in crossing the desert-furnace between Taro and Maungu, and reached the wells of the latter place "in a state of perfect exhaustion." The Bishop, however, got his men over the "terrible plain" on this occasion without any special difficulty, beyond, of course, the great fatigue of all, and reached Taita on the 22nd, or six days after the start. The little company of Wa-Taita on Ndara was still further reduced in number, and all the paths up the mountain were overgrown with thorns and vegetable rankness. The caravan had literally to cut its way through the tangle of spiked grasses and jungle which barred all upward progress.

When here—finding that Jumba Kimameta * had left Taveta—Bishop Hannington came to the conclusion that he would not himself proceed to Chagga, but that he would send Mr. Wray and Mr. Fitch forward to occupy that station, and return at once to the coast to prepare for his great journey northward to the Lake.

He had already carefully selected sites both at Moschi and other places where Stations might possibly be founded ; he had made every arrangement for the reception of his representatives by Mandara, and had negociated for the same end with other princelets of the mountain. Having laid his train to the best of his ability and sought the blessing of God upon it, he thought that he would be better employed in hastening forward the new expedition than in renewing his acquaintance with Kilima-njaro. He, therefore, determined to deny himself that pleasure, and to return without delay to Frere Town.

His return march was a very remarkable exploit, and notably worthy of being chronicled. Two years previously Mr. Thomson had made a forced march over the same ground. He says : "Leaving Ndara we performed a pedestrian feat which probably has never been equalled in the annals of African travelling." Making a great effort, he covered the distance between Taveta and Rabai at the rate of 34 miles a day. This great achievement has been since rivalled by Bishop Hannington, who walked from

---

* An Arab trader who had greatly assisted Mr. Thomson, and whom Hannington desired to consult with regard to his journey over the same route.

Ndara to Rabai at the extraordinary rate of 40 miles a day. The distance, estimated to be 120 miles, was accomplished by him in exactly three days and half an hour !

But we must let him describe his own adventures.

" On June 24th, the first anniversary of my Consecration, I started homeward from Taita with a handful of men and just the bare necessaries of life, leaving behind tent, bed, bath, in fact, every single thing I could do without.* Is this setting out typical of what the second year of my episcopal pilgrimage is to be ? I could rejoice if it is, if only the Lord continues to manifest His guiding and protecting care as He has done all through this journey !

" We met together and knelt in prayer, and then I had literally to run out of the place at 7 a.m., for I was beseiged with requests and questions from the porters whom I had left to go forward. My feet had got painfully blistered on the way up, and this was not a pleasant prospect in view of the rapid return I hoped to make. However, we had the donkey as a last resource, and I found that after walking a short distance the pain much decreased. My donkey, I may as well say, here as elsewhere proved of but little personal use to *me*, for some of the men got blisters or thorns, so they had to ride to get them along at all. The first day, in spite of its being cloudless and terribly hot, I covered thirty-five miles, and laid me down to rest on the lap of mother earth. But oh, she is hard and ungiving to weary bones !

" The next day walked another thirty-five miles. I had the unusual good fortune to kill five guineafowl at one shot, and that, too, in the midst of our worst desert track,

---

* He did not wish to diminish the stores of the caravan bound for Chagga more than was absolutely necessary, and so took with him the barest provisions for his journey. The object of this hot haste homeward was to catch the *Henry Wright* before she started for Zanzibar, and so save some weeks of time.

so we had a good meal. Toward the end of this day's march I felt desperately weary, but we continued till 8 p.m., stumbling along and hurting our feet sadly over the rough ground. But it was well : it had the effect of making the ground feel softer than the night before. *Then* I found it hard sleeping without a bed ; this evening I was far too tired to think about it at all, and, in spite of a heavy shower of rain, soon fell asleep.

"*June 26th.*—Off at daylight. On and still onwards ; arrived at Samburu without difficulty, but the men now began to show signs of great weariness. Seventy miles in the last two days had told upon them, although they were carrying next to nothing, and the guinea-fowls had been a great addition to their food. When we entered a camp at 10.30 a.m., though some were more than willing to march a little farther, I felt it to be really unkind to ask them to do so, and therefore said that I would leave them to rest awhile, and march on alone to the coast. Two, however, volunteered to accompany me, and also a third, with a big heart but poor feet, whom I did not accept. It was well that I declined him, as one of the others had to ride the donkey for a time. I put the last two biscuits, some dates, and a little cheese into a box, and giving the men some heads of Indian corn, away we went. But we were not to starve, for another guinea-fowl fell to my gun, and when we halted at 7 p.m., we cooked it in the hot ashes. One of the men cut off the breast and handed it to me in his fingers, all burnt and covered with ashes as it was, and I ate it in my fingers—and was it not delicious ! Then I knelt down and thanked God for His mercies, and, creeping into a little grass hut, lay down between the two men and rested for a couple of hours. I couldn't sleep because I had made my coffee myself, and had made it too strong. Then we shook ourselves together and started again, on through the night. It was a weird march. The roar of a lion made the ground shake with its tremendous thunder; and once or twice we checked at the cry of a night bird, as we neared the war-paths of Masai, whom, with our small party of three, we had not the slightest inclination to encounter. Presently the dew began to fall, and I was soon wet through, so, as we reached the sixth camping place at about 4.30 a.m., we halted and lighted a large fire, at which the men dried my clothes, while I wrapped myself in my mackintosh.

"We were now all very tired: the donkey, too, which I had been reserving for an emergency, showed signs of fatigue. However, apologizing tenderly to him, I told him that I really must have a short ride. Then followed a heavy shower of rain, which made the ground slippery, and the donkey and I rolled over together more than once. But we were now close to Rabai, and in a few minutes were welcomed by our astonished friends, who thought that I was safe at Chagga—120 miles in three days and half an hour! I did not stay there, as I heard important news about Mbaruk, which required instant attention; so, after a bath, a meal, and a nap, I walked another five miles to the boat, and a row of three hours brought me safe and sound to Frere Town.

"Everybody was amazed to see me. However, the object of my journey appears after all to have been defeated, as the *Henry Wright* left for Zanzibar two days ago."

This was enough, surely, to have tried the patience or the most stoic of mortals. The immense effort of the last three days had been wholly frustrated by an unexpectedly early start of the little Mission steamer. He seemed doomed to lose some weeks of time, and to remain gnawing his nails at Frere Town when his caravan should already be a-preparing at Zanzibar. But, he writes :

"I refused to be disappointed, feeling sure that all would come right, and, indeed, I am being taught never to be disappointed, but to Praise ; and now H.M.S. corvette *Kingfisher* most unexpectedly steamed into the harbour, and the captain offered me a passage. It is wonderful how God has appeared for me over and over again, and wonderful, too, what health and strength I have had. If all goes well, I ought to be off in three weeks' time for Masai Land."

The *Kingfisher* was upon an expedition after some slave dhows reported to be in the neighbourhood, and as she touched at Zanzibar, the captain most courteously placed a cabin at the Bishop's disposal.

The last entry in the June monthly diary is: "Hope we shall catch some prizes."

"Writing, writing, writing ; " so begins the diary of the voyage. Whatever spare time he had was filled up with his now voluminous correspondence. As one of our English Bishops is said to have written most of his letters upon his knee in railway carriages, so Bishop Hannington wrote many of his in his travelling tent, or bivouacking by the light of a camp fire, or on board the steamers which bore him back and forth between Mombasa and Zanzibar.

In the midst of his official correspondence he found time for not infrequent letters to the wee ones at home. The following is an example, with fac-similes of the pen-and-ink sketches with which such letters were generally embellished :

"MY DEAREST CHILDREN,— . . . . I was obliged to walk for a long distance through a Mangrove swamp-

Mangrove trees are very curious; they let down from their stems and branches many roots, which bind them to the

soft, black mud, and keep them from being washed away by the tide; for they always grow in the salt water creeks within reach of the tide. On their roots hang a great many oysters. In these parts we almost always have our doors and windows wide open, so a great many different insects come flying into the rooms. There are some black hornets that come and make nests of earth on the beams. They do not sting one, or do any harm beyond making a little dust, which is easily cleared away. They kill a great many caterpillars and other insects with which to feed their

young, holding them in this fashion. I rather fancy that they sting the caterpillars first of all, and make them insensible. I hope that you have all been very good and obedient to your mother, and that God has

blessed you with much happiness. I think a great deal of you, and am always happy to know that my dear little pets pray for their father who is so many miles away. God is love, and watches over us, although we are absent from one another. Love and kisses to your dearest Mother.

" I remain, sweet children, your very affectionate

FATHER."

We may here let the Bishop give some of the reasons

which induced him to make this perilous journey through a land known to be occupied by the most lawless of savages, and which had only once been entered by a European, and by him traversed for only part of the way.

We have seen that he was, very soon after his arrival at Frere Town, struck with the immense superiority of the new route into the interior, from a health point of view, over the old route. This opinion was confirmed by his journey to Mount Kilima-njaro. He was overjoyed to find that none of the terrors which haunted the footsteps of the traveller upon the lower road—rheumatic and malarial fevers and dysentery—which rendered courage, strength, and determination almost nugatory, were to be feared upon these high uplands. Mr. Thomson had shown that the same healthy highland country continued northward and westward as far as he had penetrated. His active mind at once grasped the idea that if one had the courage to open up this new route to U-Ganda, and secure the friendly co-operation of the natives, others might easily follow ; and, the way once made, a large saving would in future be effected both in time and expense, and, above all, in valuable lives. Anybody can see, by a glance at the map, the advantage of the northerly route to U-Ganda in point of directness ; and those who have read the account given in this book of the Bishop's first journey to the south end of the Lake, with its weary record of sickness and suffering and death, and will compare it with Mr. Thomson's account of his healthy journey to Kavirondo,* cannot but feel with the Bishop that it was worth while to risk something to secure so great an advantage. Added to this was the prospect, never absent from Hannington's heart, that a new tract of country,

---

Mr. Thomson's sickness upon his return journey was occasioned apparently by over-fatigue at Lake Baringo, following upon a severe accident, rather than by any fault of the climate.

occupied by a singularly noble, if exceptionally ferocious, race of men, might be brought under the shadow of the Cross.

As early as April 21st he wrote to Mr. Wigram with regard to this journey to Chagga : " The country through which we have passed is extraordinarily healthy, as far as we can judge from our own experience, that of other travellers, and the nature of the soil. There are long, dry, waterless tracts which are difficult—but not so much so as the Wa-Nyamuezi deserts which have to be encountered on this side of Uyui—and the worst of these tracts is met with on *this* side of Taita."

He then continues : " With regard to my journey to the Lake across the dreaded land of the Masai. When up the country, I made all the inquiry that I could with regard to it, and, from what I hear, the difficulties are not so great as we have been led to imagine. The first question which would suggest itself to an ordinary mind is, Why take such a journey when the other road is well known ? The answer would be : *First*, the old route is beset by special difficulties of its own. The first month's journey lies along a most unhealthy track ; then succeeds the inhospitable region of U-Gogo ; then the long, dangerous deserts of U-Nyamuezi ; then, after leaving Uyui, there is always great doubt as to which road to the Lake will be open ; and lastly, there are the two hundred miles of water, with the difficulty about obtaining canoes. Stokes' caravan was, as you know, attacked by robbers, and several men were killed ; and how many caravans have reached U-Ganda in anything like entirety ?

" The new road, on the other hand, is, as we have every reason to believe, perfectly healthy. With its desert tracts we are already well acquainted, as they lie early in the journey. It should be, moreover, *at least* six weeks shorter in point of time. Its almost only danger is the Masai ; and I have learnt that Swahili caravans of all sizes are constantly passing and repassing without incurring much greater risks than elsewhere.

" Now compare the losses, trials, expenses, and dangers of Wilson's party with those of Thomson's across the Masai. If Thomson's route, as he affirms, will not be open for fifty years, Wilson's * ought not to have been opened for a hundred !

" *Secondly.* If this route be opened up, our work will be much more centralized. We could then work all our caravans from Frere Town and Rabai. We could thus give regular employment to many of our Christian men, and we could keep a well-trained staff of responsible head-men.

" The present Station at the south end of the Lake might then be transferred to Kavirondo. Uyui might be taken charge of by a neighbouring Mission, and Mpwapwa and Mamboia treated as branch Missions.

" If this route is to be opened, I can see no one but myself at present to do it. To the Lake I must go, and I somewhat dread the old route of illness and misery.

" There is the question of hongo to be considered, and there will undoubtedly be a large hongo to pay. But I believe that the shortness of the journey will far more than compensate for this."

Later. " I have just had an interview with Sir John Kirk ; he is anxious that we should advance, and leans strongly to the new road."

---

* The Rev. C. T. Wilson, B.A., whose party reached U-Ganda in 1877 by the route already described. On this journey Dr. Smith died, and Mr. Mackay was for some time incapacitated by sickness.

The following was written to the Committee of the
C. M. S. on May 7th :

" GENTLEMEN,—I hear that my first letter concerning the
journey across the Masai county was not sent *via* the Cape,
and therefore should reach you at the same time as this.   In
the interval matters have been developing.   I have had more
time for counsel and consideration, and now I want you to
listen to me.

"I appeal most earnestly to you, to my Commissaries,
and to all friends of Africa, to stand by me in an effort
which I feel ought to be made to open up the country for
the Gospel of Christ Jesus.   I want £1000 to relieve you
from any extra burden which might arise from the journey ;
and I am sure that, even in these troublous times, it will be
forthcoming, and yet more, if necessary.

" The serious part of the matter is this : I am venturing
to take the responsibility of the action on myself, so that
before this letter reaches you I shall, unless our loving
Father directs differently, be on the road.   I hope I may be
able to satisfy you that this course is not so blameworthy as
it appears at first sight.   I have taken counsel with all possible on the subject, and the feeling of all, without exception,
is Go, for the time seems come to make the attempt.

" We have weighed the matter here over and over
again.   I have had a long interview with Sir John Kirk and
Mr. Wakefield, whose lengthened experience of Africa
makes them most valuable counsellors. ; also with Jumba
Kimameta, who so staunchly supported and helped Thom-
son ; with the Vice-Consul ; and last night the V.-C. and
I were closeted with Martin (who accompanied Mr.
Thomson) for three hours ; and Martin says, Go.   Again,
William Jones strongly feels that the time has come ; and
further, the Sultan's expedition under General Matthews to

Kilima-njaro seems, as far as I can tell, to be further opening up the way.

"And now let me explain why I have not waited for your opinion. The reason is this. June is the best month for travel. Ramadan begins on the 14th, and, as soon as it is finished, the Swahili caravan, under Jumba Kimameta, will start. To this caravan I want to attach myself. It is, in fact, *then or never*, as regards this year.

"I hope, almost immediately after the Ordination which should take place on Trinity Sunday, May 31st, to start, and take with me Mr. Taylor and Mr. Fitch, and at Taita to pick up Mr. Wray, whom I hope to settle at Chagga. I want then to join Jumba Kimameta's* large caravan, and in his company, with Mr. Taylor, to proceed to Naivasha, and probably thence to Sendege, in Lower Kavirondo. As to future policy, I look forward with longing eyes to a Station in the heart of the Masai country, at Ngongo a Bagas, at the foot of Mount Lamuyu, and to another in Kavirondo ; but for this we are not yet ripe.

"I am afraid you will repent you of your Bishop, or at least wish that you had clipped one of his wings and shod his feet with leaden soles ; but I say, while I have health and strength, let me spend it in this work. May I there-

---

* After consideration, Bishop Hannington resolved to travel independently of Jumba. That noted trader has acquired his influence over the Masai by laying claim to the possession of magical powers, and practises rites in which no Christian teacher could participate, yet which his very presence in the caravan must appear to sanction. Rather than avail himself of such dubious assistance, and perhaps, thereby, hamper all his after-work, the Bishop determined to do without Jumba's co-operation. As the event showed, he was quite able to pass through the Masai un-aided, and on beyond Kavirondo Jumba's name would have availed nothing.

fore crave even more energy and more prayer on our behalf at Home?"

Again, in a letter to Mr. Wigram, on May 12th :

"My hope is to catch Jumba, and a delay even for a telegram might set all this wrong. With regard to expense, I hope that this journey may really cost less than by the other way. If I open the road, we shall save thousands of pounds in the end. This time it is possible I may incur large extras. I calculate that if I go round by the old road, I cannot do with less than a hundred or more men with their cloth, to take me up and down, and enable me to remain a season in U-Ganda ; and whoever is located in U-Ganda would require as many. Thomson's expenditure was, I know, enormous ; but then his journey took eighteen months, and his expedition was much more elaborately fitted out than mine will be. If the friends of Africa will give me £1000, I believe that the C. M. S. will be saved money by the expedition."

It will be seen from the above extracts that the only serious danger of which the Bishop had any apprehension was from the Masai. It never entered into his head to suppose that his entry into U-Ganda from the North-East would be opposed. He was not aware of the alarm which existed in the minds of the tribes of Central Africa with regard to a European invasion. He did not know that the chiefs were busily instilling into their young King Mwanga the duty of repelling any attempt of white men to enter his kingdom by the " backdoor " of Kavirondo. Nor could he suppose that the report of German annexations had reached the far interior, and excited the people to the verge of panic. For such difficulties as he foresaw he made proper preparations, and, as he had anticipated, he overcame them successfully, and arrived without disaster at what he had always·

considered to be the end of the perilous part of his journey
—the frontier of U-Ganda.

No one, then, can justly accuse him of rashness. His
plans were laid with prudence and forethought. They were
carried out with boldness and decision. They were completely successful. The blow which struck him down was
wholly unexpected. It was as though a bolt had fallen from
a clear sky. For the final disaster it would, therefore, in
presence of the heroic dead, not only be ungracious, but
unjust, to hold the Bishop responsible.

CHAPTER XXII.

THE LAST JOURNEY.

(1885. JULY–OCTOBER.)

"Can you face this Olympic contest? Are your thews and sinews strong enough? Can you face the fact that those who are defeated are also disgraced and whipped?"   EPICTETUS.

"He begrudgeth not to get a probability of victory by the certainty of his own death ; and flieth from nothing so much as from the mention of flying. And though some say, He is a madman . . . . . our soldier knows that he shall possess the reward of his valour with God in heaven, and also, making the world his executor, leave to it the rich inheritance of his memory."

FULLER ("*The Good Soldier*").

THE next three weeks were spent partly in Zanzibar and partly in Frere Town, in hastening forward preparations for the great journey. We have already attempted to give some idea of the amount of trouble entailed in the organization of a caravan. Added to the endless work and worry which falls to the lot of every traveller into the interior, was the dread which the porters entertained of entering the country of the Masai. Both Thomson and Hannington have proved that the turbulent and troublesome El-Moran can be dealt with by a white man without much greater risk than other savages ; but the terror of them lies like a nightmare upon the minds of their own countrymen. These truculent young bloodshedders and cattle-lifters have as fiendish a reputation throughout North-East Africa as even such blustrous swaggerers could desire. To go to Masai

Land is, in the opinion of the Zanzibari, like going into a sort of Inferno—"All hope abandon, ye who enter here."

Bishop Hannington, however, by dint of patience and tact, succeeded in getting together about two hundred porters, some for Chagga, some to accompany him to Kavirondo, and of whom he says, "They were a very nice lot of men." Many of them, poor fellows, shared his fate, and met their death far away from their homes—but it was not at the hands of the dreaded Masai.

Mr. Copplestone, who joined his Bishop at Zanzibar, and accompanied him back to Frere Town, writes to me :

"On my arrival at Zanzibar there were letters awaiting me from the Bishop asking me if I would join him in his journey to U-Ganda, but failing health prevented my accepting his proposal. We thought then that he was at Chagga, but, quite unexpectedly, while I was thinking over the contents of his letter, he turned up. We then discussed the whole question, and he appointed me to Chagga to assist in the formation of the new Station. We had many conversations with regard to his proposed journey, and eventually he decided to travel *alone*, so that if he got into any difficulty or trouble he would not involve any of his friends in the result—*so utterly unselfish was he*. We then left together for Frere Town, having settled that I should return to Zanzibar in about ten days and bring up the porters.

"When, however, the day came for me to go for the porters and make final arrangements about the caravan, he decided to accompany me.

"On our way back to Frere Town I had another manifestation of his love and sympathy, which also revealed to me that he felt some anxiety with regard to his journey. We were on board the *Henry Wright*, in the Pemba channel ; the night was dark and stormy. The Bishop was lying on a seat in the saloon, and I was reading the 146th Psalm. The Bishop was silent and preoccupied. I read to him a few verses of the psalm. When I came to the 9th verse, ' The Lord preserveth the strangers,' the Bishop suddenly exclaimed with evident relief, ' Praise God ; He has sent me His message to night. *The Lord preserveth the strangers.* My poor men are strangers, but the Lord preserveth them.' The verse came like a direct message from God, and a relief from the anxiety which was in that hour weighing upon h'm.''

Such a reminiscence is priceless. It reveals the man. How many travellers are there who, upon the eve of an eventful journey, upon which hang great results affecting both themselves and the cause which they have at heart, would let the fate of their bearers, the human beasts of burden who are to carry their loads, weigh upon their minds ? Had he been an ambitious man, his thoughts at that moment would have been quite elsewhere. Had he been a mere Ecclesiastic, a man of one idea, the Promoter of a great Cause, he would not have thought hundreds of such lives too dear a price to pay for the attainment of his Object. But in this man we recognize something higher. He had evidently drunk deeply of the spirit of Him of whom we hear again and again in his letters as " our loving Father," without whom " not a sparrow falls to the ground." As Mr. Copplestone well says : " Applied to him, the words of the Apostle are singularly fitting, ' *Besides all these things that are without, that which cometh upon me daily, the CARE of all the Churches.*' ''

As Mr. Copplestone refers to the fact that he had not seen his way to accept the Bishop's proposal to accompany him to Kavirondo—as, indeed, his health, barely restored after a prolonged residence at Uyui, scarcely warranted that he should—I may quote here a passage from a letter, written shortly before, to Mrs. Hannington, in which the Bishop mentions the subject. He says : " I am now beginning to wonder what Copplestone will do : whether he will accompany me or go by the other road ; he will have had time to think it over by the day I arrive at Zanzibar. It will be a great comfort to you to think of him as with me, but my feeling is that I would rather be alone, as the anxiety is rather increased than otherwise by another man, however good he may be. I feel this—that another man could add nothing to my safety. *In Jesus' keeping I am safe.* And so, if you hear that Brother C. takes the other road—well and good ; it will be a race between us as to who will get up first."

As we have seen, the Bishop, after talking the matter over with Mr. Copplestone, resolved to place him at Chagga, instead of in U-Ganda ; but eventually, his health again broke down, and he returned to England.

The strain of this unceasing work was beginning to tell upon Hannington, but he did not allow himself to bend for a single instant, lest he should collapse into ruins. His great spirit kept him up. He wrote to Mr. Wigram from Zanzibar :

" Mandara (I have had letters) turns out a little troublesome, but it is not more than I expected, so you must not be discouraged, but believe that we shall leave no stone unturned to make matters succeed. Mine is an intensely arduous and anxious post. I long to be in telegraphic communication with you, but suppose it to be impossible. I greatly need your prayers and all the support you can give me ; otherwise I shall —— Well, never mind, I *must* succeed somehow or other, the Lord being my helper."

He writes to his wife in much the same strain :

" Work, work, work. I am nearly driven to death. I have been very much overdone, and was as near as possible to a break-down yesterday ; but to-day I am revived, and am able to send an excellent account of myself. I was delighted to think that you can trust me in His hands, who has hitherto led me by the way."

On Thursday, July 23rd, the Bishop led the way out of Rabai at the head of a caravan two hundred strong—an army of peace, yet marching to the " pulling down of strongholds." The usual caravan troubles, of course, fell upon him during the first few marches from the coast. Many of the porters enlist merely for the sake of the earnest money, or advance wages which are given them before they start, and make up their minds to desert upon the first favourable opportunity. The closest watch has, therefore, to be kept upon them until they have got so far inland that retreat is more difficult for them than advance, when they may be trusted to proceed tractably enough. At first, too, being out of condition and lazy, they make every excuse to throw down their burdens and cast themselves prostrate under the shade of any available bush. Especially is it a formidable matter to get a large caravan of porters across the burning desert of Taro. The men have no idea of self-restraint, and drink up all the water intended to last them for two days in as many hours ; and then have to be driven, half dead with the thirst that consumes them, to the far distant wells. A caravan leader needs the arms of a Briareus, and the sleepless vigilance of an Argus, to keep his men together during the early stages of a journey into the interior.

Hannington says : " Starvation, desertion, treachery, and a few other nightmares and furies, hover over our heads in ghostly forms." However, Mr. Jones, the newly-ordained native clergyman whom he had decided to take with him, proved a great help and comfort, taking out of his hand many of the lesser responsibilities of the management. And, for the rest, he did not let these things disturb the flow of his spirits. All the way during that march to Taita his letters reveal him to us, till we seem to see him as he strides ahead with that springy step of his. Arms swinging, eyes ever on the alert to notice anything new or remarkable— now a snatch of song, again a shout of encouragement—a leap upon some rare flower or insect—the very life and soul of his company ; while ever and anon his emphatic voice would be raised in the notes of some old familiar tune, and the wilderness would ring to the sound of a Christian hymn—

> " Peace, perfect peace, the future all unknown ;
> Jesus we know, and He is on the Throne."

He writes to his wife from Maungu ; and the tone of this letter, which he had reason to think would be his last before he reached the end of his journey, is very touching to those who know how little he was given to "sentimentalizing" in his correspondence. "I have just finished forty-five miles, have cleared away the bushes and lighted a fire with my own hands. You must not be surprised if I am rather hazy. I have had scarcely any food for eighteen hours, and have not had a wash for two days, nor do I see much chance of getting more than a ' lick ' for two days more. I am afraid, however, that hardships have not even commenced. God is just giving me a merciful rest after the terribly severe strain I have had to go through during the last twelve months." (His idea of a " rest " is pathetic.) " How gracious God has been in giving me so good a wife and such dear children and relatives ! "

His reference in the same letter, to the now near

25

approach of his separation from his colleagues and plunge into the unknown district is of much interest. " Everything I hear makes me think that the dangers of the road are greatly exaggerated. It is not the danger that I fear in the least, but the want of food, or a sufficient stock of beads, or something of that kind, which might turn us back. I have not been able to take as much as Thomson took, and he found that his store was soon exhausted. I am not, however, conscious yet of any neglect on my part, so I am content to leave the issue in His dear Hands."

How correct was his judgment the result has clearly shown. His danger did not lie among the Masai.

He continues : " I hope the dearest ones keep well—as well as their father; then they will do." Then follows reference to some friends who, he hopes, will forgive him for not writing to them, on the plea that his hands were *very* full of business. " I wonder if I delude myself in this respect. We sometimes fancy we are busy when we are only idle. I leave them to judge. God bless them all." (Such words need no comment—but they irresistibly recall to our minds the words of the Master, "*When the fruit is ripe*, immediately he putteth in the sickle, because the harvest is come.") " And now, fare thee well, for a time. You must scarcely venture to expect another letter for a month or two, but just leave me in His Hands."

A day or two later, however, he found another opportunity of scribbling a few lines in pencil from Taita. " I am hoping," he says, " before long to advance to where I don't exactly know, but along Thomson's homeward route to Ndi and Ukambani. Food seems the great difficulty, as the country has not recovered from the famine."

But even this was not to be the last letter. Another chance of getting a word home occurred at Kikumbuliu and from there he sent his last lines both to his wife and to his friends the workers at Frere Town.   To the former he writes :

" KIKUMBULIU,

"*Aug.* 11, 1885.

"MY DEAREST,—There is a remote chance of this reaching the coast.   I have found a man who says that he is going before very long, so you may get it.   The burden of my song must be Praise, and the teaching of every lesson has been Trust : so comfort your heart during my absence. But to the journey.   We left Taita on Thursday, July 30th. We mistook the road a little, as far as I can make out, and kept too much to the east, camping on the banks of the Voi.   The next day we had intense difficulty in forging through the bulrush-fringed banks, and again took a wrong road, which led us nearly due west, but it led after all in the right direction, and conducted us to Ndi (of Thomson), where we found plenty of food, and were able, without strain on our resources, to rest both Saturday and Sunday.   Here we obtained a guide, but all to no purpose, for on Monday, Aug. 3rd, soon after starting we found ourselves lost over and over again.   The fact is, that the famine has decimated the country and many of the roads have perished.*   We got scattered as we forged our way through the dense jungle, so I took the lead, and climbing a tree got a survey of the country ; and so was able to strike for a mass of rock that formed a landmark.   Finally, after firing guns to collect the stragglers, we found ourselves together at sunset, after a very fatiguing day for some of us.   The men, fortunately, were not over-taxed, as they rested while we explored or broke through the jungle.   On the next day, the 4th, we made

---

* The Rev. W. Jones says :—"All is saddening.   The Jimba of 1883 is not Jimba of 1885.   All its beauty is gone.   All its fine sugar-canes are gone.   Its fields are turned into wild jungle.   All is dreary and desolate.

our way as straight as we could across country, and arrived long before I had dared to hope at the river Tsavo.   Here I was a little feverish, from over-anxiety and walking in a very hot sun through a forest more shadeless even than that of Taro.   It is no small thing to lose yourself in a waterless desert.   The Tsavo is broad and clear, and full of fish, some of which we caught.   Here we struck the main U-Kamba road, which passes the south-east side of the Taita Hills, so all anxiety about getting lost again was at an end.

"We were told here that we should not get any more water until the third day; but we had a cool day for our start, and the next day we quite unexpectedly reached a fine pool.   This helped us along wonderfully.*   The next two nights we camped without water; but on Saturday, Aug. 8th, we arrived at some villages of the Wa-Kamba.   Here we learned that food was exceedingly short.   Anxiety tried to press upon me; but again the good Hand of our God was upon us, and we got enough to enable us to rest there over Sunday.   Yesterday, Monday, the 10th, we reached a densely populous district (Thomson's Nosanga) where food was plentiful.   Another three days, and we should be at Ulu; there report says people are dying of famine : if this is so we shall have difficulty in getting through, and there seems to be no game of any sort to help out the men.   My one fear is insufficiency of stuff.   If I had been *permitted* to start with fifty men less I should have been more san-guine, but I can see less hope of retreat.   So, with God's help, speedy advance must be the word.   I am quite aware that this is the easy part of the journey, and that far greater difficulties from hongo-demanding natives are ahead, but if this is God's time for opening up this road, *we shall open it up.*

---

* Note in pocket-book : This pool "cannot be reckoned upon."

" ' We are a little poor,' as Jones says. My watch has gone wrong. The candles and lamp oil were forgotten and left behind, so that the camp fire has to serve instead. My donkey has died, so that I must walk every step of the way. Well! Having no watch, I don't wake up in the night to see if it is time to get up, but wait till daylight dawns. Having no candle, I don't read at night, which never suits me. Having no donkey, I can judge better as to distances, and as to what the men can do ; for many marches depend upon my saying, ' We will stop here and rest, or sleep.'

" My greatest trial is that I have a very inefficient staff of headmen, and nobody with me who really knows the road. Of course, I was assured before we started that many whom I had engaged had been over the road again and again. One man was said to have been over it *five* times.

" And now, just leave me in the Hands of the Lord, and let our watchword be, ' We will trust, and not be afraid.'

" Many kisses.

" Your most affectionate Husband,

" James."

And here all correspondence ceases. His friends heard no more of him until that fatal telegram received from Zanzibar on New Year's Day, 1886 :

" Bishop Hannington, who left Mombasa in June last, in order to find, if possible, a new road to the Victoria which will obviate the long detour by Unyanyembe, has been seized by order of the king, within two days' march of U-Ganda. The latest report is that the king has given secret orders to have the Bishop executed."

Happily, his own tiny pocket diary, with its daily jottings, has been recovered by a Christian lad at Rubaga, who bought it from one of the band that murdered him.

Happily, also, his native friend, the Rev. William Jones, who accompanied him as far as Kwa Sundu, kept a journal, which is now in my hands. From these two sources we are enabled to gather much of what occurred from day to day almost until the end.

Mr. Jones' pencilled diary of the journey is full of interesting details. I wish that space permitted to quote from it more fully, but, as it is, many of the following extracts have been condensed. He has written, as a kind of title upon the fly-leaf, the words, " Behind my Bishop through Masai Land "; and the tone of the entire narrative abundantly testifies to his love and devotion to " his Bishop." A testimony, no doubt, to the worth of the man himself, about which all seem to agree ; but an additional evidence also of the strange attractive power which Hannington exercised over all who were brought into contact with him. When they were leaving Taita, one of the Wa-Zaramo boys who had been engaged to carry food for the caravan, and who were all paid off and discharged near Taita, insisted that he would follow the Bishop. No arguments availed. " Whither thou goest I will go," and finally the poor lad was taken. Hannington did not need painfully to exact homage from his dependents after the manner of other mortals ; it was yielded to him spontaneously, and as his due.

Mr. Jones describes in the following manner the constitution of the caravan bound for the Lake. First the amount of goods (*i.e.*, the equivalent of money), and necessary food, etc. Cloth, 24 loads. Wire, 51. (This is greatly in demand among the Masai, and is worn by the women as armlets, leglets, and necklets.) Provision boxes, 19. Powder, 10. Shot, 1. Beads, 21. Baskets, 5. Bishop's personal luggage, 6. Fowl box, 1. Cooking pot, 1. Washing tub, 1. Rice, 4. Beans, 13. Millet, 5. Shells, 7.

Salt, 2. Dates, 1. Bishop's cot, 1. Biscuit boxes, 5. Jones' personal luggage and tent, 6.

The headmen of the caravan were Ibraim, Arthur, Bedui, Hassani, Asumani, and Kiongozi (also the interpreter). The under headmen were Gilbert Juma, Mbaruku, Mwandzingo, Tosiri, Abdalla, and Tofiki.

The caravan was divided into three sections : First, Zanzibar and Mombasa Mohammedans, 106. Second, Rabai men, 66. Third, Kisauni, 54. In all 226 men ; the Bishop and Jones bringing up the total number to 228.

It will be easily understood that the feeding of such an army in a famine-stricken district can have been no simple business. The " anxiety " to which the Bishop refers in his letter was not uncalled for. It must have been a very real relief when the caravan reached parts in which food was once more obtainable upon the usual terms.

We may now, by the aid of the Bishop's brief jottings, supplemented by Mr. Jones' diary, continue our narrative from the date of his last letter.

Aug. 12th.—One of the men fell ill, and had to be left behind, supplied with enough cloth to enable him to return home. " Poor fellow ! he was very sorry to part from his old companions in the caravan." The rest started at six a.m., and after a hard march of eleven hours, reached a fine stream—the Kuombi, or Kiumbi—two hours from which they halted. The Bishop writes : " Game abundant ;" and Jones describes how, during the march, they shot a number of guinea-fowl, and supplied the camp with fresh meat ; he then goes on to say, " To-day, for the first time in my life, I saw the mountain of Kilima-njaro. It looked like a large table covered with a great white sheet." On this day a grave misfortune happened. The boy who bore the medicine chest was nowhere to be found. The Bishop would not believe that the boy had run away, nor did it seem probable that he would do so in that remote region. The medicine, too, could not be dispensed with ; so he offered six doti of cloth to any man who would find the boy, and detached ten men from his own party to retrace their steps as far as the last camp.*

During the whole of Aug. 14th, they fought their way through an obstinate jungle that lies between the Kiangeni River and Ulu, at which latter place they arrived at four p.m., and camped at the foot of the Nzawi Hill by the River Chamela. The country here is beautifully wooded, and the climate temperate, the mornings and evenings being cold enough to cause the Coast porters some discomfort. The people tried to be troublesome, and wanted to exact a large hongo. The Bishop offered them three doti, which they accepted scornfully and asked for more. He immediately ordered the hongo to be taken from them, and walked off to his tent. The elders were confounded, not being accustomed to be treated otherwise than with humble deference by passing caravans. When, however, they saw that the Mzungu (white man) was in earnest, they called for the interpreter, and begged that his master would not be angry, but would let them have the three doti.

This was repeated more than once at different stages of the journey through Ulu. On one occasion, when the Bishop moved steadily on, and refused to listen to their plaguing demands, they could not conceal their surprise and bewilderment. But they soon came to their senses when they saw their hongo vanishing with rapid strides into the jungle. So much so that one of the most importunate turned to Jones and said, " I was only making fun " ; whereupon he at once replied, " And so, of course, was I," and matters were amicably settled by the payment of a moderate sum.

---

* " The search appears to have been to no purpose. Hannington writes, " I suppose I ought to turn back ; but no, not yet."

Aug. 16th being Sunday, the Rabai men and others who were willing to attend Service were summoned by the sound of Mr. Jones' whistle. He says: " I preached to them both morning and evening, and we sang the hymn, ' For ever with the Lord.' " Nor could a more suitable camp hymn be possibly chosen. We may here mention that every day was begun and concluded with public prayer.

On Aug. 18th, at about 11 a.m., their way was blocked by a mob of armed men. Mr. Jones writes: " They demanded most vehemently that we should not pass till something had been given to them. Halt, halt, they cried; if not, we will fight. Our interpreter trembled from head to foot, and said to me, Do not resist them, or we shall all be killed. On and on I moved, followed by the whole caravan, threatened on every side by the infuriated crowd. The bearer of the Union Jack trembled fearfully, and heartily wished himself away. I stopped the caravan that we might discover where the Bishop was, for the throng was so dense that we could not see each other. By and by the Bishop appeared. At the sight of his lordship the barbarians gave way like a cloud before the wind. They were all amazed to see the Bishop, for many of them had never seen a white man in their life. They stood thunderstruck and gazing at him. The Bishop made his way through the crowd. Then many of them resisted him with all their might, without any respect or regard for his dignity. I was close to him, and began to be anxious for his lordship; but he walked rapidly on quite regardless of their yellings and ferocious cries. Twice they barred our way with a human fence, and twice we passed through them to their great astonishment. The Bishop all this time was quite calm, and only smiled at all their gestures and menaces. At last we came to a stream which divided one district from another. They refused to let us pass, but the Bishop went straight ahead, and was followed by all the caravan. We arrived safely at Mboni towards 3 o'clock in the afternoon, and were not sorry to have reached a resting-place. I was greatly amused to see the very men who had given us so much annoyance an hour ago come round to our camp to barter and dispose of their goods. We bore them no enmity, but hospitably invited them in."

It then appeared that one of the men had picked up an empty ostrich egg which lay at the foot of a large tree by the wayside. This egg was a charm, and hongo was demanded from the unwitting culprit. As the Bishop's party were now in a position of security, the matter was easily settled by a trifling present.

On Aug. 19th they started to try and reach Machako's Hill, but were misled by some guides and came short of their goal. They passed the night in a deep valley about six miles distant. "On the way we passed through high, lonely hills, which all trend toward the north. It is difficult to say how beautiful the Ulu country is. It is a country full of water and cattle. All provisions are plentiful and cheap."

"*Aug.* 20.—Reached Machako's Hill. Densely populated : pies much in request ; beads will pass for a few things, and all kinds of wire. Climate suitable for Europeans. Very cold at night, and the days sometimes so cloudy that the sun is not seen at all."

Aug. 21st was spent in buying food for three days, as the march to Ngongo a Bagas is across a plain where nothing can be obtained. Jones describes this district as "one vast plain extending for miles westward, and dotted with small hills." On these grassy prairies the Masai pasture their immense herds of cattle. Across this plain they steered by compass, making a straight line for Ngongo.

The Bishop and his Chaplain presently sighted a rhinoceros, and as the caravan wanted meat, they tried to stalk him. They succeeded in creeping within twenty yards of the formidable monster, so dim-eyed and so keen-scented, and then he seemed to sight them. Down they both dropped into the grass. "Fire, my lord!" said Jones. "No," replied the Bishop, "as he stands I cannot get a good shot; wait." It is not pleasant to kneel face to face with a rhinoceros in an open plain, with the knowledge that if the brute makes out your whereabouts he will come thundering down upon you like an express locomotive. Jones got nervous. "Fire, my lord!" he whispered anxiously. But the Bishop would not, and the two remained in their uneasy position, as Jones says, "like two devotees of Siva, with their knees bent," before the grim idol. At last the great beast got their wind, and dashed round with a snort. The Bishop leaped to his feet and fired, but failed to stop it, and, after a short chase, had to return to the greedily expectant caravan without his rhinoceros steaks.

A few days later the Bishop had a narrow escape from another rhinoceros, which charged him almost home. A shot in the head produced no effect, and the second shot, which turned him, was delivered point-blank at four yards distance. Mr. Jones bears an admiring tribute to his Bishop's perfect coolness in such situations of danger. The plain of Kapté abounds with game of every kind. The whole caravan was held once in astonishment at an enormous herd of zebras, some two thousand in number, the playful beasts careering back and forth and in and out, like cavalry going through some intricate evolutions.* Here, too, they sighted a herd of elephants.

---

* The Masai do not kill them, and they are, in consequence, extremely tame.

Aug. 25th.—" Arrived in the evening at Ngongo a Bagas." This place is situated on the borders of Masai Land and the country of the Wa-Kikuyu. Here is the source of the river Athi. The Wa-Kikuyu inhabit the forest-clad uplands which here abut upon the plains of the Masai country. Mr. Thomson, who camped at this spot for some three weeks in company with a huge caravan of Swahili traders, accuses them of treachery, and, indeed, not without reason. He describes the extreme precautions which had to be adopted in protecting the camp against a night assault, and how the traders entrenched themselves within a ditch and a strong palisade of tree trunks before they considered themselves safe. It is only, however, fair to add that there are two sides to this story. Let us hear what Mr. Jones has to say : " The greedy Swahili last time they were here, as they were in great force, took advantage of the poor Wa-Kikuyu, and when they came down to sell their goods caught them and made slaves of them. Some of these were redeemed by their relations ; the remainder were taken down to the coast. The Swahili traders followed this up by attacking the Wa-Kikuyu in their forest homes, killing some and kidnapping others ; so that there is little wonder if they have lost faith in the Swahili caravans." It seems clear that if Jumba Kimameta and his friends have suffered occasionally from this forest tribe, they are only reaping what they have themselves sown. The Bishop was very anxious to hold some intercourse with the Wa-Kikuyu, but they dared not venture down to his camp. He therefore went up to them with an escort of only ten men. Even then he failed to gain their confidence. So far from attempting to do him any violence, the unhappy Wa-Kikuyu fled before him everywhere. His camp was reduced to the verge of starvation. With the greatest difficulty, after several days, and by carefully divesting himself of every appearance of being about to use force, he succeeded in buying a few sweet potatoes, and so staving off what threatened to be a real disaster. The men were absolutely without food, and the camp resounded with their wails. At last the elders of the caravan were summoned to a council, and, at their recommendation, the Bishop resolved to "eat muma "* with the natives. This he attempted to do, but in vain ; their fears were not to be allayed. But Mr. Jones must tell his own story : " The Bishop returned, thoroughly disheartened, disappointed, and discouraged. ' Bwana,' he said, ' bring me a gun-cap tin box.' He then took all our remaining grain, and measured it out. He found it to be 70 small teacups. 'Three times that is 210 ? ' ' Yes, my lord.' ' Well, call the men, and give each a cap-box full.' I summoned our starving people together, and distributed the grain accordingly. After being the whole day without food, a cap-box full of grain would seem to be nothing. But to our men it was something. They all moved away to their fires, and ate with less gloom upon their faces. Few of them, however, slept that night. Some cried, ' Let us go back.' Others asked, ' Is this our last place ? Have we been brought here to die ? ' Of course they knew that they could not go back, and that there was no retreat. The camp was filled with cries and weeping. The elders were again summoned, but could recommend nothing. So the Bishop bid them again to try and get food from the Wa-Kikuyu ; they were then dismissed, and I whistled for our Rabai men to come to prayers. After prayers the Bishop and I, as a rule, sit down by our fire and talk over the day's work, and now and then peep into Thomson's book, to see what he says. We are very

---

* This is a ceremony by which friendship is supposed to be sealed. Blood is extracted from the arms of both parties to the contract, and a piece of meat dipped in the mingled blood is eaten by each. The two then are accounted " brothers."

much indebted to that author for many good suggestions. The result of this night's talk was that I started off early in the morning with 20 men, as the Bishop told me not to take more lest I should alarm the natives. I took a few strings of beads, and some cloth, and iron wire. We crossed the stream, made our fire upon a rock, and sat down. Like Heralds at Ear-Gate, we fired our guns as a salute, though we could see no one through the impenetrable undergrowth. After waiting two hours, a single man came out from the forest, with fresh leaves in his hand, as a mark of submission and peace. We also plucked leaves and waved them, after which he drew near. He said the Chief was close by, and wanted to know whether we had come to fight or to buy grain. We explained, and the man flew to his friends, to tell them that we wanted to buy food and not to fight. Three men next stepped out of the wood, told us the Chief was coming, and disappeared. Then the Chief came towards us, a man of about fifty years old, and half-drunk, reeling to and fro like a ship in a storm. He first spat in his hand,* and, with its filthy contents streaming down, this savage potentate shook hands with me. I was not at all inclined to reach my hand to him, but it could not be helped. I asked to eat muma with him and his people, after which I would give him the present I had brought for him. They refused to eat muma with us, and clamoured for the presents, which I gave them ; after that they promised to bring food for sale. Off they went, and in a quarter of an hour buying and selling began. Trade had scarcely become brisk, however, when the natives showed signs of hostility. They threatened us from a distance with their shields, throwing arrows in our direction and brandishing their swords. We took no notice, though I kept my

---

* Spitting upon a stranger in this district is a mark of friendship, and the highest compliment.

eye upon them. But, as arrow after arrow was thrown at us, I gave orders to the men to hold their guns in readiness, which they did. The Wa-Kikuyu shouted, and made the women who were selling return back. The children all fled. None remained but men, who all began to yell and throw their arrows at us. My men were panic-stricken. We had a dense jungle behind us, and some of them retreated into it, which, of course, encouraged the natives. They drew closer, and their poisoned arrows fell among us. I told the men not to fire, and we retreated slowly with the food we had bought, keeping our faces toward the enemy, lest our backs should be turned into targets. Happily, they did not follow us into the jungle. With our guns we were more than a match for them, had we chosen to fire ; but I felt that I should do nothing which would grieve the Bishop and give our caravan a bad name. I picked up eight poisoned arrows that fell among us.

" When I reported myself to the Bishop, I found that the Masai had come into camp. They had just found us out, and wanted presents. They promised to bring ngombe (cattle) for sale next day. In the evening, the Bishop called the elders together and told them that he did not consider that the danger from the Wa-Kikuyu was anything great, and he would go the next day armed only with his umbrella and encounter them. From this we with much difficulty dissuaded him, and the next day, August 31st, a hundred men left the camp with orders to go and buy food. After a few volleys the Wa-Kikuyu came down in great numbers, and a brisk market began. This looked better. We really thought our troubles were going to end ; so I went hunting with three men, and left all buying food as fast as they could. When I returned, some hours later, the Bishop called me, and I saw at once that something was wrong. As soon as I entered the tent I saw a Zanzibar man with two sword cuts upon his thigh and several wounds upon his body. Another man had his skull fractured with a club. I was not, I confess, much surprised. There had been an attempt to steal, and our men had lost their heads and got roughly handled.

"The men were now all very anxious to get away, but the Bishop, who knew that it would be impossible to advance further to the North unless we succeeded in getting a supply of food, insisted that another effort should be made. The elders of the caravan were again taken into consultation, and signified their readiness to abide by what the Bishop might determine. On Tuesday, Sept. 1, therefore, he started with a hundred men to re-open negotiations with these abominable Wa-Kikuyu. The presence of the Bishop made them behave somewhat better, but by and by one of the headmen saw a man making off with his upper garment, and ran after him, firing a charge without a bullet to stop him. Immediately the market broke up and the Wa-Kikuyu fled in all directions into the jungle. Our men seeing this, rushed forward to seize their goods. But the Bishop, seeing what would follow if the men were allowed to do what they pleased, ran and stood where the natives had piled their saleable things, and prevented any of our men from snatching them. He then ordered the men to march home and leave him there alone. Presently a native peered out of the thicket, and, when the Bishop beckoned to him, drew near, and the Bishop gave all the goods belonging to his people into his hands, and then returned to camp, very angry with our men. But for their disobedience the market might have been continued much longer. The man who fired at the native had his gun taken from him, and was severely reprimanded. He was afterwards forgiven at the intercession of the elders in behalf of their brother. A gun taken from the Wa-Kikuyu was also returned to them.

"On Sept. 2nd the Bishop went out again with seventy men. This time he determined to purchase everything himself. When the natives came down, he concentrated our men in one spot, from which he forbade them to move, while he bought what was necessary. So things went for a while very smoothly, though our famishing men were hard to restrain ; till suddenly the cry of Masai was raised, and a number of warriors leapt from the jungle with spears and shields. It was a false alarm, but the Wa-Kikuyu took fright, and again the market was stopped. The Bishop returned weary and disgusted. The men were daily grow-ing weaker and weaker. It would soon be impossible to move from this place either forward or backward. The same tactics were, however, patiently adopted during the next three days. The apparently desolate forest was in reality swarming with the Wa-Kikuyu ; but they live in impenetrable fastnesses. Even the Swahili traders, with all their pretences, have not succeeded in peeping into their huts, and the formidable Masai cannot cope with them in the recesses of their own forest highlands. On Monday the 7th a more successful attempt was made to purchase food. The Bishop again went out with about a hundred men, whom he caused to sit in a circle while he dealt with the natives. The plain was soon crowded with the Wa-Kikuyu, who pressed in on every side. Our men, who had no trust in them, laid each his loaded gun by his side. It was, how-ever, almost impossible to prevent things from being stolen by these thievish people. The Bishop had great confidence in natives,* and believed that they would not try to kill a

---

* He writes : "They never attempt to offer me the slightest show of insult. Half a mile from our men, I was not unfrequently alone with them ; while, if a black man is with me, it is with the utmost difficulty that they keep their hands off him, nearly stabbing him at my side."

European ; but he was to-day roughly undeceived ; for the men who had completed their own sales began to assume a defiant attitude, and raised their war cry. The women at once fled. The Bishop ran to the front and waved some grass in token of peace, and for a time order was restored. Looking round, however, he saw a group of men close behind him, with their bows bent, and on the point of shooting. When they caught his eye they retreated. We had by this time purchased enough to make a move, and so, after a fortnight's delay, and being brought to the verge of starvation by these provoking Wa-Kikuyu, we packed up our goods, and on Tuesday, the 8th, resumed our march to Mianzini."

The foregoing extract from Mr. Jones' diary affords a good illustration of the patience and cool courage with which Bishop Hannington would encounter a serious difficulty. It is a no less remarkable instance of the method which he consistently adopted in dealing with the natives. He was determined, at all costs, to win their confidence, and to teach them, by firm and just treatment, that the good faith of a Christian might be implicitly relied upon. On this occasion, he had to deal with a case of unusual difficulty. Not only were the natives of a peculiarly timid, treacherous, and wolfish nature, but they had been accustomed to have to do with the slave-taking Swahili traders, and to hold intercourse with their caravans much as a pack of shrinking, snarling jackals might try to snatch a mouthful in the presence of the lion.

On Tuesday, Sept. 8th, the long caravan was again in motion. The greatest care had now to be taken to guard against an attack from the rear. The path skirted the forest for a long distance, and every bush concealed a lurking foe. Mr. Thomson's caravan was here set upon and very roughly treated, while some of his cattle were killed. Mr. Jones writes :

"As we were descending a steep track, a rush was made upon the sick, who were being carried in the rear, by a host of Wa-Kikuyu. The men in charge of the sick fled, but they, strange to say, revived and flew for their lives, escaping with a few blows from clubs. When we heard the alarm, the Bishop and some of our men ran back to the scene of action, and a volley put the enemy to flight. At the end of the plain there is a fine tree, towards which all our men at once made, to rest beneath its shadow. They had scarcely sat down when they were attacked furiously by an enemy worse than the Wa-Kikuyu. A vast swarm of bees came down from the tree, and settled upon the caravan in thousands. The men ran for their lives, many of them dropping their loads. The bees covered the ground for some two hundred yards in every direction from the tree. The Bishop bid the men who had dropped their loads return and fetch them ; but though they tried, they found it simply impossible to do so ; many of them actually cried like children, and called upon their mothers ; everyone was stung more or less. The Bishop made the attempt to reach the deserted loads himself, but was driven back. He then draped himself in his mosquito curtains and tried again, but before he got the loads he was stung most pitifully. My own eyes were so closed by the swelling from stings that I was almost totally blind for two days."

On Wednesday, Sept. 9th, they crossed the River Kedong. Mr. Jones continues : "We slept in a Masai kraal for the first time. The kraal caught fire owing to the carelessness of the men, and we were burnt out."

On Sept. 10th they camped within sight of Lake Naivasha. The next day they were introduced, in the neighbourhood of that lake, to the notorious Masai. Mr. Jones writes : " Though their name is a terror to all surrounding countries, yet in their own land they are not so savage. The married men are hospitably inclined toward strangers, and if the hongo is paid in time all is peace and pleasantness. As soon as we reached Naivasha, we were surrounded by the young warriors, whom they call El Moran ; it is from these that trouble comes. I said to the Bishop that, after all, they did not seem to be so bad as they had been described. ' Wait,' said he, ' you have not seen them yet.'

" The morning of Sept. 12th broke most gloriously, but little peace was in store for us. By 7 a.m. our camp was filled with Masai women, bringing all kinds of things for sale. They talked and trafficked with our people most freely. As they poured into the camp, they brought with them swarms of flies. We soon found that our boma (fence) was too weak ; but that could not now be remedied. The El Moran, too, began to flock in, and to sing war songs and shout vociferously. The El Moran is an idle creature, who looks upon himself as born into the world for no other purpose than to shed blood. He regards all the other tribes as infinitely beneath him. He expects to be treated with great respect and consideration by all the caravans which enter his country, and regards the coast porters with huge contempt. His body is smeared with red earth, and an oil called mbuu ; his hair is twisted into tails which hang down his forehead and shoulders. He possesses a fine-shaped head, which approaches, in many respects, that of the Anglo-Saxon, though his cheekbones are very high and prominent. As a rule, the El Moran is tall, and, as he lives on nothing but flesh and milk, his body is remarkably strong and solid. He lives in a separate kraal, with his girl companions of his own age. At this stage, the El Moran has no thought of marriage, till his time as a warrior is served out. He does not, generally, marry until about thirty years of age, after which

A MASAI WARRIOR (EL-MORAN).

he lays down his spear, and counts himself unfit for the
field. . The only nation he regards with any respect is the
European. He calls the white man Ngai, which may be
said to mean a son of the gods. He is not an atheist, but
worships the Supreme Being. When a caravan arrives, El
Moran comes with great pride and dignity of demeanour to
demand a hongo, which has to be given, or mischief will soon
follow. About a thousand, or even three thousand, of these
El Moran, and their girl consorts, live together in a circular
kraal. They never go about alone either at home or to the
battlefield, but by twos. It is considered shameful and de-
grading that an El Moran should return alive if his chosen
companion has been killed in battle.

" Such are the Masai as young warriors ; but as soon as
they marry they put off their fierceness and settle down to
a peaceable life. They are no longer ferocious, blood-thirsty,
and turbulent, but are very remarkably kind to strangers,
and especially to any women who may be in a caravan.
They go about shaking hands most heartily with the
foreigners, and are fond of entering into conversation
with them." So writes Mr. Jones, and his words form
an interesting addition to what Mr. Thomson has
written on the same subject. He continues : " How to
bring the knowledge of God's truth to this nomadic tribe—
but, the time will come." Mr. Jones and the interpreter
approached the group of young braves seated, each with his
broad-bladed, glittering spear stuck in the ground by his
side. " They arrogantly told us that they were the young
warriors of the Masai, and had come to demand a hongo
from the foreigners. They sneered at us when we tried to
reduce the enormous tax they wished to extort from us.
I told the trembling interpreter to say that I was not in a
position to offer more than my Bishop had set apart for the
purpose. No sooner did they see the presents than they all

sprang up as if in a towering rage, moved back a few yards, and again sat down. 'We will show you how to respect us,' they cried. The interpreter was dreadfully frightened, and his body seemed to shake from head to foot. 'Why,' said he, with his two hands stretched out imploringly to me, 'why not give them what they want?' The present refused consisted of forty coils of iron wire, six pieces of calico, and forty strings of white and blue beads. More and more of the young warriors poured in upon us, and the situation seemed to be getting critical. I went in to the Bishop, and told him that we were having difficulty with the warriors, so he came out himself and tried to reason with them. They most insolently replied that they did not care whether he were a Swahili or a European; what they wanted was their hongo, and that they meant to get. On such occasions the Bishop was wont to take matters most patiently, and patience was sorely needed now. The whole camp was in trouble. The Masai men and women thronged everywhere, till our own people were not visible among them; so, after some discussion, the Bishop yielded, and more goods were given to these hungry wolves. They were now satisfied; but a few more beads were still asked for as a gift, which the Bishop gave to them. At about 10 a.m. a second gang turned up, and began shouting to us from without the stockade. They had, it appeared, come from a different quarter, and wanted the same hongo as the first. Abdallah and a few others were busy in my tent cutting the wire and cloth and arranging the loads, and by and by we paid off this second detachment. It was now midday. The Bishop had not had an instant to rest. His tent was stormed by Masai elders, who seated themselves upon everything. The boys did not know what to do. Nobody dared to tell a Masai to move. My own tent was guarded at both entrances, but they peeped under the flaps, and pulled out whatever they could lay hold of. Everywhere they were pilfering. Whenever the men tried to resist them they pointed their spears at them. All got nervous ; all were hungry, but none dared to sit down and eat. Our visitors began to tear open the loads and turn over the boxes, while the guards were shamefully handled. I could not sit for a minute ; my heart would not let me rest. Every moment I anticipated an attack. Our men were all on tenterhooks of apprehension. The Bishop himself was puzzled and confused. His tent was filled. The chair, the cot, the wash-tub, bags, biscuit-boxes—all held Masai. One could not go through. The cloth of the tent was spoiled by the red earth and oil with which their bodies were daubed, and everything was more or less smeared with it.

"The Bishop retreated to a tree and sat down upon his stool. Soon the guards over our goods began to disperse through the pressure upon them ; my boy Assumani was fast getting mad in trying to keep people out of my tent. The iron pegs of the Bishop's tent were being pulled up and stolen. A Masai seated himself behind Pinto the cook, and coolly stole a table-knife. He was running off, when I saw him and gave chase, and with difficulty got it back. Suddenly the guards shouted, 'A load of wire is going,' and a group of young warriors was seen bearing it off among them, none daring to resist them. I ran after them, and flinging myself into their midst, dashed the load to the ground without regarding their threatening spears. They were greatly astonished, but then gave way, and I bore the load back in triumph to camp. One of our men got his head cut open with a spear thrust ; another had his clothes taken ; but I saw the thief, and made him return the garment.

"A *third* gang of warriors now appeared, and were chanting their mournful songs. The Bishop asked me to return and settle with them, and when I came back to him I was utterly surprised to see two ancients seated with him and conversing in the most serious mood. I brought the interpreter and left them together. It was now 3 p.m., and we all looked toward the sun and longed that it should go down. No day surely passed so slowly as that day. The third gang was satisfied; but now the Masai seemed bent on robbery. They threatened our men with their spears, and teased and insulted everybody. All of a sudden a cry was raised that the women should leave the boma. They at once retreated, and the El Moran stood to their spears. As many of our men as were bold enough held their guns in readiness, but more than half of our strength was away, as the men were hunting by the lake. Happily the riot was quelled somehow, and nothing came of it.* Lastly came the 'doctor.' 'The old and the young have got their hongo. Where is mine as doctor of the nation?' said he, defiantly smiling. After almost endless discussion he was paid off. Then another, who declared that he had been useful in some way or another, put in a claim. More discussion, and *he* at length was satisfied. Then the Masai boys had to receive strings of beads.† . . . . Hungry

---

* The Bishop writes : "I strove in prayer, and each time trouble seemed to be averted."

† The Masai boys, until the age of fourteen, are called El-Aiok. They are then circumcised and attached to the warriors' kraals as general assistants, and are termed El·barnodi. Between about the ages of seventeen and twenty-five or thirty they serve as warriors, and are known as El-Moran. After marriage the Masai becomes an El-moruo, and generally quits the war path and becomes a staid and respectable member of society. The unmarried girls, who live in promiscuous intercourse with the El-Moran in their special kraals, are called En-ditto (pl., En-doye). The Masai are not governed by chiefs, but by elders elected by popular vote, and who hold their office only so long as they give general satisfaction. They may, therefore, be termed republicans !

and thirsty the Bishop and I sat down to our evening meal.
The place at length seemed clear. But no, our friends came
in to see us eat. They touched and befouled everything
eatable with their filthy fingers. We were at our wit's
end. It was not till dark that we finally cleared the camp."

The Masai were pleased to express their admiration of
the Bishop, notwithstanding their scurvy treatment of him.
As they examined him closely, stroked his hair and smoothed
his beard, and then drew back to contemplate his manly and
well-set figure, rivalling their own tall race in height, they
would murmur, "Lumuruo Kitó!" (a very great old man!)
It is possible that much of their teasing and besmirching
attention was intended as a compliment, but if so, it was a
species of compliment that would soon have rendered the life
of its object unbearable. To live among the Masai is like
moving among a troop of lithe and beautiful, but half-tamed
leopards. The traveller has to be ever on the alert, or he
will be pinned by the throat. Not yet had the caravan
passed a' more trying day. Every man in it was utterly
exhausted. Never had they so longed for the evening. All
watched with feverish anxiety till at length the great red
disc of the sun set behind the mountain range of Mau, and

> " Slowly by God's hand unfurled
> Down around the weary world
> Fell the darkness."

One such day was enough. The next morning the
camp was broken up, and the caravan was on its way northward with the rising sun. The way led through "deep
valleys, as if they had been excavated."

On the 14th they saw the last of the troublesome Masai,*

---

* Three Masai brought an ox for sale. With these the Bishop
made great friends, and allowed them to pass the night in his
tent. He writes : " Having strewed the floor with the leaves of the
sweet-scented Caleshwa, we laid us down, their spears and shields

and camped at a place where, some years ago, "a caravan of a thousand men was surrounded and cut to pieces by the Masai."

On the 15th they continued their way almost due north toward Njemps, passing through the volcanic region near Lakes Elmeteita and Nakuro.

On the 16th, the Bishop writes: "Misled by Thomson's map, I took a wrong direction, going too much north. A great corner may be cut off by management. Reached Doreta."

Mr. Jones writes: "On Sept. 18th we discovered a new lake, as we marched a little out of Mr. Thomson's road. It is not mentioned or marked by Mr. T. We slept on its banks. This lake lies south-east of the hot springs which are seen before reaching Njemps.

"At about midday we came across a herd of elephants. The Bishop saw an opportunity of supplying the hungry caravan, and at once charged them. A cow elephant, in return, charged his lordship furiously. While the Bishop was thus engaged with the elephants, two rhinoceroses started up and made straight towards where he stood. I was standing upon a high precipice, from whence I could see all that was going on below. I shouted to the Bishop to beware of the two rhinoceroses, who were coming down rapidly upon him. But both he and Brahim, who was with him, failed to see them. Just as the cow elephant was charging the Bishop, the rhinoceroses got in between, and the elephant at once turned her attention to them, and charged down upon them instead of the Bishop. And now,

---

at their sides. They packed themselves away like sardines in a box, and I covered them over, first with a leopard's skin, then with a grass mat, and finally with a waterproof sheet. They fell almost immediately into a most gentle sleep. I soon followed their example. Wherever we meet we are to be brothers."

from the top of my rock, I witnessed a very singular spectacle. The Bishop running and volleying the elephants; the elephants chasing the rhinoceroses; a leopard hunting my dog Tom; and the caravan men dashing down their loads and scattering in every direction before the great beasts! It was soon over, however, for the Bishop bagged his elephant, and almost brought down a second.

"When our hungry people saw the elephant fall, they shouted for joy. That elephant was soon disposed of. The men scrambled forward with their knives, and in a few minutes the huge beast was cut in pieces. Some of the men ate the meat raw, while others made large fires, and sat round to enjoy their feast. . . . . As they were not allowed to camp there, almost every man made up an extra load of meat to carry on with him."

The next two days were spent in fruitless wandering. The party went astray in following what seemed a good lead, but which turned out to be a *cul de sac*, from which they only extricated themselves after some desperate work, clambering over a steep hill of a thousand feet, which brought them once more upon the plain.

The Bishop writes : "I seem to see now why we lost our way. The game which we had shot supplied us with meat and enabled us to spend Sunday here in a beautiful spot, free from natives, and in peace and quiet; otherwise we should have been in Njemps in the thick of worry and bustle. The heat is intense, as Baringo lies in a deep hole. We have descended 3000 feet since last Sunday. We had our two pleasant Services, and the day passed in the most absolute rest and peace. I lay stretched on my back in quiet contemplation and sweet dreams of dear ones at home, and often longing, often wondering whether I shall be permitted to see them."

After resting throughout Sunday, the Bishop entered

Njemps, near Lake Baringo. There are two villages of that name. The caravan made its way to the smaller. The Wa-Kwafi of Njemps are by extraction Masai, but, having lost their cattle in a war with a tribe of the latter, they have become tamed, and have settled down to agriculture. They are a simple-minded and inoffensive people, and extremely trustworthy, so that their villages offer a delightful resting-place to the traveller weary of the violence and importunity of the Masai hordes through which he has struggled thitherward.

On Sept. 22nd they left the beehive huts of Njemps, and set their faces towards Kavirondo. The men were all well laden with the food which they had purchased for their journey into the almost unknown country which they were now entering. Mr. Thomson's men did their utmost to dissuade him from penetrating further into this perilous region ; but then they had the large caravan of the Swahili traders to fall back upon. Bishop Hannington's porters well knew that for them there was no retreat. Between them and home lay the dreadful Masai. Their only hope of safety now lay in pushing on to the Nyanza. There were, therefore, no protesting voices, but all braced themselves up to meet whatever dangers the next fortnight might have in store for them.

They crossed the river Guaso Tigirish, scrambled over the rocky terrace that divides it from the Guaso Kamnyè, and made for Kamasia. That evening they rested at Mr. Thomson's halting-place of Mkuyu-ni.

On Sept. 23rd they started at daybreak, and climbed along the steep and thorn-impeded track to the summit of the mountain pass of Kamasia.

On the 26th they passed through Kaptè, and the hills of Elgeyo lay before them, seeming to stretch in one long line of stupendous precipices from north to south. They camped at the foot of the Elgeyo escarpment, and spent the Sunday there. The Bishop writes : " Hongo rather hotly demanded by a fresh party, stirred up by Wa-Kwafi. I resisted a long time, but, for the sake of a quiet day,* gave way."

On Monday, the 28th, the Bishop and his party ascended the precipitous lava cap of the Elgeyo escarpment. They seem to have hit upon an easier point of ascent than that which gave so much trouble to Mr. Thomson,† for the Bishop's pocket-book has this sole reference to the event, " Climbed to the top without difficulty " ; and Mr. Jones does not in any way expatiate upon any special peril or labour incurred in surmounting the obstacle. He does, however, allude to the fact that the night spent upon the height above was extremely cold, as indeed would necessarily be the case at that great elevation.

The following day was spent in crossing a wide, tree-less plain, the Rangata Nyuki, or Red Plain of Guas' Ngishu, a kind of inlet of Masai Land, which runs up between the steep mountain ranges of Elgeyo on the east and the Surongai Hills on the west. The river Kiborum, which bounds the plain on the west, is neck deep and rapid, and gave them some trouble to cross it. Next day a man was missed. Searchers were sent and found him a short distance in the rear, dead, and already half eaten by hyænas.

The Bishop notes that he saw one of those beautiful and rare monkeys, the *Colobus guereza.* He had met with it before only on the forest-clad sides of Kilima-njaro. It is specialized by a stripe of long white hair running along the

---

* " As a sign how tired one can be, on Friday last, when going to bed, I took a bite from a biscuit and fell asleep with the first mouthful still in my mouth, and the rest in my hand."

Bishop's Diary.

† *Through Masai Land,* p. 465.

sides and meeting at the tail, which is also white and bushy.
Its skin is much affected by the warriors of Moschi.

When they reached the summit of the range of hills
above the river, their journey seemed almost finished.   Kavirondo lay stretched beneath their feet.*

The village of Kabaras was reached at nine o'clock on
the morning of the 4th.   The simple-minded people had
apparently exhausted their curiosity and fear at the sight of
a white man over Mr. Thomson, for they greeted the Bishop
in a frank and friendly manner, and supplied him cheaply
with what provisions he was willing to buy.

The country of Kavirondo, through which they were
passing, is thickly inhabited.   Villages are to be seen everywhere dotting the grassy plain.   The inhabitants are the
nakedest in the whole of Africa.   Strangely enough, they
are also the most moral.   Both Mr. Thomson and Mr.
Jones make special allusion to these facts.   The chief,
Sakwa, received the Bishop and his present most graciously,
and sent him on his way towards Kwa Sundu in peace.

Kwa Sundu is only two hours distant from Kwa Sakwa.
The people were a little shy at first, as the whole country
had suffered terribly from the wretched Swahili slave
hunters, who had carried fire and sword among the villages
not long before.   When, however, they found that the Bishop
had no connection with such they were at once friendly, and
admitted the caravan into their pleasant village, upon a tree-
clothed hill-top near the rapid flowing river Nzoia.

Bishop Hannington writes: "Naturally the natives

---

* Hannington writes, with unconscious prophetic meaning:
"There lay Kavirondo before us—

"'As when the weary traveller gains
    The height of some o'erlooking hill,
His heart revives if 'cross the plains
    He sees the goal, though distant still.'"

seem good-natured and polite to strangers, and are by no means importunate. Oh that we might possess fair Kavirondo for Christ ! "

A halt was made at Kwa Sundu until the 11th. We may gather what followed from Mr. Jones' diary :—

" Soon after arriving, the Bishop decided that he would proceed to the Lake alone, and leave me behind in charge of the caravan. Accordingly he began to pack those things which he thought to be most necessary for himself and the 50 men whom he chose from the 200 porters to accompany him. He said that he would try to cross the Lake after reaching Lussala (Massala of Mr. Thomson), and go to U-Ganda. At Rubaga he would ascertain if any of the brethren wished to return to the coast, in which case they might take the new route by Kavirondo. They would then be able to take the caravan back with them. The Bishop himself intended, when he returned, to do so by the old Unyamwezi route, and visit the churches which were established to the south of the Lake.

" *Oct.* 12*th.*—To-day the Bishop left me. He was not at all well. An abscess had formed in his leg which gave him considerable pain. He would not, however, listen to my entreaties that he should wait until his leg was healed, but started with his fifty picked men. They were all loaded lightly, in order that they might be able to carry him should it prove that he was unable to walk.

" *Oct.* 13*th.*—To-day some natives arrived from Sindi and reported that the Bishop and his caravan had passed that place all well. Sindi lies due North-west, and is about fifteen or twenty miles distant.

" *Oct.* 20*th.*—No news of the Bishop. The guide who went with him has returned, but brings no message. Probably the man has run away from the Bishop's camp. I am daily looking for a messenger with a line from the Lake.

" *Oct.* 22*nd.*—To-day a man reported to me that one o the Bishop's porters is at Sindi. Who he may be I cannot tell. Very likely he was left behind through sickness. No letters from the Bishop, though to-day is the twelfth since he left us for the Lake. I pray that all may be well with him.

" *Oct.* 25*th.*—No letters from the Bishop. I have only 152 men with me. With these, if the Bishop does not come this way, I shall have to return by the same way that we came. Wherever we passed our caravan was laughed at, owing to our small numbers. What will they say when they see us still less in returning?

" *Oct.* 28*th.*—No news from the Bishop. It is becoming a matter of great anxiety.

" *Oct.* 30*th.*—Still no news. Last night Arthur reported that one had told him that the Bishop had been attacked by a neighbouring tribe, but of his safety nothing is said. It is now nineteen days since he left us. The tribe that is said to have attacked the Bishop is only four days distant, and we should have heard of any disaster long before this. I therefore regard this report as utterly false.

" *Nov.* 3*rd.*—All is silent.

" *Nov.* 7*th.*—Not an air of news! I am very anxious. To-day it is twenty-seven days since the Bishop left, and not a line has he sent. Every now and then I hear from people coming from Tunga's quarters that the party has passed that place, but no more. It *may* be that the party have reached the Lake, and that, owing to the Bishop's bad leg, everything is brought to a state of stagnation.

" *Nov.* 8*th, Sunday.*—After service, and just as I had finished writing in my journal, precisely at 12 noon, Bedue, one of the men, came to me sighing and breathing hard.

'What's the matter?' I said to him, rising. 'Two men have come to me,' Bedue continued, 'with the report that the Bishop and his party have been killed!' 'Where are they?' I demanded; 'bring them to me at once that I may learn the truth of their story.' Bedue flew away, but somehow the two men came to me before he returned. They said that they had been a long distance in search of a doctor for their chief, who is now ill; on their road they picked up three of our men who had managed to escape when the Bishop and his men were being killed. 'Where are the three men?' I asked, though I could scarcely speak for nervousness, and my whole body shook fearfully. The men replied that they were at Sindi's. 'Why have you not brought them?' I said; 'then I might have given you a handsome present. You have only got the news of the Bishop's death, but no eye-witness who saw him die, or who has seen his dead body.' They then asked me to give them wire and beads, and said they would go and fetch the men. I hoped even then that these men might be playing me a trick, so I refused to give them anything, and said that I would make arrangements about any men who might be at Sindi's.

"I immediately sent to the chief and asked for men to go to Sindi's village. Before the chief could return an answer, one of the men from Sindi's appeared. Now we could no longer regard the report as false, or how should he have come entirely stripped of everything? The man came in and sat down. 'Now,' said I, 'Senenge, where have you come from? and where is the Bishop?' (I asked these questions with trembling lips—the Bishop *dead*!—). Senenge said that the Bishop and his party reached this side of U-Ganda safely. He wanted to go on, but the people prevented him until they had sent a message to their chief. The Bishop refused to be kept long waiting; however, he was compelled to yield, and wrote a letter which he desired them to send to the missionaries in U-Ganda. On the eighth day the reply was brought that the chief had sent word that the European should proceed to see Mtèsa.* Early on the ninth day the Bishop and his party were tied and confined in different places. Towards 5 p.m., first the Bishop and then the men, one by one, were killed at some distance from the village!

" Before he had finished this tale, the two remaining men arrived from Sindi's. One of them had been speared in the right arm. They give the same report as to the Bishop and Pinto being killed, but different accounts as to *how* he was killed. Senenge says he saw none of the men killed. The other two say that thirteen men were killed and the rest taken for slaves. That before they were led to be killed they were stripped of their guns, tied together in threes, and made to sit in one place. The Bishop, they all say, was confined by himself in a place where the other men could not see him. All the goods were taken to the house of the chief Rua. The place of the murder they say is three days from U-Ganda. They say that October 31st is the day on which the Bishop died.† Senenge says the Bishop was speared and Pinto shot. The other two, that the Bishop was shot with two guns, Pinto with one."

"After hearing all this dreadful report of the dear Bishop, I cross-examined the men as to how they managed to escape. To this I could get no satisfactory reply. As we were surrounded by eager natives all listening, I gave

---

* Probably Mr. Jones meant Mwanga, for he knew of Mtèsa's death, but wrote "Mtèsa" from long habit, as his name has always been associated with the U-Ganda Mission.

It is now almost certain that the 29th was the day of his death.

it out that this report was not true, and that these three men had wickedly deserted the Bishop, and instructed all my people to represent the report as untrue to the people of the village."

" *Can it be true that the Bishop is killed ?* "

CHAPTER XXIII.

HOW IT CAME TO PASS.

" 'And do you think that a spirit, full of lofty thoughts, and
privileged to contemplate all time and all existence, can possibly
attach any great importance to this life?'

" 'No ; it is impossible.'

" 'Then such a person will not regard death as a formidable
thing, will he?'

" 'Certainly not.' "   PLATO : *Repub.*

Ἐμοὶ γὰρ τὸ ζῆν, Χριστὸς, κὰι τὸ ἀποθανεῖν, κερδος.—*Phil.* i. 21.

WE must now transfer our thoughts to the capital of
U-Ganda, and inquire how matters had been going on
there since Bishop Hannington's visit to the Lake in 1882.
We shall in this manner be able to understand how it came
to pass that the Bishop, after that the journey which he had
so daringly and skilfully undertaken had been brought to a
triumphant conclusion, and when he had the best reason for
believing that all danger was over, was seized and put to
death by the very men whom he regarded as his friends.

I very heartily wish that space permitted me to give a
detailed and full account of this, the most interesting of
modern Missions, and fullest of the romance of real life.
Chiefly for the sake of those who have not read Mr. Mackay's journal-letters, which have been published from time to
time in the *C. M. Intelligencer.* It is not likely that those
who have followed the varying fortunes of the Mission as narrated in his graphic and thrilling letters will require me to add
anything to their knowledge. Perhaps, however, they will

pardon me if, for the sake of the less accurately informed, I attempt to trace out, as briefly as may be, the sequence of events which led to so great a disaster, and to the loss of a noble man over whom the Church Universal has mourned.

On the 10th of October, 1884, about a month before the Bishop sailed from England, an event occurred which most seriously affected all Church work in Central Africa, and to which may be attributed the disaster of October 29th, 1885. Mtèsa, king of U-Ganda, died, and was succeeded by his son, Mwanga. This Mwanga is a mere boy, possessing none of his father's strength of character, and has proved to be almost wholly under the influence of his Katikiro (vizier) and council of chiefs.

Christianity had been making great strides in U-Ganda ;* and that in spite of the perplexing divisions caused by the French priests of the Roman Church, the bitter opposition of the Arabs, and the scarcely disguised disfavour of the chiefs. Mtèsa was a man of a marvellously large heart— for an African potentate—and he was inclined to let all parties have a fair field and no favour. Our Churchmen were not slow to make hay while the sun was shining. They set up their printing-press, and distributed everywhere portions of the New Testament, hymns, prayers, etc., in Luganda. It soon became fashionable to learn to read. The store-houses and offices of the Court were literally converted into reading-rooms. Lads might be seen everywhere, sitting in groups, or sprawling on the hay-covered floor, all reading— some the Book of Commandments, some the Church prayers, others the Kiswahili New Testament. Nor were these books and papers given to them for nothing. They were both ready and eager to *buy* whatever literature they could get.

On March 18th, 1882, the first five converts were baptized, and in the year following several more. At the

---

* Compare pages 193—196.

end of 1884 the native Church consisted of eighty-eight members. Among these was no less a personage than one of Mtèsa's own daughters, "Rebecca" Mugali. This the king had not bargained for, and for some time the little Church was in real danger. But, after a while, Mtèsa's natural breadth of mind led him to accept the logical conclusion of his tolerance, and things went on as before. Then occurred his death. What immediately followed is a very remarkable testimony to the hold which Christianity had, even in this brief time, acquired over the minds of the people. The invariable custom hitherto had been to indulge in mutual and indiscriminate pillage, rapine, and murder during the brief interregnum, and until the new king was installed. The heads of the Mission were warned by several of the converts, who hastened to announce the king's death, and bid them fortify themselves and prepare for the worst. After united prayer and consultation, they resolved to await events, without resisting any officially authorized attempt to pillage them. To their wondering thankfulness, the expected carnival of blood was "honoured in the breach." It was made known that the young king had spared the princes his brothers, whom custom would have permitted him to exterminate, and that there was to be no slaughter. Such a thing had never been known before, and a bright prospect of a good time coming seemed to open out before the Mission. But then came a time of trouble. Mwanga, immensely puffed up by his elevation, and indulging himself in all possible vanities and vices, proved to be of a feeble and vacillating character; passionate and vindictive, timid and suspicious, he soon became a tool in the hands of his designing courtiers. The chiefs, intensely conservative of all customary abuses by which they maintained their special privileges and victimized the people, were alarmed at the progress which enlightened Christian

views were making. They did not find it very difficult
to arouse Mwanga's suspicions and work upon his fears.

Unhappily, a pretext was soon forthcoming for an attack
upon the Church. Mr. Mackay had been permitted to sail
in the Mission boat *Eleanor* to Msalala, at the south end of
the Nyanza, to meet three of his companions who were
reported to be upon their way to U-Ganda. They had not,
however, penetrated so far, as their services were required
at the various Mission Stations along the road. When Mr.
Mackay returned without them, it was at once suggested by
the unfriendly chiefs that he had never intended to bring
them back, but had used the opportunity of leave of absence
to communicate with the king's enemies. (The most
puerile reports are enough to set an African kingdom in a
blaze.) Some sort of colour was given to this story by a
rumour of white men in U-Soga, at the north-east corner of
the Lake. This was Mr. Thomson's party, which penetrated to Upper Kavirondo in 1883—84. The chiefs of
U-Ganda have always looked upon an approach to their
country from the north or north-east with extreme suspicion
and dislike. They regard the Lake as a natural barrier
against invasion from the south; they do not as yet entertain any great fear of danger from the west, though the
new Congo State may probably before long excite their
alarm; but they are very nervous about any advance of
another nation from the east or north. When Egypt was
enlarging her borders southward they were in a state of
panic. A single white man is looked upon as a host in himself, and as such to be most rigorously excluded if he should
make his appearance from the two forbidden quarters. Even
Mtèsa used sometimes to twit the white men at Rubaga,*
asking them if they would like to see the country behind

---

* Mwanga has removed his capital, and built his "palace" at a
place called Mengo, a mile and a half S.E. of Rubaga, which is

U-Soga, and assuring them that they should not. Mr. Thomson escaped even more narrowly than he at the time realized. Perhaps he owes his safe return to the fact that he reached the borders of U-Ganda about the time of Mtèsa's death. At all events, it is certain that the chief who was responsible for letting him go, and omitting to bind and bring him before the king, has since been charged with the offence and degraded from his office.

Such being the state of feelings in Mtèsa's time, it was not hard for the chiefs to instil all kinds of vague fears into the feeble-minded Mwanga. Mr. Mackay was charged with sending his friends to U-Soga, there to collect an army, while he stole away the hearts of the people in U-Ganda from their king. Mwanga was enraged to find that all his pages, with the exception of two or three, were pupils of the Missionaries ; he complained to them that they had ceased to respect his majesty, that they counted Jesus as their king, and himself not much better than a brother ! Matters soon reached a crisis. Mr. Mackay had obtained permission again to cross the Lake, and was proceeding with some of the Mission boys to the port, when he was forcibly arrested by order of the Katikiro. The instrument employed was one Mujasi, captain of the body guard, who had once been sent on an embassy to General Gordon at Khartoum, and not meeting from that great Governor the distinguished consideration which he thought that his own highness merited, had returned with a perfect hatred of all white men, and a deep-seated loathing for their religion. He was rejoiced at this opportunity of showing his contempt for the Christian teachers, and used them with the utmost rudeness, dragging them forcibly before the Katikiro. They only averted the utter destruction of the Mission premises by a timely present

now a bare, uninhabited hill. The C. M. S. Mission Station is at Natete, a mile and a half N.W. from Rubaga.

to the authorities. Their boys, however, had been seized upon the pretext that as Christians they were joining with the white men against the king. They made the utmost efforts to obtain their release, but all to no purpose. Three of the younger were at last returned to them, but the other three were shamefully tormented and done to death. The lads who escaped described the scene to their teachers. But Mr. Mackay must himself narrate the terrible facts : " They were taken, with Kakumba and Mr. Ashe's boy, and also Serwanga, a tall, fine fellow who had been baptized. These three were then tortured, their arms were cut off, and they were bound alive to a scaffolding, under which a fire was made, and so they were *slowly burned to death.*" As they hung in their protracted agony over the flames, Mujasi and his men stood around jeering, and told them to pray *now* to Isa Masiya (Jesus Christ) if they thought that He could do anything to help them. The spirit of the martyrs at once entered into these lads, and together they raised their voices and praised Jesus in the fire, singing till their shrivelled tongues refused to form the sound, *Killa siku tunsifu* :—

> " Daily, daily, sing to Jesus,
>   Sing, my soul, His praises due ;
> *All He does* deserves our praises,
>   And our deep devotion too.
> For in deep humiliation
>   He for us did live below ;
> Died on Calvary's cross of torture ;
>   Rose to save our souls from woe." *

---

* One of the hymns translated into the musical language of U-Ganda, The book of hymns and prayers has upon its title-page the happily-conceived monogram :

```
            M
            A
        I S A
            I
            Y
            A
```

Little wonder that Mr. Mackay should write: "*Our hearts are breaking.*" Yet what a triumph! One of the executioners, struck by the extraordinary fortitude of the lads, and their evident faith in another life, came and asked that he also might be taught to pray. This martyrdom did not daunt the other Christians. Though Mwanga threatened to burn alive any who frequented the Mission premises, or adopted the Christian faith, they continued to come, and the lads at the Court kept their teachers constantly informed of everything that was going on. Indeed, when the Katikiro began to make investigation, he found the place so honey-combed by Christianity * that he had to cease his inquisition for fear of implicating chiefs and upsetting society generally. One man, named Nua, who had gone to the Court to confess himself a Christian and take the consequences, was sent home in peace, and his accuser, Mujasi, rebuffed. This discovery did not, however, as one may suppose, incline the chiefs to look with any greater favour upon the new religion.

Such was the state of affairs in U-Ganda in the spring of 1885, when the Bishop was contemplating his journey thither through Masai Land.

He was quite ignorant of the strength of the prejudice which existed there against permitting an entrance into the country through U-Soga. It is evident that Sir John Kirk and all in Zanzibar, as well as the Missionaries at Frere Town, were also in ignorance of this. They were all apparently unanimous in their recommendation that the new route should be tried, and if the country of the Masai were safely passed, they did not see any reason to doubt that

---

* In July, 1885, a large church had been built, which was over-crowded. The daily school was so largely attended that it was impossible to teach properly all who came. Mr. O'Flaherty writes that on July 26th no less than 35 persons openly *communicated.*

the Bishop would be received in a friendly manner into U-Ganda.

Yet all this time the danger was *increasing*, until, had the Bishop known it, he might as safely have walked into a den of lions as have ventured into U-Soga. We have mentioned the effect produced by Mr. Thomson's expedition, and the manner in which Englishmen in U-Ganda suffered in consequence; but to the general vague fear of invasion by white men was now added the definite report of the high-handed proceedings of Germany at Zanzibar.* Mtèsa, when he was pressed by his chiefs to take measures against the Europeans, who, they averred, were only waiting until they had sufficient forces at their command to declare hostilities, and eat up his country, would wisely reply : " If they intended to take the country, they would not begin with the interior. I shall wait until I see them commence upon the coast." Well, *now*, apparently, the dreaded Bazungu had begun to " eat up " the coast. " Alarm was at its height," writes Mr. Mackay ; " the Court counselled killing all the Missionaries, as we were only the forerunners of invasion." Mr. Mackay did all in his power to convince the king and his chiefs that Englishmen were a different race from the Germans, and taking a large school map, pointed out to them the various divisions of Bulaya (Europe). His arguments were to little purpose. To the tribes of Central Africa all white men seem to be of one race ; all are called Bazungu (Europeans).

When information reached the Mission party that their Bishop was about to visit them, and had determined to enter by U-Soga, they were naturally alarmed. They took counsel together, and decided to tell the king, and explain to him the object of the Bishop's visit before a garbled

* Germany had demanded from Seyyid Barghash the port of Bogamoyo—and threatened to take it if he would not sell.

account should reach his ears. This they did in September. They mentioned that their Superior and chief of their Church was coming that way probably to avoid the Germans, and did all that was possible to remove from the king's mind the suspicion that they had any connection with the Germans themselves.

The next morning, the king summoned a council of his chiefs. After some consultation they unanimously came to the conclusion that white men were all of the same race. That the white teachers were only the forerunners of war ; and that they were waiting for their head-man to arrive, when they would commence at once to eat up the country. One proposed to go out and fight the Bishop. Another thought that all the white men in U-Ganda should be first killed, and so the evil stamped out with one blow. Another remarked that though it had been said that to kill a white man would bring disaster upon the land, yet that several had been killed with impunity, and nothing had happened. All were agreed that the Bishop should not be allowed to enter the country, especially as he was coming by the "*back door*," through Busoga.* It was finally decided that the Bishop's party should be conducted round to the south of the Lake, to Msalala, and there await the pleasure of the king.

In the meantime, Mr. Ashe, with Mr. O'Flaherty and Mr. Mackay, were not idle. They realized the peril in which their Bishop would stand, and constantly sought interviews with Mwanga to induce him to allow them to meet him and conduct him themselves to the capital. It was terrible to think that their friend was rapidly advancing into the snare, and that they were utterly helpless to give him warning.

On Oct. 25th, one of the Court pages came to the Mission house with the news that a tall Englishman had

---

* In U-Ganda the prefix B is added. Thus, U-Ganda, Wa-Ganda, U-Soga, etc., become Buganda, Ba-ganda, Busoga.

arrived in Busoga, and further stated that it was said he had lost a thumb.* There could be no doubt who this might be. The king held a council, and it was decided that the stranger should be put to death. Mwanga was at first unwilling, and suggested that the white man should simply be turned back. To this the Katikiro replied, " Will you let their goods go also ? " So, for the sake of the plunder, the order went forth. Soon one of the pages whispered to his teacher that the white men had been all put in the stocks ; and, as Mr. Ashe and Mr. Mackay hastened to the palace to seek Mwanga, a lad whispered, as they entered the enclosure, " Men have already been sent to kill the white men." The king refused to see them, and they were assured that their white friends would be quite safe and would merely be escorted out of the country.† Sorrowfully they departed, knowing that they were being deceived, since they had obtained reliable information through one of their young friends the pages that orders had been given " to kill the white man and his whole party, letting none escape, and to count their goods."

We have not space here even to summarize what Mr. Mackay has written since that terrible 29th day of October, with regard to his own position and that of his brethren in

---

* It was at first reported that there were *two* white men.

† The following extract from a letter written by Père Lourdel, the Superior of the Jesuit Mission, refers to this : " Quelques jours après, nous apprenons que des blancs viennent par la route de Busoga. Les missionaires anglais, qui savaient que le blanc signalé était M. Hannington, vont, mais inutilement, intercèder auprès du roi pour qu'il revienne sur la sentence ; mais ils ne purent, pendant deux jours qu ils attendirent à la cour, obtenir une minute d'audience. Ils eurent alors recours à moi et me prièrent d'aller intercéder en leur faveur pour la vie de leur évêque. Comme alors le roi me recevait facilement, je me rendis à leurs prières, et, à force d'instances, j'obtins de Mwanga qu'il ne ferait pas périr les blancs, mais le chasserait simplement en leur envoyant l'ordre de retourner sur leur pas. Mais la promesse du roi

U-Ganda. It must suffice to say that they have been in daily
peril of their lives, and the only fact which has apparently
stood between them and death on several occasions has been
that Mwanga imagines that they do not know the fate which
has befallen their Bishop. The Christians have been very
faithful and devoted, and though the persecution has broken
out afresh, and as many as *thirty-two* converts have been
heaped together and burned alive in one great funeral pyre,
conversions do not stop, and brave souls still confess Christ,
seeking baptism at the risk of death in its most awful form.
How this will end, God alone knows. In His keeping
this band of Christian heroes may be left with confidence.

We must return to the Bishop. The accounts of his
death which were given to Mr. Jones by the men who
escaped from the massacre, and those given to the Mission
party in U-Ganda by persons who professed to have been
eye-witnesses of the deed, are *substantially* in agreement.

It will be remembered that Mr. Jones states that the
Bishop was suffering from an inflamed leg, which had confined him " to the outside of his bed " for nearly a week.
He, nevertheless, made every preparation for an immediate
start with his fifty men for the Lake. His own journal, so
happily and so unexpectedly recovered, supplies us with
full and accurate information as to all that happened from

était-elle fausse, ou l'ordre était-il déjà exécuté ? Le fait est que
nous apprenions, quelques jours après, que le meurtre était con-
sommé. Le blanc venait d'être massacré avec la plus grande
partie de son escorte, une quarantaine d'hommes environ."

Also with regard to Mwanga's state of mind :

" Le pauvre Mwanga ajoutait, le matin même de cette séance.
C'est moi qui suis le dernier roi de Buganda ; les blancs s'em-
pareront de mon pays après ma mort. De mon vivant, je saurai
bien les en empêcher. Mais, après moi, se terminera la liste
des rois nègres du Buganda.' "

the moment when he left Kwa-Sundu to within, probably, a few hours, or even minutes of his death. He writes :—

" *Oct* 12*th, Monday.*—Nine hours, eighteen miles. At daylight, and almost before, I made a dash at my boot, and with fear and trembling, laced it up, and put foot to the ground. I stood, I walked, and without great pain, so I organized a start. . . . . Arrived at Mtindi's at 5 p.m., tired, but none the worse. . . . . Immense Masai town close at hand."

During the next week the Bishop walked about a hundred and seventy miles. On the second day he writes : "Climbing a hill, the Lake burst suddenly upon us, long before I expected it, for hills which we saw miles away proved to be islands. We found ourselves to the west of the deep Sio bay." The country was densely populated, and the people, on the whole, friendly, but inclined to hinder the rapid march westward of the impatient European. Each petty chief of a district endeavoured to compel him to halt and remain for a day or two. The Bishop, however, pushed resolutely on, and refused to be detained. It was terribly anxious work, as he was perpetually surrounded by a crowd of obstructives, who seemed to be ever on the point of resorting to violence. His men were terrified, but he, generally with a well-assumed smile, or seeming-hearty laugh, sometimes with a demonstration of fist or stick, shouldered his way onward to the Nile. On Oct 17th he found himself unexpectedly on the shore of the Lake, and writes :—

" I found an enormous market in full swing, and canoes from the islands, but none of my inquiries satisfied me as to where we were, though I have strong suspicions that we have only reached a deep inlet opposite (Uvuma Island ?). . . . We are in the midst of awful swamps, and mosquitos as savage as bees ; the Lord keep me from fever ! "

" *Oct* 18*th*, *Sunday.*—I can hear nothing about the Nile. Nobody has heard of a river running north, nor of the Ripon Falls. . . . . . I passed a very restful and pleasant day, although it was difficult not to fidget myself nervous about the swamps and bad water. The nearer I get the more anxious I seem, wrongly, to be about arriving, though I am sure I ought not to be so, since God has been so very gracious to me, and has thus far led me by the hand.

" *Oct.* 19*th*, *Monday.*— . . . . . Presently we came upon symptoms of war, and finally we fell in with a Wa-Ganda mob sent to subdue U-Soga. Their excitement at seeing me was intense. Many of them knew Mackay. Most of their leaders were drunk, and in a most dangerous mood, coming round me, shouting and yelling, and ordering me about. Whereupon I took the high hand, and in spite of overwhelming numbers, I refused to stop, shook my fist in the faces of the most noisy, gathered my scattered men, and pushed through the mob. . . . . . All the neighbour-hood is decimated by war ; hundreds of fine banana trees cut down, and huge bunches lying about rotting. We camped between the two war-parties. I could hear them both, and was in a very dangerous situation, as it was dark, and my men such fools that they would not keep still.

" *Oct.* 20*th.*—Through the mercy of God—and every step of the way is through His mercy—nothing happened during the night, but I fear we have arrived in a trouble-some country. . . . . We have, however, made fine progress to-day, and almost all in the right direction that should bring us to the Nile, near about the Ripon Falls ; and I don't think I am much out of my reckoning. Here, at least, we seem to have peace for a night.

" *Oct.* 21*st*, *Wednesday.*—About half an hour brought us to Lubwa's. His first demand, in a most insolent tone, was for ten guns and three barrels of powder ; this, of course, I refused. They then demanded that I should stay three days ; this I refused, and when the same demands were made, I jumped up and said, ' I go back the way I came.' Meantime the war drums beat. More than a thousand soldiers were assembled. My men implored me not to move, but, laughing at them, I pushed them and the loads through the crowd and turned back. Then came an imploring message that I would stay but for a short time. I refused to hear till several messages had arrived ; then, thinking things were turning my way, I consented ; said I would give a small present and pass. My present was returned, and a demand made that I would stay one day ; to this I consented, because I fancy this man can send me on in canoes direct to Mwanga's capital, and save a week's march. Presently seven guns were stolen from us ; at this I pretended to rejoice exceedingly, since I should demand restoration not from these men, but from Mwanga. A soldier was placed to guard me in my tent, and follow me if I moved an inch. I climbed a neighbouring hill, and to my joy, saw a splendid view of the Nile, only about half an hour's distance,* country being beautiful ; deep creeks of the Lake visible to the south. I presently asked leave to go to the Nile. This was denied me. I afterwards asked my headman, Brahim, to come with me to the point close at hand whence I had seen the Nile, as our men had begun to doubt its existence ; several followed up, and one, pretending to show me another view, led me further away, when suddenly about twenty ruffians set upon us. They violently threw me to the ground, and proceeded to strip me of all valuables. Thinking they were

---

* It seems clear from the above that Bishop Hannington penetrated further than was at first supposed ; in this edition, therefore, the blue line upon the map has been prolonged almost to the right bank of the Nile.

robbers, I shouted for help, when they forced me up and
hurried me away, as I thought, to throw me down a precipice close at hand.   I shouted again, in spite of one
threatening to kill me with a club.   Twice I nearly broke
away from them, and then grew faint with struggling, and
was dragged by the legs over the ground.   I said, ' Lord, I
put myself in Thy hands, I look to Thee alone.'   Then
another struggle, and I got to my feet, and was thus dashed
along.   More than once I was violently brought into contact with banana trees, some trying in their haste to force
me one way, others the other, and the exertion and struggling strained me in the most agonizing manner.   In spite
of all, and feeling I was being dragged away to be murdered
at a distance, I sang ' Safe in the arms of Jesus,' and then
laughed at the very agony of my situation.   My clothes
torn to pieces so that I was exposed; wet through with
being dragged along the ground ; strained in every limb,
and for a whole hour expecting instant death, hurried along,
dragged, pushed, at about five miles an hour, until we came
to a hut, into the court of which I was forced.   Now, I
thought, I am to be murdered.   As they released one hand,
I drew my finger across my throat, and understood them to
say decidedly No.   We then made out that I had been
seized by order of the Sultan.   Then arose a new agony.
Were all my men murdered ?   Another two or three hours'
awful suspense, during which time I was kept bound and
shivering with cold, when to my joy, Pinto (the Portu-
guese cook) and a boy were brought with my bed and
bedding, and I learnt that the Sultan meant to keep me
prisoner until he had received word from Mwanga, which
means, I fear, a week or more's delay, nor can I tell whether
they are speaking the truth.   I am in God's hands."

The man who enticed the Bishop away from his
followers, a few of whom had accompanied him to the

summit of the hill, was one Masudi bin Suleiman, a rene-
gade Mahommedan, who has renounced his race and creed,
and cast in his lot with the heathen.   He is well known
as a violent opponent of Christianity in U-Ganda.   The
Bishop was dragged by a circuitous route to the village; but
one of the men, who happened to be wandering, was a
horrified witness of his master's fate.   He ran to tell his
companions, and soon all was confusion and dismay.   The
panic-stricken men lost all nerve, and some of their goods
were at once scrambled for by the natives.   They were then
all seized and detained as prisoners.   The Bishop continues :

" *Oct. 22nd, Thursday.*—I found myself, perhaps about
ten o'clock last night, on my bed in a fair-sized hut, but
with no ventilation, a fire on the hearth, no chimney for
smoke, about twenty men all round me, and rats and
vermin *ad lib.* ; fearfully shaken, strained in every limb;
great pain, and consumed with thirst, I got little sleep that
night.   Pinto may cook my food, and I have been allowed
to have my Bible and writing things also.   I hear the men
are in close confinement, but safe, and the loads, except a
few small things, intact.   Up to one o'clock I have received
no news whatever, and I fear at least a week in this black
hole, in which I can barely see to write.   Floor covered
with rotting banana peel and leaves and lice.   Men relieving nature at night on the floor ; a smoking fire, at which
my guards cook and drink pombe ; in a feverish district ;
fearfully shaken, scarce power to hold up small Bible.
Shall I live through it ?   My God, I am Thine.
"Towards evening I was allowed to sit outside for a little
time, and enjoyed the fresh air ; but it made matters worse
when I went inside my prison again, and as I fell exhausted
on my bed I burst into tears—health seems to be quite
giving way with the shock.   I fear I am in a very caged-

lion frame of mind, and yet so strained and shattered that it is with the utmost difficulty I can stand; yet I ought to be praising His Holy Name, and I do.

" Not allowed a knife to eat my food with. The savages who guard me keep up an unceasing strain of raillery, or at least I fancy they do, about the Mzungu.

" *Oct. 23rd, Friday.*—I woke full of pain and weak, so that with the utmost difficulty I crawled outside and sat in a chair, and yet they guard every move as if I was a giant. My nerves, too, have received such a shock that, some loud yells and war cries arising outside the prison fence,* I expected to be murdered, and simply turned over and said : ' Let the Lord do as He sees fit; I shall not make the slightest resistance.' Seeing how bad I am, they have sent my tent for me to use in the daytime. Going outside I fell to the ground exhausted, and was helped back in a gone condition to my bed. I don't see how I can stand all this, and yet I don't want to give in, but it almost seems as if U-Ganda itself was going to be forbidden ground to me— the Lord only knows. Afternoon.—To my surprise my guards came kneeling down, so different to their usual treat-ment, and asked me to come out. I came out, and there was the chief and about a hundred of his wives come to feast their eyes on me in cruel curiosity. I felt inclined to spring at his throat, but sat still, and presently read to myself Matthew v. 44, 45, and felt refreshed. I asked how many more days he meant to keep me in prison. He said four more at least. He agreed, upon my earnest request, to allow me to sleep in my own tent, with two armed soldiers at each door. The object of his visit was to ask that I would say no bad things of him to Mwanga. What

---

* Since the publication of the first edition, the recovery of the Bishop's sketch-book has enabled us to give a facsimile of his drawing of the hut in which he was confined.

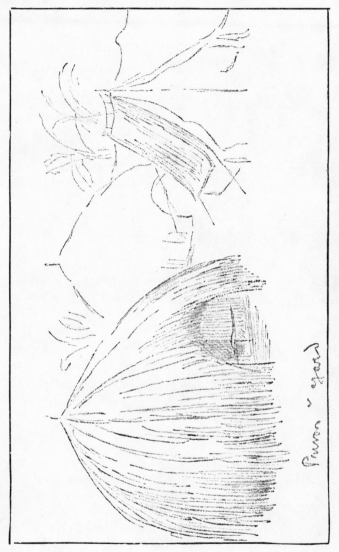

FACSIMILE OF THE BISHOP'S SKETCH OF HIS PRISON.

can I say good ?   I made no answer to the twice repeated
request.   He then said if I would write a short letter, and
promise to say nothing bad, he would send it at once.   I
immediately wrote a hasty scrawl (I scarce know what),
but said I was prisoner, and asked Mackay to come.   God
grant it may reach.   But I already feel better than I have
done since my capture, though still very shattered.

"*Oct. 24th, Saturday.*—Thank God for a pleasant
night in my own tent, in spite of a tremendous storm and
rain flowing in on the floor in streams.   Personally I quite
forgave this old man and his agents for my rough treatment,
though even to-day I can only move with the greatest discomfort, and ache as though I had rheumatic fever.   I have,
however, to consider the question in another light ; if the
matter is passed over unnoticed, it appears to me the safety of
all white travellers in these districts will be endangered, so
I shall leave the brethren, who know the country and are
most affected, to act as they think best.   The day passed
away very quietly.   I amused myself with Bible and diary.

"*Oct. 25th, Sunday.*—(Fourth day of imprisonment.)
Still a great deal of pain in my limbs.   The fatigue of dressing quite knocks me over.   My guards, though at times
they stick to me like leeches, and, with two rifles in hand,
remain at night in my tent, are gradually getting very careless.   I have already seen opportunities of escape had I
wanted so to do, and I doubt not that in a few days' time,
especially if I could get a little extra pombe brought to
them, I could walk away quite easily, but I have no such
intention.   I should be the more inclined to stop should
they say go, to be a thorn in the old gentleman's side, and
I fear from that feeling of contrariness which is rather inborn.   I send him affectionate greetings and reports on my
health by his messengers twice a day.   What I fear most
now is the close confinement and utter want of exercise.

When I was almost beginning to think of my time in prison as getting short the chief has sent men to redouble the fence around me. What does it mean? I have shown no desire or intention of escaping. Has a messenger arrived from Mwanga? There is just time for him to have sent word to tell them to hold me fast. The look of this has cast me down again.

" One of my guards, if I understand him rightly, is making me offers of escape. He has something very secret to communicate, and will not even take my boy into confidence. I do not, however, want to escape under the present circumstances ; but at the same time I take great amusement in watching and passing by various little opportunities. My guards and I are great friends, almost affectionate, and one speaks of me as ' My whiteman.'

" Three detachments of the chief's wives, they say he has 1000 nearly, have been to-day to see me. They are very quiet and well-behaved, but greatly amused at the prisoner. Mackay's name seems quite a household word ; I constantly hear it.

" My men are kept in close confinement, except two who come daily backwards and forwards to bring my food. This they take in turns, and implore, so I hear, for the job.

" *Oct. 26th, Monday.*—(Fifth day in prison.) Limbs and bruises and stiffness better, but I am heavy and sleepy. Was not inclined to get up as usual, and, if I mistake not, signs of fever creep over me. Mackay should get my letter to-day, and sufficient time has passed for the chief to receive an answer to his first message sent before I was seized, the nature of which I know not, probably—White man is stopping here. Shall I send him on? Waiting your Majesty's pleasure. If they do not guess who it is they will very likely, African fashion, talk about it two or

three days first of all, and then send a message back leisurely
with Mwanga's permission for me to advance.

"About thirty-three more of the chief's wives came and
disported themselves with gazing at the prisoner. I was
very poorly and utterly disinclined to pay any attention to
them, and said in English, 'O ladies, if you knew how ill
I feel, you would go.' When my food arrived in the
middle of the day I was unable to eat. The first time, I
think, since leaving the coast I have refused a meal. To-
day I am very broken down both in health and spirits, and
some of the murmuring feelings which I thought that I had
conquered have returned hard upon me. Another party of
wives coming, I retired into the hut and declined to see
them. A third party came later on, and being a little better
I came out and lay upon my bed. It is not pleasant to be
examined as a caged lion in the Zoo, and yet that is exactly
my state at the present time. My tent is jammed in
between the hut and high fence of the Boma, so scarce
a breath of air reaches me. Then at night, though the
tent is a vast improvement on the hut, yet two soldiers,
reeking with pombe and other smells, sleep beside me, and
the other part of my guard, not far short of twenty, laugh
and drink and shout far into the night and begin again
before daylight in the morning, waking up from time to
time to shout out to my sentries to know if all is well.
I fear all this is telling on my health tremendously.

"*Oct. 27th, Tuesday.*—(Sixth day as prisoner.) All I
can hear in the way of news is that the chief has sent men
to fight those parts we passed through. I begin to doubt if
he has sent to Mwanga at all, but thinks I am in league
with the fighting party, and is keeping me hostage. I
begin the day better in health, though I had a most disturbed
night. I am very low in spirits; it looks so dark, and
having been told that the first messengers would return *at*

the latest to-day. Last night the chief's messenger said perhaps they might be here as soon as Thursday, but seemed to doubt it. I don't know what to think, and would say from the heart, ' Let the Lord do what seemeth to Him good.' If kept here another week I shall feel sure no messengers have been sent, and if possible shall endeavour to flee, in spite of all the property I must leave behind and the danger of the undertaking.

"Only a few ladies came to see the wild beast to-day. I felt so low and wretched that I retired within my den, whither they, some of them, followed me; but as it was too dark to see me, and I refused to speak, they soon left.

"The only news of to-day is that two white men, one tall and the other short, have arrived in Akota, and the Sultan has detained them. It is only a report that has followed me. I am the tall man, and Pinto, my Goa cook, the short one ; he is almost always taken for a white man, and dresses as such. I fear, however, with these fearfully suspicious people, that it may affect me seriously. I am very low, and cry to God for release.

" *Oct. 28th, Wednesday.*—(Seventh day's prison.) A terrible night, first with noisy drunken guard, and secondly with vermin, which have found out my tent and swarm. I don't think I got one sound hour's sleep, and woke with fever fast developing. O Lord, do have mercy upon me and release me. I am quite broken down and brought low. Comforted by reading Psalm xxvii.

" In an hour or two fever developed very rapidly. My tent was so stuffy that I was obliged to go inside the filthy hut, and soon was delirious.

"Evening ; fever passed away. Word came that Mwanga had sent three soldiers, but what news they bring they will not yet let me know.

" Much comforted by Psalm xxviii.

4th day of imprisonment — I should I think count Wednesday because after capture I was guarded all day **Sunday 25** long, until ordered off and seized — about 5 P.M.

Still a great deal of pain in my limbs the fatigue of dressing
quite knocks me over. my guards though at times they stick to
me like leeches and two, rifles in hand, remain all night in
my tent are gradually getting very careless & have already seen
opportunities of escape had I wanted so to do I doubt not that
in a few days time especially if I could get a little extra food
lent to them I could walk away quite easily but I have no
such intention. I am more inclined to stop where they say go
like a thorn in the old gentleman's side and I fear from that
feeling of contrariness that is rather inborn. I send him
affectionate greeting & reports of my health by his messengers
twice a day. What I fear most now is the close confinement &
utter want of exercise. The Sultan sent a detachment of 70
more of his wives to inspect the prisoner after they had feasted
their eyes & made their remarks they respectfully retired
When I was almost beginning to think of my time in prison as getting short the
chief has sent men to re-build the fence around me what does it mean
I have shown no desire or intention of escaping. has a messenger arrived
from Mwanga there is just time that it should be so to tell them to hold
me fast. the look of things has cast me down again
One of my guards if I understand him rightly is making me
offers of escape he has something very secret to communicate &
will not even take my boy into confidence. I do not however
want to escape under the present circumstances but at the
same time I take great amusement in watching & passing
by various little opportunities. My guards and I are
great friends almost affectionate & one calls me when
he speaks of me as "my whiteman"
3 detachments of the chief's wives they say he has a 1000 wives
have been today to see me they are very quiet & well behaved
but greatly amused at the prisoner. Mackay's name
seems quite a household word I constantly hear it
but of the others I scarce ever hear a word
the men are kept in close confinement except about
two who come daily backwards & forwards to bring my food
this they take in turns and implore to be sent for the job

FACSIMILE OF A PAGE OF THE BISHOP'S DIARY.

(*Exact size.*)

"*Oct.* 29*th, Thursday.*—(Eighth day's prison.)   I can hear no news, but was held up by Psalm xxx., which came with great power.   A hyena howled near me last night, smelling a sick man, but I hope it is not to have me yet."

This is the last entry in the little pocket diary.*   The few lines of almost microscopic writing do not occupy quite an eighth part of the page.   It is quite clear, from the different colour of the ink, that each day's entries were made, not at the close of the day, but at various times, as the writer found strength and opportunity.   Thus, in the entry of Wednesday, the 28th, the eye can almost trace the phases of the sick man's suffering in his writing.   The ink is faint in which he wrote : "Fever fast developing.   O Lord, do have mercy upon me."   There he seems to have laid down the pen—in what bodily weakness who can ever know ?   The following words—" and release me ; I am quite broken down and brought low.   Comforted by reading twenty-seventh Psalm "—were evidently added at night, after the delirium of the fever had passed away.   The comparative briefness of the entry made on the 28th tells an eloquent tale of weakness and physical distress.   For the first time since he left the coast, three months before, his old enemy, fever, had found him out, and threatened to overwhelm his faculties at the moment when he most desired to be in the full possession of them.   It is just possible that a second attack of fever may have incapacitated him from

---

* The book is one of Letts' monthly pocket diaries, very thin, and only 4½ inches by 2¾ ; with an entire page for each day.   Into this small space the Bishop has managed to get as many as forty-six lines to a page, each line averaging twelve or thirteen words.   The writing is very minute ; indeed, a lens was found almost necessary to decipher some parts of it.

writing more on the 29th.   But as no hint is given of recurring symptoms it is most probable, indeed, well-nigh certain, that the entry of that day was cut short by his death. The ink may still have been wet when his guards led him forth to die.

It is needless to add anything to these words of his which have come to us from the antechamber of death.   During that testing time the man reveals himself to us in all the grand simplicity of his sublime faith.   Almost torn to pieces, deprived of every comfort and all the decencies of life, latterly racked by fever, and with the shadow of an unknown doom darkening his heart, he never seems for a single instant to have wavered in his confidence in his God.   When " quite broken down " by bodily outrage and the sickness of hope deferred, when " brought very low " by superadded fever, he could be comforted by such Psalms as xxvii—xxx, and apply to himself the words : " I had fainted, unless I had believed to see the goodness of the Lord in the land of the living.   Wait on the Lord.   Be of good courage.   Wait, I say, on the Lord."

It seems that until the very end Hannington had little or no suspicion that Mwanga was concerned in his arrest. He looked forward to the return of the messengers sent to U-Ganda as the signal for his immediate release.   On Wednesday, the 28th, there had been much drumming and shouting among the natives.   When the Bishop's men asked the meaning of the demonstration, they were told that the king had sent word that the Mzungu (European) should be allowed to proceed to U-Ganda.   They were much relieved, and hoped that their trouble was over.   Probably the same story was told to the Bishop on the following day as an excuse for hurrying him out of his prison-hut to the place of execution.   Until the last moment he would have had no idea that he was irrevocably doomed to death—that

this Lubwa was but the poor cat's-paw by the employment
of whom Mwanga hoped to escape the responsibility of the
actual massacre. When, therefore, he was conducted to an
open space without the village, and found himself surrounded
once more by his own men, we can well imagine that he
concluded that the worst was now over, and even began to
turn his thoughts toward the recovery of the valuable goods
which he had brought so far for the use of the brethren in
U-Ganda.

He was not, however, long left in doubt as to the
fate which was in store for him. With a wild shout
the warriors fell upon his helpless caravan-men, and their
flashing spears soon covered the ground with the dead
and dying. In that supreme moment we have the happiness of knowing that the Bishop faced his destiny like a
Christian and a man. As the soldiers told off to murder him
closed round, he made one last use of that commanding mien
which never failed to secure for him the respect of the most
savage. Drawing himself up he looked around, and as they
momentarily hesitated with poised weapons, he spoke a few
words which graved themselves upon their memories, and
which they afterwards repeated just as they were heard.
He bade them tell the king that he was about to die for the
Ba-ganda, and that he had purchased the road to Buganda
with his life. Then, as they still hesitated, he pointed to
his own gun, which one of them discharged, and the great
and noble spirit leapt forth from its broken house of clay,
and entered with exceeding joy into the presence of the
King.

*   *   *   *   *   *

Every morning during that hard-fought journey he had
greeted the sunrise with his "travelling psalm," "*I will lift
up mine eyes unto the hills, from whence cometh my help.*"
NOW his feet were planted upon the battlements of the

everlasting hills, and the weary traveller saw what it is not granted to eyes of flesh to see.

How often had he encouraged his companions, in times of doubt or difficulty, with the words : " Never be disappointed, only Praise." Was he disappointed now, when, standing upon the very verge of the land he had come so far to see, he was yet forbidden to enter it ; and when the prize of his endeavour was snatched from his grasp in the very moment of victory ? " *The Lord shall preserve thy going out and thy coming in from this time forth for ever more.*" That day was the day of his "coming in," not to the land which he had hoped to reach before he died, but to a far better land. For henceforth " he shall dwell on high, his place of defence shall be the munitions of rocks : bread shall be given him : his waters shall be sure ; for his eyes do see the King in His beauty ; and they behold the Land that is very far off."

*   *   *   *   *   *

Out of the fifty men who accompanied the Bishop only four were suffered to escape. These made their way back, as we have seen, to Kwa Sundu, and carried the tidings of the massacre to Mr. Jones. The only reason which he had for not at once believing their tale was that they failed to give him a satisfactory account of the manner in which they had avoided the fate of their companions. This is partially explained by Mr. Mackay, who says that three or four men were spared in order that they might show their captors how to open the boxes which contained the Bishop's goods. It is easy to understand that they might have been ashamed to confess that they had purchased their lives upon such terms. Hence their equivocation upon this point only.

Mr. Jones, faithful and devoted to his Bishop to the last, waited at Kwa Sundu for about a month after he received

the report of his death—hoping against hope, and unwilling
to leave while the most remote chance of his being alive
should remain.   It would have been utterly impossible for
him to have penetrated into U-Soga.   To have done so
would have been to sacrifice his entire caravan, without
even the prospect of achieving anything.   On the 8th of
December, therefore, he sorrowfully turned his face from
the Lake, and began to retrace his steps along the backward
route.

*   *   *   *   *   *

On the 4th of February, 1886, at sunrise, the Christians
at Rabai were wending their way churchward to the early
Service, when they were startled by the sound of guns ; and
presently some messengers—weary men, and with the marks
of long travel upon them—came in to say that the Bishop's
caravan was at hand.   The Bishop's caravan without the
Bishop!   While these were being eagerly cross-examined,
other guns signalled from the valley, very distant, but volleying nearer and yet more near ; and the whole settlement ran
down to meet their returning friends.   Among them were
sad-faced and distracted women, who had gleaned from the
first-comers that their husbands had perished in the great
disaster.   As the two Englishmen in charge of the Mission
Station hastened forward, they met one bearing a blue
pennon—the African symbol of mourning—whereon was
sewn in white letters the word ICHABOD.   Behind the
sad standard-bearer, amid a crowd of weeping and distraught
women and friends, limped a straggling line of sorry-looking
men, staggering beneath their diminished loads ;—a feeble
crew, lean and weary and travel-stained—most of them
garmentless or clothed in hides.   Behind them came a
battered white helmet, and the Bishop's friend and sharer in
his peril was grasping their hands, and taken into their arms.
None of them were able to say much: all were thinking of

him who had gone out so hopefully, and whose great heart
was now stilled for ever.

*   *   *   *   *   *

When the news reached England, the report of the
Bishop's death was at first received with general incredulity.
The public did not believe that any African king would
deliberately, and in cold blood, murder a European dignitary.
Others had, indeed, lost their lives, but—as in the case of
Shergold Smith and O'Neill—this was rather owing to their
having become in some way, however unintentionally,
implicated in tribal feuds, than to any desire on the part
of the natives to injure them. There was no quarrel
between U-Ganda and England. Envoys had been sent
from thence to our Queen, and had returned loaded with
her favours. The British Consul was in communication
with Mtèsa, and his name was one to conjure with at his
court. At the first blush the tidings seemed absurd.

Nor did those who knew Hannington intimately believe
that he had been killed, until they were forced to do so by
overwhelming evidence. We had great confidence in the
man. That he should have suffered from his own hardiness
and extreme contempt of danger did not seem improbable,
but that he should have been put to death at the bidding of
any native chief appeared very unlikely. His presence of
mind and readiness of resource were, we thought, sufficient
to extricate him from most perils of this sort. We were
then as ignorant as he was when he planned his last journey,
that the young king of U-Ganda and his chiefs had assumed
such an attitude towards Europeans that it would be almost
certain death for any stranger to approach their dominions
from the forbidden East.

When, at last, our countrymen were compelled to accept
the fact, it was received with quite universal sorrow. The

young Bishop had not lived long enough to be known much beyond the circle of his own personal friends, but all were aware that a man of no ordinary parts, brave and self-devoted beyond most others, had been suddenly cut down in the actual consummation of a great achievement.

His death seemed to be a martyrdom. And indeed it was. As an ambassador of Christ he started, and as an ambassador of Christ, the recognized chief of that growing party in U-Ganda who served "another King, Jesus," and who were ready to confess His name in the fire, he was met and murdered. His dying testimony will not be forgotten on the shores of the great Lake. His words are passed from mouth to mouth : " I am about to die for the Ba-ganda, and have purchased the road to them with my life."*

So his death was lifted out of the list of ordinary deaths which happen to men in the course of their duty ; it was understood that he had devoted himself in no ordinary manner, and his name at once found a place, with that of Gordon, Patteson, Gardiner, and other Christian heroes of this generation, among the ranks of the noble army of martyrs.

By and by, from all sides, poured in the testimony of his friends. It was noticed that those who had been brought into closest contact with him were most impressed by his

---

* Mr. Ashe writes from Natete, Buganda : "We were fortunate in obtaining our dear Bishop's Bible. One of our Christians bought it of a man who had taken it from the Bishop. An incident connected with it is worth mentioning. One or two of those who were present when I was giving the cowrie shells for the book expressed a desire to share in the cost of redeeming it. They said it was our brother's, and they would like to do this. I mentioned before that one of the members of our native Church Council wrote to me a letter, saying *he quite understood that the Bishop had lost his life in endeavouring to benefit them.*"

single-minded self-devotion and unselfishness; and many who knew him only by name began to feel that they had lost in him a friend and a brother. Among many such testimonies we may quote that of Mr. Wray, who, it will be remembered, accompanied his Bishop to Chagga. He says : "The more I knew him, the more I loved him. Oh, that loving, tender-hearted, winning soul ! I cannot forget those feet which trod over a hundred miles of desert that I might be carried in his own hammock. He saved my life ! "

There were some who thought that he had rashly thrown his life away ; that he had incurred an unwarrantable amount of danger for no corresponding advantage. We are all prone to be wise after the event. We can all see *now* that he placed his head within the very jaws of the lion. We can all give a score of excellent reasons why his journey should never have been attempted at all. But then we are in possession of information which was not in the hands of either Bishop Hannington or his advisers. Sir John Kirk, than whom no living man has had a larger experience of Africans, and missionaries who had spent many years in dealing with the natives, concurred with the Bishop in his opinion that the only danger to be apprehended was from the wild and turbulent Masai tribes. These once passed, the success of the journey would be, they thought, assured. Against this danger the Bishop made preparation by thoroughly studying the manners and customs of these people ; he arrived at the conclusion that they would prove troublesome rather than dangerous, if met in a friendly spirit ; and that he was not wrong in this estimate of the perils of the way has been abundantly shown, both by his own quick upward progress, and by Mr. Jones' safe return with the shattered remnants of the originally small caravan.

And even had the peril been greater than the Bishop and his advisers thought it to be, he would not have hesi-

tated to incur it, if he might thereby have conferred a great
and lasting benefit upon the Church of Central Africa.   The
lower road to the Lake is not only circuitous and difficult,
but has dangers of its own which are more to be feared than
the spear of the Masai.   Bishop Hannington could not contemplate with equanimity the inevitable sufferings and probable death of those who, like himself two years before, were
bound to fight the spectral army of disease which barred the
way into the far interior.   He thought it worth while to
incur some risk in order that he might in his own person
prove or disprove the practicability of the short and healthy
road to U-Ganda.   But for the stupid ignorance and short-
sighted greed of the boy-successor of the great Mtèsa, he
would in all human probability be now hailed as the successful explorer who by one bold stroke had saved to the pioneers
of Christian Civilization many thousands of money and
many invaluable lives.

In these days of advanced civilization, when so much
painful forethought is expended upon the upbringing of a
single man, it is not unnatural that we should have formed
a high opinion of the value of life.   It seems to us a pitiful
thing that the masterpiece which has been turned out as the
result of long years of patient and costly toil should be
shattered—dashed into fragments in a moment.   We are
inclined to be impatient with the man who unduly exposes
himself to danger ; and the word "rash" carries with it
a sense of opprobium unknown to our courage-loving
ancestors.

It is of course impossible that we should value life too
highly ; but is there no danger lest we should value life too
much ?—too much as *mere living ?*   A life is not always
"thrown away" when it is poured out—poured out as was
the water of the well of Bethlehem at the feet of the great
king ; otherwise the costly missile from the great piece of

ordnance would be " thrown away " when, in breaking down the wall of the enemies' fortress, it is broken itself.

And what did he achieve, this martyr-bishop of the modern Church ? He died at the early age of thirty-eight. He had not time to do many things, and yet we may truly say that he did *much*. Not to mention the deep impress of his own personality which he has left upon those who were brought into close contact with him, he has given to the Mission in East Africa an impulse of which we may confidently expect that it will not lose the momentum. He has completed the circle of that great ring of Christian stations of which the signet stone is the Victoria Nyanza, and, in joining the two ends, has welded them together with his death.

When the present panic has subsided, and the chiefs of the Nyanza States have learned to regard their white teachers as their truest friends—and it is a safe prophecy to predict that this will be the case before many years have passed —then the messengers of the Church will make their way to the furthest outpost of her dominions along the healthy upland stretches of that Northern route. They will then remember whose feet first trod that path for Christ. It may be that the time is not far distant when a memorial cross will mark the spot where the brave Bishop fell, and that native Christians from U-Ganda will take their children there to point out to them the hallowed ground on which a martyr died.

To us he has bequeathed the priceless legacy of a devoted life. His splendid example will not have been set before this generation in vain. As he himself was stirred by the early and violent death which closed the faithful labours of Shergold Smith and O'Neill, so we are persuaded that others will be stirred by the recital of his gallant attempt, and his fall on the very ramparts of the fortress, to step forward and uplift the banner that has dropt from his dying hands.

As for him, we commit him to the Lord, in whom he trusted. He shall not be confounded. What if his busy hands and feet, torn from his body, now rattle in the wind above the gateway of some savage town! What if the bleaching skull, wherein once his active brain wrought for the good of all, now hangs like a beacon from the leafless arm of some withered tree! He would have been the first to tell us that no such things could affect his *life*. For that was hid with Christ in God. The world is his tomb. Somewhere upon its circumference lie his mortal parts. Wherever that may be we know that his sleep is sweet. *Obdormivit in Christo.*

His last words to his friends in England—words scribbled by the light of some camp fire—were :

" If this is the last chapter of my earthly history, then the next will be the first page of the heavenly—no blots and smudges, no incoherence, but sweet converse in the presence of the Lamb! "

There, then, in that blessed Presence, we may leave him, only asking for ourselves that which it was granted to him so abundantly to enjoy—

> " That blessed mood
> In which the burden of the mystery,
> In which the heavy and the weary weight
> Of all this unintelligible world,
> Is lightened."

THE END.

SIMMONS & BOTTEN, Printers, Shoe Lane, E.C.